HUMILIATION, DEGRADATION, DEHUMANIZATION

LIBRARY OF ETHICS AND APPLIED PHILOSOPHY

VOLUME 24

For futher volumes:
http://www.springer.com/series/6230

HUMILIATION, DEGRADATION, DEHUMANIZATION

Human Dignity Violated

Edited by

PAULUS KAUFMANN
University of Zurich, Switzerland

HANNES KUCH
Freie Universität Berlin, Germany

CHRISTIAN NEUHÄUSER
Ruhr-University Bochum, Germany

and

ELAINE WEBSTER
University of Strathclyde, UK

Springer

Editors
Paulus Kaufmann
Universität Zürich
Ethik-Zentrum
Zollikerstr. 117
8008 Zürich
Switzerland
kaufmann@philos.unizh.ch

Hannes Kuch
FU Berlin
SFB Kulturen des Performativen
Grunewaldstr. 35
12165 Berlin
Germany
h.kuch@fu-berlin.de

Christian Neuhäuser
Ruhr-University Bochum
Department of Philosophy
Universitätsstraße 150
44780 Bochum
Germany
Christian.neuhaeuser@rub.de

Elaine Webster
University of Strathclyde
Law School
St James' Road
G4 0LT Glasgow
The Lord Hope Bldg.
United Kingdom
elaine.webster@strath.ac.uk

ISSN 1387-6678
ISBN 978-90-481-9660-9 e-ISBN 978-90-481-9661-6
DOI 10.1007/978-90-481-9661-6
Springer Dordrecht Heidelberg London New York

Library of Congress Control Number: 2010936345

Printed on acid-free paper

Springer is part of Springer Science+Business Media (www.springer.com)

Foreword

Human dignity is the main philosophical foundation of human rights, as expressed in the Charter of the United Nations, the Universal Declaration of Human Rights and many other documents. The concept of human dignity is meant to distinguish human beings from other creatures, notably animals. It underlines the uniqueness of human beings among all creatures, above all their free will, individual autonomy and capability of independent decision-making based on reason and free moral choice. But philosophers disagree on how to define human dignity and, as with human rights, the concept is often regarded as a Western one not applicable to other cultures. On the other hand, with the recognition of poverty and climate change as major violations of human rights and faced with certain challenges to the uniqueness of humanity caused by modern science and technology, notably biomedicine and genetic engineering, the concept of human dignity features again more prominently in the contemporary human rights discourse.

On the occasion of the 60th anniversary of the Universal Declaration of Human Rights, the Swiss Foreign Minister presented an Agenda for Human Rights entitled "Protecting Dignity" which had been drafted by a Panel of Eminent Persons from all world regions.[1] While reaffirming that "human dignity, which is inherent in all human beings, is the moral and philosophical justification for equality and other universal human rights", the Agenda recognizes at the same time that "only certain violations of human rights constitute an attack on human dignity". As a consequence, the Agenda "primarily aims at addressing human rights issues directly linked to human dignity", such as poverty and climate change, migration and urbanization, armed conflicts and weapons of mass destruction, racism, genocide, war crimes, ethnic cleansing and crimes against humanity, terrorism and counter-terrorism, organized crime and human trafficking, inhuman prison conditions, arbitrary detention, torture and enforced disappearance.

By identifying these most serious human rights violations as attacks on human dignity, the drafters of the Swiss Agenda for Human Rights follow a similarly negative approach as the authors of the present book. By focussing on violations of human dignity, they address the question what it means for human beings all over

---

1 www.UDHR60.ch.

the world to be degraded, humiliated and dehumanized. What do victims of slavery and torture, poverty and starvation, armed conflict and domestic violence, corporal and capital punishment, racism and genocide, arbitrary detention and enforced disappearance, rape and human trafficking have in common? In my opinion, it is the experience of absolute powerlessness which creates the feeling among the victims of certain gross human rights violations to have lost their dignity and humanity. As the slave holder exercises absolute power over slaves, the torturer, the rapist, the genocidaire, the trafficker exercises absolute power over their respective victims. Many victims of torture, rape, trafficking, female genital mutilation, corporal punishment and inhuman prison conditions whom I interviewed in my function as Special Rapporteur on Torture in all world regions had reached a stage in which they regarded death as a relief compared to the suffering of being further dehumanized. That is why the right to human dignity seems to be even more important than the right to life and why "ticking bombs" and similar scenarios can never be used to balance security and saving lives of individuals against human dignity.

By addressing various aspects of human dignity and ways how human beings continue to be deprived by other human beings of this essential aspect of being human, the present volume constitutes an important contribution to the contemporary inter-disciplinary discourse on the relationship between human rights and human dignity.

Vienna, January 2010

Manfred Nowak (Ludwig Boltzmann Institute
of Human Rights, University of Vienna;
U.N. Special Rapporteur on Torture and other Cruel,
Inhuman or Degrading Treatment)

Contents

Contributors

Marcus Düwell Department of Philosophy, University of Utrecht, Netherlands, M.Duwell@uu.nl

Tamara Enhuber Department of Anthropology, University of Trier, Germany, tamaraenhuber@yahoo.com

Steffen K. Herrmann Department of Philosophy, Freie Universität Berlin, Germany, s.k.herrmann@fu-berlin.de

Paulus Kaufmann Centre for Ethics, University of Zurich, Switzerland, kaufmann@philos.unizh.ch

Samuel J. Kerstein Department of Philosophy, University of Maryland, USA, kerstein@umd.edu

Hannes Kuch Department of Philosophy, Freie Universität Berlin, Germany, h.kuch@fu-berlin.de

Andreas Maier Centre for Ethics, University of Zurich, Switzerland, andreas.maier75@gmail.com

Julia Müller Department of Philosophy, University of Potsdam, Potsdam, Germany

Christian Neuhäuser Department of Philosophy, Ruhr-University Bochum, Germany, Christian.neuhaeuser@rub.de

Sophie Oliver University of Konstanz, Germany, Sophie-Anne.Oliver@uni-konstanz.de

Arnd Pollmann Institute of Philosophy, Otto-Von-Guericke-University Magdeburg, Germany, arnd.pollmann@ovgu.de

Ivana Radačić Ivo Pilar Institute of Social Sciences, Centre for Croatian Studies, University of Zagreb, Croatia, ivana_radacic@yahoo.com

Peter Schaber Centre for Ethics, University of Zürich, Switzerland, schaber@philos.uzh.ch

Kirsteen Shields London School of Economics and Political Science, Centre for the Study of Human Rights, UK, k.shields@lse.ac.uk

Ralf Stoecker Department of Philosophy, University of Potsdam, Germany, Ralf.stoecker@uni-potsdam.de

Elaine Webster Centre for the Study of Human Rights Law, University of Strathclyde, UK, elaine.webster@strath.ac.uk

About the Authors

Marcus Düwell studied Philosophy, German literature and theology in Tübingen and Munich. He received his PhD in philosophy for a thesis about the relation between ethics and aesthetics. From 1993 to 2001 he was Academic Coordinator of the International Centre for Ethics in the Sciences and Humanities at Tübingen University. Since 2002 he has held a chair in Philosophical Ethics at the Department of Philosophy at Utrecht University and is research director of the Ethiek Instituut at Utrecht University and director of the Netherlands Research School for Practical Philosophy. Some Publications: *Ästhetische Erfahrung und Moral* (Aesthetical Experience and Morality) (Alber 1999); *Bioethik – Methoden, Theorien, Bereiche* (Bioethics-Methods Theory, Dimensions) (Metzler 2008). *Handbuch Ethik* (Metzler, 2002, 2. Aufl. 2006); *Bioethik – Eine Einführung* (Suhrkamp 2003); *Bioethics in Cultural Contexts* (Springer 2006); *The Contingent Nature of Life* (Springer 2008), in preparation: *Cambridge Handbook on Human Dignity* (Cambridge University Press 2011).

Tamara Enhuber, M.A. Sociology. Studied at Hamburg School of Economics and Politics and at the Graduate Faculty, New School, New York. Has worked as a consultant for UN agencies, international human rights organizations, development agencies and trade unions. Currently doctoral candidate at the University of Trier. Research interests are contentious politics, subaltern studies, collective identities, and bonded labour in south Asia, drawing from the fields of political, historical and industrial sociology, anthropology, social psychology, and south Asian studies. Award of various fellowships in Germany and the U.S.

Steffen K. Herrmann, M.A. Philosophy. Is research assistant at the Department of Philosophy at the Freie Universität Berlin and member of the interdisciplinary research project "Performing Culture". Within this context he works in the research project "The Performance of Linguistic Violence". He studied philosophy, sociology and literature in Frankfurt/Main and Berlin. His main research interests lie in the field of social philosophy, namely theories of recognition and otherness; philosophies of language and performativity; studies on power and violence. Currently he is working on his dissertation "Symbolic Vulnerability. Recognition and Misrecognition in Hegel and Levinas". He is co-editor of two anthologies on language and violence: *Verletzende Worte. Die Grammatik sprachlicher*

Missachtung (Words that Wound. The Grammar of Linguistic Misrecognition) (Transcript 2007); *Philosophien sprachlicher Gewalt. 21 Grundpositionen von Platon bis Butler* (Philosophy of Linguistic Violence. 21 Key Concepts from Platon to Butler) (Velbrück 2010).

Paulus Kaufmann studied philosophy and Japanese studies at the universities of Hamburg, Zurich and Fukui. He is now research assistant at the Center for Ethics and at the Institute for East-Asian-Studies, both at the University of Zurich, and wrote his PhD-thesis on using people merely as means. His research focuses on normative ethics and premodern Japanese thought, especially on Kukai.

Samuel J. Kerstein is Associate Professor of Philosophy at the University of Maryland, College Park. His main interests lie in ethical theory, bioethics, and the history of philosophy, especially Kant. In several articles and a book, *Kant's Search for the Supreme Principle of Morality*, he has examined the foundations of Kantian ethics. He is now elaborating and defending moral principles inspired by Kant's Formula of Humanity. With the help of these principles, he is engaging with issues in bioethics, such as how we ought to distribute scarce, life-saving resources and the moral permissibility of offers to purchase organs for transplanation.

Hannes Kuch is research assistant at the Department of Philosophy, Freie Universität Berlin, and member of the Research Centre "Performing Culture". Within this context he works in the research project "The Performance of Linguistic Violence". His main interests lie in the social philosophy of recognition, power and performativity. He is currently working on his PhD-thesis on Hegel's figure of "Master and Slave" as a theory of symbolic power. He has co-edited two volumes on the relation of violence and language: *Verletzende Worte. Die Grammatik sprachlicher Missachtung* (Words that Wound. The Grammar of Linguistic Misrecognition) (Transcript 2007); *Philosophien sprachlicher Gewalt. 21 Grundpositionen von Platon bis Butler* (Philosophy of Linguistic Violence. 21 Key Concepts from Platon to Butler) (Velbrück 2010).

Andreas Maier is a graduate student at the University of Zurich and currently finishing a PhD-thesis on the concept of human dignity. Research interests include the role of normative concepts in moral practice, the free will problem, and methods of ethics.

Julia Müller is a PhD-student at the Department of Philosophy, University of Potsdam, Germany. She is currently working on a thesis on the relationship between human dignity and extreme poverty. Her research interests are applied ethics and political philosophy.

Christian Neuhäuser is assistant professor at the Ruhr-University of Bochum. He works and publishes in the field of practical philosophy, including on business ethics and global justice, human rights and dignity, environmental ethics and democracy. He also has a keen interest in action theory and questions of collective responsibility. For more information you can visit his digital self on the university homepage.

Sophie Oliver has recently completed an interdisciplinary PhD at the University of London, funded by the UK's Arts and Humanities Research Council. Her doctoral research examined the possibility of an ethics of secondary witnessing, in particular in relation to cultural memory and the experience of embodiment. Awarded a Research Fellowship by the Alexander von Humboldt Foundation, she is currently working on a new project about the aesthetics of secondary witnessing in relation to memorial culture in Berlin. She has published a number of articles in peer-reviewed journals, and is a contributor to various edited books on a range of themes including human rights, cultural theory and media representations of trauma.

Arnd Pollmann is Assistant Professor of Practical Philosophy at the Otto-von-Guericke-University of Magdeburg, Germany. His main interests lie in ethical theory, moral philosophy, political philosophy, human rights, human dignity and bioethics. He is also co-founder of the interdisciplinary "Arbeitsstelle Menschenrechte" (Working Group for Human Rights) at the University of Magdeburg and co-editor of the "Zeitschrift für Menschenrechte" (Journal for Human Rights). Publications include: *Integrität. Aufnahme einer sozialphilosophischen Personalie* (Transcript 2005); (together with Christoph Menke) *Philosophie der Menschenrechte. Zur Einführung* (Junius 2007); *Unmoral. Ein philosophisches Handbuch. Von Ausbeutung bis Zwang* (C.H. Beck 2010).

Ivana Radačić holds a LLB from the University of Zagreb, MPhil in criminological research from the University of Cambridge, LLM from the University of Michigan and PhD in law from University College London. She is senior research assistant at the Ivo Pilar Institute for Social Sciences in Zagreb and a lecturer at the Centre for Croatian Studies, University of Zagreb. She also teaches at the Centre for Peace Studies and the Centre for Women's Studies, and she was a visiting professor at UN University for Peace and UCL. Ivana previously worked as a lawyer at the European Court of Human Rights, and has held interships with Human Rights Watch, New York, and Interights, London. She is a Council of Europe expert on human rights and she cooperates with a number of NGOs in Croatia on strategic litigation and human rights education. She has published a number of articles, contributed to two books and edited a book on feminist legal theory. Her research interests are: human rights, specifically women's human rights and European human rights law, as well as feminist legal theory.

Peter Schaber is Professor for Applied Ethics at the University of Zurich. He has worked on different topics in normative ethics as well as in applied ethics. His publications deal with issues of global justice as well as with bioethical issues. Together with a colleague he edited a volume on *World Poverty and Ethics* (2007) and is planning to edit one on *Migration and Ethics*. He just has finished a manuscript on "Instrumentalization and Human Dignity" and is currently working on a book on "The Ethics of Physician-assisted Suicide".

Kirsteen Shields is Fellow in Human Rights at the London School of Economics. She writes on the relationship between trade and human rights and she teaches on the regulation of corporations in respect of human rights and the environment at the School of Law within the University of London.

Ralf Stoecker is professor of philosophy at the University of Potsdam, Germany. He has worked on various topics in philosophy ranging from metaphysics and ontology to anthropology and applied ethics. His areas of research are philosophical action theory, matters of life and death, and the role of human dignity in ethics. His publications on the latter theme address applied topics such as: human dignity in embryos, human dignity and capital punishment, human dignity and brain death, honour killing; as well as more theoretical articles, e.g. about human dignity and self-respect and human dignity and the paradox of humiliation. He is the editor of *Menschenwürde – Annäherung an einen Begriff* (Wien 2003). Stoecker's contribution "Three Crucial Turns on the Road to an Adequate Understanding of Human Dignity" was completed while he was a fellow of an interdisciplinary research group on human dignity in modern medicine at the Center for Interdisciplinary Research, Bielefeld.

Elaine Webster is Director of the Centre for the Study of Human Rights Law and Lecturer in Public Law at the University of Strathclyde in Glasgow, Scotland. Her research focuses on Article 3 of the European Convention on Human Rights prohibiting torture, inhuman or degrading treatment or punishment. In particular, on interpretation of the right not to be subjected to degrading treatment in which the concept of human dignity is understood to act as a guiding force in the European Court of Human Rights' teleological interpretation. Elaine studied Law and French Language (L.L.B. Hons) at the University of Glasgow, International Politics (M.A.) at the Université Libre de Bruxelles, Belgium, Human Rights and Democratisation (M.A.) at the European Inter-University Centre for Human Rights, Venice, Italy/Catholic University of Leuven, Belgium and a PhD at the University of Edinburgh, Scotland.

Chapter 1
Human Dignity Violated: A Negative Approach – Introduction

Paulus Kaufmann, Hannes Kuch, Christian Neuhäuser, and Elaine Webster

The concept of human dignity is one of the few philosophical notions that has gained popular currency beyond specialist academic discourse. From the writings of Pico della Mirandola, Immanuel Kant and other philosophers it has found its way into our colloquial vocabulary. Appeals to human dignity are an important part of ethical, legal and political discourse nowadays and appear frequently in national constitutions and UN documents, in newspapers, NGO publications and in human rights discourse. But what is it that *motivates* all this talk about human dignity?

A look at the philosophical literature from whence the concept has emerged often yields contradictory and disappointing answers to this question. For example, we find a debate between philosophers who claim that human dignity is a metaphysical property possessed by all human beings serving as the fundamental foundation for the whole of morality (Kass 2002, President's Council on Bioethics 2008) and philosophers and scientists who dismiss talk about dignity as useless, stupid or even dangerous (Macklin 2003, Pinker 2008). But debates such as this suffer from various shortcomings. Firstly, in these debates the role of human dignity is often characterized as *either* the supreme foundation of morality *or* as nothing at all. Alternative and more specific roles are ignored and the many dimensions of the concept thereby drift out of sight. Secondly, the debate is often restricted to examples from the area of bioethics and applied only to contested topics such as abortion, euthanasia and genetic enhancement. Thirdly, the theoretical discussion about human dignity usually starts with abstract values such as the sanctity of life or with human capacities such as autonomy, rationality or moral agency. While all of these debated topics are certainly important, they somehow seem to miss our primary interest in human dignity. UN documents, newspapers and NGO publications that address the question of human dignity refer to humiliation and degrading treatment, torture and war, poverty and slavery. The philosophical notion of human dignity has entered these discourses because the concept seems particularly apt as part of a description of such morally repugnant acts and practices that form a part of our modern experience of

---

P. Kaufmann (✉)
Centre for Ethics, University of Zurich, Switzerland
e-mail: kaufmann@philos.unizh.ch

P. Kaufmann et al. (eds.), *Humiliation, Degradation, Dehumanization*, Library of Ethics and Applied Philosophy 24, DOI 10.1007/978-90-481-9661-6_1,

the world. It is our conviction that any satisfactory conception of dignity should be able to explain the reality of its violation and should not be detached from concrete occurrences and interpretations in social life, since this is what motivates us to talk about dignity in the first place.

In this book, therefore, we propose to look more closely at dignity violations and adopt what we call a "negative approach to human dignity". In his contribution to this anthology Ralf Stoecker will provide one detailed view of what this approach may amount to. At present, we will confine ourselves to a few remarks on the main characteristics of this approach.

Instead of deducing moral principles from an abstract conception of human dignity, all of our contributions start from some act or practice that often is or can be characterized as a violation of human dignity. They take the contemporary discourse on human dignity as a starting point and draw their material from legal sources, historical documents, testimonies and many other kinds of literature that employ the concept of human dignity. The contributions to this book can all be said to proceed from philosopher Avishai Margalit's insight that we learn most about human dignity when we look at its violations and focus on what it means for people to be degraded, humiliated and wronged in many other ways (Margalit 1996). The contributions thereby stress the phenomena that make us care about dignity rather than analyzing abstract values and capacities.

Of course, in order to develop a philosophical conception of human dignity abstract values and human capacities have to be considered as well. Something has to be said about the grounds for human dignity and about the structure of a moral theory that rests on such a conception. We do not want to deny the importance of these matters and are well aware of the shortcomings of philosophical approaches that confine themselves to analyzing concrete cases. But at the same time, we want to emphasize that the phenomena should not be lost from sight. The contributions in this volume demonstrate the complexity of the phenomena that may be labelled "violations of human dignity". But they also show how conceptions of dignity can bring order to this complexity.

To be sure, the studies in this book do not pretend to show the only way in which certain violations of human dignity can be approached and understood. Furthermore, the different studies are underpinned by different conceptions of human dignity and, as such, cannot and do not purport to provide a unified picture of human dignity and its violations. But by concentrating on concrete phenomena these studies help us to better understand what must be explained by any ambitious account of human dignity. What an existing theory of human dignity can glean from our book is not a rival theory; rather, this book is a collection of reflections on various forms, dimensions and practices of dignity violations, and thus it provides some raw material that comprehensive theories should deal with, either by integrating it or by arguing against its relevance for a comprehensive account. We do not believe, therefore, that a unitary theory can be derived from our studies on dignity violations, but that it can be enriched by it. We believe that any such theory will be enhanced insofar as it takes account of at least some of the phenomena that make us think about human dignity in the first place.

This book consists of three parts. In the first part we proceed from what we understand to be some general forms of dignity violations such as humiliation, degradation or dehumanization. These concepts are often used to characterize dignity violations in general or to point to the feature that makes dignity violations wrong. By studying these general forms more carefully the contributions of this part aim to overcome the first shortcoming of the contemporary debate on human dignity: They aim to gain insights into the varied roles and dimensions that dignity displays. Kaufmann and Webster, for example, analyze instrumentalization and degrading treatment respectively. From very different starting points both draw attention to the role that the concept of dignity might play in describing the wrong that is captured in these general expressions of dignity violations. For example, they point to the close interrelation between dignity and autonomy and suggest that we need both concepts to explain instrumentalization and degradation. Neuhäuser shows in his contribution that certain forms of humiliation cannot be adequately understood without accepting the idea that the dignity of a collective can be violated as well as the dignity of an individual. He argues that this collective dimension of human dignity is obscured by a one-sided diet of examples and a confusion of methodological and ethical individualism. Kuch and Oliver analyze two paradoxes that seem to arise from the concept of dignity. Kuch asks how we can make sense of the observation that in some atrocious circumstances people are afforded so little recognition that they accept insult rather than endure the complete absence of recognition. He argues that a conception of dignity based on autonomy cannot explain this voluntary violation of one's own dignity and that dignity should instead be understood as a special form of vulnerability due to the human desire for recognition. Thus, Kuch highlights the symbolic dimension of dignity violations, since recognition is essentially related to symbolic acts of addressing one another. Oliver focuses on the fact, documented by many testimonial accounts, that victims of dignity violations are often described – by themselves, by perpetrators, or by bystanders – as having lost their humanity. This description seems to be at odds with the idea of human dignity (perceived as the key attribute of the human) as inalienable. Oliver argues that this logic of dehumanization should be resisted by engaging with alternative understandings of human dignity as embodied rather than merely transcendent. The contributions to this section, focusing on varied examples from different fields of scholarship, aim to unearth certain features of, functions exercised by, and conceptual relationships associated with the notion of human dignity.

The contributions of the second part deal with practices that can be seen to violate human dignity. The chapters differ widely in method and context, but what these chapters share is a starting point and a common objective: they begin from concrete examples of what are, or might be considered to entail, dignity violations in social life. They analyze these phenomena carefully and demonstrate the sense in which they should be perceived as dignity violations. By dealing with various forms of dignity violations this second part of the book aims to overcome the current debate's emphasis on a select few examples, especially from the field of bioethics. On one hand, the chapters will examine practices that are cited regularly as violations of human dignity. Maier discusses the uncontroversial example of torture as a violation of human dignity, and incorporates media references and international law approaches into a discussion that highlights that an explanation of the wrongness of torture must address the question of moral recognition. Radačić deals with another prime example of human dignity violation: rape. She analyses human rights jurisprudence on rape and lays open various failures of the mainstream human right bodies. On the other hand, some of the chapters look at practices and conditions which cannot so easily be understood as violations of human dignity. Shields delves into international labor standards to highlight the perception of labor exploitation as a dignity violation on the basis of a lack of consent. Enhuber focuses on cases of bonded labor in India and finds that domination is the prevailing feature of such working relationships. Highlighting the dimensions of agency and identity, she further considers the ways in which cumulative relations of subjugation appear to be entrenched – but also resisted. The contributions of Schaber and Müller and Neuhäuser deal with poverty, which is less often conceptualized as involving violations of human dignity. These authors argue that we need the concept of human dignity to fully explain the moral dimensions of absolute poverty and relative poverty respectively. Herrmann situates a particular form of social exclusion as a dignity violation through a discussion of National Socialist politics of the personal name. These reflections on some examples that can be considered as violations of human dignity highlight particular features of these practices that give rise to human dignity connotations, and at the same time illustrate the value of reflecting on the substance of the phenomena themselves.

The last part of the book takes a fresh starting-point. In the chapter by Düwell entitled "Human Dignity and Human Rights", we have included a text that is very critical of our approach (especially the approach as outlined by Stoecker), but which is deemed to add a valuable, critical voice to the dynamic topic to which the book aims to contribute. Whilst it is believed that the negative approach adopted in the book offers a fruitful asset to any concept of human dignity, it is of course clear that this position will not be universally shared. The book will not engage in this metatheoretical debate beyond the inclusion of this chapter. Instead this volume provides space in which a negative approach can take shape, and in doing so, we hope that it becomes clear why and how we think the negative approach can be useful and indeed quite essential to a concept of human dignity. Moreover, in the final section we include two other texts that also try to establish a positive account, but that are more sympathetic towards the negative approach and see it as a valuable asset in their undertaking. These two contributions start from insights into concrete practices and examples, thereby showing the importance of careful observation of the phenomena. They aim to build comprehensive accounts of human dignity that address the complexity that these phenomena exhibit. The value of personhood is the focus of Kerstein's contribution. By discussing the examples of heroic self-sacrifice and actions of privileging the young over the old in the distribution of scarce, life-saving resources he aims to overcome some of the difficulties of the traditional Kantian conception of human dignity. Pollmann starts from the twentieth century experience of totalitarian mass destruction and moves towards an innovative account of human dignity that questions the traditional picture of dignity as inalienable and equally distributed amongst all human beings.

Though varying greatly in their method, focus and conclusions, the contributions to this anthology are united in their shared conviction that the widening of interest in dignity beyond the gaze of specialist academic philosophy is to be welcomed. The concept now figures prominently in political debates on many social and moral problems of global concern. All of these debates have certainly profited from the work of philosophers and their efforts to form a feasible conception of human dignity. But we have now reached a point where philosophy can no longer ignore the life of the notion beyond the academy; rather, academic philosophy can in turn profit from a consideration of those phenomena, and expressions of their wrongness, that are regarded as representing violations of human dignity.

References

Kass, Leon. 2002. *Life, liberty and the defense of dignity*. San Franciso, CA: Encounter Books.
Macklin, Ruth. 2003. Dignity is a useless concept. *BMJ* 327: 1419–1420.
Margalit, Avishai. 1996. *The decent society*. Cambridge, MA: Harvard University Press.
Pinker, Steven. 2008. The stupidity of dignity – Conservative bioethics' latest, most dangerous ploy. *The New Republic* 238: 28–31.
President's Council on Bioethics. 2008. *Human dignity and bioethics*. Washington, DC: President's Council on Bioethics.

Chapter 2
Three Crucial Turns on the Road to an Adequate Understanding of Human Dignity

Ralf Stoecker

Abstract Human dignity is one of the key concepts of our ethical evaluations, in politics, in biomedicine, as well as in everyday life. In moral philosophy, however, human dignity is a source of intractable trouble. It has a number of characteristic features which apparently do not fit into one coherent ethical concept. Hence, philosophers tend to ignore or circumvent the concept. There is hope for a philosophically attractive conception of human dignity, however, given that one takes three crucial turns. The *negative turn*: to start the inquiry with violations of human dignity. The *inductive turn*: to consider the whole range of applications of the concept of human dignity in different areas of ethics. And finally, the *historical turn*: to take into account the historical bonds between human dignity and traditional conceptions of dignity. Taken together they point in the direction of an understanding of *human dignity as universal nobility*.

2.1 Introduction

> *I could strangle him with my bare hands! Yet, I decide for a more subtle revenge. Normally we use two washcloths: a bright one for the face and upper part of the body and a dark one for the legs and genitals. He, however, gets the dark washcloth for his bum as well as for his face.*
> (Temsch 1994, my translation)

In the following article I shall pass in review the history of the concept of human dignity and its philosophical shortcomings, before I argue that there is still hope for an attractive conception of human dignity, if one is careful to take three crucial turns that lead to it.

R. Stoecker (✉)
Department of Philosophy, University of Potsdam, Germany
e-mail: Ralf.stoecker@uni-potsdam.de

P. Kaufmann et al. (eds.), *Humiliation, Degradation, Dehumanization*, Library of Ethics and Applied Philosophy 24, DOI 10.1007/978-90-481-9661-6_2,

2.2 The Roots of Human Dignity – A Standard Account

Historical accounts of human dignity typically distinguish four different sources: the Greek and Roman heritage culminating in Cicero's notion of "*dignitas*": the biblical conception of man and woman as being created in the image of God; Kant's *Würde* as opposed to price; and, finally, the concept of dignity that turned up after 1945 in numerous declarations and constitutional laws (for a good recent example, see Schulman 2008). Although not unrelated, at first sight these traditions point in quite different directions.

"*Dignitas*" in ancient Rome was a social concept, describing the particular social role of a person. The bearers of the role and the people around them had to pay duty to this social role in their behavior (Pöschl 1989). Cicero's famous letter to his son Tullius, "De Officiis", was one big guide to the numerous considerations and duties that belonged to the dignified life of a Roman aristocrat. What made Cicero's letter the founding document of human dignity, though, is his claim, adopted from the Greek Stoics, that part of our obligations towards ourselves and to others is due merely to our being human, which meant for him in the first place: being rational.

Human dignity in the biblical tradition shared two features of the Roman understanding: first, dignity was regarded as something of high value which, secondly, made strong demands on the bearer of dignity herself. In contrast to the Roman conception, however, *human* dignity was not merely a basic, residual dignity at the bottom of all shades of social nobility. Quite to the contrary, the assumption that every human being was created by God as well as in the image of God was meant to trump and annihilate all social ranks instead. This view rarely had any political implications, though. Human dignity for the best part of the history of Christianity was merely regarded in terms of its bearing on the appropriate behavior of the dignitary herself, and for a long time emphasis was put on the notorious failures of meeting these demands due to human sinfulness, weakness and misery. With the dawn of Humanism and Renaissance, however, this bleak conception of humanity was countered by writers (like Giovanni Pico della Mirandola) who praised the particular ability for self-creation as the basis of human dignity – although it was still a long way to go until these ideas had a political impact in the human rights movements.[1]

The role that dignity plays in Kant's philosophy is notoriously difficult to elucidate.[2] In the "Groundwork to the Metaphysics of Morals," he nowhere mentions the expression "human dignity" ("*Menschenwürde*"); it is in this book, however, that he develops his understanding of dignity. Following Seneca he distinguishes two kinds of value: On the one hand, the price of something, which allows for its substitution by something of similar price, and on the other hand, dignity, which forecloses such

[1]Dignity also played an important (but presumably different) part in the Gospels, when Jesus repeatedly exposed himself to situations that were considered as deeply undignified and humiliating.

[2]For a profound presentation, see Von der Pfordten (2006).

an exchange. Almost everything of value merely has a price, according to Kant, yet only persons – strictly, their humanity, their having reason – have dignity because the categorical imperative puts us under the obligation never to treat someone's humanity as a mere means (i.e. as in principle exchangeable). In his later "Metaphysics of Morals," Kant tried to draw conclusions concerning ethical applications from this conception of human dignity; it is not clear, however, whether he really succeeded.

What is usually regarded as the fourth source of our moral conception of human dignity is to be found in a number of legal documents published in the early years after World War II. Almost without precedence in the history of jurisprudence, dignity adopted a prominent role in the UN Charter, in the German *Grundgesetz* and in the Universal Declaration of Human Rights, to be followed by many other declarations and constitutions. At least with respect to the recent German debate on human dignity, it seems fair to say that this debate would not have taken place if human dignity had not had such an outstanding position in the very first article of the German *Grundgesetz*, which states that human dignity is inviolable. But in spite of the prominence that these documents accord to human dignity, they remain remarkably silent about its content.

2.3 Problems with the Concept of Human Dignity

Given that these four traditions are usually regarded as the sources of our modern concept of human dignity, it is easy to understand why moral philosophers have found it so difficult to incorporate this concept into a promising normative ethical theory.

Evidently, normative ethics can hardly rely on a special relationship to God, or on any other religious presumption. Moreover, the genuinely hierarchical Roman understanding of dignity, treating universal dignity merely as a residual claim to basic decency, seems to be in stark contradiction to the magnitude of the role we would now accord to human dignity. In both respects, at any rate, referring to dignity appears unhelpful.

Kant's understanding suits the modern esteem for human dignity much better. Yet at the same time his reliance on the faculty of reason seems to disclose many people from the shelter of dignity, some of whom have been in particular need of this shelter during history (e.g. severely mentally disabled people). In this sense, Kant's understanding of dignity is thus missing the universality we ascribe to human dignity.

Human dignity, as it is employed in the legal documents, certainly has the required universality; here the problem is that human dignity is merely stated without any hint of how it should be construed or what particular role it is supposed to play (i.e. whether it is meant to be a human right itself or even the very basis of all human rights).

In recent years, there have been a number of philosophical attempts to circumvent these difficulties and to develop a satisfying conception of human dignity. Religious philosophers have tried to strengthen the idea of man and woman being created in the image of God and have even argued that there could not be a non-religious justification of human dignity (or of morality at all) (Spaemann 1987 [1985], Gelernter 2008). Ronald Dworkin has advocated an understanding of human dignity associated with sanctity (Dworkin 1993: 238–240). Some philosophers have suggested that we should construe human dignity as a demand to have one's basic needs fulfilled (Gewirth 1992, Nussbaum 2006). Others have opted for reductionism, according to which human dignity is a label for our fundamental human rights (Birnbacher 2004, Stepanians 2003). And finally, Kant's association of human dignity with reason has continued to attract many adherents who are confident that it may last without the problematic parts (Habermas 2001).

But beneath these attempts there has always existed a temptation either to steer a radical course and to dismiss the notion of human dignity altogether or (much more frequently) to simply ignore it. Even a cursory glimpse into some of today's most prominent textbooks in applied ethics reveals that human dignity is only rarely mentioned at all, and where it is, it is usually shrugged off as being genuinely unclear, polemical and philosophically useless (examples are Frey and Wellman 2003, LaFollette 2003, Rhodes et al., 2007, Beauchamp and Childress 2009). In particular in the United States, it seems, for a long time many philosophers showed no motivation to engage with human dignity at all. But why should they? Answering this question will help us to find a satisfactory account of human dignity.

2.4 The Negative Turn

For Kant, his claim that we have a dignity that has to be respected by others was a result of his metaphysical survey in the Groundwork. This is one possibility for arriving at the necessity to care about human dignity: We find good theoretical reasons to assume that we have it; i.e. our best moral theory entails that there is something like human dignity to be respected. But, as indicated, from most theoretical perspectives in moral philosophy today there is no felt need to care about human dignity.

Yet, there is another possibility of being led to human dignity in ethics. It is exemplified by the quotation at the very beginning of this chapter. The passage is taken from the report of a young man who worked in an outpatient nursing service in lieu of military service. In this surprisingly frank document, he describes how he took his revenge on a senile old man with whom he had been annoyed: He used the washcloth first for the lower parts of the old man's body and then the same cloth also for his upper parts, particularly his face.

The author's openness is so strange because, evidently, he has severely maltreated his victim. That he nonetheless lacked any sense of guilt is certainly a reason of societal concern. But the example also bears a philosophical challenge: the difficulty of accounting for the obvious reprehensibility of the young man's behavior. Due to his dementia, the client presumably never realized what had been done to him. Moreover, there is no evidence in the report that the treatment harmed the old man's health. Hence, from a consequentialist perspective there is little reason to complain. And although the client certainly would never have consented to having been washed with just one washcloth, it sounds somewhat forced to maintain that what is morally at stake in the example is merely a violation of autonomy. The young man's deed was so bad not just because he treated his client in a way that he would not have agreed to but because the treatment was deeply humiliating; it violated the old man's dignity.

This is the point of the example: It is important for moral philosophy to find a satisfactory account of human dignity because there are numerous instances of vile and reprehensible behavior that could not be morally accounted for at all, or at least not adequately, except as violations of dignity. Excremental assaults provide typical examples, as well as some insults and sexual abuses (Des Pres 1976: passim, Silver et al. 1986). Other examples are to be found in the public humiliation of members of disdained minorities. When the Nazis forced Jewish citizens to scrub the sidewalks, they certainly scared them and put them under duress, yet it is doubtful that these aspects adequately explain why these treatments were so abominable. What is missing, obviously, is the deeply humiliating character of being forced into such a situation (Stoecker 2003).

The challenge of accounting for dignity in moral philosophy, if there are instances of morally bad conduct that could not be dealt with adequately without recourse to dignity, immediately leads to the first heuristic turn I want to suggest for an adequate inquiry into human dignity: If we want to understand human dignity, we should start with instances of its violation. Instead of attempting to derive a conception of human dignity from our normative ethics (as Kant did) or anthropology, we should choose a *negative approach*, i.e. start from situations which we are inclined to describe as violations of human dignity and then ask what it is that makes it so appealing to use this concept instead of referring to, for example, harming, infringing autonomy or violating human rights.

2.5 The Inductive Turn

In Germany the debate on human dignity flared up some 10 years ago as part of the bioethical discussion on the status of the human embryo, particularly in the context of stem cell research and preimplantation diagnostics. It was not surprising, therefore, that the debate was focused only on very few characteristics of human dignity. For example, a comprehensive and widely esteemed anthology explicitly started with the assumption that what is at stake in this discussion is merely human dignity as the foundation of the prohibition of killing (Damschen and Schönecker 2003). Yet, although only few participants in the debate took notice of it, the notion of human dignity had been present in very different areas of philosophy (as well as in social sciences, politics and theology) during the previous decades. In the 1960s and 1970s, for example, nobody in Germany would have expected that a conversation about human dignity concerned embryos. In those days people were worried about violations of human dignity in Latin America, the USSR, or Vietnam, for example. Or they used the notion to describe the situations of the inhabitants of psychiatric clinics and jails. And 20 years before that, as I already noted, the notion of human dignity had entered into numerous declarations and constitutions, because, to many people, this notion of human dignity was necessary and appropriate to express the horrendous nature of the deeds of the Nazis.

What this shows is that we have to beware of approaching human dignity in a way that is too narrow-sighted, in particular in bioethics. Any philosophically satisfying explanation of human dignity has to take into account how broad the scope of its application is. Even a coarse survey shows many different areas in which we are confronted with morally questionable actions that we are inclined to describe as violations of human dignity: terror and torture, killing and rape, slavery, racism, sexism, severe hunger and poverty, hard and monotonous work, endemic unemployment, political and religious suppression, the refusal of citizenship, being prohibited from maintaining personal relations, state control and the restriction of liberty, flagrant injustice, disregard of privacy, instrumentalization, isolation, insult, the transgression of the borders between humans and animals, interference in our biological make-up, and so on. No doubt these cases differ considerably in several respects, but they have in common that they are occasionally regarded as threats to our human dignity, and, moreover, that there is no other ethical principle or feature that could adequately account for their shared moral impropriety.

At first sight, the apparently broad scope of the concept of human dignity shows how difficult is the task of finding an adequate account that does justice to all of these different applications. Yet, the broadness of the concept also provides us with ample material for such an account. In order to understand what human dignity is, we should therefore approach it from different angles, from the various areas where we are apparently confronted with human dignity violations. In short, we should supplement the negative approach with an *inductive strategy* that ideally will lead from the scattered applications to a unified concept, in tune with our pretheoretical intuitions.

However, the fact that we are inclined to fall back on human dignity in many different areas of moral concern has not always provoked an interest in a profound examination of the concept. Instead many authors took it as evidence that there is not much more to human dignity than a moral verdict presented with special emphasis. According to them, the claim that a particular behavior violates someone's dignity is a sort of conversation stopper, saying something like: This behavior is evil, period.

Hence, advertising the negative-inductive approach is not enough in order to justify our confidence that one may find an ethically attractive concept of human dignity. In the next two sections, I shall therefore try to say something more about the content this concept might have. First, I will defend another heuristic move, namely that we should observe something that has usually gone unnoticed in the discussion: the intimate relationship between human dignity and dignity proper in the recent history of the concept. Secondly, I will give a sketch of where the route to an adequate conception of human dignity might lead us, given that we obey the three crucial turns.

2.6 The Historical Turn

There is something peculiar in the historical sketch I gave at the beginning of my contribution. It leaves us wondering why the concept of human dignity gained its unprecedented prominence after World War II at all. As a matter of fact, neither Kant nor Cicero played an important part in the political debates that led, for example, to the Universal Declaration of Human Rights or the *Grundgesetz*. Christian convictions certainly were influential, but there were also strong Anti-Christian currents in these debates; hence, it could not have been merely the religious tradition that accounts for the attractiveness of the concept of human dignity (Vögele 2000).

At least part of the answer, I believe, is to be found in another historical root that has been oddly underestimated: the role that the notions of dignity and human dignity played in social and political thinking during the last 200 years, and which, no doubt, the authors of these documents vividly had in mind. In the context of this contribution, I can only give a few hints of what I have in mind. As far as I know, there has been no systematic survey in the histories of ideas on this topic yet.

In Germany, the first prominent occurrence of the expression "*Menschenwürde*" is in Friedrich Schiller's drama "Don Carlos." One of the heroes of the play, the Marquis of Posa, has rejected an offer of an influential and powerful position at the court of the Spanish king, Philip II. Astounded by this unforeseen refusal, the king cannot help but suspect a particularly clever kind of flattery. Thereupon Posa says:

> I am well aware, Sire, of how low and mean you regard *human dignity*, seeing a free man's speech merely as the mean trick of a flatterer. And I presumably know why you are entitled to think so. Men forced you into it; since they voluntarily gave up their nobility, they voluntarily descended to this low rank (Schiller 2005: 122, my translation and emphasis).

For Schiller, "*Menschenwürde*" is obviously a special kind of dignity, or nobility as he described it. And the same goes for many authors of the late eighteenth and throughout the nineteenth century. To mention just one further example, in 1860 the Swiss historian Jacob Burckhardt wrote in his famous book "Die Kultur der Renaissance in Italien":

> But by the side of all this there appeared in Italian poetry, towards the close of the fifteenth century, signs of a more realistic treatment of rustic life. This was not possible out of Italy; for here only did the peasant, whether laborer or proprietor, possess *human dignity*, personal freedom, and the right of settlement, hard as his lot might sometimes be in other respects (Burckhardt and Günther 1989: 348).[3]

---

[3]The translation is taken from the Gutenberg Project: http://www.gutenberg.org/dirs/etext00/corii10.txt (2.8.2009), my emphasis.

Again, *Menschenwürde* is far from being a mere moral status, something innate, which we inevitably own and which we cannot lose or forfeit. Quite to the contrary, according to Burckhardt, the peasants outside of Italy did not have it, because they lived under circumstances that would not have allowed them a minimum of nobility, necessary for writing poetry. And, according to Schiller, we can also forfeit it ourselves, by not behaving appropriately, for example, by toadying to the king.

In a sense, *Menschenwürde* for these authors is quite similar to what Cicero called "*dignitas*", yet with the crucial difference that everybody is entitled to it. It is an ideal of *universal nobility* and, it must be added, it is this universal human nobility that counts most in human relations, much more than the other, traditional, unequally distributed kind of nobility. According to Schiller, as long as we keep our human dignity, we can easily meet even a powerful king like Philipp II at eye level.

As I suggested, the strong continuity of the concept of human dignity with the traditional understanding of dignity as a characteristic of noblemen is usually ignored in the current debate. A prominent exception is Jeremy Waldron who has recently argued for a strong connection between human dignity and rank:

> [...] once associated with hierarchical differentiations of rank and status, "dignity" now conveys the idea that all human persons belong to the same rank and that that rank is a very high one indeed, in many ways as high as those that were formerly regarded as ranks of nobility (Waldron 2007: 201).

However, given that the observation is correct in that the ideal of dignity as universal nobility has played a prominent role in the development of postwar constitutions and declarations, the project of developing an ethically attractive notion of human dignity seems to be doomed to fail. As long ago as the late Middle Ages, rebellious peasants asked (according to a traditional rhyme): When Adam delffid and Eve span, who was than a gentilman? Why, after all, should we maintain that in fact both Adam and Eve were the "gentilmen", instead of simply assuming (as the rhyme suggests) that there were not any noblemen around at the onset of the world and that it would have been better if they were not around any longer? Luckily enough, we do not live in the stratified societies of Schiller and Burckhardt any longer. Hence, the assumption of universal nobility must appear unnecessarily roundabout, and politically as well as metaphysically dubious.

In order to explain how the idea of human dignity as a kind of universal nobility might still be worked into a satisfactory conception, I shall in the next section give a very rough sketch of what I expect to be its central elements.

2.7 Human Dignity and the Personal Self

To be sure, when Adam delffid and Eve span, nobody was the gentilman. But what happened to the noblemen at the end of their times, in the transition to our modern societies? According to the sociologist Niklas Luhmann, it is a crucial feature of modern societies that their members are expected, not only to fill one or another social position, as in the old stratified societies, but to fuse different social roles into one individual identity (Luhmann 1965). According to this account, our "*Menschenbild*" is individualistic, not in the sense that we have left behind all social dignities, but in the sense that we possess an individual dignity in conjunction with our professional, family-related, political and other dignities.

From a sociologist's perspective, therefore, individual dignities define tasks conferred to the individual by the society: we are supposed to act according to a dignity. The modern state, in turn, should better enable its citizens to fulfill these tasks in order to secure its proper functioning. This is, according to Luhmann, the functional role of Article 1 of the *Grundgesetz*.

From the perspective of a moral philosopher, though, it would obviously be unjustified to simply follow social practice and to state a moral obligation to obey whatever behavioral demands flow from individual identity. Our identities are subject to continuous reconsideration and reconstruction; they are neither sacrosanct to us nor to others. What is not so morally innocuous is whether we care about our identities at all, since this is at the very heart of our conception of self-respect: Self-respect is an evaluative attitude we have towards our individual dignity. And from the ethical perspective, self-respect is something valuable that has to be respected.

Displaying self-respect, however, may be an easier or a more difficult task according to the circumstances. On the one hand, these circumstances could be so demanding that almost nobody could stand upright, heroically saving her or his face (for example, in concentration camps, under torture, in situations of great pain and terror). On the other hand, one may find oneself in very special situations – such as weakness, illness, confusion, or even unconsciousness – in which one is unable to take care of oneself and hence is dependent on the help of others to save one's face.

In both kinds of situation, human dignity is typically at stake. Although nobody has an unconditional right to keep his individually chosen dignity (frauds, bigmouths and stuck-up peacocks may very well be cut down to size), it is of utmost importance to give everybody the possibility to keep a minimally decent identity, an identity that does not comprise situations in which, for example, one might fall victim to mordant offences, wild cruelty or total helplessness.

Jean Amery, a member of the resistance against the German occupation in Belgium, once described his experience of the Gestapo torture as follows: "Whoever fell victim to torture will never feel at home in the world again. The shame of the annihilation can never be wiped out" (Améry 1977: 73). It is this existential and, according to Amery, incurable harm to the victim's life prospects, and therefore to his or her self, which makes torture such an extreme case of a violation of the demand of human dignity and, hence, makes it under all circumstances atrocious, in addition to, and perhaps even above, the physical and mental pain it causes.

Torture, of course, is not the only way of violating human dignity. Perhaps the most common violation of human dignity is world hunger and poverty, since almost every individual personality is dependent on a sufficient satisfaction of the person's basic needs.

And there are still many other violations of human dignity, most of which may be described as less severe violations, yet they all share the basic feature of cutting into a person's ability to keep a decent identity. Avishai Margalit, who has developed his account of a decent society on very similar considerations, has discussed a number of different, familiar cases in which a state might threaten its citizens' dignity: for example, racism, unemployment, bureaucracy (Margalit 1996). Erving Goffman has described the mechanisms of stigmatization that do not allow proper identities (Goffman 1963). And, finally, examples like the one of the old man who has no choice but to live the life of someone who has his own feces smeared into his face show how human dignity can be violated by nurses and medical staff (Agich 2007, Franklin et al., 2006).

I merely wanted to sketch the understanding we arrive at if we take the three turns that I regard as crucial in the inquiry into human dignity. The negative turn, i.e. to start with violations, not only provides us with a philosophical motivation to look into human dignity but also gives us an idea of which features may be essential. The inductive turn, i.e. to consider the whole range of applications in different areas of ethics, is a good antidote to rash solutions. And finally, the historical turn, i.e. to take into account the historical bonds between human dignity and traditional conceptions of dignity, leads in the direction of an understanding of human dignity as universal nobility, which in my eyes probably points to the best way of seeing ourselves.[4]

References

Agich, George J. 2007. Reflections on the function of dignity in the context of caring for old people. *Journal of Medicine and Philosophy* 32(5): 483–494.

Améry, Jean. 1977. *Jenseits von Schuld und Sühne: Bewältigungsversuche eines Überwältigten*. Stuttgart: Klett-Cotta.

Beauchamp, Tom L., and James F. Childress. 2009. *Principles of biomedical ethics*. New York, NY: Oxford University Press.

Birnbacher, Dieter. 2004. Menschenwürde – abwägbar oder unabwägbar? In *Biomedizin und Menschenwürde*, ed. Matthias Kettner. Frankfurt/Main: Suhrkamp.

Burckhardt, Jacob, and Horst Günther. 1989. *Die Kultur der Renaissance in Italien*. Frankfurt/Main: Deutscher Klassiker Verlag.

Damschen, Gregor, and Dieter Schönecker. 2003. *Der moralische Status menschlicher Embryonen: Pro und contra Spezies-, Kontinuums-, Identitäts- und Potentialitätsargument*. New York, NY: De Gruyter.

Des Pres, Terrence. 1976. *The survivor: An anatomy of life in the death camps*. New York, NY: Oxford University Press.

Dworkin, Ronald. 1993. *Life's dominion – An argument about abortion and euthanasia*. Hammersmith: Harper Collins.

Franklin, Lise-Lotte, Britt-Marie Ternestedt, and Lennart Nordenfelt. 2006. Views on dignity of elderly nursing home residents. *Nursing Ethics* 13(2): 130–146.

Frey, Raymond G., and Christopher Heath Wellman. 2003. *A companion to applied ethics*. Malden, MA: Blackwell.

[4] I want to thank the editors of this volume not only for their patience but primarily for their numerous helpful suggestions and remarks that have definitely improved whatever quality there is in this paper.

Gelernter, David. 2008. The religious character of human dignity. In *Human dignity and bioethics*, ed. President's Council on Bioethics, 387–405. Washington, DC: President's Council on Bioethics.

Gewirth, Alan. 1992. Human dignity as the basis of rights. In *The constitution of rights – Human dignity and american values*, eds. Michael J. Meyer and William Parent. Ithaca, NY: Cornell University Press.

Goffman, Erving. 1963. *Stigma. Notes on the management of spoiled identity*. Englewood Cliffs, NJ: Prentice-Hall.

Habermas, Jürgen. 2001. *Die Zukunft der menschlichen Natur*. Frankfurt/Main: Suhrkamp.

LaFollette, Hugh. 2003. *The Oxford handbook of practical ethics*. Oxford and New York, NY: Oxford University Press.

Luhmann, Niklas. 1965. *Grundrechte als Institution*. Berlin: Duncker & Humblot.

Margalit, Avishai. 1996. *The decent society*. Cambridge, MA: Harvard University Press.

Nussbaum, Martha Craven. 2006. *Frontiers of justice: Disability, nationality, species membership, the tanner lectures on human values*. Cambridge, MA: The Belknap Press of Harvard University Press.

Pöschl, Viktor. 1989. *Der Begriff der Würde im antiken Rom und später*. Heidelberg: Carl Winter Universitätsverlag.

Rhodes, Rosamond, Leslie Francis, and Anita Silvers. 2007. *The Blackwell guide to medical ethics*. Malden, MA: Blackwell.

Schiller, Friedrich. 2005. *Don Carlos*. Stuttgart: Reclam.

Schulman, Adam. 2008. Bioethics and the question of human dignity. In *Human dignity and bioethics*, ed. President's Council on Bioethics, 3–18. Washington, DC: President's Council on Bioethics.

Silver, Maury et al. 1986. Humiliation: Feeling, social control and the construction of identity. *Journal for the Theory of Social Behaviour* 16(3): 269–283.

Spaemann, Robert. 1987 [1985]. Über den Begriff der Menschenwürde. In *Das Natürliche und das Vernünftige*, 77–106. München: Piper.

Stepanians, Markus. 2003. Gleiche Würde, gleiche Rechte. In *Menschenwürde – Annäherung an einen Begriff*, ed. Ralf Stoecker, 81–103. Wien: Öbv & Hpt.

Stoecker, Ralf. 2003. Menschenwürde und das Paradox der Entwürdigung. In *Menschenwürde – Annäherung an einen Begriff*, ed. Ralf Stoecker, 133–151. Wien: Öbv & Hpt.

Temsch, Jochen. 1994. Das wird schon wieder. *Die Zeit* 25(11): 1994.

Vögele, Wolfgang. 2000. *Menschenwürde zwischen Recht und Theologie*. Gütersloh: Chr. Kaiser.

Von der Pfordten, Dietmar. 2006. Zur Würde des Menschen bei Kant. *Jahrbuch für Recht und Ethik* 14: 501–517.

Waldron, Jeremy. 2007. Dignity and rank. *European Journal of Sociology* 48(2): 201–237.

Part I
Conceptions and Theories

Chapter 3
Humiliation: The Collective Dimension

Christian Neuhäuser

Abstract There are two possible understandings of the idea of a collective dimension of humiliation. One is: *Can collectives violate human dignity?* And the other is: *Can someone violate the (human) dignity of a collective?* The first understanding points to the familiar direction of collective agency and collective responsibility. We ask questions like: Are the Germans responsible for the Holocaust? Is the United States to blame for Guantanamo Bay? And: Do men add to the subjection of women by tolerating or downplaying its importance? There is an ongoing debate over the question whether there can be collective agency and responsibility and how it should be understood if it exists at all.[1] Although this is surely an important debate, it is not the question I want to focus on. My concern here is the second understanding of the question: Can someone violate the human dignity of a collective? The initial response to this question seems to be *no*, because collectives have no dignity and certainly nothing like human dignity. I think this answer is plainly wrong because it rests on a confusion of methodological and ethical individualism (Lukes 1973). It is correct that collective entities do not have dignity apart from their human members, but this does not mean that we have to look at individuals alone and not at groups when being concerned about humiliations. In what follows, I will explain how an account of collective or, rather, shared dignity can be understood and why this is not an issue ethical individuals need to fret about. First, I will describe three ways in which a group can be humiliated. I will then assess how the third and most indirect way, namely group humiliation through the humiliation of individual members, can be understood. Finally, I will outline how an account of shared dignity might help us to understand the role of a concept of special group rights within the family of human rights.

C. Neuhäuser (✉)
Department of Philosophy, Ruhr-University Bochum, Germany
e-mail: Christian.neuhaeuser@rub.de

[1]Recent accounts of shared intentions and collective or corporate responsibility can be found in an anthology by Peter French (French and Wettstein 2006).

P. Kaufmann et al. (eds.), *Humiliation, Degradation, Dehumanization*,
Library of Ethics and Applied Philosophy 24, DOI 10.1007/978-90-481-9661-6_3,

3.1 Three Ways of Humiliating a Group

At first sight it seems to be strange to assume that a collective can be humiliated. A collective might be able to act and might even be a responsible agent, but it certainly is not a fully-fledged person with dignity. I do not want to argue this point and, therefore, concede that it is better to talk about groups when it comes to dignity and about collective or corporate agents only when it comes to responsibility. The question of collective humiliation is, therefore, not whether a collective has personal dignity but whether groups have something like shared dignity. I think it can be shown that individuals indeed share dignity within groups (Bayertz 1996, Kretzmer and Klein 2002, Stoecker 2003). A good way of pointing to this fact is by looking at ways in which groups are humiliated.

I will follow Margalit in using humiliation as a normative concept and not only as a psychological one: "Humiliation is any sort of behaviour or condition that constitutes a sound reason for a person to consider his or her self-respect injured" (Margalit 1996: 9). Someone can feel humiliated without in fact being humiliated. And one can respond to a humiliation with different feelings, or stoic indifference. It is important to see what humiliations in the normative sense are about: They attempt to lower someone below the status of a human being as a person with dignity through an improper attitude or treatment. In this normative sense, humiliation is close to dehumanization, and not all kinds of degrading treatment can be understood as humiliating. On this understanding, I see three different ways of humiliating a group.[2]

1. The first case can be called *direct group humiliation*, since in this case all members of a group are directly humiliated precisely because they are members of this group. Imagine that special sections are opened at airport controls for people who appear to be of Islamic religion and that they are checked in an especially thorough way because they are rated as possible terrorists.[3] Such a treatment would be humiliating for each and every affected individual. However, this procedure can also be regarded as a form of group humiliation because the individuals are humiliated *as* members of a group (namely people of Islamic faith). I think it is rather important to point out the role of the group here. It is by virtue, and *only* by virtue, of being a member of this group that these individuals are humiliated. The humiliation depends on the attributes that are ascribed to the group and the humiliating attitude

[2]My thanks go to the colloquium on applied ethics at the University of Potsdam for pointing out that there is a strong need to separate these cases.

[3]Some people have suggested to me that thorough controls in themselves are not humiliating. I think this is somewhat isolating the example from its social context. Consider that these people are singled out just because of their religion and see in the eyes of all other people from whom they are separated the fearful question: Are you a terrorist? This clearly has to count as a humiliation, because these persons are not judged for what they are but for the worst anybody could be and they have no way of telling the other customers: Look, this is just a weird misunderstanding.

towards the group that is perceived in such a way. A struggle for recognition must therefore focus on the group level and should not isolate the affected individuals.[4]

It should be clarified whether a threat of direct group humiliation exists for all groups or only for those Margalit and Raz call encompassing groups (Margalit and Raz 1990: 439–461). Encompassing groups play a significant role in their individual members' lives and are important for their self-definition. This is why hurting an encompassing group amounts to damaging the self-image of its individual members. Margalit asserts that a decent society does not reject legitimate encompassing groups, i.e. groups that are not humiliating others (Margalit 1996: 141). I agree that a group must be legitimate in this sense to earn the right not to be rejected, but I do not think that direct group humiliation can only exist when it comes to encompassing groups. The reason for this is quite simple: The direct humiliation of a group can transform a group into an encompassing group and any group, however random, can be directly humiliated. Imagine that the special airport controls are not designed for people of Islamic religion, but for those with green eyes who are taller than 180 cm. Before this regulation there was probably no such an encompassing group of tall, green-eyed people at all. But when the regulation is enforced, it will quickly become obvious what kinds of people are singled out and that this is all they have in common. It is by virtue of those attributes that they are humiliated, and those attributes lead them to form an encompassing group exactly because this group becomes important for their self-definition through the shared fate of humiliation at airports.[5]

One objection might state that this account of direct group humiliation overlooks the fact that not all people of Islamic religion would be humiliated by selective airport controls, because many people never fly. One answer would be to construct smaller groups, namely those who fly and are of Islamic religion, or those who are tall and green-eyed. This, however, would mean to overlook an important difference between the two groups of people of Islamic religion, on the one side, and Muslims who fly, on the other. It is not only the case that everyone should be allowed to fly without being humiliated, Muslim or not. It is furthermore the case that even those of Islamic religion who do not fly are potentially humiliated, because flying is something that might well fit into their self-concept and could come about instantly. I will come back to potential problems regarding the treatment of Muslims in Western societies when I discuss representative group humiliation later.

2. The second case can be called *symbolic group humiliation*. Here, not all members of a group are directly confronted or threatened with humiliating acts. Instead,

---

[4]This is also clearly captured in the social and political theory of recognition developed by Axel Honneth (1996).

[5]This is not meant to negate that in fact the groups that are humiliated for certain reasons, because they are of different faith for instance or are of a lower social status. In fact there is always a story behind humiliating attitudes and behavior and it is important to look at this history when one wants to overcome this indecency.

a symbol of the group is in some way defiled, which then constitutes a humiliation for all members of this group and therefore a group humiliation in the sense of a humiliation of shared dignity. There are many cases of this kind of symbolic group humiliation. Think of the defilement of a Jewish graveyard or the abasing picturing of homosexuals on TV. These are clear cases, but things get more complicated when we think of the burning of American flags or the ridiculing of religious leaders. Normally, we do not take these acts to constitute serious humiliations, but rather something like maybe tolerable, maybe insulting mocking. Why are the first two examples cases of symbolic group humiliation and not the other two?

One suggestion would be that the first two cases are indeed threatening, only in an indirect way. The rejection from humankind is not only pictured but connected to some real danger. In the case of the homosexuals, they were and in some ways still are not treated as equals in our societies. And the history of the Holocaust is still very much alive today. Therefore, the defilement of a group symbol must be connected to a real threat in order to constitute a symbolic group humiliation and not merely a form of mocking.[6] Only then the symbolic action bears the power that warrants calling it a rejection from humankind. This is why the burning of American flags is not humiliating, even if it is intended to be so. It may still be perceived as insulting, but that (as I will argue later) is another matter.

It is important to note that the existence of a real threat is not enough to establish this connection between symbolization and humiliation. There must be a closer conceptual link. For instance, many people think the Muhammad caricatures were not humiliating even though people of Islamic religion might be subject to diverse threats in Western societies. They were not humiliating because they were not intended to humiliate, but only to mock. This accounts for a striking difference between direct group humiliations (and representative group humiliations), on the one hand, and symbolic group humiliations, on the other. Normally, humiliations do not have to be intended as humiliations and not even to be perceived as humiliations in order to be humiliating. It is enough to see from an external perspective that someone is rejected from humankind or not granted proper self-control. In the case of symbolic humiliations, a direct connection between the symbolic act and the humiliation of the victims is absent. This connection has to be established through intentions.

In cases of symbolic group humiliations, the humiliation is dependent on the displayed connection to real threats. This display must be intended otherwise the perception of the connection is only a misunderstanding. Take again the example of the defilement of Jewish graveyards. This is humiliating, because it reminds one of the Shoah, and, moreover, it is threatening as a matter of fact when someone goes as far as besmearing gravestones. What else is he ready to do?[7] But even a caricature

[6]Note that the idea of a connection does not necessarily imply that there is a precursor of a future violation, it can also point at past violations in order to be humiliating, but it must be linked to those grim memories in order for that to be so (Thompson 2002: 101–113).

[7]An act that is intended to humiliate, like the defilement of Jewish graveyards, does not have to lead to felt humiliation, but can lead to other feelings like anger or fear. In many cases, anger might

of defiled Jewish graveyards would be humiliating, because we cannot imagine that someone would do this without thinking of the Holocaust. It is reasonable to assume that to produce such a caricature was intended to be and therefore *is* humiliating. Following this line of thought, it is questionable if in the light of Abu Ghraib and Guantanamo Bay the Muhammad caricatures must be intended to be humiliating. I don't want to take a stance here and think that it is open to further debate if the link between those incidents is tight enough or not. The crucial question here is: Were and are the prisoners mistreated because they are seen as evil terrorists or because they are seen as Muslims, or both? What is very troublesome about this group of cases is that some people seem to lose sight of the fact that the two groups are totally different, which already constitutes a major humiliation of a whole group of many millions of religious people.

3. The third case can be called *representative group humiliation*. Here a whole group is humiliated through the humiliation of one or more of its members. In cases that belong to this category the specific elements of the other two forms of humiliation are often combined. Individual persons are humiliated because they are members of a specific group, and at the same time this individual humiliation constitutes a symbolic group humiliation. I think the case of representative humiliation is the most difficult to understand, because it is far from self-evident how the humiliation of some individuals can constitute the humiliation of a whole group. I also think that this case provides the strongest argument for specific group rights. This is why I will take a closer look at representative group humiliations in the next section before discussing the role of group rights within the family of human rights.

3.2 Can the Humiliation of Some Individuals Violate the Dignity of a Group?

We have already seen that this question seems to be very strange because a collective certainly does not have dignity. This is certainly true, but there is still something to be said for the idea of representative group humiliation. I will start out with a rather innocent example to establish the more basic points of what this idea might be about. From there I will consider different attempts to formulate a concept of representative group humiliation, whereas rejecting the first attempts lead to a more comprehensive account of representative group humiliation.

If we say that one soccer team humiliated another one, this sounds metaphorical not only because soccer teams normally do not humiliate each other (as individual players appear to do – remember the Zidane-Materazzi case). This way of talking (a soccer team is humiliated) is also metaphorical because the team itself cannot be

---

be an appropriate reaction to an attempt to humiliate. Nonetheless, the act of defilement of Jewish graveyards still qualifies as humiliating in a normative sense. I thank Guy Stroumsa for pointing this out to me.

humiliated. Of course not, one feels inclined to add, because evidently only the individual members of the team as beings with dignity can be humiliated. This seems to be true, since without the players there would be no team, and, moreover, it is the players who feel the stain of dishonor and not some strange collective entity. Again, this is certainly the case, but still something strange is happening. Think of the players on the bench or the fans in the ranks. Without doubt they also feel humiliated, at least if they are good team members and real fans. But how can that be? They did not play; they did not get beaten, smashed and crushed. To summarize: No act of humiliation was carried out against them. The answer to this little puzzle is quite obvious and straightforward: They feel debased because they identify with their team. They are all part of it and whether they play an active role does not matter in the least. "They live and die with their band," so to say.

Following these suggestions, an initial way of explaining the idea that a collective can be humiliated shows up. I will follow this thread of thought and give a number of possible understandings of representative group humiliations ranging from number A to D, where the first three suggestions (A–C) prove inadequate but eventually lead to the fourth, complete understanding of representative group humiliations (D). The initial approach goes like this:

(A) If one member or some members of a group are humiliated, the whole group is humiliated.

Although the point of identification with a group seems to be well captured in sentence (A), there is a problem, namely that its content is certainly too strong. Think again of the maybe humiliating comment Materazzi made to Zidane (or the other way round). Let's say, for the sake of the argument, that it was indeed a humiliating comment. Still, only Zidane was affected, maybe also some of his family members, but certainly not his team or the whole French nation. Sentence (A) must be wrong because it would include lots of cases where in fact no group was humiliated.

Although (A) is not the formulation I am looking for, however, there is a trouble-free pass to improvement. As we have seen, the humiliating comment made to Zidane had nothing to do with the team, but only with him and maybe his family. Therefore, we can infer, the humiliation of a group member must somehow be directed at that group in order for the group to be humiliated. It is tempting to connect collective humiliation to the intention not only to humiliate the individual but the whole group. In my view, this does not work out, and I will now have to put the example of football aside and move on to more troubling examples to show why. It is difficult to talk about such gruesome cases in philosophical papers because it is hard to pay due respect to their sad significance and to grasp their full reality. I think it is nonetheless important to deal with them because, in the end, ethical theorists should be especially concerned about such cases and learn to develop the sensitive language that is needed to deal with them, especially when it comes to concepts like humiliation and dignity.

There are cases where the intention to humiliate the whole group does play an important role. The systematic use of rape as a means of inhuman warfare is an example of such an intended group humiliation and, moreover, an example of the inhumanness of warfare (Human Rights Watch 2000, Barstow 2000). Although intentions to humiliate the whole group certainly play a role, this is rather on a psychological and not on a normative level. Margalit uses the example of the contented slave Uncle Tom to emphasize that humiliations need not be felt in order to exist (Margalit 1996: 35–39). In the case of Uncle Tom, we would say that he is humiliated and that it is much worse because he does not even know. We would say so because his enslavement expresses that he is not seen as a fully accepted member of humankind and that he does not possess the form of self-control necessary for self-respect and that in itself is humiliating. This is the difference between a normative and a psychological notion of humiliation, already hinted at earlier.

One may argue that there might be a difference between individual and group cases when it comes to the question of intention, but that does not seem to be the case. If women live in a society where they are treated as subhuman compared to men, this is humiliating. It does not have to be intended as being humiliating; it can even be intended as appropriate treatment, like Aristotle thought of the treatment of women and slaves (Schofield 2005: 91–120). Even a woman who personally lives in a loving and caring environment and is treated as equal, as might have been the case with Aspasia, the wife of Pericles, has a right to see herself as humiliated in a society where women generally are not seen as equal human beings. I will, therefore, move forward with the account of representative group humiliation without using intention but only a weaker notion of directedness. The importance of the shared part of identity can then be expressed like this:

(B) If a humiliation is directed against a collectively shared part of identity, the whole group is humiliated and not only the violated individual.

This formulation sounds somewhat better than sentence (A) because it emphasizes the link between the humiliated individual and the humiliated group. But it is still too strong. To explain why it is not appropriate, I will refer to the difference between humiliation and insult, also introduced by Margalit. To insult someone means to diminish his social position. To humiliate someone means to diminish her self-respect (Margalit 1996: 119–120). The first might be an attack on his honor, but only the latter is an attack on her human dignity. So it is not only important that a humiliation is about a shared part of identity, but it has to be a shared part that is constitutive for self-respect.

When exactly is a shared identity constitutive for self-respect? I think there is no easy answer to this question because it is difficult to draw a clear line between social honor and human dignity. Margalit names three ways to humiliate someone: "(1) treating human beings as if they were not human – as beasts, machines, or subhumans; (2) performing actions that manifest or lead to loss of basic control; and (3) rejecting a human being from the 'family of Man'." (Margalit 1996: 144) The problem with the differentiation between dignity and honor in light of this understanding of humiliation is that taking away someone's social honor is not only insulting or degrading sometimes but can also be humiliating in the fundamental sense that it is violating human dignity. Think of the rather peculiar group of bird lovers. One bird lover might not think that his being a member of a group of bird lovers is a big deal for him. If, for instance, he is ridiculed by his colleagues for his intense bird loving, then he probably feels insulted, but not humiliated, because he is not rejected from humankind. But imagine he learns that in another company some bird lovers are not promoted for the sole reason that they are bird lovers, or they are given the meanest and lowest jobs despite their qualifications and desire for much better jobs. In this case, he might think that this indeed is humiliating for bird lovers in general.

Whether something is humiliating or only insulting for a group cannot depend, therefore, on the importance of the group and whether this group is somehow of existential importance and connected to the innermost needs of an individual. It has to depend on the kind of behavior that is directed against the group members. A fairly unimportant group can become really important when it is humiliated. Although this is already captured in the normative notion of humiliation, it might be helpful to point out that there needs to be a link of a special kind between the acts carried out against the members of the group and their self-respect in respect to what is shared in this group. The cases in which the humiliation itself constitutes the importance of the shared identity that makes it constitutive for self-respect are then included in such a clarification. The formulation can therefore be changed as follows:

> (C) If a humiliation is directed against a collectively shared part of identity that is constitutive for the self-respect of the members of this collective, not only the violated individual but the whole group is humiliated.

This is getting close to what I am looking for, but there still is a problem, because the tie between the self-respect of an individual and a group still seems to be too tight. Consider this: Whenever an individual is humiliated, and this is directly connected to a part of her shared identity, all those who share this part are also humiliated. It is certainly true that this formulation now excludes many cases, but there are still some other cases that need to be excluded. This is because in some cases the humiliation of one person is humiliating for those who share her identity in a relevant way; there are others where it is only insulting, and there are those where it might not have any (justified) group effects at all.[8]

[8]Samuel Kerstein suggested that the humiliation of a group member might be welcomed, even when it is directed against a shared part of identity that is constitutive for the self-respect of the members of the group. This could be the case when one member of a group is just taking it much too far in being proud of having this identity. Likewise Marcus Düwell suggested that it might be called for to humiliate those who are themselves very humiliating in their attitude. I think a group can rightfully want one of its members to be insulted, but not to be humiliated. And it might be that there are cases where humiliation is the only response to prevent humiliation and, therefore, some kind of self-defence. But I have no clue how such cases would look and how it can be made certain that those members of the group who do not humiliate are also not humiliated. Moreover, I think both have something similar in mind that is degrading but not humiliating. There are probably many cases where degrading someone can be justified; there are no cases where it is justified to humiliate someone, or, at least, I can think of none.

How can this be the case? The humiliation of one group member is insulting for the whole group when there is some strong sense of a common fate, including a feeling of solidarity that leads to profound sympathy. If such a connection between members in a group is lacking, a humiliation of one member might be perceived without any reaction at all. This would explain why the feeling of being insulted is sometimes present and sometimes absent, and always justified when present. It does not explain why the humiliation of some members of a group is not always humiliating for all members of the group in the normative sense of the notion.

I believe the difference comes from the role played by social reactive attitudes in the construction of self-respect. We need to know how and where we stand in society, how we are perceived by the dominant culture, and if our way of living is recognized as acceptable and respected as such (Stoecker 2004: 107–119). When a humiliation is not sanctioned by a society or not strongly opposed, then this reactive attitude or its lack constitutes a collective humiliation. Why is this the case? What does society have to do with self-respect? The idea is quite simple. As pointed out above, I need to have the feeling that I am recognized as an equal human being with self-respect by the society that I belong to. If a member of a group with which I identify is humiliated as a member of this group and I happen to live in a society where nobody cares about this humiliation, then I am humiliated too. This is because my identity is not respected in the society I belong to – even if I myself might still be treated as an equal human being, this is only due to chance and I am therefore not a full member of society. Since being a recognized member of society is constitutive for my self-respect, I am humiliated when I have reason to feel excluded from society, which is the case when those with whom I share my identity are not cared for in times of grave mistreatment. If, on the other hand, the humiliation is not carried out by representatives of the society I belong to and if there is an adequate social reaction to it, then I do not have any reason to feel humiliated. I might still have a reason to feel insulted if I feel strong sympathy with the insulted individual, since the act of humiliation is so closely connected to an identity I share. And although my self-respect is not diminished, the humiliation of someone who is so much like me might by itself give me a reason to feel insulted on his or her behalf and on behalf of what we have in common. This leads to the following series of claims:

> (D^1) If a humiliation is directed against a collectively shared part of identity that is constitutive for the self-respect of the members of this collective, not only the violated individual but the whole group is either insulted or humiliated.
>
> (D^2) An act is humiliating for a group when it is sanctioned on a social level, or no appropriate measures against it are taken.
>
> (D^3) An act might be insulting for a group when appropriate measures against the humiliation of one of its members are taken.

I think these statements capture the collective dimension of human dignity when it comes to representative group humiliations. This final account of representative group humiliation can be rephrased in the following way:

(I) The humiliation of some members of a group is humiliating for the whole group, if:

(II) the humiliation is directed against a collectively shared part of identity;

(III) this shared part of identity is constitutive for the self-respect of the members of this group;

(IV) the humiliation is sanctioned on a social level and/or no appropriate measures against it are taken.

Before I move on to clarify some open points and discuss whether group humiliations can be a basis for group rights, I want to examine three examples for representative group humiliations.

Until as late as 1997, it was not legally forbidden in Germany for men to force their wives into sexual intercourse as long as no serious physical harm was done, because spousal rape was not legally recognized.[9] Such a rape is humiliating for women in the normative sense of the notion, regardless of being recognized as such, because women are not treated as autonomous agents with self-respect when they have no control over their sexual activities. Even a woman in a loving and caring relationship who is not threatened in this way has a right to see herself as humiliated in a society in which spousal rape is not recognized as something that is humiliating and legally forbidden. This is the case because society tells her that in some way women should not or need not have control over themselves as men do. Such an attitude is an attack on the self-respect of women as equal human beings, and, therefore, they are seen as subhuman in this respect.

Now what if a spousal rape is carried out, but is condemned and sanctioned on a social level? The raped woman is humiliated by her husband, but other women are not humiliated, because society shows that it sees the act as what it is: the humiliation of a woman by her husband and therefore as a violation of her right to be treated as a person with self-respect. Out of a sense of solidarity and sympathy other women might still feel insulted by that act, but that is another matter. Moreover, the raped woman is humiliated in the normative sense, but the reactive attitude on a social level also tries to tell her that she does not need to feel humiliated in the psychological sense because society recognizes the way she is treated as a violation of her rights. Rights that she is still capable to make full use of on a normative level, once she is protected from her husband.

Another example is the turmoil that is often caused by the mistreatment of individuals by the police. In 1992, the Los Angeles riots started after four white policemen were acquitted despite the fact that they had beaten up a black person. In the present context, it is an interesting fact that the riot did not start directly after the beating became public but only when it turned out that the policemen would not be punished. This can be seen as a response towards a social reactive attitude which was experienced as a representative group humiliation. This is not to say that the riots were justified in any way – in fact, many serious crimes were committed;

---

[9]For data on rapes in marriages: Vergewaltigung in der Ehe: "Wer den eigenen Mann anzeigt, setzt sich nicht mehr an den gemeinsamen Tisch." *Der Tagesspiegel*, 26 July 2000.

at least 53 persons were killed, many more injured, and a lot of private and public property destroyed. The judges, attorneys and members of the jury made two mistakes. First they did not sentence the four policemen, who obviously committed a serious crime. Second they were not aware of the public dimension of the case. They did not foresee that many people would identify with Rodney King, not because he was a criminal but because he was black. Those people saw King as a black person mistreated by white policemen. In their eyes this mistreatment was a humiliating act because he was not treated as white criminals would have been. When the policemen were not punished for their crime, society sanctioned this humiliation and it became a case of representative group humiliation.

A third example I already touched upon earlier might be the treatment of some people of Islamic religion in the course of what is now called the war against terrorism. In Guantanamo Bay, people are treated as prisoners of war without any acknowledged legal status and in a way that is harshly criticized by many human rights groups and activists. During the war in Iraq, some American soldiers tortured Iraqi prisoners in Abu Ghraib. The goal of this torture was not to acquire information, which is also humiliating. The goal was no other but to humiliate the prisoners.[10] These are humiliating acts, and in my understanding torture is never justified, and even the most dangerous prisoners should never be treated the way they are in Guantanamo Bay. I do not wish to discuss the connection between damaged pride and the desire to humiliate others, which often goes hand in hand on an individual level and might also be an important explanation on a social level. I am more concerned with the question of whether or not Guantanamo Bay and Abu Ghraib can be seen as cases of representative group humiliation. I think that they should not be understood in this way for two reasons. First, in Guantanamo Bay, the victims are seen as terrorists. This is not to say that there is no danger that Western society is on the edge of committing cases of representative group humiliations. I think it is imperative to move very carefully here by being especially clear that terrorism and Islam have no internal connection at all. Not only are group humiliations morally as bad as individual humiliations, but, moreover, severe damage is done to peaceful and respectful relations between two groups of people when members of one humiliates members of the other.

This danger gives additional urgency to the question whether special group rights are justified that apply when a group is humiliated or threatened with humiliation. In order to discuss this point I want to clarify some aspects of the normative account of humiliation presented above and discuss the difference between group rights that have their basis in ethical holism and group rights that have their basis in ethical individualism.

[10]There are now many books on Guantanamo Bay. One by an activist insider is: C. Stafford Smith (2007) One that explores the ethical dimension of the case: C. Butler (2007). There are even more books published on Abu Ghraib. For an investigative journalist's perspective: M. Danner (2005). For interesting reflections of an art historian: S. F. Eisenman (2007). Material on both cases can be found in: W. F. Zimmerman (2004).

3.3 The Normative Account of Humiliation and Group Rights

By now it should be clear that in my opinion there clearly are cases of collective humiliation. Dignity can be shared in groups, and our self-respect is highly dependent on the social role played by those groups we belong to. First, individuals belonging to a group can be humiliated because every member of this group in a certain situation will be humiliated. This I called direct group humiliation and gave the example of special and degrading airport controls. Second, whole groups of individuals can be humiliated through the mistreatment of certain symbols of the group when this mistreatment is connected to past humiliations or the threat of present humiliations. This I called symbolic group humiliation and gave the example of the defilement of graveyards. Third, whole groups can be humiliated when one or more of its members are humiliated and that is somehow sanctioned by society. This I called representative group humiliation and discussed at length, giving the examples of spousal marriage, racist policemen, and torture in Abu Ghraib and Guantanamo Bay.

But does this account of group humiliation and shared dignity give rise to special group rights, or can the importance of this collective dimension of dignity be captured in individual rights? The right to form and take part in non-humiliating groups, for instance, is an individual right and not a group right. The same is true for the right to be treated as an equal human being with dignity, regardless of what kind of non-humiliating groups one belongs to. So maybe there is no need for group rights, even though dignity as such might be essentially social. One of the important implications of the normative concept of dignity is indeed that *only* individual human beings and *all* individual human beings have dignity. If one accepts that human dignity is the fundamental basis for human rights, then all basic rights have to be justified with reference to individual dignity and not to the cultural or other importance of some group. However, it would be a misunderstanding to think that ethical individualism blocks the possibility of special group rights that are based in the dignity of individuals. The idea of shared dignity and collective humiliation might help us in figuring out whether we need such rights. Before I turn to the question of how group rights can be understood in the light of shared dignity, I want to clarify two points concerning the normative idea of dignity and humiliation. These clarifications are needed in order to stress the importance of the collective aspect of dignity and to point out that this does not lead to normative collectivism or holism, as Popper designated the enemies of his open society, which is primarily a society of ethical individualists.

Above, I have followed Margalit's claim that there is a difference between dignity and honor, but I have also claimed that diminishing social honor can be humiliating. This seems to confuse the distinction between insult and humiliation. Indeed, there seems to be a problem with the clear differentiation between humiliation and insult as conceived by Margalit. I think there are ways of diminishing someone's social honor that are not only insulting but humiliating. This is the case because being an honorable member of a society can be essential for someone's self-respect as a human being. Consider the case of a respectable school teacher suspended from his duty because he believes in the "wrong" religion. This is an attack on his social honor, but it is also humiliating because it destroys the former teacher's self-respect. The destruction is not due to the fact that he cannot teach anymore – maybe he did not like teaching at all; the way people look at him in public is the real problem. Still, the teacher is not rejected from humanity but only from the group of those who are thought to be fit to be teachers. Maybe people think: Well, he is a good man and fellow citizen, but we cannot let someone with such a religion instruct our children. Being a teacher is not essential to live a good life and also not essential to be respected as a human being. If the person never was a teacher then, for him, this would not be a problem at all. But we would still say that it really is humiliating for this person to be suspended from his duties just because of his religion.

The answer to this puzzle lies in the notion of social dignity. When Margalit only talks about dignity, on the one hand, and social honor, on the other, he neglects something like social dignity, which lies in-between. Social dignity is *dignity* and not only honor, because without it someone is not a fully respected member of a society. But it is *social* and not human dignity, because this does not necessarily mean that someone could not be a respected member in another kind of society of humans. The rejection depends on the standards of this particular society and not on the fundamental idea of being human. For instance, not having any shoes to put on certainly is debasing in our society, but it does not have to be an issue at all in a totally different society. The distinction between the two kinds of dignity can also be seen as the background for the differentiation between absolute poverty, which is a problem from the perspective of human dignity, and relative poverty, which is a problem from the perspective of social dignity (Ladwig 2002). These examples should make clear that what counts as humiliating is sometimes dependent on social conditions. It is not the case that some basic material conditions just have to be fulfilled and above that bottom line questions of humiliation do not arise anymore. When women do not have equal access to public offices this is humiliating because it implies that women are not seen as equal beings and are somehow subhuman compared with men.

The concept of social dignity can be seen as an argument for group rights to equal treatment and recognition and special policies that lead to the fulfillment of rights like, for instance, affirmative action. This is because whether a society is confronted with a humiliating discrimination or not can only be seen on a group level and not on an individual level, or to put it in other words: Only then the structural discrimination which constitutes the humiliation becomes visible.

There is another issue that needs to be solved. Of course, there are cases where members of a group feel humiliated, when in fact they are not. These cases resemble those where individuals feel humiliated, when in fact they are not. The point is that they ground their self-respect in the wrong things – things that have nothing to do with their ability to live a decent life as a human being in a particular society. When someone thinks that he needs to have a very nice handbag or she needs to have a very expensive car in order to have reason to respect him- or herself, that person is surely mistaken (at least in most societies). If, for instance, the car or the handbag is taken away from them for whatever reasons, and if they are still able to dress and travel properly, no humiliation has taken place. They may have been insulted, but that is a completely different issue.[11]

A good example for such a misunderstanding of group humiliation is provided by Turkish criminal law. According to article 301 of the Turkish penal code, it is a crime to insult "Turkishness." For instance, the writer Orhan Pamuk was charged with insulting "Turkishness" when stating that: "Thirty thousand Kurds and a million Armenians were killed in these lands and nobody but me dares to talk about it."[12] Article 301 makes at least two mistakes. First, there is nothing like "Turkishness" that can be insulted or humiliated, and the same is true for states, nations, churches, religions, and so on; neither they nor any other institution can be humiliated. It is only individual beings that can be humiliated, because only they have dignity grounded in the fact that they are sentient beings, free agents, and autonomous persons.[13] Second, it is wrong to accuse someone of humiliation where, in fact, no humiliation has taken place, even if there are feelings of humiliation. To state that some group committed serious crimes is not humiliating for any individuals, though it can be controversial and felt to be insulting when wrong, and then it calls for an apology. The consequences, if the accusation is correct, might be degrading, for instance, because reparations have to be paid and attempts of reconciliation made (Thompson 2002), but insulting or degrading someone is different from humiliation because it does not have to be, and often is not, connected to dehumanization.

Following this line of thought, the question arises how humiliating groups should be treated. In my view, even with humiliating groups humiliations have to be avoided, in a similar way in which the humiliation of individual beings always has to be avoided. This is the case because in a certain fundamental sense dignity is something that nobody can ever lose, which demands that this person or group should be treated with some respect and not in a humiliating way.[14] It might still be acceptable to insult a humiliating group or to degrade it, but that still is another matter.

So what about group rights? To ground a possible account of group rights in human dignity and the protection from humiliation certainly rules out those group

---

[11] One might think that they are not treated as rational agents when treated like this, but this is not the case given that rational reasons are given for this action. One might also think that they are not treated as autonomous agents. I think this is also not the case because one of their autonomous decisions is not respected, which is different from not treating some as a person with autonomy.

[12] In the end, the case was dropped. See: "Court Drops Turkish Writer's Case," BBC, 23 January 2006.

[13] This account is obviously based on the Kantian idea that our dignity stems from our nature as rational beings and, therefore, as free agents. It also extends this account, however, because it recognizes that we are sentient beings with rationality in the Kantian sense (Baumann 2003: 19–34, Schaber 2003: 119–131).

[14] This idea also goes back to Kant and his idea that everything has a price (*Preis*) while only human beings have dignity (*Würde*). In the German constitution this is captured in article 1, paragraph 1: "Human dignity is inviolable. To respect and to protect it is the duty of all state authority." This leads to the problem of the paradox of humiliation, i.e. the question why dignity matters when it cannot be violated. A solution to this problem is presented by Ralf Stoecker (Stoecker 2003: 133–151).

rights that are themselves humiliating. It cannot be the case that some groups have special rights because they see themselves as more human or in any other way ethically superior to other groups. This is why the special rights of, for instance, apartheid can never be justified and are ruled out by any account of shared dignity based on ethical individualism. Group rights based on human dignity can therefore never help to justify the superiority of any group. Instead they have an enabling aspect. Non-humiliating groups that are not recognized as equals in their social environment are violated in their fundamental rights, and this gives rise to certain claims to affirmative action to put it differently: When groups are humiliated and not treated as equals as they should, a duty to grant them this equal status arises. Moreover, group rights based on human dignity are also protective. When a group is threatened in its status as a recognized part of the social whole, it has a right to protective actions, like campaigns raising awareness or the persecution of those who humiliate its members or symbols. These measures are precisely what I call social reactive attitudes in the context of representative group humiliation.

As a consequence, it can be claimed that there should be special enabling rights for women as long as they are not treated as equals. As soon as they have the same access to the same social positions without affirmative action, this special treatment has to be stopped in order to avoid new inequalities. The same holds for poor people. Being poor disables one from exercising one's rights as a citizen. This disability can easily be removed and is, therefore, humiliating. Affirmative action is needed to help poor people out of their poverty and provide them with the material basis necessary to be able to live as equal citizens in their society. As soon as this is achieved, redistribution cannot be grounded in social dignity anymore. One might think that further redistribution is still needed, but then it would have to be grounded in different principles provided, for instance, by a stronger account of social equality. These are examples for enabling rights. Let's turn to protective rights: For instance, the elderly or people of Islamic faith might have a claim to special protective rights. In my view, they are not seen or treated as subhuman (yet), but there is a certain danger in our societies' present attitude of Westernism and anti-aging rhetoric. Examples like these highlight the importance of group rights as a political measure to end or prevent the humiliating treatment of legitimate groups or groups that are constituted by their humiliating situation.

Although there is much more to be said about group rights, I will end here and summarize. The view I presented on the different forms of the humiliation of groups, of shared dignity, and of group rights can help us to overcome the danger of an evanescence of dignity which could come about through an attitude of radical individualization. On such an account, persons are seen as atomic entities that do not need to have social ties in order to live a decent or even a good life. The alternative account of shared dignity and the three ways of humiliating groups show that this is false. At the same time it should be clear that group rights have to be based in ethical individualism in order to overcome totalitarian tendencies and the attempted justification of humiliating attitudes towards other groups. Only under these conditions will a peaceful coexistence of culturally diverse groups that nonetheless respect each other become possible.

References

Barstow, Anne. 2000. *War's dirty secrets: Rape, prostitution and other crimes against women.* Cleveland, OH: Pilgrim.
Baumann, Peter. 2003. Menschenwürde und das Bedürfnis nach Respekt. In *Menschenwürde. Annäherungen an einen Begriff,* ed. Ralf Stoecker, 19–34. Wien: Öbv & Hpt.
Bayertz, Kurt, ed. 1996. *Sanctity of life and human dignity.* Dordrecht: Kluwer.
Butler, Clark, ed. 2007. *Guantanamo bay and the judicial-moral treatment of the other.* West Lafayette, IN: Purdue University Press.
Danner, Mark. 2005. *Torture and truth: Abu Ghraib and America in Iraq.* London: Granta.
Eisenman, Stephen. 2007. *The Abu Ghraib effect.* London: Reaktion.
French, Peter and Howard Wettstein, eds. 2006. *Shared intentions and collective responsibility. Midwest Studies in Philosophy*, vol. XXX. Boston, MA: Blackwell.
Honneth, Axel. 1996. *The struggle for recognition: The moral grammar of social conflicts.* Cambridge, MA: MIT.
Human Rights Watch. 2000. *Kosovo: Rape as a weapon of "ethnic cleansing".* New York, NY: Human Rights Watch.
Kretzmer, David and Eckart Klein, eds. 2002. *The concept of human dignity in human rights discourse.* The Hague: Kluwer Law International.
Ladwig, Bernd. 2002. Arm und Reich. Eine Normative Betrachtung. In *Was Reichtümer vermögen. Gewinner und VerliererInnen in Europäischen Wohlfahrtsstaaten*, ed. Die Armutskonferenz, 12–28. Wien: Mandelbaum.
Lukes, Steven. 1973. *Individualism.* New York, NY: Harper & Row.
Margalit, Avishai. 1996. *The decent society.* Cambridge, MA: Harvard University Press.
Margalit, Avishai and Joseph Raz. 1990. Self-determination. *Journal of Philosophy* 87: 439–461.
Schaber, Peter. 2003. Menschenwürde als Recht, nicht erniedrigt zu werden. In *Menschenwürde. Annäherungen an einen Begrif,* ed. Ralf Stoecker, 119–131. Wien: Öbv & Hpt.
Schofield, Malcolm. 2005. Ideology and philosophy in Aristotle's theory of slavery. In *Aristotle's politics. Critical essays,* eds. Richard Kraut and Steven Skultety, 91–120. Lanham, MD: Rowman and Littlefield.
Stafford Smith, Clive. 2007. *Bad men: Guantanamo bay and the secret prisons.* London: Orion.
Stoecker, Ralf, ed. 2003. *Menschenwürde. Annäherungen an einen Begriff.* Wien: Öbv & Hpt.
Stoecker, Ralf, 2004. Selbstachtung und Menschenwürde. *Studia Philosophica* 63: 107–119.
Thompson, Janna. 2002. *Taking responsibility for the past. Reparation and historical justice.* Cambridge: Cambridge Polity.
Zimmerman, Frederick, ed. 2004. *Basic documents about the treatment of detainees at Guantanamo and Abu Ghraib.* Ann Arbor, MI: Nimble Books.

Chapter 4
The Rituality of Humiliation: Exploring Symbolic Vulnerability

Hannes Kuch

Abstract Following the thought of G.W.F. Hegel, this article attempts to look at "human dignity" as a particular form of vulnerability – a symbolic vulnerability, which has its roots in a desire for recognition. My reflections follow two objectives, the starting point for both of which is Hegel's "struggle to death". (1) What does it mean to speak of "dignity" in terms of vulnerability? It means to look at human dignity not as worth or as a strength, but rather as a specific fragility. For Hegel, the longing for recognition implies a dependency on recognition. This dependency may even go so far that human beings accept being insulted. Thus, a person may be recognized so little that an act of humiliation is taken as an act of recognition. From the viewpoint of an autonomy-perspective on human dignity, this openness for humiliation might itself appear to be humiliating. This paradox is discussed by contrasting two readings of Hegel: one which brings him closer to Kant, and one which refers to Judith Butler's account of recognition. (2) My second objective is to point to the *symbolic* dimension of violations of human dignity. This "rituality" of humiliation has its roots in the symbolic dimension of recognition. In recent social theories, the "act of recognition" is spelled out in symbolic terms: To be recognized is to be addressed by the other. This is the reason why not only acts of recognition but also acts of misrecognition, and of humiliation, have a constitutive symbolic dimension. We can indeed be humiliated by simple words. But even mere violence can have a certain ritual dimension – and it is perhaps this very dimension that constitutes its humiliating force.

4.1 Introduction

The photographs of Iraqi prisoners who were tortured by US-soldiers in the course of the third war in Iraq were appalling in various ways. Not just because of the maltreatment and physical violence they showed, but also because of the humiliating

H. Kuch (✉)
Department of Philosophy, Freie Universität Berlin, Germany
e-mail: h.kuch@fu-berlin.de

P. Kaufmann et al. (eds.), *Humiliation, Degradation, Dehumanization*, Library of Ethics and Applied Philosophy 24, DOI 10.1007/978-90-481-9661-6_4,

gestures and postures the victims had been forced to take on. The photographs showed naked bodies piled up on one another, or prisoners being kept on a leash like dogs. These humiliating postures were of central importance with regard to what was going on in Abu Ghraib. They point to a "theatrical" dimension, to a moment of staging within the ritual of humiliation. Of course, this does not mean that the actions were "merely posed" as if they were not real or effective. On the contrary, I think the treatment of the prisoners of Abu Ghraib was humiliating precisely to the extent that humiliating postures and gestures were involved. Moreover, what was frightening was not only what the photographs depicted, but above all the very fact that there were photographs at all. The photographs did not just show what was going on, as if an arbitrary external observer just happened to have taken them, on the contrary, they constituted a crucial part of the scenery. The perpetrators could be seen looking into the camera, even smiling towards it. Maybe the camera was even a spur to stage the humiliations (for more on this question, see Butler 2007). And this spur must have been intense as the photographs were taken under the risk of being used as evidence. Obviously, the importance of the photographs as part of the humiliation offset the peril that these very photographs could become evidence for the maltreatments. If the photographs were crucial for the humiliations in Abu Ghraib, then it is because they brought in an audience that could see or witness the actions. In this sense, I think the photographs of Abu Ghraib point to a symbolic dimension implied in the violation of human dignity: Such violations are often exercised in rituals – that is to say, they are staged like a play in front of an audience.

In what follows, I will try to explain why we should conceive dignity as a *symbolic* vulnerability. We can indeed be humiliated by simple words. But even mere violence can have a certain ritual dimension. This symbolic vulnerability has its basis in the importance of recognition in gaining dignity. I will trace this idea of a dependency on recognition back to its roots in Hegel's "struggle to death". In so doing, I will use the concept of humiliation as a paradigmatic form of violation of human dignity (in such a way that it may even be an overall term for various forms of violations of human dignity); and although humiliation is closely related to the loss of recognition, we will see that not every loss of recognition is humiliating.

However, before I proceed to explore the idea of a constitutive *symbolic* vulnerability (4.3), I would like to enquire into what it means to look at dignity as *vulnerability*. We will see that this idea suggests that we consider human dignity not so much as worth or as a form of strength but rather as a specific fragility. In order to spell out the fabric of this vulnerability, I will contrast it with an approach that looks at human dignity as worth. In fact, both perspectives can be traced back to Hegel. While Hegel's struggle to death can be read as a demonstration of the freedom of human beings, it can, at the same time, be seen as a struggle for recognition. In this latter approach, the struggle for recognition has its roots in an essential dependency of humans on recognition (4.2).

4.2 Vulnerability

4.2.1 The Struggle to Death as a Demonstration of Autonomy

In the primordial scene of Hegel's struggle to death, two subjects meet, and each is willing to kill the other, thereby risking to be killed himself. The aggressiveness of the encounter need not be thought of as a result of a striving for biological survival or a conflict about material goods, as someone like Thomas Hobbes might suggest. For Hegel, the struggle to death is something like an existential demonstration of man's ability to be free. In putting one's own life at risk, one proves oneself to be free of all natural constraints – even the most basic: one's own physiological life. In Hegel's own words: "[. . .] from this perspective, it is only by putting himself as well as others in danger of death that man demonstrates his capacity for freedom" (Hegel et al. 2007 [1830]: 220). Of course, for Hegel, the importance of this scene of struggle lies not in the fact that it might be of empirical relevance. For him, it is already significant that this struggle might happen at all. What is of analytic interest is the fact that we *can* think of human beings as being able to engage in that kind of struggle. Furthermore, the crucial issue for Hegel is not so much the fact of putting one's life at stake in struggling, but rather the fact of being able to commit suicide. In his early writings, Hegel is more explicit about this point: "To him as consciousness it appears that in this he must intend the *death* of the other, although it is his own death that is at issue – suicide, in that he exposes himself to danger" (Hegel 1983 [1805–1806]: 117; see also Kojève 1980: 247–248).

This scope of our autonomy is, according to Hegel, the reason why we recognize the other as person. If the other, in the struggle to death, proves to be willing to risk his own life, we acknowledge or recognize this other as an equal human being. To some extent, Hegel comes close to Kant's notion of respect here.[1] For in a Kantian approach, is freedom of the will: the capacity of an autonomous subject to make rules or "legislative laws" that govern his or her actions the most basic human quality: "The will is therefore not merely subject to the law, but is so subject that it must be considered as also *making the law* for itself and precisely on this account as first of all subject to the law (of which it can regard itself as the author)" (Kant 1964 [1785]: 431). In Kant's view, this is the basis of human dignity, and the source of respect for other persons:

> But the law-making which determines all value must for this reason have a dignity – that is, an unconditioned and incomparable worth – for the appreciation of which, as necessarily given by a rational being, the word '*reverence*' [*Achtung*] is the only becoming expression. *Autonomy* is therefore the ground of the dignity of human nature and of every rational nature. (Kant 1964 [1785]: 436)

[1]In this, I am following a suggestion made by Ernst Tugendhat in "Self-consciousness and Self-determination" (1986: 306).

Autonomy, in this sense, is the reason for the worth of humanity, an incomparable worth which demands respect. Respect for another subject is thus not related to his or her merits; it is related to the most basic human ability, the ability to be free.

Hegel somewhat follows Kant here, yet he spells out this capacity for freedom in more concrete, more radical forms. While Kant emphasizes that autonomy formally means to act according to the laws which one has made for oneself, and therefore being able to act detached from the laws of nature, Hegel pushes this idea to its extreme when he states that in risking their own life human beings are able to act on the basis of their free will even against one of the most basic laws of nature – the drive for physiological self-preservation.

Of course, the heroic gesture of the Hegelian struggle to death might look rather odd nowadays. But one can find certain radical cases of this "capacity for death" even in modernity. In fact, there are extreme conditions such as those that were found in Nazi concentration camps or in slavery, conditions under which human beings may choose death instead of giving in to oppression. Referring to Hegel's master/slave-dialectics, Paul Gilroy takes the life of Frederick Douglass, a famous nineteenth century abolitionist and former slave in the confederate plantation slavery, as an example for the preference of the possibility of death to the condition of slavery. Douglass risked his life in effectively resisting his master: "For him the slave actively prefers the possibility of death to the continuing condition of inhumanity on which plantation slavery depends" (Gilroy 1993: 63). Another example is Bruno Bettelheim, a psychoanalytic theorist, who himself survived a concentration camp. He writes:

> But to survive as a man not a walking corpse, as a debased and degraded but still human being, one had first and foremost to remain informed and aware of what made up one's personal point of no return, the point beyond which one would never, under any circumstances, give in to the oppressor, even if it meant risking and losing one's life. (Bettelheim 1961: 157)

We can see that these extreme cases illuminate Hegel's idea of a capacity for freedom which is revealed in risking one's life. But what if someone is not courageous enough, for whatever reasons, to risk his or her life? If the (potential) capacity for freedom demands that one be recognized or respected, may it not in turn be possible that the (actual) inability to prove this capacity could become a source of contempt or abhorrence? An undertone of this contempt is obvious, for example, in the reflections on the notion of humiliation by Maury Silver and his colleagues. While they refer positively to the prisoners of Nazi concentration camps who fought to live up to their ideals and standards, they write about those who are not able to maintain their agency: "This lack [of power; H.K.] does not make us evil, it may not be our fault, but it makes us ugly, deformed [...]" (Silver et al. 1986: 279). One might even say that a person who is so openly submissive that he or she accepts to be humiliated actually deserves this humiliation. Indeed, Hegel bluntly justified slavery in this way: "Those who remain bondsmen suffer no absolute injustice; for he who has not the courage to risk his life to win freedom, deserves to be a slave [...]" (Hegel 2007 [1830]: 161). The entire scope of the contempt against those who do not stand up and risk their lives to prove their freedom finally becomes obvious if one reads what SS-overseers of Nazi extermination camps said about their Jewish prisoners. In fact, Franz Stangl, the commandant of Treblinka, compares Jewish prisoners with lemmings:

> They were so weak; they allowed everything to happen – to be done to them. They were people with whom there was no common ground, no possibility of communication – that is how contempt is born. I could never understand how they could just give in as they did. (Franz Stangl, in Sereny 1977: 232–233)

Hegel, with his struggle to death as a demonstration of freedom, participates in a perspective that runs the risk of holding those in contempt who are not able, for whatever reasons, to resist. In this sense, this positive account of dignity (dignity as worth) may help to induce the very opposite of that at which it actually aims, resulting in contempt instead of respect. Indeed, praise for the "upright carriage" [*der aufrechte Gang*] (Bloch 1987: 174) can tacitly entail contempt for the broken human being.[2]

Yet there is a second reading of Hegel's struggle to death. Although both readings depart from this struggle, we will see that they are in some respects opposed to one another.

4.2.2 Hegel's Idea of Recognition

In this second reading, the struggle to death can be seen as a struggle for recognition. The two opponents demonstrate that they put their social being above their physiological being; the self reveals that under certain conditions it subordinates everything to its desire to be recognized – even its mere survival. Hegel puts this existential absoluteness in this way: "Self-Consciousness exists in and for itself when, and by the fact that, it so exists for another; that is, it exists only in being acknowledged [*als ein Anerkanntes*]" (Hegel 1977 [1807]: 111). The demand for recognition might become so strong that I am willing to put my life at risk simply for the sake of honor. Historically, this was, of course, the case in rituals of dueling, which allowed a man to re-establish his honor.

According to Hegel, these struggles are based in the fact that identities can be threatened or wounded by acts of misrecognition or disrespect. This is because recognition is constitutive of social and personal identity (Honneth 1995). In this context, for Hegel, to recognize [*anerkennen*] goes beyond the meaning of "identification", it means even more than "to acknowledge someone"; above all, it means "to value" or "to respect" the status of a certain being. Moreover, in an even stronger sense, it means "to esteem", "to honor" or "to love someone" (Inwood 1992). In this sense, we can refer to Alexandre Kojève: human beings love to be loved; they

[2] Margalit clearly points to the peril of any notion of dignity. He writes that any trait with which one tries to justify respect for human beings "[. . .] must not be of the sort that it can be abused – namely, that it can provide a reason for abhorrence or disrespect" (Margalit 1996: 62).

want to be wanted (Kojève 1980: 5–6). For Kojève, the desire for recognition is essentially the desire *to be desired.* In Kojève's view, animal desire is directed at an object – for example, a certain food to satisfy the feeling of hunger. Human desire in contrast is not only directed at another *subject*, but at another subject's *desire*.

Hegel's basic idea was that subjects can only relate to themselves through the medium of recognition. This is why recognition is, under certain conditions, demanded so radically. The self only comes into existence within the dynamics of recognition. This idea of the constitution of the self through recognition has a long history. Starting off with Hegel, it was elaborated in the direction of social psychology by George Herbert Mead (1995 [1934]), whilst from a more psychoanalytic perspective it was Jacques Lacan (2003 [1953]) who followed this Hegelian thought. More recently, the theory of recognition has been renewed by Axel Honneth (1995) and Charles Taylor (1994). The idea of the constitution of the self through the mediation of recognition includes at least three facets: *Firstly*, the self-relation at stake in the procedure of recognition is not epistemic and cognitive, but normative and practical. Thus it is rather about a person saying, "I know that I am good in mathematics" than about someone saying, "I know that I am six feet tall" (Tugendhat 1986: 18–21). *Secondly*, if recognition makes up identity, identity presupposes a social world. If one is to take a normative relation towards oneself, one has to live in a normative context (Honneth 1995). In this sense, reflexivity presupposes reflection: reflection not in the meaning of introspection, but the reflection that is mediated by another person (Margalit 2001). *Thirdly*, due to the dependency on significant others in recognition dynamics, the becoming self relates to the world above all affectively. In the early stages of subject-formation, the infant initially takes the world in as a social world where it emotionally invests in the other and those objects which it takes as substitutes for him or her (this is Lacan's reading of Freud's game *Fort! Da!*, see Lacan (2003 [1953]: 113)). It is only through this detour via the social world that a cognitive, objectifying reference to the world becomes possible (Honneth 2008: 40–44).

Within the horizon of recognition theory, we can conceive dignity preliminarily as a fundamental aspect of identity. The relation to oneself, which makes up identity, is, as we have seen, a normative relation. This normative dimension is grasped in terms like "self-respect" or "self-worth". Both of these terms refer to internal relations of a person to herself, but both terms also have an external dimension (Margalit 1996: 44–53). While self-worth is visibly embodied and displayed in a social context as pride, self-respect is equally embodied and displayed socially and overtly, albeit differently: as dignity (Margalit 1996: 51–53). While self-respect refers to an internal relation of a person to herself, dignity is the external, "lived" embodiment of self-respect.[3] Respect for others is the necessary source of the possibility to gain

[3] Although I am obviously following Margalit and his conception of self-respect to a certain extent here, it is not at all clear how he understands the relation between recognition (or respect) and self-respect. Margalit even seems to question the importance of recognition: "Why should other people's recognition be important to one's self-respect? After all, we are not talking about a person's self-esteem, which must be validated through interaction with others. Self-respect, in contrast

a normative relation towards oneself, not just in the sense of a feeling of self-worth but also in the sense of self-respect.

In being the productive force in the formation of the self, recognition has, on this account, a "productive", i.e., "constitutive", dimension. In this sense, dignity, as embodied self-respect, is not so much the ground for respecting persons but rather its result.[4] But if so, who is it, then, to whom we owe respect? If there isn't any antecedent trait (for example, autonomy) which demands respect, then we do not know any more whom to recognize at all. Why shouldn't we, for example, recognize certain animals that until now have been excluded from our framework of recognition (say worms)? If we take a look at Hegel once more, we can read his idea of a struggle for recognition as an answer to this question. The struggle for recognition, then, is a practical conflict in which the scope of the sphere of recognizable beings is negotiated. Here it becomes obvious which beings need to be recognized or respected. It is the struggle for recognition that shows us which beings care about being respected or not. Obviously, in the future there may be beings other than human beings that demand recognition (cyborgs, perhaps, one day). If someday we get in touch with these beings and experience that they are beings that need to be respected, then, I assume this would lead to a widening of our usage of the term "human" – even if these beings may not necessarily "look" like "us". If our frames of recognition were to change, we would restructure our human world and "form" or "constitute" within our practices of recognition a new group of human beings.[5]

The fundamental question, therefore, is how to refine our sensitivity to how different demands for recognition could become manifest. I think Hegel's idea of a *struggle* for recognition is too narrow an answer. I will later argue that a demand for recognition may take extremely bizarre forms which would not at all fit into Hegel's aggressive pattern of struggling. Albeit in its bizarre manifestation, a certain behavior may articulate a demand for recognition, and the crucial question is whether or

to self-esteem, is the honor a person grants herself solely on the basis of the awareness that she is human" (Margalit 1996: 24). But later, his argument is, quite on the contrary, that self-respect ultimately depends on social contexts because this context is necessary to make it possible for someone to articulate a concept of the human which everyone needs in order to be able to see himself as human. And Margalit coins this social context in terms of recognition: He states that the "skeptical justification for respecting human beings is rooted in the fact that we all *recognize* one another as part of humanity and for this reason and this reason alone we deserve respect" (Margalit 1996: 124, my emphasis).

[4]In recognition theory, there is an ongoing debate between an "attributive" (or "productive") approach to recognition which argues that certain beings are formed or constituted (or at least constituted as selves) in recognition dynamics, and a "receptive" (or "reproductive") approach which assumes that recognition is the acknowledging of an antecedent value or characteristic (see Honneth 2007: 331–332).

[5]Of course, we cannot satisfy all demands for recognition. There is a difference between the basic demand for being recognized as equal being and demands for being recognized in one's special qualities and merits. While the former principle of recognition is (or should be) distributed equally and universally, the latter is distributed differentially and unevenly (see Honneth 1995: 92).

not we are able to see or recognize in this behavior a demand for recognition. I will return to this question later.

Until now I have presented two different readings of Hegel's struggle to death. While from the autonomy-perspective, the freedom of the will of the person is of central importance, the recognition-perspective looks on the struggle to death as a struggle for recognition. The two readings think of the overcoming of the struggle – both parties recognizing each other – in a different way: While in the first reading, it is the autonomy of the other person that is respected, in the second reading, it is the person as desiring being that is respected. The two differing accounts entail different ideas of what humiliation is about. The autonomy-perspective looks at dignity violations as restrictions or denials of other persons' autonomy. My dignity is violated when others treat me only as a means, and not as an end, because this is a way of denying my autonomy. In contrast to this, recognition theory understands humiliation as a radical loss of recognition that may be effected through practices of exclusion.[6]

4.2.3 Longing for Humiliation

We have seen that Hegel's primordial scene of the struggle to death can be read as an answer to the question of which beings we do recognize or respect, or, at least, to which we morally owe recognition. We respect (or we should respect) those beings who prove themselves to depend on respect. The struggle to death is *one* answer to the question of which beings really demand to be recognized. But obviously it is too narrow to presume that the desire for recognition would *only* or *primarily* manifest itself in a struggle to death. Perhaps Hegel in this respect was too much caught up in the rituals and practices of his times (maybe having honor duels in mind). Thus, instead of presupposing a heroic fearlessness – as in putting one's life actively at risk only for the sake of honor – one can also choose to widen the framework of recognition. Then, more passive expressions of the desire

[6]There are, however, cases that may look at first sight like examples of humiliations (in the sense of a loss of recognition) but that turn out, after a closer look, to be examples of a loss of self-control (i.e., as a restriction of autonomy). If we take a look at a racist insult, for example, we may assume that the insulted person knows that the expression was a mere insult and that it is not true, but nevertheless may feel humiliated – and this may be mainly because of the fact that he or she is not able to meet the challenge and throw back another, equally humiliating insult. That is to say that the insult as such may not be humiliating, but the inability to return the challenge actually is. "Our humiliation consists, at least in part, in the particular sort of powerlessness that not answering the challenge represents – weakness, cowardice, lack of wit etc." (Silver et al. 1986: 273). In other words: In this perspective, it would not be the loss of recognition that is humiliating but the loss of autonomy. Yet I think this objection overestimates the dimension of autonomy here. The problem in the example is not so much the loss of control but the specific content of what is said about the insulted person. Of course, experiencing a loss of self-control is a bad thing, but this experience would have been a lot less bad if the insult had been a mere personal insult against some individual weak point.

for recognition come into focus. In fact, there are human beings who have preferred death to the possibility of being ashamed (Lynd 1958: 29). The shame of being humiliated, of living in a state of non-recognition, can be so unbearable that the ashamed person chooses death. This, too, is a version of Hegel's idea of the primacy of recognition over physiological life. But it would, indeed, be an important modification of his account of recognition, as it implies a shift from heroism to passivity. But there may be even more bizarre manifestations of the desire for recognition.

It is Judith Butler's idea that under certain circumstances the desire for recognition may turn into a desire for humiliation. And this desire for humiliation may appear itself – and that is a crucial, and even tragic, point – to be humiliating, contemptible, or undignified. To put it in other words: The trait on account of which someone should be respected (that is, because she or he depends on being respected) could turn into a reason to hold him or her in contempt. It is this radical inversion of our longing for recognition that makes a deepening or widening of our sensitivity for the vulnerability of others so necessary.

But how can that be? How can the desire for recognition turn into a desire to be humiliated? Let us look at two narratives – one more historic, the other more fictional. The first is a story which tells of the days when the Nazi concentration camps were liberated by the allies. A little Jewish girl is found by soldiers; they ask her for her name. She answers: "Jewish pig" [*Judensau*]. The second example is taken from a crucial scene in the film "Happiness" (directed by Todd Solondz, USA 1998). Billy's father sexually abuses one of his son's friends. As the offence is revealed, Billy makes his father explain himself. But Billy does not directly accuse his father of the abuse. Instead, he appears rather to reproach him for having raped his friend and not him.

Both examples deal with exceptional situations, and while the latter is obviously fictive, neither is the historic truth of the former certain. Moreover, both narratives are about children, beings who are extremely dependent on others. Nevertheless, I think both examples reveal something – even if they are purely fictional, even if they depict extreme and exceptional situations. Indeed, both scenes reveal extreme possibilities within the dynamics of recognition: that there can in some cases be so little recognition between humans – the demand for recognition thus so great – that even an act of humiliation is taken as an act of recognition. Under particular circumstances, it could better to be "enthralled" than to have no social existence at all (Butler 2004: 4–5). Something that may hurt us even more than insults is the complete closure of communication, that is, social death in silence. In this sense, humiliation is at the very least a minimal form of recognition – which may be still more bearable than not to be recognized at all. In her reflections on hate speech, Judith Butler points to that possibility:

> There is no way to protect against that primary vulnerability and susceptibility to the call of recognition that solicits existence, to that primary dependency on a language we never made in order to acquire a tentative ontological status. Thus we sometimes cling to the terms that pain us because, at a minimum, they offer us some form of social and discursive existence. (Butler 1997a: 26)

With this idea Butler radically transforms Hegel's heroism. While the Hegelian autonomous subject might say: "It is better to die than to be subjected to someone", Butler's subject of recognition would say: "It is better to be subjected to someone than to die" – and this death being not the *physiological* but the *social* death of the subject (for her notion of "social death" see Butler 2000: 73–74).

The Hegelian struggle to death thus leads to two opposed accounts. As a demonstration of autonomy, one can say that the struggle reveals the dignity of human beings – understood as their capacity for freedom or autonomy. As a struggle for recognition, however, it leads to the idea of a dependency on recognition – a dependency that renders us vulnerable to the insults or humiliations of others. And this dependency on recognition may go so far that human beings accept their own subjection. From the viewpoint of the first perspective – the autonomy-perspective – this openness for subjection might itself appear to be humiliating. A person who readily accepts an insult would demonstrate no self-respect or integrity. From the autonomy-standpoint, the servility of the dependent subject may even result in contempt. Such an attachment can appear to be utterly undignified. It is for this reason that I am reluctant to say that the demand for recognition "is" or "constitutes" human dignity. The dependency on recognition entails an attachment which can appear to be humiliating as such – at least to some extent, however minor. The notion of dignity can imply an idea of strength, and it is this idea of strength which could – unintentionally – help to make us turn away from those who are overtly dependent on others, susceptible to the gestures of others even if they are humiliating. Within the horizon of recognition theory, this inability to resist, this susceptibility for subjection can itself be brought up by our dependency on recognition – which is, in this perspective, at the same time the reason why we are vulnerable to humiliation at all in the first place.

Do I propose, then, to do away with the notion of dignity altogether? I am not sure. Of course, at this point, one could argue that this focus on vulnerability only makes it necessary to restate the concept of dignity in negative terms. In fact, there are approaches which are "negative" in the sense that they take a certain "lack" or "weakness" as the criterion which renders human beings dignified. Sometimes this lack is spelled out in terms of "recognition" or "respect": we are beings who need the respect of others (Baumann 2003). Sometimes this lack is seen in the fact that we are beings who need justifications (Forst 2005). Sometimes it is seen in the fact that we are beings who can suffer humiliation (Schaber 2003). I doubt, however, that our ordinary language can be extended in a way that the term "dignity" designates a lack or a weakness at all. In a non-moral context, we speak of a "dignitary" (*Würdenträger*) when we refer to priests or judges – that is, to social positions of high rank and authority. Or we say: "He maintained his dignity despite his great defeat" (in a football game, for example).[7] In these and similar cases, the term dignity signifies a certain greatness or (inner) strength; by no means a lack.

[7]For these and similar, convincing examples of our ordinary usage of "dignity" see Roughley (1996: 784) or Schaber (2003: 120).

However, there still is a possibility to rethink dignity as vulnerability (that is, as lack). Perhaps it is necessary to underline the fact that certain beings are *able* to be humiliated. In fact, Richard Rorty sees the most basic human essence in "our shared *ability* to suffer humiliation" (Rorty 1989: 91, my emphasis). Of course, it seems paradoxical to show a certain weakness or fragility to be an ability. But maybe this is exactly the decisive conceptual move here. In this sense, the term vulner*ability* would indeed designate an "ability". Yet, it would definitively not refer to the positive capacities, abilities, and faculties, the attributes and qualities, which have been at the centre of philosophical reflection on human nature for such a long time – be this faculty or quality, this "pouvoir" or "avoir", as Jacques Derrida called it, reason, autonomy, or language (Derrida 2002). The negative approach to dignity presented here would rather point to a dimension in which certain creatures are *more* vulnerable than others – nevertheless, it would be a distinctive, that is, extraordinary, characteristic. Symbolic vulnerability, though indicating a weakness, does in fact comprise a sensitiveness which exceeds the sensitiveness of other creatures. Perhaps, then, our picture of the moral notion of dignity should not refer to, say, the solidity of an old tree (which stands there perfectly poised and self-contained) or the sublime movement of a person (for instance an aristocratic lady) but rather to the dignity of a gracefully delicate, wafer-thin porcelain vase – the fragility of which is overtly visible. For, perhaps, it is precisely this openness to see fragility that would allow room for the potential to recognize – and thereby respect – such gracefulness.

4.3 Symbolic Vulnerability

4.3.1 Speech, Gifts, and Recognition

Until now I have discussed the fabric of the specific human vulnerability which renders us sensitive to the humiliations inflicted upon us by others. I have situated this vulnerability within the context of the dependency of human beings on recognition. Having dealt with vulnerability in this sense, I will now move on to enquire whether, and if so in what sense, we should look at this vulnerability as symbolic vulnerability.

In his "Decent Society," Avishai Margalit aptly pointed to "the fact that human beings are creatures capable of feeling pain and suffering not only as a result of physically painful acts but also as a result of acts with symbolic meaning" (Margalit 1996: 84–85). For him, humiliations are cruelties – not in the sense of physical cruelties, but symbolic cruelties. In this context, he refers to the example of mimicking a person's stammer (Margalit 1996: 88) which for him is an act of humiliation, and obviously one constituted by mere words. It is this idea brought by Margalit and others that I want to explore in what follows.[8] To point to the symbolic dimension

[8]Although Margalit is one important philosopher amongst others who have introduced the idea of a symbolic vulnerability, he does not really tell us why human beings are vulnerable in this specific

of violations of human dignity does not mean that there would be an isolated class of humiliating acts which are symbolic actions while other violations of human dignity would be non-symbolic. Violations of human dignity are symbolic as such. Of course, the term "symbolic" here does not mean "non-effective" or "non-serious" (as we could use the term "symbolic" to mean, for example, the "token price" of real estate when it is sold for nearly nothing). My thesis is that only those actions which are to some extent symbolic actions violate human dignity. To be sure, violence – for example, under torture – inflicts physical pain, but if the violence is meant to humiliate the victim, it has a symbolic dimension. The same is true of poverty: Of course, poverty can lead to bad nutrition, or even to hunger. But the humiliating dimension of poverty lies in its symbolic impact. As we will see, all these actions and conditions humiliate insofar as they constitute a certain gesture of exclusion.

This symbolic dimension of humiliation has its roots in the fabric of recognition. In recent social theories, the "act of recognition" is spelled out in symbolic terms: To be recognized is, in this view, to be addressed by the other. The primal scene of this addressing is the act of being given a proper name. It is the proper name that introduces us into the social and which locates us in a social context. The proper name makes it possible to be addressed by others – not only now, but within the duration of time. While "you" only refers to a concrete addressee here and now (and to another addressee in another situation), the proper name makes our social existence persisting (Butler 1997b: 101–103). In more general terms, one can look at language not only as a means of transferring "information" or of making statements with propositional content. Rather, it is about opening up social relations. Language, or more precisely, the interplay between demand and answer, can be seen as an exchange of gifts and thus as a ritual of recognition. To "*give* an answer" would then literally mean the giving of a *corporeal* thing, a *gift*. This, for example, is exactly what rituals of greeting are about: The "Hi, how are you doing?" is not so much concerned with propositional content; it is just about opening up a relationship between self and other, and in this it is a ritual of reciprocal recognition. The idea of conceiving recognition as a symbolic act was most prominently introduced by the French psychoanalyst Jacques Lacan (who himself was deeply influenced by Kojève's famous lectures on Hegel's "Phenomenology" in the 1930s at the *École des Hautes Etudes* in Paris). According to Lacan, a baby's crying for food indicates a *need* for nourishment. But this need is exceeded by the human desire for recognition

sense. Margalit just gives a vague reference to the work of Ernst Cassirer (Margalit 1996: 85). Why doesn't he connect the question of symbolic vulnerability to his idea that the constitution of self-respect depends on a normative social context (Margalit 1996: 124)? What is even more difficult is the problem that Margalit is rather vague about the idea of humiliation as symbolic cruelty itself. In fact, later on in his "Decent Society," he seems to associate the impact of humiliations with the threat to the physiological life of the affected person: "The existential threat implicit in the humiliation must be taken seriously, but not the humiliation itself. The victim has no reason to see any flaw in human value, but only a danger to his existence, or to his basic human condition" (Margalit 1996: 123).

(Lacan 2003 [1958]: 317). The baby not only cries out for food, it also strives to be nourished with care and tenderness. That is why a baby's nourishment by its parents is always both a donation of food and the giving of love. The baby's *need* is directed at the object, but the baby's *desire* aims at the object as a gift: Food is thus a symbol for the baby, a symbol of love. In turning into a symbol, the object de-materializes. The symbol is, to put it in Lacanian terms, the death of the object (Lacan 2003 [1953]: 114).

Of course, at this point one might object that recognition in this view is "merely" symbolic. This objection is important as there are indeed social practices in which symbolic recognition functions as an ideological dispositive (this is discussed at great length in Honneth 2007). Consider, for example, recent discourses in which employees are increasingly addressed as entrepreneurs of their own labor-power [*Arbeitskraftunternehmer*]. This interpellation addresses the employees as subjects with greater autonomy, with a larger agency, with more hope for individual self-realization. At the same time, one can clearly see that the working conditions themselves have not been very much improved beyond renaming the status of the employees. In fact, working conditions may even have worsened: Demands on employees may have increased (in terms of working hours or unpaid overtime, intellectual demands, or responsibilities) while the "material" conditions in terms of payment, for example, may have been kept at the same level. In this sense, ideological, "merely" symbolic recognition can function as means to give esteem to the addressees to make them accept "material" changes for the worse. For these reasons, Axel Honneth concludes that "an act of recognition cannot consist in mere words or symbolic expressions [...]" if it is not supposed to function ideologically (Honneth 2007: 329). Acts of recognition remain insufficient if "they do not go beyond the merely symbolic plane to the level of material fulfillment" (Honneth 2007: 346). This is certainly true. But that does not render recognition merely symbolic. On the contrary, one ought to take into account the fact that "material fulfillments" are part of the process of recognition and that, in this respect, they too count as symbolic. The persons concerned take these fulfillments as a societal expression of their esteem. In turn, the absence of material fulfillment is primarily experienced as social disrespect, which means that it too is experienced as symbolic.[9] In the end, the objection does not contradict but, on the contrary, supports my argument: Even material goods and conditions can turn into symbols of recognition; that is, they can function as symbols.

But not only must we take into account the fact that goods and objects can turn symbolic – the symbolic, too, has its own materiality. In the context of his reflections

[9] Although Honneth's argument aims at a different direction, he involuntarily supports my argument when saying that "material fulfillments" should "lead to modes of behavior that give real expression to the actual value articulated in the original act" (Honneth 2007: 345, my emphasis). In his discussion with Nancy Fraser, Honneth argues that the societal distribution of goods is not opposed to the cultural sphere of recognition, but instead one part of it. In other words, the distribution of goods is itself a medium of the social expression of esteem (Honneth 2003: 150–159).

on recognition, Lacan clearly articulates this idea. While in the circulation of recognition, the object becomes symbolic, the symbol at the same time turns, to some degree, into a corporeal thing: "Speech is in fact a gift of language, and language is not immaterial. It is a subtle body, but body it is" (Lacan 2003 [1953]: 95). The corporeality of speech lies in the fact that the linguistic gift is not so much about semantic content; for the recipient, the significance of an expression lies, to begin with, in the event of being addressed at all.

4.3.2 The Rituality of Humiliation

If it is true that acts of respect or recognition have a constitutive symbolic dimension, the same is true for acts of disrespect. Humiliations are always communicative acts; they communicate the radical disrespect of an actor towards the addressee (see, for example, Baumann 2003: 28). Of course, humiliating acts or conditions are not always as such purely symbolic. Poverty and torture are only two examples in a wide range of humiliating practices which are not at all merely symbolic. Yet, in what follows, I want to explore the idea that humiliations always have at least a symbolic dimension. And it is precisely the symbolic dimension of these "material" practices or conditions which render them humiliating. Moreover, the symbolicity of humiliation is not an additive or contingent supplement but rather a constitutive element.

In order to gain a first impression of the symbolic practices of violating human dignity, it is helpful to take a closer look at the notion of honor. Despite some fundamental differences, there are, as we have seen, important overlaps between dignity and honor. While the modern notion of dignity points to the fundamental equality of every human being, the notion of honor includes a hierarchical and asymmetric relationship between those who "have" and those who do not have honor (Berger 1973, Margalit 1996: 41–43). But honor as well as dignity can be seen as constituted by a symbolic sphere surrounding a person to which others have to pay attention in their behavior and which can easily be threatened by the actions of others, namely by their symbolic actions. Thus, an insult may be nothing more than a mere word; however, it is, in its essence, an assault on honor (Berger 1973). In honor cultures, your name can be "spotted", for example, when you are insulted. The slur "darkens" a person's good name, leaving "stains" on his or her honor – and thus giving rise to the cultural demand to "clear" it (Benedict 2005 [1946]: 145–176). Another example is the importance of rituals in honor societies. For instance, the ritual of the appropriate greeting is extremely important in these societies. In turn, the absence of a response to one's greeting is dishonoring. In the words of Hans-Georg Gadamer, an unreturned greeting

> [. . .] would be fatal for one's consciousness of self. Think of the feeling of humiliation when a greeting is not returned, be it because the other refuses to take cognizance of you – a devastating defeat for your consciousness or self – or because he is not the person you thought he was but someone else and hence does not recognize you [. . .] (Gadamer 1996: 159).

Besides obviously symbolic cases like that of the gauntlet (which is thrown to initiate an honor-duel), one can also look at rather intricate practices of dishonoring. A slap in the face, for example, is not only dishonoring (even more so when you are slapped with the back of the hand), it is also situated at the threshold to physical violence. But no matter how slight a slap in the face might be in physical terms – never can it be insignificant. This is because the slap does not mainly aim at the body, it rather aims at a symbolic sphere: It hits the face, and thereby make's one "lose face". While the slap in the face may be physically violent, the humiliating dimension, its threat to the "face", is purely symbolic.

Returning from the pre-modern concept of honor to modern concepts of dignity, we can see that even here its violation can be effected by mere words. Racist discrimination does not, of course, only function through discourses and words, but it is significant that discriminating speech acts do play an important role (Graumann 1998). It is for this reason that the proper name has often been a target of humiliation (see Chapter 10 by Herrmann, this volume).

But what about "material" violations of human dignity, like poverty or torture? Some people say that these cases do not concern questions of dignity, simply because there are other factors at stake which weigh much more than dignity violations. The involuntary suffering of physical violence or the deprivation of vital goods are such radical forms of social injustice which need not be criticized in terms of dignity. Let us first take a look at the case of poverty. It is the very problem of relative poverty which raises questions of dignity and which makes clearer the symbolic dimension of violations of human dignity. That is different with absolute poverty. Of course, absolute poverty is closely connected to humiliation. For example, when a person is forced to eat what others throw away (see, for example, Margalit 1996: 228). Nevertheless, the problem of absolute poverty resides primarily elsewhere, that is, in the material consequences of poverty: hunger, the danger it presents to one's life, its effects on one's health. It would be too little to criticize absolute poverty only as a violation of human dignity, because absolute poverty concerns a dimension which is even more fundamental than human dignity – the dimension of an existential viability.[10] This is different with relative poverty. The justification of a critique of relative poverty in terms of its "material" consequences is obviously more difficult than is the case with regard to absolute poverty. This is because it is possible that the relative poverty of a group may have increased although its prosperity may have too. Nevertheless, relative poverty can be criticized in terms of dignity, and this is exactly because of the symbolic dimension of

[10]This example again sheds light on Hegel's "struggle to death". Of course, this struggle might have suggested that humans always put their autonomy or their recognition above their physiological life – or in other words: that recognition is more fundamental than life. Yet I think it only shows that human beings are able to put their recognition above their life; but that neither means that they always actually are willing to risk their life or to commit suicide, nor that they should do this, nor that recognition as such is more fundamental than life. Besides, I have tacitly criticized Hegel and his whole narrative of the struggle because of its heroic undertone, while I have, at the same time, tried to save his idea of the importance of recognition

humiliation. In recognition theory, the societal distribution of goods counts as an expression of social esteem (see Chapter 12 by Müller and Neuhäuser, this volume). To be relatively poor thus means to receive very little recognition. If this imbalance in the general prosperity of a society is too strong (what exactly this means is not relevant here), relative poverty can be humiliating. The symbolic dimension of humiliation, in this case, lies not only in the fact that the socio-economic inequality can be seen by the persons concerned as social misrecognition. It has also to do with the relationality of relative poverty: A certain amount of goods is not as such humiliating but only in reference to other amounts of goods.

Let us move on to another example of humiliation, which, at first sight, does not look symbolic at all, that is, torture. Torture can roughly be understood as the act of inflicting physical pain on someone, deliberately and systematically, against his or her will, and as inflicting pain in a way that does not necessarily lead to the death of the affected person. This is not to say that torture is a less extreme form of physical violence than murder. On the contrary, the endless extension of inflicting pain – together with the concomitant aim to keep the victim alive and conscious – is definitively one of the most extreme forms of physical violence. How, then, should there be any symbolic dimension at all? And if there were, is it this dimension that constitutes the humiliating impact of torture? Here again, just as in the case of absolute poverty, the forced suffering of pain can be criticized as such without reference to human dignity. But torture as a violation of dignity is humiliating exactly as a result of its symbolic dimension. A whole variety of symbolic actions are part of the torture. For example, a typical aspect of torture is the demonstration of the instruments of torture (Scarry 1985: 27). And even though torture, at least in modern societies, has withdrawn into the cellars of power and is thus no longer a public spectacle (as was the case in pre-modern times), it still has to some extent a "theatrical" dimension (Zirfas 2004). There is abundant evidence that even in modernity tormentors find theatrical metaphors for the sites of torture. For example, the scene of torture is called "cinema room" or "blue lit stage" (Scarry 1985: 28). The theatrical dimension is also evident in the use of photographs in Abu Ghraib, as referred to at the beginning of this paper. Furthermore, the postures, which the victims are often forced to take on, play an important role. Kneeling down or taking the posture of a dog, for example, are highly coded positions; they designate, above all, humiliation. Finally, we can find further symbolic actions which are of crucial importance to torture, such as the forced eating of feces, for example, with feces being one of the most abject objects in human society.

Nevertheless, all these elements could be seen as merely additional and contingent, sometimes accompanying the actual violence in torture, sometimes not. This may be true, yet within the realm of torture, violence itself is symbolically charged with meaning. This is because in most cases violence in torture is an end in itself. Compared to the violence in a holdup, for example, it is often not a means to an end (as in the case of the holdup, say, a means to steal someone's money). Surely, at first sight, torture appears to be about extorting a confession out of someone. However, in most cases, it is not (Scarry 1985: 28). Either the tormentor already knows what he finally comes to hear. Or the victim tells the tormentor anything, just to have something to confess at all. Whatever information gleaned from a torture victim may just as well be misleading, for the tormentor knows that the victim will eventually say anything the tormentor might want to hear – just to make him end his cruelty.[11] Violence is thus no means to an end in torture. It is an end in itself. Precisely this is the primary reason why violence in torture is always at the same time symbolic. In assuming a symbolic meaning, the violence then stands for something. As a "spectacle of power" (Scarry 1985: 27), torture is thus not just about inflicting pain, it is at the same time a demonstration of inflicting pain. The tormentor acquires absolute power, while the victim may have no agency left at all – his will broken, his integrity damaged, not even being able to commit suicide, this last little bit of freedom human beings normally have, but instead reduced to begging the tormentor to let him die, which he, the tormentor, refuses. The tormentor demonstrates his absolute power, while the powerlessness of the victim is overtly exposed (see also Chapter 8 by Maier, this volume). To be sure, one could argue that this is the right track, though the argument, from a certain point on, is carried too far. The humiliation, according to the objection, is just about losing one's power, one's freedom. In torture, there is no agency left at all, and that is its humiliating core.

Yet this argument does not go far enough. Torture is not just about absolute power and absolute powerlessness, it is about demonstrating absolute power and being exposed in one's powerlessness. This exposed powerlessness, on the one hand, and the demonstrated power, on the other, is the humiliating truth of torture (Schick 1997). In this sense, torture has an essentially symbolic dimension. And this demonstration of powerlessness has to do with recognition, or, more specifically, with a loss of recognition. To be exposed in one's absolute powerlessness implies, precisely in its symbolic dimension, a radical loss of recognition. Autonomy, freedom, or agency are of central importance in our cultural values, and their loss may be a reason for far-reaching devaluation; that is, an extreme loss of recognition. Here again, I follow Avishai Margalit who argues that the loss of self-control is more like a sub-category of exclusion from the "human commonwealth" (Margalit 1996: 115). If torture, then, is constitutively linked with symbolic, theatrical, or ritual elements as well as with the question of recognition and its loss, where is the body left? To be sure, if torture is about inflicting pain, then the body does indeed play a crucial role. The body is the site of the violence of torture – not just in the sense that the body is the target or object of violence, but also, and maybe even more importantly, in the sense that the victim is reduced to being a mere bodily being, a being reduced to an animal-like corporeality:

> The purpose of torture is not only to make a person talk, but make him betray others. The victim must turn himself by his screams and by his submission into a lower animal, in the eyes of all and in his own eyes (Sartre 1958: 24).

In the course of torture, the victim loses more and more his reference to the world, being thrown back to his own bodily existence. The victim thus gradually loses his or her human voice (Scarry 1985: 35). At the end, he or she can but scream like

---

[11] I am indebted to the helpful notes of Steffen Herrmann.

an animal, or only just breath and stutter. This, again, is a dimension of the loss of recognition which the victim suffers: to be excluded from humankind by being reduced to a merely bodily being (Throta 1997: 29).

It is this rejection or exclusion that lies at the heart of humiliation. Exclusion is one form of a deep loss of recognition. Surely, not every loss of recognition is humiliating. An insult constitutes a "weak" form of loss of recognition which threatens a person in her honor or prestige, but not yet in her dignity (Margalit 1996: 115–116). An important practical realization of strong forms of disrespect is the practice of exclusion (see Chapter 10 by Herrmann, this volume). Exclusion, in this view, refers to an essentially social process, as it is linked with recognition, or, more precisely, with misrecognition. Of course, exclusion can be understood literally, as spatial segregation, when we think of ghettos, for example. In the perspective of social exclusion, however, the process of exclusion is internally linked with the problem of recognition. In this account, Axel Honneth understands exclusion mainly in terms of legal non-recognition, in the sense that certain social groups are denied basic equal rights (Honneth 1995: 131–139). But he also deals with more daily and subtle forms of exclusion in the shape of social invisibility, for example. For him, invisibility can be part of everyday racism and is experienced by the concerned person as if others would behave towards him or her as if he or she were physically absent: you are not greeted, for example, or you get the feeling that others look through you (Honneth 2001). Avishai Margalit also deals with various forms of exclusion, of which the most extreme form ends in the extermination of the Jews in Nazi-Germany (Margalit and Motzkin 1996). A more widespread practice of exclusion for him is discrimination against what he calls "encompassing groups" (Margalit 1996: 135–143), that is, the humiliation of those groups which are integral for the identity of their members. Within recognition theory, it is Judith Butler who, in her recent writings, works out the notion of "social death" (Butler 2000: 73–74). With this term she refers to a form of "non-intelligibility" to which certain groups are subjected (Butler 2004: 146–147). To fall out of our established frames of sexuality (in the case of gays and lesbians) or to fall out of our usual frames of gender-identity (in the case of transgender-identities) is, for her, a position of non-recognizability. All these various forms of exclusion are, in the recognition-account, held as ways in which certain persons are humiliated, because excluding practices can bring about a more or less severe loss of recognition.

References

Baumann, Peter. 2003. Menschenwürde und das Bedürfnis nach Respekt. In *Menschenwürde. Annäherung an einen Begriff*, ed. Ralf Stoecker, 19–34. Wien: Öbv & Hpt.

Benedict, Ruth. 2005 [1946]. *The chrysanthemum and the sword: Patterns of Japanese culture*. Boston, MA: Houghton Mifflin Harcourt.

Berger, Peter L. 1973. Excursus: On the obsolescence of the concept of honor. In *The homeless mind. Modernization and consciousness*, ed. Peter L. Berger, Brigitte Berger, and Hansfried Kellner, 83–96. New York, NY: Random House.

Bettelheim, Bruno. 1961. *The informed heart: Autonomy in a mass age*. New York, NY: Free Press.

Bloch, Ernst. 1987. *Natural law and human dignity*. Cambridge, MA: MIT.
Butler, Judith. 1997a. *Excitable speech. A politics of the performative*. New York, NY and London: Routledge.
Butler, Judith. 1997b. *The psychic life of power: Theories in subjection*. Stanford, CA: Stanford University Press.
Butler, Judith. 2000. *Antigone's claim: Kinship between life and death*. New York, NY: Columbia University Press.
Butler, Judith. 2004. *Precarious life: The powers of mourning and violence*. London: Verso.
Butler, Judith. 2007. Torture and the ethics of photography. *Environment and Planning D: Society and Space* 25(6): 951–966.
Derrida, Jacques. 2002. The animal that therefore I am (more to follow). *Critical Inquiry* 28(2): 369–418.
Forst, Rainer. 2005. Die Würde des Menschen und das Recht auf Rechtfertigung. *Deutsche Zeitschrift für Philosophie* 53(4): 589–596.
Gadamer, Hans-Georg. 1996. Hegel's dialectic of self-consciousness. In *Hegel's dialectic of desire and recognition*, ed. John O'Neil, 149–168. Albany, NY: State University of New York Press.
Gilroy, Paul. 1993. *The black Atlantic. Modernity and double consciousness*. London: Verso.
Graumann, Carl F. 1998. Verbal discrimination: A neglected chapter in the social psychology of aggression. *Journal for the Theory of Social Behaviour* 28: 41–61.
Hegel, Georg Wilhelm Friedrich. 1977 [1807]. *Phenomenology of spirit*. Oxford: Oxford University Press.
Hegel, Georg Wilhelm Friedrich. 1983 [1805–1806]. *Hegel and the human spirit: A translation of the Jena lectures on the philosophy of spirit (1805-6) with commentary*. Detroit, MI: Wayne State University Press.
Hegel, Georg Wilhelm Friedrich. 2007 [1830]. *Hegel's philosophy of mind*. Oxford: Oxford University Press.
Honneth, Axel. 1995. *The struggle for recognition: The moral grammar of social conflicts*. Cambridge, UK: Polity Press.
Honneth, Axel. 2001. Invisibility: On the epistemology of "recognition". *Supplement to the Proceedings of the Aristotelian Society* 75(1): 111–126.
Honneth, Axel. 2003. Redistribution as recognition. In *Redistribution or recognition? A political-philosophical exchange*, eds. Nancy Fraser and Axel Honneth, 110–197. London: Verso.
Honneth, Axel. 2007. Recognition as ideology. In *Power and recognition. Axel Honneth and the tradition of critical social theory*, eds. Bert van den Brink and David Owen, 323–347. Cambridge, MA: Cambridge University Press.
Honneth, Axel. 2008. *Reification. A new look at an old idea*. Oxford: Oxford University Press.
Inwood, Michael. 1992. Recognition and acknowledgement. In *A Hegel dictionary*, ed. Michael Inwood, 245–247. Oxford: Blackwell.
Kant, Immanuel. 1964 [1785]. *The groundwork of the metaphysic of morals*. New York, NY: Harper.
Kojève, Alexandre. 1980. *Introduction to the reading of Hegel: Lectures on the phenomenology of spirit*. Ithaca, NY and London: Cornell University Press.
Lacan, Jacques. 2003 [1953]. The function and field of speech and language in psychoanalysis. In *Écrits. A selection*, 33–125, London and New York, NY: Routledge.
Lacan, Jacques. 2003 [1958]. The signification of the phallus. In *Écrits. A selection*, 311–322. London and New York, NY: Routledge.
Lynd, Helen Merrell. 1958. *On shame and the search for identity*. New York, NY: Harcourt, Brace & Co.
Margalit, Avishai and Gabriel Motzkin. 1996. The uniqueness of holocaust. *Philosophy & Public Affairs* 25(1): 65–83.
Margalit, Avishai. 1996. *The decent society*. Cambridge, MA: Cambridge University Press.
Margalit, Avishai. 2001. Recognizing the brother and the other. *The Aristotelian Society. Supplementary Volume* 75(1): 127–139.

Mead, George H. 1995 [1934]. *Mind, self, and society: From the standpoint of a social behaviourist*. Chicago, IL: University Press of Chicago.
Rorty, Richard. 1989. *Contingency, irony, and solidarity*. Cambridge, MA: Cambridge University Press.
Roughley, Neil. 1996. Würde. In *Enzyklopädie Philosophie und Wissenschaftstheorie*, eds. Jürgen Mittelstraß et al., vol. 4, 784–787, Stuttgart: Metzler.
Sartre, Jean-Paul. 1958. Preface. In *The question*, ed. Henri Alleg, 11–28. London: John Calder.
Scarry, Elaine. 1985. *The body in pain: The making and unmaking of the world*. Oxford: Oxford University Press.
Schaber, Peter. 2003. Menschenwürde als Recht, nicht erniedrigt zu werden. In *Menschenwürde. Annäherung an einen Begriff*, ed. Ralf Stoecker, 119–131. Wien: Öbv & Hpt.
Schick, Frederic. 1997. On humiliation. *Social Research* 64(1): 131–146.
Sereny, Gitta. 1977. *Into that darkness: An examination of conscience*. London: Pan.
Silver, Maury et al. 1986. Humiliation: Feeling, social control and the construction of identity. *Journal for the Theory of Social Behaviour* 16(3): 269–283.
Taylor, Charles. 1994. The politics of recognition. In *Multiculturalism: Examining the politics of recognition*, 25–73. Princeton, NJ: Princeton University Press.
Throta, Trutz von. 1997. Zur Soziologie der Gewalt. In *Soziologie der Gewalt*, ed. Trutz von Throta, 9–56. Opladen: Westdeutscher Verlag.
Tugendhat, Ernst. 1986. *Self-consciousness and self-determination*. Cambridge, MA: MIT.
Zirfas, Jörg. 2004. Rituale der Grausamkeit. Performative Praktiken der Folter. In *Die Kultur des Rituals: Inszenierungen, Praktiken, Symbole*, ed. Christoph Wulf and Jörg Zirfas, 129–146. München: Fink.

Chapter 5
Instrumentalization: What Does It Mean to Use a Person?

Paulus Kaufmann

Abstract In Kant's moral theory we find a close connection between the concept of human dignity and the prohibition to use people merely as means. My chapter follows Kant in tracing this connection. But in contrast to Kant, for whom the prohibition to use people covers the whole range of perfect duties, I present an account of using people that seems to be closer to our common sense understanding in that it only covers a limited range of such duties. I will argue that, nevertheless, we need the concept of human dignity to explain why it is at least prima facie wrong to use people merely as means. The peculiar work that the concept of human dignity fulfills in explaining the wrongness of these acts does not consist in making them wrong directly. The concept of human dignity is rather necessary to explain how certain other properties can make acts wrong. By applying the concept of human dignity to the case of using people, we not only become able to explain the wrongness of using, but we also see that the concept of human dignity does play an important role in moral philosophy as a whole.

5.1 The Role of Dignity in Moral Theory

In this paper, I deal with three questions: First, I will ask what role the concept of dignity can play in moral theory. Second, I will consider the question of what it means to use a person. And thirdly, I will examine how the concept of dignity and the concept of using people are connected. I will present one conception of dignity, and I will argue that we need this conception of dignity to understand the intuitions behind the idea that it is wrong to use other people merely as means.

What role can the concept of dignity play in moral theory? There is, of course, more than one possible answer to this question. The word "dignity" has many different aspects, and moral philosophers when using this word differ significantly in which of these aspects they stress. One therefore finds a great variety of conceptions

---

P. Kaufmann (✉)
Centre for Ethics, University of Zurich, Switzerland
e-mail: kaufmann@philos.unizh.ch

P. Kaufmann et al. (eds.), *Humiliation, Degradation, Dehumanization*, Library of Ethics and Applied Philosophy 24, DOI 10.1007/978-90-481-9661-6_5,

of dignity in philosophical literature. And one also finds a great variety of roles the concept of dignity is meant to play in different moral theories. I will not examine all, or even the most important, of these different roles of dignity in my paper. Instead, I wish to focus on *one* role that seems particularly important to me. This role can be easily shown by a scheme that seems to capture one understanding of dignity, the understanding we refer to when we say that some entities *have* dignity.[1]

According to this scheme, a thing has dignity if it has certain properties and these properties lead to the thing having a higher status than other things. This status requires a special kind of behavior towards it. An account of dignity in the relevant sense has then three elements: a class of things, a class of properties, and a class of implicit or explicit rules of behavior that define the special status of the things in question. An account of dignity may thus be characterized by three questions: (1) Who has dignity? (2) What properties underlie dignity? and (3) What behavior fits with dignity?

Here are some examples: Sometimes we speak about the dignity of certain social positions, as, for example, the dignity of a judge. We could then answer the three questions by saying that *judges* have dignity because of their *role in society* and that this dignity demands that we, for example, *stand up* when the judge enters the court room.

In another sense, we might say that someone has dignity if he tends to react in a certain way to social or natural adversities. In such cases, we sometimes say that the person in question has the *virtue* of dignity. In this account of dignity, the three questions are answered in the following way: First, it is all the people with a certain character who have dignity. Second, this dignity is due to the disposition to react to adversities with the right balance between submission and resistance. And third, this dignity requires of us esteem and emulation.[2]

And a last example: Some people speaking about *human* dignity[3] mean to say that all members of the human species have dignity just because they belong to this species, and that this dignity requires the compliance with certain rules such as the strict prohibition of killing and the duty to help.

These examples illustrate a common feature of all accounts of dignity that fit with the scheme I have presented: Dignity gives us reasons to act. Or more precisely: Dignity is due to certain properties, and these properties give us reasons to treat the bearer of these properties in a certain way. The relevant properties may give us reason, for example, to stand up when a judge enters the room or not to kill a human embryo. But these practical reasons are reasons of a particular kind. They are not reasons to bring something about, but they are reasons to respect the bearer of certain properties. While the fact that something is pleasant, for example, might

---

[1] Different conceptions of dignity may for example be drawn from expressions such as "to live under undignified circumstances" or "to be bereft of one's dignity." In the following, I will not address these conceptions and their relation with the conception I am presenting.

[2] For the definition of dignity as a virtue, see Beyleveld and Brownsword (2001: 58–60).

[3] There are of course other accounts of human dignity that are less speciesist than this one.

give us a reason to bring it about, the properties that underlie dignity do not give us a reason of this kind. This distinction between two kinds of reasons is, of course, Kant's, who distinguishes between *ends to bring about* and *ends to be respected.*[4] It is not at all easy to say exactly what it means to respect an end or the bearer of certain properties, and I will not try to give a comprehensive answer to this question here. Yet it seems to be intuitively plausible to say that if there are reasons to respect something, these reasons put at least certain *constraints* on our behavior such as the constraint not to destroy or hinder the property in question.[5]

What role is assigned to dignity within this scheme? According to the scheme, the fact that someone possesses dignity does *not* provide an actor *directly* with reasons to treat him in any way. The reasons for a certain treatment are the properties that underlie his dignity. It is not the judge's dignity that gives us a reason to stand up when he enters the court room. Rather it is the fact that he plays a certain role for society that makes this behavior necessary. What then is the role of the concept of dignity here? To explain this role it will be helpful to call to mind that it is not immediately evident that the possession of certain properties by some person or other being might give reasons for action. If we think about properties that give us reasons for action, we naturally think of properties of the act itself or of the states the act may bring about. But the property in question is no property of any act at all. Neither is it a state that anyone wishes to bring about. It is a property that exists independently of the wishes and deeds of the actor. How can such a property provide reasons for action? What I claim in this paper is that it is *the role of dignity to explain how this is possible*. I will claim that certain properties can provide reasons for action because they *bestow dignity* on the bearer of these properties. The bearer then has a different status, so that he may not be treated in certain ways, although it is legitimate to treat other things in these ways that do not possess the relevant properties.

Thus, the central idea behind the conception of dignity I am presenting here is the idea of *properties bestowing status*. This idea is certainly rather vague, but instead of giving a definition, I want to give an example of how dignity can explain the existence of certain constraints on behavior by making use of the idea of bestowing status.

Before I proceed to the second question, the question of what it means to merely use a person, let me stress one preliminary point: The constraint not to use other people merely as means is just *one* constraint among others. It is not only wrong to use people merely as means but also to insult, neglect or humiliate them. On my reading, to respect dignity means to comply with the constraints with regard to the bearer of certain properties. One thing that follows from this understanding

---

[4]See Kant (1902: IV.437): "[. . .] *so wird der Zweck hier nicht als ein zu bewirkender, sondern selbstständiger Zweck, mithin nur negativ, gedacht werden müssen, d.i. dem niemals zuwider gehandelt* [. . .] *werden muss.*"

[5]Kant expresses a similar idea when he says that a being with dignity "limits all choice" ("[. . .] *mithin sofern alle Willkür einschränkt*") (Kant 1902: IV.428). The close relation between respect for persons and constraints on our behavior is also stressed by Stephen Darwall (1977, 2004).

of respecting dignity is that the non-observance of a constraint cannot be offset by bringing that property about in another person or nourishing an already existent property. Another way of saying this would be that no person may be used in order to improve overall respect for others. According to this understanding of dignity, the particular constraint on using persons follows from the meaning of constraints in general, but it does *not* follow that all particular constraints can be expressed by saying that people shall not be used. It seems clear to me that *we do violate constraints due to the dignity of persons* if we neglect, insult or humiliate them. *But we do not thereby use them.*[6] Let me now explain which cases of violating constraints are, in my account, also cases of using people.

5.2 Using People

I propose to clarify our common sense understanding of the expression "to use a person" by comparing it with our use of the expression "to use a tool." Unsurprisingly, both expressions have many features in common. According to my analysis, in order to say that somebody uses a person or a tool, three conditions have to be fulfilled:

First, I only use a tool if I do something with the tool. If I only look at a hammer or talk about it, I do not thereby use it. Similarly, I only use a person if I interact with that person. This condition should be understood to imply that an act of mine has some foreseeable effect on that other person.

Second, in our interaction we pursue a goal that is not directed towards a state of the tool itself. That is, we do not use a knife if we sharpen it because the sharpness we are aiming at is a state of the knife itself. Similarly, A does *not* use a person B if in interacting with him she is finally aiming at a state that is supposed to be good or even at a state that is supposed to be bad for B. Consider the following two examples:

> *Christmas*: In December, Ron and Jill are doing some shopping. Jill gets enthusiastic about a scarf but does not buy it. Half an hour later Ron pretends that he forgot something, but, in fact, he goes back to the shop and buys the scarf as a Christmas present for Jill.

> *Insult*: A young man on a bicycle drives in the middle of the road thereby preventing a car from overtaking. When the car finally manages to pass the bicycle, the car driver opens the window and shouts derogatory words to the cyclist.

It seems clear to me that in none of these situations we would speak of someone using another person. In *Christmas*, Ron tricks Jill to realize one of his goals. But as his goal is to make Jill happy, we would not say that Ron uses Jill. In *Insult*, the car driver wants to offend the cyclist but he does not use him. The reason for our hesitation to speak of using in this case seems to be due to the fact that the driver's act is directed against the cyclist. These two points may be taken together

[6]Here I disagree with Robert Nozick, for example, who seems to suggest that we use a person whenever we violate a constraint that the properties of this person impose on us (Nozick 1974: 31–32).

by claiming that for A to use B, A must pursue a goal that does not essentially refer to B.[7]

Third, we only use a tool if we interact with it because we believe it to be useful for our purposes. We do not use a hammer, for example, if we take it out of the tool box to have more space to look for the screwdriver. In this case, the hammer is not useful to us but an obstacle to pursuing our goal. Similarly, A only uses a person B if A believes that B can contribute to his goal. B's presence or participation must play a role in A's plan towards his ends,[8] as the following examples may illustrate:

> *Pollution*: The chemistry company Chisso introduces industrial waste polluted with mercury into the open sea close to the city of Minamata, Japan. Approximately 10,000 people are severely harmed.
>
> *Assassin*: Trevis wants to kill the president. He stands in the crowd and shoots at the open car of the president. He aims badly and would have missed the president if the driver would have continued to drive at the same speed. But the driver suddenly slows down and the bullet hits the president.

Chisso interacts with the people of Minamata and pursues a goal that does not refer to these people. Yet it would have been a lot easier for Chisso to realize its goal without these people. Thus Chisso did not use them. In *Assassin*, the driver's participation is necessary for the success of Trevis' project. Yet Trevis does not use the driver as the driver's behavior was not part of his plan.

To summarize these results I would say that A uses B if and only if A interacts with B because he believes that B's presence or participation can contribute to the realization of his goal but that this goal does not essentially refer to B.

These three conditions tell us what it *means to use a person*, but they certainly do not already name a property that makes acts wrong. There are many cases where using a person – in the sense just defined – is morally innocent: The conditions I mentioned are, for example, fulfilled when I climb on a friend's back to pick an apple or when I take a taxi to get to work. In both cases, I interact with another person believing that this person's presence or participation can help me to realize a goal that does not point to this person. But in such cases I am usually not acting wrongly. So it is still necessary to draw the line between morally permissible and impermissible cases of using people. Many authors including Kant mark this distinction between permissible and forbidden use by calling the latter a "mere use."[9] This wording is warranted by ordinary language where we use expressions such as, "You were *just* using me." What then distinguishes using a person from *just* or *merely* using her?

To answer this question it is helpful to notice that climbing on a friend's back is not always morally innocent, as it seems at first glance. If we judge this case to be morally innocent, we do so because we presuppose the friend's consent. If I climb

---

[7] A goal essentially refers to a person if it cannot be spelled out without linguistically referring in any way to the person in question, be it by using proper names or definite descriptions.

[8] Quinn (1989: 343, 348–349) and Scanlon (2008: 106) refer to a similar condition.

[9] See, for example, Parfit (forthcoming, Chapter 8). On Kant see Paton (1948: 165), Ross (1969: 49) or Timmermann (2007: 96).

on a friend's back without his consent, almost all of us would say *that I do interact with him in a morally impermissible way*. Thus it seems that the person I use must give his consent that we have an interaction at all and must agree about what kind of interaction we have.

The morally required consent can be expressed in diverse manners. In many cases, consent is given verbally, of course, but in suitable situations a nod, a kiss or even staying silent can be acts of morally transformative consent (Wertheimer 2003: 152–153). Besides, in some cases it is not necessary to actively ask for consent. If Peter wants to climb on Paul's back to pick an apple, and if both friends know each other very well and have many times undertaken similar actions, then we will not require Peter to explicitly ask for Paul's consent. In any case, Peter must believe that Paul agrees to the interaction and its conditions and *he must be justified in this belief.*[10] Sometimes this justification might be grounded in profound knowledge of the other and many similar common experiences, but in most cases we can only be justified in believing that the other is consenting if we explicitly ask him.

On my interpretation of the expression "to merely use a person" there are thus two elements that define its content: The context of using and the condition of justified belief about the consent of the person used. Even if this account of merely using someone seems to capture many of our intuitions and provides a rather clear-cut concept, it is still not obvious what is wrong about merely using another person. Let us therefore move on to my third question and ask how the concept of mere use and the concept of dignity are connected.

5.3 Using People as a Violation of Dignity

In the first section of this chapter, I claimed that one role dignity fulfils is to explain the existence of certain constraints on our behavior. In the following section, I specified one particular constraint, namely the prohibition not to use people merely as means. Now, how does dignity fulfill its role with regard to this particular constraint? How does it explain the existence of the constraint on merely using people?

Let me note first that the word "explain" might give rise to exorbitant expectations. I certainly cannot give an ultimate justification for the constraint in question, nor can I convince inveterate skeptics about dignity. But what the concept of dignity, as I understand it, *can* achieve is to structure an answer to the question of what is wrong about merely using people.

So far I have characterized dignity by a scheme according to which a thing has dignity if it has properties that bestow a status on its bearer, where this status imposes certain constraints on how to treat him. What are the relevant properties in the case of the constraint on merely using people? This becomes clearer if we take note of a feature of the expression "to use a person" that I did not mention

---

[10] With "justification" I do not mean moral but only epistemic justification. A similar idea is expressed by Kerstein (2009).

before: Compared to the talk of using tools or even animals, it does not sound good to talk about using *persons*. We feel uneasy when we say "I'm using you," and in general we try to avoid this expression. Where does this hesitation come from? According to my analysis, it is conceptually true that when I use a tool or a person I am pursuing an end that is not essentially related to the thing that I use. Now what is questionable about using persons seems to be the fact that in using a person for my ends I am using a being that is capable of pursuing ends itself. A hammer as well as a taxi driver can help me in realizing some of my goals. However, in contrast to the hammer, the taxi driver also pursues a set of ends and continuously decides how to realize them and how to weigh them against each other. Thus, when I make him serve one of my ends, I may bar him from pursuing his ends. Thereby, I somehow put myself above him and treat him as a tool. This seems to evoke the above-mentioned negative moral responses towards such interactions. The property that is impeded by merely using a person is thus the capacity to set and follow ends.

If merely using someone is a violation of dignity, in my sense, this property must bestow a special status on its bearer and thereby impose constraints on how to treat her. To understand the mere use of a person as a violation of dignity, we therefore have to show that the capacity to set and follow ends really bestows status and thereby imposes constraints. To show this, I want to consider what would follow if we suppose that it does not.

It would, of course, *not* follow that we have no conceptual means to prohibit most of the acts that are in fact prohibited by the constraint on merely using people as I understand it. It would *not even* follow that our moral theory would have no place for the peculiarity of the capacity to set and follow ends. Instead of referring to the idea of bestowing status, one might simply say, for example, that this capacity is *valuable in itself* and should therefore never be impeded or destroyed. By saying this we would not presuppose that the capacity to set and follow ends *bestows a special status* on its bearer, thereby imposing constraints on how to treat him. If we do so, we arrive at a constraint that is significantly different from our constraint and, as I would like to show, one that does not capture its intuitive plausibility. So I want to show that we need the idea of dignity to explain the existence of the prohibition of merely using people, a constraint I suppose to have intuitive appeal.

So what prohibition would follow if we say instead that the capacity to set and follow ends is valuable in itself?[11] It is my impression that the resulting prohibition would face some major obstacles. First of all, such an approach would have to confront the question of what would be so valuable about setting and following ends. The value of this capacity seems to be reducible to the value it has for its bearer or for anybody else. The claim of an intrinsic value thus needs an extra justification that seems hard to provide. Even if we accept the special value of this capacity, we confront an even bigger problem: We would have to explain why we cannot set off the

[11] There might of course be other proposals than the one I am presenting: namely, the proposal to obtain a similar prohibition by presupposing the capacity to set and follow ends to be valuable in itself. I here assume that any proposal that does not refer to this capacity at all would be even less capable of capturing our intuitions with regard to the constraint on merely using people.

impeding of this property in one person by nourishing it in another? If the property is valuable in itself,[12] it seems plausible to demand the bringing about of as much of this property as possible. If we concede this, then it becomes clear that the resulting prohibition would have nothing to do with the prohibition of merely using people. It would follow that it might be legitimate to set off the impeding of the valuable property in one person by nourishing it in another. But that clearly contradicts one of the features of the prohibition of merely using people. The prohibition of mere use specifically forbids the use of one person for the sake of others. A prohibition that dispenses with the idea of bestowing status therefore seems to be incapable of expressing the intuitions behind the prohibition of merely using people.

Let me further clarify this argument by pointing to the difference between the intrinsic value of a property and the status, or value, of a person or other object. Properties are abstract objects that are instantiated in particular things. They can be instantiated to different degrees, and they can be instantiated in any number of objects. Particular objects cannot be instantiated and so it seems less plausible to conclude from their intrinsic value that their number should be multiplied. Now the idea of dignity implies that it is the bearer who has a special status and not the property in question. We thus need the idea of dignity to explain why certain constraints on our behavior cannot be offset by maximizing the implementations of certain valuable properties.

So how can we explain the peculiar wrongness of using people if we *include* the idea of properties bestowing status on their bearer, thereby imposing constraints on their treatment, i.e. how can we explain the peculiar wrongness of using people if we do make use of the concept of dignity?

To answer this question, let us look at what our constraint on using people actually demands of a potential user. It demands of any potential user to seek the consent of the person she is going to use. The important point about consent is that the negative connotations that the talk of "using a person" arouse, as previously suggested, completely vanish if the used person freely and fully consents to the interaction in question. Recall the taxi driver. In general it is perfectly innocent to use him to get to the desired destination. The taxi driver does not want to go where he drives me, but as I pay him, and as the conditions of the interaction are transparent, the driver can choose the interaction as a means to his own ends. To go where I want to go becomes his end too and our interaction becomes morally innocent. Due to the act of consent, the used person is not a tool anymore but an end-pursuing person as much as I am. It is sometimes said that the peculiar work of consent consists in its transforming the normative relations between people (Archard 1998: 3–4). With regard to the case of using, we can thus say that it transforms a person-tool relationship into a co-operative one.

This consideration now helps us to explain why we have to add the idea of bestowing status to explain the wrongness of merely using people: The constraint

[12]The same consideration does *not* apply to the claim that some *particular beings* are valuable in themselves.

on merely using people demands that we seek the consent of the person used. As we have just seen, consent transforms a person-tool relationship into co-operation. The constraint therefore demands of us that we treat the used person as a person and not as a tool, i.e. it demands that we recognize the peculiar *status* of the other. To demand the consent of another person thus already presupposes the idea of status. Someone whose consent counts is of a higher status than other things and should not be treated in certain ways.

The idea of consent shows that what is wrong about merely using a person is not only that it impedes some of her properties. The wrongness of merely using someone is in impeding properties that bestow a special status upon the bearer. By so acting, one makes a person into a tool. To describe the wrongness of merely using someone, we therefore need not only the concept of valuable properties but equally the idea that properties bestow a special status on their bearer, i.e. we need the concept of dignity.

References

Archard, David. 1998. *Sexual consent*. Oxford: Westview.
Beyleveld, Deryck and Roger Brownsword. 2001. *Human dignity in bioethics and biolaw*. Oxford: Oxford University Press.
Darwall, Stephen. 1977. Two Kinds of Respect. *Ethics* 88: 36–49.
Darwall, Stephen. 2004. Respect and the second-person standpoint. *Proceedings and Addresses of the American Philosophical Association* 78: 43–59.
Kant, Immanuel. 1902. *Gesammelte Schriften*. Berlin: Königlich-Preussische Akademie der Wissenschaften zu Berlin.
Kerstein, Samuel. 2009. Treating others merely as means. *Utilitas* 21: 163–180.
Nozick, Robert. 1974. *Anarchy, state, and utopia*. New York, NY: Basic Books.
Parfit, Derek. forthcoming. *On what matters*. Oxford: Oxford University Press.
Paton, Herbert James. 1948. *The categorical imperative*. Chicago, IL: The University of Chicago Press.
Quinn, Warren. 1989. Actions, intentions, and consequences: The doctrine of double effect. *Philosophy and Public Affairs* 18: 334–351.
Ross, William David. 1969. *Kant's ethical theory*. Oxford: Clarendon.
Scanlon, Thomas. 2008. *Moral dimensions*. Cambridge, MA: Harvard University Press.
Timmermann, Jens. 2007. *Kant's groundworks of the metaphysics of morals*. Cambridge: Cambridge University Press.
Wertheimer, Alan. 2003. *Consent to sexual relations*. Cambridge: Cambridge University Press.

Chapter 6
Degradation: A Human Rights Law Perspective

Elaine Webster

Abstract This chapter focuses on a number of common questions relating to the concept of degradation, against the backdrop of that concept as it has developed in the jurisprudence of the European Convention on Human Rights, specifically in relation to the prohibition of degrading treatment within Article 3. The prohibition of torture and inhuman or degrading treatment or punishment is commonly understood, and is expressed in case-law, as having an intimate connection with the concept of human dignity, the language of which underpins the modern human rights regime. The basic structure of the Article 3 understanding of degradation is outlined, alongside examples of its practical application, in order to highlight significant conceptual relationships. Questions concerning the significance of the individual emotion of degradation, the relevance of autonomy in understanding degradation, and the relevance of the idea of social dignity can be illuminated by a contextualized discussion of the jurisprudence. It is suggested in this respect that the scope of what can be understood as degradation is not limited primarily by the victim's emotional experience, that the jurisprudence draws our attention to one particular facet of autonomy, and that the essence of the concept of degradation is helpfully captured in the idea of abuse of equal rank.

6.1 Introduction

Human rights law provides an example of the conceptual interaction between degradation and human dignity, embodied in the interpretation and application of the prohibition of degrading treatment, one form of harm within the prohibition of torture and inhuman or degrading treatment or punishment. This chapter will draw upon the jurisprudence that has been developed in this respect by the European Court of Human Rights (hereafter "the ECtHR" or "the Court") in the

E. Webster (✉)
Centre for the Study of Human Rights Law, University of Strathclyde, UK
e-mail: elaine.webster@strath.ac.uk

P. Kaufmann et al. (eds.), *Humiliation, Degradation, Dehumanization*, 67
Library of Ethics and Applied Philosophy 24, DOI 10.1007/978-90-481-9661-6_6,

context of Article 3 of the European Convention on Human Rights (ECHR), which incorporates this prohibition.[1] This context will be used as a resource in reflecting upon questions that are deemed to be significant for an understanding of the concept of degradation. The premise is that degradation encapsulates a violation of human dignity, as is indeed visible in the ECHR context. It is assumed that degradation expresses a *particular form of violation* of human dignity. A particular substantive content of the concept of degradation is identifiable via the degrading treatment jurisprudence of the ECtHR. The Court's case-law suggests the contours of the wrong that is deemed to merit the label of degradation. This can provide valuable insight since our common sense understanding of degradation is vague, and our ability to coherently identify its occurrence is precarious. A simple and familiar example will suffice as an illustration: that of the woman who is on the receiving end of male attention of a sexual nature, be it a whistle or a "friendly tap" and accompanying comments. A series of intriguing questions come into view, to which our common sense understanding of degradation provides only ambiguous answers: Is she *degraded* by this? And/or is it something else? Could it involve more than one form of violation of human dignity? Where are the overlaps? Or is it just plain unpleasant, without being remotely close to degradation? What does degradation actually look like in concrete terms? What do we understand to be the characteristics of degradation? A central question relates to the significance of the individual experience of degradation: is it not the case that what I, as a woman, find degrading, you, as a woman, might find mildly irritating, or even gratifying? This alludes to the question of when degradation can be said to exist: If you *feel* degraded, does this imply that you have been degraded? If you do not *feel* degraded, does this imply that you have not been degraded? Is the context important? Does it matter, for example, if the woman is young? Religious? Vulnerable? Could it be argued not only that this is degrading for a particular woman but that such a situation is always degrading for any woman? Does the idea of autonomy in some form, whose restriction is often associated with a violation of dignity, have any relevance here at all? A different question concerns the term degradation itself and its link to human dignity in the human rights context: is the idea of grade important; of rank in the sense of social dignity? We see allusions to the idea of rank in dictionary meanings of the term degrading: "To reduce from a higher to a lower rank, to depose from a position of honour or estimation."[2] Yet there may be a seeming contradiction here from a human rights perspective in that the idea of rank tends to denote not equality of status amongst human beings but differentiated status, whereas it is clearly expressed in the foundational instruments of international human rights law that human dignity has a dimension in which it is equal amongst all human beings. This raises a question concerning the relevance of the idea of rank in understanding degradation and

[1] Some reference will also be made to the former European Commission of Human Rights, although examples will primarily be drawn from the legally binding decisions of the Court.

[2] *The Compact Edition of the Oxford English Dictionary*. Oxford: Clarendon Press (all dictionary references in the present chapter refer to this edition unless otherwise stated).

brings us full circle to re-engage with the concept of human dignity. The reflections that follow can shed light on all of these questions, from the very specific to the more general.

The principal criteria for motivating the discussion by these particular questions is, firstly, that they often form the basis of challenges to arguments on the scope of application of the right not to be subjected to degrading treatment. It is commonly objected that degradation means different things to different people, that whether degradation has taken place depends entirely on individual perceptions of the experience, which will differ according to each individual's particular sensibilities. The degrading treatment jurisprudence under the ECHR says something interesting in response to such questions and allows us to address such objections. Secondly, an attempt to articulate answers to these questions will assist in gaining a better understanding of the core conceptual meaning of degradation. This is valuable if we are to understand as fully as possible the conceptualization of degradation as a violation of human dignity.

This analysis, therefore, takes place within the particular situated context of supranational human rights law. Indeed, this is seen as the very value of the exercise. The pronouncements of the ECtHR are not, of course, philosophical texts, and the intention is not to suggest that the substance of the concept of degradation beyond the legal human rights sphere is, or should be, wholly or exhaustively the same as the concept as it is construed in the context of the ECHR. But the ECHR is a valuable site of analysis from which insight can be drawn into degradation as a moral concept. The judgments of the Court are testament to the practical interpretation and use of the concept of degradation within a strong and established system of binding human rights protection that encompasses 47 states of the Council of Europe. It has been noted that the ECHR is a leader of the wider international approach to the prohibition of torture and inhuman or degrading treatment or punishment (Evans and Morgan 1998: 74). There is a wealth of jurisprudence that has engaged with practical individual and inter-state complaints in light of the Convention rights, and in light of the principles and purposes underlying the Convention. The Court operates at the interface of interpretation and application of a right whose purpose has been declared by the Court as one of protecting human dignity. This example of practical application of the moral concept of degradation within international human rights discourse, in light of the influential nature of the Court's interpretation and the wide geographical scope of the Court's jurisdiction, is an informative resource.[3]

In providing insight from the case-law into the above series of questions, the ECHR approach to the concept of degradation will be outlined (including relationships and principles that have been established in the case-law) and examples will

---

[3]See the work of Peter Cane in the context of the concept of responsibility, which is illuminative in this respect. Cane discusses the particular value of common law approaches to responsibility, deriving from the uniqueness of the institutional legal setting, for understanding responsibility beyond law as a complex moral concept (Cane 2002: 9–28). I would like to thank my colleague Simon Halliday for drawing the work of Cane to my attention.

be given of situations in which degradation has been identified. Three key ideas that emerge from the jurisprudence will be highlighted and drawn upon: firstly, the value of a distinction between feeling and being degraded; secondly, the relevance of the concept of autonomy in one particular dimension; and thirdly, the sense in which the notion of rank is a significant conceptual tool when tied to the idea of equal, rather than social, dignity. The intention is to demonstrate that the ECHR interpretation can contribute valuable insight into our understanding of degradation as a violation of human dignity.

6.2 Degradation in the Jurisprudence of the European Court of Human Rights

The ECtHR uses the term "degrading treatment" rather than degradation. For the purpose of exploring the concept of degradation from a human rights law perspective, however, "degrading" can be seen as its equivalent. A number of authors in the human rights field have indeed elided the two terms.[4] The significance of the term "treatment" is linked to the possible sources of degradation within the Article 3 context and is tied to the question of the obligations and responsibility of the state in a vertical system of international human rights protection – points that need not concern us presently. Degradation is unquestionably the conceptual core of the right not to be subjected to degrading treatment protected by Article 3.

The ECtHR, in the process of interpreting and applying the prohibition of degrading treatment, approaches the idea of degradation through the lens of a number of conceptual points of reference that are repeated, individually or in conjunction with one another, in its judgments. The ECtHR relies upon a characterization of degradation that has remained largely constant since the 1970s. The principal measure of degradation amongst these was established in the inter-state case of *Ireland v. United Kingdom*, in which a number of interrogation techniques used by UK security forces in Northern Ireland in the early 1970s were found to be degrading:

> [They] were also degrading since they were such as to arouse in their victims feelings of fear, anguish and inferiority capable of humiliating and debasing them and possibly breaking their physical or moral resistance.[5]

Although this is the primary approach to degradation, an earlier formulation was introduced in 1969 by the Court's former sister organization, the European

[4]This is visible, for example, in an article on degrading treatment entitled "The Limits of Degradation and Respect" (Lawson and Mukherjee 2004) and in an article entitled "Punishment, Dignity and Degradation" (Duff 2005). See also Susan Millns' reference to dignity and degradation as two sides of the same coin (Millns 2002).

[5]*Ireland v. United Kingdom*, 18 January 1978, Series A, no. 25, para. 167.

Commission of Human Rights, and continues to be invoked by the Court: degradation as involving the victim being driven to act against her will or conscience.[6] A further element that is used to characterize degradation is the suffering by an individual of contempt or lack of respect for her personality.[7] The Court looks for the existence of one or more of these points of reference in order to determine whether the event or situation being complained of might entail degradation within the bounds of Article 3. It does not go beyond these statements to explicitly stipulate the substance of humiliation (although this particular concept has been elaborated upon through the development of certain principles), being driven to act against will or conscience, etc. The Court's focus is on the practical application of the right.[8] Nevertheless, when one looks holistically at the jurisprudence and on this basis works towards deeper accounts of the concepts relied upon, the conceptual foundations of the right are apparent.

Some interesting observations can be made: the most evident concerns the inclusion of the prohibition of degrading treatment alongside the prohibition of torture; both are clearly seen to be closely related. It is clear from the jurisprudence that Article 3 as a whole is interpreted as being directed towards protection of dignity (as will be evident in the citation from *Tyrer v. United Kingdom* below). It is also interesting to note that degrading treatment is seen to be a different form of harm than inhuman treatment (captured in the concept of dehumanization?); both are related – both are side-by-side within the same prohibition – but often treated as distinct.[9] It is notable that humiliation is explicitly associated with degradation and has in fact been selected as part of the definition of degradation. Given that humiliation might be seen as a separate, self-standing violation of human dignity, it is intriguing to note this relationship. These points form the foundations of how degradation is understood and delineated in the ECHR forum. Much is left open and unarticulated, but the relevance of *particular* concepts within the conceptual framework of degradation is visible, as is a basic view of the relationships between these concepts.

[6] *Greek Case*, Commission Report of 5 November 1969, Yearbook of the European Convention on Human Rights XII (1969), Chapter IV, section A(2), p. 186; *Keenan v. United Kingdom*, no. 27229/95, ECHR 2001-III.

[7] *Abdulaziz, Cabales and Balkandali v. United Kingdom*, 28 May 1985, Series A, no. 94, para. 91.

[8] This is unsurprising; such elaboration is not to be expected given that the Court is primarily concerned, now that the principles are firmly established, with the concrete application of the law to very particular facts in concrete complaints before it. Martha Nussbaum makes this point in relation to a jury deciding upon a case involving emotions, where a more general exploration of the emotional concepts involved is not an immediate concern (Nussbaum 2004: 67–68).

[9] Applicants have often argued, and the ECtHR has arrived at, conclusions of inhuman *and* degrading treatment (for example, in *Ireland v. UK*). However, a distinction between "inhuman" and "degrading" is evident where the ECtHR classifies treatment or punishment specifically as one form or the other (see, for example, *Yankov v. Bulgaria*, no. 39084/97, ECHR 2003-VII (degrading treatment) and *Bilgin v. Turkey*, no. 23819/94, 16 November 2000 (inhuman treatment)), and it is also visible in the different conceptual points of reference that have been established by the ECtHR.

Furthermore, since this forum revolves around application, we also gain a picture of how these ideas and relationships translate into practice.

6.3 What Does Degradation Look Like?

The question of how degradation is played out in practice could be viewed as one of the simpler ones on the above list – is there not a sense in which we all know degradation when we see it? But then what do we respond when asked to give a practical example of degradation? The articulation of an example necessitates engagement with a myriad of questions, beginning with the question of what kind of harm degradation encapsulates and how this is judged in relation to oneself, but also to others, and so on. Nevertheless, it is difficult to relinquish the idea that one could identify a degrading situation if one were presented with it. The case-law in which a finding of degrading treatment or punishment has been reached provides ready-made examples of degradation that have been identified in the Article 3 context.[10]

A first example of degradation in practical form concerns detention conditions, which have been a common cause for concern. Such cases tend to involve complaints about a combination of factors that, taken together, are degrading: including, for example, poor and/or non-private sanitary facilities, vermin or insects in detention cells, overcrowding, and lack of movement.[11] The use of unwarranted physical force by state agents has been found to be degrading, even where the victim suffered no serious injury.[12] The manner of conducting a search of an individual in detention was also found to have inflicted degradation:

> Obliging the applicant to strip naked in the presence of a woman, and then touching his sexual organs and food with bare hands showed a clear lack of respect for the applicant, and diminished in effect his human dignity.[13]

A lack of respect for an individual's well-being as a result of a failure to provide adequate medical care is a further example.[14] In the late 1970s, in the *Tyrer* case,

---

[10]The case-law research on which this chapter is based focuses primarily on outcomes of degrading *treatment*, rather than punishment, in cases before the Court. Judgments of degrading treatment are more common than those on punishment, notably since treatment appears to be the broader of the two terms and capable of also encompassing punishment. This is suggested by Nowak in the context of the equivalent provision of the International Covenant on Civil and Political Rights (Nowak 2005: 159; Jayawickrama 2002: 303). Where helpful insight is provided, however, specific punishment cases will also be cited. For present purposes, it is not significant whether degradation takes the form of treatment or punishment; what is significant is the understanding of the degrading nature of the treatment or punishment.

[11]E.g. *Kalashnikov v. Russia*, no. 47095/99, ECHR 2002-VI, para. 97–102; *Peers v. Greece*, no. 28525/95, ECHR 2001-III, para. 72–75.

[12]*Barbu Anghelescu v.Romania*, no. 46430/99, 05 October 2004, para. 55–60.

[13]*Valasinas v. Lithuania*, no. 44558/98, ECHR 2001-VIII, para. 117.

[14]*Nevmerzhitsky v. Ukraine*, no. 54825/00, ECHR 2005-II. para. 100–106.

the Court for the first time held that corporal punishment of a child, also taking into consideration the anguish of anticipating the punishment, was degrading; the Court found that the punishment:

> [...] whereby [the applicant] was treated as an object in the power of the authorities – constituted an assault on precisely that which it is one of the main purposes of Article 3 [...] to protect, namely a person's dignity and physical integrity.[15]

A further example is a case involving a detainee whose hair was forcibly shaved:

> A particular characteristic of the treatment complained of, the forced shaving off of a prisoner's hair, is that it consists in a forced change of the person's appearance by the removal of his hair. The person undergoing that treatment is very likely to experience a feeling of inferiority as his physical appearance is changed against his will.
>
> Furthermore, for at least a certain period of time a prisoner whose hair has been shaved off carries a mark of the treatment he has undergone. The mark is immediately visible to others [...]. The person concerned is very likely to feel hurt in his dignity by the fact that he carries a visible physical mark.[16]

It is interesting and significant to highlight the detail and scope of such situations that have been held to entail degradation; they bring the practical manifestation of degradation into view. In addition to such cases where the Court has agreed that degradation had occurred, there are, of course, the many cases that have argued this unsuccessfully. In some it has been accepted that a situation might involve degradation but not in the circumstances of that particular case, as with discrimination, notably.[17] In others, the Court has not accepted that the harm complained of was serious enough to be recognized as degrading treatment[18]; for example, in a case concerning living conditions caused by a waste treatment plant in close proximity, the Court found that the conditions for the family must have been "very difficult" but were not degrading.[19] It should be noted that the Court's decisions are based on the circumstances of the particular case at hand; taken into account are the duration of the treatment and the effects on the individual. The age, sex, and state of health of the individual may also be relevant factors.[20] The case-law effectuates a differentiation between that which can be called degrading and that which is simply "unpleasant."[21] The examples that do result in a finding of degrading treatment or punishment reflect the substance of the concept of degradation as understood by the ECtHR.

---

[15] *Tyrer v. United Kingdom*, judgment of 25 April 1978, Series A, no. 26.

[16] *Yankov v. Bulgaria*, para. 112–113.

[17] *Smith and Grady v. United Kingdom*, no. 33985/96; 33986/96, ECHR 1999-VI, para. 121. See also the comments of the European Commission of Human Rights in *East African Asians v. United Kingdom*, Commission Report of 14 December 1973, Decisions and Reports 31, para. 207.

[18] The "minimum level of severity" is a standard requirement that is referred to systematically in Article 3 case-law; see *Ireland v. United Kingdom*, para. 162.

[19] *López Ostra v. Spain*, judgment of 09 December 1994, Series A, no. 303-C, para. 60.

[20] *Ireland v. United Kingdom*, para. 162.

[21] *Guzzardi v. Italy*, judgment of 06 November 1980, Series A, no. 39, para. 107.

In such cases, a relationship between degradation and human dignity is visible. Degradation is portrayed as a conceptual opposite of human dignity:

> [The treatment] in the Court's view, showed a lack of respect for the applicant's human dignity [. . .] the Court is of the view that in the present case such behaviour which humiliated and debased the applicant, amounted to degrading treatment contrary to Article 3.[22]

And the right is interpreted as aiming to protect human dignity; for example: "[. . .] treatment [. . .] may be incompatible with the standards imposed by Article 3 in the protection of fundamental human dignity [. . .]."[23] The way in which the Court understands dignity is not clearly articulated, but a consistent concern becomes visible through a piecing together of such insights from the case-law. Certain conditions are simply viewed as unacceptable and improper for a human being (including, for example, poor sanitary conditions).[24] The Court admonishes a lack of respect for the person, including for a person's physical and mental health.[25] The Court has criticized the treatment of a person as an object.[26] (Part of) a consistent picture emerges of an understanding of dignity and its violation in a very basic, fundamental sense. The objective of this chapter is to reflect on the concept of degradation drawing upon European human rights jurisprudence, rather than to focus on the ECtHR's understanding of dignity, but it is important to explicitly recognize that, underlying these examples of degradation and indeed all aspects of the Court's characterization of degradation, there is some understanding of human dignity. Ronald Dworkin's account of adjudication highlights that interaction with such moral concepts is an inherent feature of the process of interpretation and application (Dworkin 1977). Very conveniently taking the example of the concept of dignity, Dworkin states that his imaginary judge Hercules indeed relies upon his *own understanding* of dignity in interpretation. This point, which highlights judicial engagement with the concept of dignity, is linked to the relationship between the personal experience of degradation and the Court's judgment as to whether degradation has occurred.

6.4 The Significance of Feeling Degraded

Questions related to the significance of the individual experience of degradation are pivotal, yet they are not straightforward, and the conclusions potentially entail even less straightforward implications. Insight into this dimension of the concept of degradation emerges via the concept of humiliation in the case-law[27] (given that

---

[22] *Iwanczuk v. Poland*, no. 25196/94, 15 November 2001, para. 59.

[23] *Keenan v. UK*, no. 27229/95, ECHR 2001-III, para. 113.

[24] *Price v. United Kingdom*, no. 33394/96, ECHR 2001-VII.

[25] *Peers v. Greece*, no. 28524/95, ECHR 2001-V; *Valasinas v. Lithuania*, no. 44558/98, ECHR 2001-VIII.

[26] *Tyrer v. United Kingdom*.

[27] Humiliation is coupled in the standard characterization with debasement. The latter appears to act primarily as reinforcement. Principally, it provides a strong link to the concept of degradation in its

degradation, within the ECtHR's framework, can be identified on the basis of an individual having suffered humiliation). The significance of the individual experience in the ECHR approach emerges specifically through a discussion of a principle with which humiliation has been linked in the case-law: that it is sufficient that an individual is humiliated in his/her own eyes.[28]

This principle (like the concept of humiliation itself) is not explicitly clarified or explained in the jurisprudence, but rather is substantiated through its application. In exploring humiliation[29] and this related principle, a particularly significant point emerges from a range of humiliation literature – that humiliation is recognized as an emotion or feeling, but also as a state or social fact (Silver et al. 1986: 273, Miller 1993: 146, Waldron 1995: 1794). The distinction between emotion and social fact entails that a person can feel humiliated without being humiliated as a social fact, and vice versa (Silver at al. 1986). Recognition of this dual aspect of humiliation is indispensable. Both facets of this distinction are reflected in the principle that it is sufficient that an individual is humiliated in his/her own eyes, and also in the degradation case-law more generally. It is a valuable distinction that suitably allows us to acknowledge the subjective experience of degradation but *at the same time* accommodates a dimension of degradation that is not victim-subjective.

This principle established by the Court can be seen to reflect this emotion/social fact distinction. In the statement that it is sufficient that an individual is humiliated in his/her own eyes even if not in the eyes of others, "is" should be read as implying "feels"; an individual can feel humiliated even if no other person witnesses the humiliation. The reference to the "eyes of others" is a reference to the (far from irrelevant but not crucial) presence of witnesses to the humiliation (Silver et al. 1986: 278–279). "It is sufficient" refers to the sufficiency of feeling humiliated; it does not refer to the sufficiency of the existence of humiliation. We know this because in subsequent cases the Court has repeated this point combined with a conclusion that the applicant was *not* humiliated.[30] It can be inferred not only that humiliation can be emotionally experienced even without other individuals witnessing it but also that the existence of humiliation, as far as the judgment of the Court is concerned, is not accepted only on the basis of an emotional experience of humiliation. The latter point is significant because it moves towards articulating the respective place

visible sharing of the "de" preposition, highlighting the "down from", "off" dimension of the concept. Debasement is found in one dictionary defined simply as degradation (*The Chambers English Dictionary*. Cambridge: Chambers). Humiliation instead emerges as the core concept within this coupling.

[28] *Tyrer v. United Kingdom*, para. 32

[29] On the concept of humiliation, see Chapters 3 by Neuhäuser and Chapter 4 by Kuch (this volume).

[30] *Campbell and Cosans v. United Kingdom*, judgment of 25 February 1982, Series A, no. 48, para. 28–30.

and importance of what might be called subjective versus objective evaluations of humiliation, which then feeds into an understanding of degradation.[31]

Since degradation is understood to be characterized by humiliation, this suggests that degradation is identified, via humiliation, on the basis of more than an internally-felt emotion, as something whose existence is not dependent upon the individual's actual experience. For the Court to be able to identify a state of humiliation and degradation, an appreciation of the felt experience seems implicit, but at the same time, precedence is given to the Court's evaluation of whether the applicant had, to use Margalit's expression, "sound reasons" for feeling humiliated or degraded (Margalit 1996: 9), i.e., whether the applicant was in social fact placed in a state of humiliation or degradation.

This allows us to respond to that common challenge relating to the implications of the idea of degradation within Article 3 – the sentiment that individuals experience situations in different ways and that it is therefore impossible to label a particular *situation* as degrading, that the labeling must surely depend on one's felt experience. We can recall the questions raised in our introductory example: Is it significant or indeed problematic for judging the existence of degradation that I feel humiliated by something whereas you experience the same thing positively? Would we say that I have *been* humiliated and, as can follow from the Court's framework, degraded, and you have not? Such divergent experiences are accommodated in light of the emotion/state distinction. On this basis the answer would be negative, since the existence of a state of humiliation (and so degradation) depends *primarily* on the Court's evaluation, that is, on the Court's evaluation of the social fact, as shall be discussed further below. The conclusion can be reached that this same experience, which I might find merely irritating and you somewhat gratifying, is degrading nevertheless. We might then ask: Is it degrading for the woman to be subjected to such treatment in the example above? We might consider the particular circumstances, as indeed is the practice of the ECtHR: for example, what age was the woman? Perhaps we would be more likely to view it negatively if there was a substantial age difference between the parties. Where was the comment made? Would it be viewed as less "acceptable" in the workplace than in a bar?

Or perhaps differences in circumstances will not change our conclusion. In this sense, the question is taken one step further to ask whether a situation can be labeled as always degrading, regardless of the particular individual circumstances. A number of interesting, and likely controversial, situations could be considered in this

[31] Furthermore, the emotion/social fact distinction helps to explain the logic of a related principle that is found in the Court's case-law: that humiliation does not need to have been intentionally inflicted; see *T. v. United Kingdom*, no. 24724/94, 16 December 1999, para. 69. The emotion/social fact distinction contributes a justification for this position, simply in that the distinction makes *possible* the independence of the emotion and the social fact: The Court reserves to itself the ability to identify a state of humiliation that is not wholly dependent upon perceptions of either the "humiliator" or the victim. In the case of *Farbtuhs v. Latvia*, the Court reached a finding of degrading treatment despite both the Court and the applicant acknowledging that there had been no intention to humiliate; *Farbtuhs v. Latvia*, no. 4672/02, 02 December 2004, para. 58.

respect. Prostitution is one example. Is this something that is always, in its essence, degrading? It goes without saying that different people will give different answers to this question (likely centered on whether the individual concerned experiences it as degrading or not, which illustrates precisely the present point). The ECtHR has in fact labeled certain situations as always degrading "in principle." The case of *Yankov v. Bulgaria* can be cited again as an apt example:

> The Court thus considers that the forced shaving off of detainees' hair is in principle an act which may have the effect of diminishing their human dignity or may arouse in them feelings of inferiority capable of humiliating and debasing them. (para. 114)

This suggests that an individual will be accepted, "in principle", as having "sound reasons" for feeling degraded by such an act.

Although there is the possibility of different opinions on the answer to such a question in the judicial forum, the Court's is the legally authoritative interpretation. A question then arises: How are those socially-constructed standards, against which the existence of a social fact is evaluated, identified and used? The identification of social standards and deductions as to social facts can be illuminated by recognizing the interpretive process of the judges as engaging with what Dworkin refers to as community morality (Dworkin 1977) (or with Rawls' similar idea of public reason (Rawls 1993)).[32] Community morality comprises moral traditions and political convictions of the community (Dworkin 1977: 125–126). The substance of this morality is, as Dworkin argues, *identified* by the judge on the basis of his own judgment (distinguishing reliance on principles of community morality from reliance on the judge's personal political convictions (Dworkin 1977: 123–130)).[33] This links the substance of the idea of dignity relied upon with the idea of a network of social norms, in relation to which the existence of degradation of the individual can be judged. Again, Margalit's idea of having sound reasons in the context of humiliation is reflected here (Margalit 1996: 9). In engaging with social norms, the Court would ask whether the individual had suffered a situation that could soundly (reasonably) be seen as degrading. It is also reflected in Nussbaum's discussion of how the law deals with emotions, which highlights the link between what is reasonable in law and the idea of social standards; the idea of the "standard norms" of that person's society, and the influence of this on judgments as to reasonableness (Nussbaum 2004: 33; see also 39).

The significant point is the idea that degradation, on the basis of its association with humiliation, can be coherently understood to have a significant emotional component but can be judged to occur independently of the individual's felt experience. In the context of applications before the ECtHR, the individual(s) in question can be

---

[32] In Rawls' discussion of public reason, see note 23 on differences and similarities to Dworkin's political morality (Rawls 1993: 236–237). See also Dworkin (2006: 251–254) for a brief discussion.

[33] This view of adjudication embeds the possibility of judges arriving at different decisions on the basis of their own readings of the community morality (Dworkin 1977: 128). For further discussion, see Dworkin (2003: 67–111).

presumed to have experienced the situation negatively since an application has been made to the Court. The Court is the recognized authoritative body to judge whether degradation has or has not occurred for the purpose of Article 3.

6.5 Degradation as Restriction of Autonomy?

The concept of autonomy, which appears in a number of guises in a number of fields, is often perceived as significant in relation to dignity. Gerald Dworkin, in discussing the broad usage of the concept, notes various substantive understandings, including liberty and freedom of the will, and the association of the idea with, for example, self-assertion and the absence of external causation, amongst others. Dworkin summarizes the functions of autonomy as moral, political, and social ideal (Dworkin 1988: 6–7, 10–11). Raz additionally refers to personal autonomy and to *conditions for personal autonomy* (Raz 1986: 204). It is not the present objective, nor would it be possible, to provide an in-depth exploration of the concept of autonomy in all its guises, but it is nevertheless important in reflecting upon a conceptual understanding of degradation to question whether autonomy is a relevant concept.

Amongst the Court's conceptual points of reference in relation to degradation, the idea of being driven to act against one's will or conscience stands out as a possible source of insight; it immediately invokes associations with the basic idea of self-rule. It is an intriguing inclusion under the umbrella of degradation. Jurisprudential references are, however, scant. As a component of degradation, this has generated little discussion or elaboration. Unlike with humiliation, there are no established principles to begin from, and so there is less to engage with in this respect. However, one significant reference is identifiable, from which important considerations can be seen to emerge. This is a reference made by the European Commission of Human Rights in the *Ireland* case cited above, concerning ill-treatment of internees by UK security forces:

> The will to resist or to give in cannot, under such conditions, be formed with any degree of independence. Those most firmly resistant might give in at an early stage when subjected to this sophisticated method to break or even eliminate the will.[34]

Although brief, this allusion by the Commission might in fact be seen as particularly indicative – in its reference to *independence* of will. When viewed in the context of wider literature on the meaning and use of autonomy, the centrality of independence of will is most apparent in relation to one facet of autonomy that has been articulated. That is the latter of those mentioned above: the idea of conditions for autonomy. This facet of autonomy is presented as the basic core of the idea, which accords with the very basic, fundamental way in which the ECtHR appears to understand dignity to be violated (it is helpful also not to lose sight of the immediate context, which is that of the prohibition of torture).

[34] *Ireland v. United Kingdom*, Commission Report of 25 January 1976, Decisions and Reports 31, 402.

Raz describes conditions for autonomy as the *capacity* that is required for the realization of personal autonomy. It is alternatively expressed as, on the one hand, being an agent with a capacity for personal autonomy and, on the other hand, as leading an autonomous life (Raz 1986: 154). A similar idea is embodied in Berlin's notion of positive freedom. In the following passage, positive freedom – being one's "own master" – is strikingly tied to the idea of independence as well as to will and conscience:

> I wish to be the instrument of my own, not of other men's, acts of will. I wish to be a subject, not an object; to be moved by reasons, conscious purposes, which are my own, not by causes which affect me, as it were, from outside. I wish to be somebody, not nobody; a doer – deciding, not being decided for, self-directed and not acted upon by external nature or by other men as if I were a thing, or an animal, or a slave incapable of playing a human role, that is, of conceiving goals and policies of my own and realizing them [. . .]. I wish, above all, to be conscious of myself as a thinking, willing, active being, bearing responsibility for my choices and able to explain them by references to my own ideas and purposes. I feel free to the degree that I believe this to be true, and enslaved to the degree that I am made to realize that it is not. (Berlin 1969: 131)

The simple fact of the inclusion of the condemnation of being driven to act against one's will or conscience in the characterization of degradation, and the Commission's reference to the idea of independence, support the relevance of restriction of autonomy as capable of engendering degradation. Furthermore, the primary relevance of autonomy is arguably found in this one particular facet of autonomy – the basic capacity for autonomy, or what is memorably captured in Berlin's description of positive freedom. Much more should indeed be said on this purported relationship[35]; the intention has simply been to pose the question and to suggest that this is a form of autonomy that is arguably at the heart of the idea of being driven to act against one's will or conscience in degrading treatment jurisprudence. But regardless of the details, the most significant point is to suggest not that autonomy is indeed relevant in some sense but that it might *only* be seen as relevant in a very particular sense. It is important in applying the label of degradation to consider the demarcation of this concept, which involves consideration of the sense of restriction of autonomy it should appropriately be used to encompass.

---

[35] As noted above, the concept of autonomy is commonly viewed as relevant to understanding human dignity. Also common is a concern with the implications of a *dependent* link between dignity and autonomy – if dignity is violated by restriction of autonomy, what are the implications of this for those who are designated as lacking autonomy? This is an important question, yet one that is hindered by a lack of precision in how the terms are employed. The implications of such an objection depend upon what is understood by autonomy (including when, why, and by whom certain human beings are labeled as non-autonomous in some sense), upon how dignity itself is understood, and upon how the nature of the link between autonomy and dignity is viewed. Nevertheless, it can be noted in the context of the above example that there is no necessary implication that violations of dignity in the form of degradation are *always* characterized by restriction of the capacity for autonomy.

6.6 Degradation and Social Dignity

Etymologically, degradation is constructed on the idea of "grade" and "gradation". It is often associated with social standing or reputation. On the basis that degradation expresses a violation of human dignity, this raises the further question of whether degradation might be concerned with a conception of social dignity,[36] with ranking on the basis of social position? From a human rights perspective, this would be a strange proposition. The seminal Universal Declaration of Human Rights recognizes in its first substantive Article that, "All human beings are born free and equal in dignity and rights." This equality of dignity is a cornerstone of the human rights regime; it is quite simply incompatible with the idea of dignity as conferred on the basis of merit or social position.

The content of degrading treatment case-law indicates that dignity in this social sense is not the concern of degradation in the human rights law sphere. As stated above, a theme is apparent in this case-law in terms of what is viewed as reprehensible and as signifying degradation in the eyes of the ECtHR. This does not involve damage to reputation or standing acquired on the basis of merit due to one's position in societal affairs. The Court's understanding of degradation appears to be defined by the violation of something basic and fundamental, by treating a human person in a way that is considered inappropriate for a person to be treated. Cases such as those outlined above concerning detention conditions provide a good illustration of this point: In stipulating that certain conditions are "objectively unacceptable,"[37] this suggests that degradation can result when the person in question is not treated in a way that is befitting of persons. The case-law seems to proceed on the basis that there is something special about human persons – although, as is characteristic of international human rights law generally, the nature of that special quality is not made explicit (McCrudden 2008: 675–678). It is significant, nevertheless, that social dignity is given no audience.

For example, in the Commission's report in the *East African Asians* case, the definition of degrading treatment *offered by the applicants* was considered and rejected: It was argued that treatment could be degrading if it lowered the victim in "rank, position, reputation or character" (the definition found in the Oxford English Dictionary), which might suggest a sense of social dignity. The response of the Commission is indicative: The Commission was of the opinion that this general definition could be a useful starting point but stressed that the purpose of the prohibition of torture and inhuman or degrading treatment or punishment was to "prevent interferences with the dignity of man of a particularly serious nature" and suggested that the definition offered must be narrowed to take account of this.[38] In a later report, the Commission again mentioned lowering of rank, position, reputation, or

---

[36] Attributed on the basis of social position or role; see Pollmann (Chapter 17, this volume) for a brief summary of the origins of this conception.

[37] *Peers v. Greece*, para. 75.

[38] *East African Asians*, Commission Report, para. 189.

character, stipulating that this must be of such a degree as to interfere with human dignity. It also referred to the question of whether contempt or lack of respect had been shown for the applicant's personality.[39] In the judgment in this case, the Court did not adopt the notion of lowering of rank, position, reputation, or character, but instead relied upon the notion of adverse effect on the applicant's personality.[40]

Contempt or lack of respect for the applicant's personality in the context of the prohibition of degrading treatment is arguably best understood as expressing concern for the entity of the person. The government in the case of *Raninen v. Finland* denied that the treatment complained of showed contempt for "the applicant *as a person*."[41] On the term "personality", Gordon W. Allport writes that the wide range of meanings of "persona" and "personality" are situated on a continuum of references to the external and internal self, referring to this combination as the "outstanding characteristic" of the term (Allport 1937: 29). The relevant sense of personality in relation to degradation can be seen to sit halfway along this continuum as something that captures the essence of the person and its external display. If this reading is correct, it demonstrates that, in preferring the idea of contempt for personality over rank, position, reputation, or character, the ECtHR rejects the relevance of social dignity in understanding degradation in favor of a sense of equal dignity that demands that human persons, as persons, are treated with a certain degree of respect.

In relation to rank, position, reputation, or character, however, the Commission's statements suggest that this *is* potentially relevant – but only if it is tied to human dignity. Waldron has recently, and convincingly, reinvigorated the notion of rank in relation to understanding human dignity.[42] This discussion of the idea of rank and its relevance in a human rights context is illuminative, since it raises the possibility of maintaining a meaningful link between dignity and the idea of rank (Waldron 2007). Waldron's invocation of the notion of rank is helpful, firstly, in understanding the *form* of violation of dignity that the concept of degradation can be seen to encapsulate. It can indeed be seen to maintain the idea of "grade" and lowering of rank. Alongside those dictionary meanings that refer explicitly to rank, others contain reference to the idea of lowering: "To lower in estimation, to bring into dishonour or contempt"; "To lower in character or quality: to debase." This is echoed in what is in fact the most common domain of invocation of the term degradation: in relation to environmental harm; to the degradation of land or natural resources. It is used to express deterioration of something valuable. This idea of *lowering* can be seen to capture precisely the key feature of the idea of degradation.

[39] An indicator of degradation that had in the meantime been established by the Court.

[40] *Raninen v. Finland*, no. 20972/92, Commission Report of 24 October 1996, para. 50-52; *Raninen v. Finland,* no. 20972/92, 16 December 1997, *Reports* 1997-VIII, para. 55.

[41] *Raninen v. Finland*, para. 54 (emphasis added).

[42] Waldron has also recently engaged, in what is a rare discussion, with the idea of degradation; see Waldron (2008).

Secondly, Waldron's approach to the term rank is useful in that it presents a tie between the idea of rank and use of the concept of dignity in the human rights context (see Chapter 2 by Stoecker, this volume). In a rich discussion, which highlights notably the contribution to the idea of *equal high rank* amongst human beings given by Gregory Vlastos, Waldron concludes that dignity can be associated with the idea of rank, but: "[...] specifically with a sort of universalization, for all humans, of privileges that have historically been associated with particular ranks of nobility" (Waldron 2007: 233). The suggestion, therefore, is that although the idea of rank was indeed the core notion behind ideas of social dignity and status differentiation, the meaning of dignity itself has now evolved. In its now prominent form, where the core of dignity is seen as equality, the idea of rank nevertheless remains relevant to understanding the essence of what is captured in the evolved use of the term "dignity". Whereas degradation previously involved a person being brought down in social status, degradation against a backdrop of equal dignity involves a person being brought down from one's equal status as a human being. This can be summarized in the idea of abuse of equal high rank – a description that arguably encapsulates the essence of the concept of degradation.

6.7 Conclusion

This chapter has aimed to briefly reflect on a number of related questions deemed to be interesting from the perspective of deepening conceptual understanding of, and stimulating further debate on, the concept of degradation as it expresses a violation of human dignity. It has done so by considering one very particular, but influential, instance of the use of the concept. There are undoubtedly other questions that could and will be posed, and degrading treatment jurisprudence also contains further avenues for exploration.

The jurisprudence can be interpreted as supporting the identification of degradation, via humiliation, independently of the individual emotional experience, as supporting the relevance of a particular facet of autonomy within the meaning of degradation, and as supporting the idea of degradation as abuse of equal rank. The Court should not be seen to rely upon an isolated understanding of human dignity. Dworkin's approach is again helpful here: Hercules relies upon his own understanding of dignity in interpretation, constituted by being part of the community in which he operates, or by "collecting" an understanding of dignity "from its life" in "political rhetoric and debates of the time" (Dworkin 1977: 127).

The understanding of degradation that is found in the Court's jurisprudence is, of course, open to criticism. It is undeniable, however, that it has considerable practical weight. And to enrich our understanding of the concept of degradation alongside human dignity, human rights law presents itself as a relevant and intriguing forum for analysis. The fundamental insight from the degrading treatment jurisprudence of the ECtHR lies in the characterization of degradation in terms of *particular* conceptual relationships between degradation, humiliation, autonomy, and rank.

The nature of these relationships is a constituent of the substantive contours of degradation itself. At the core of this exercise is the contention that considering the way in which the term degradation is employed and discussing how it, and related terms, should be demarcated – in terms of the substance that they are understood to embody – contributes to conceptual clarity. And crucially, this facilitates meaningful debate.

References

Abdulaziz, Cabales and Balkandali v. United Kingdom, judgment of 28 May 1985, Series A, no. 94.
Barbu Anghelescu v. Romania, no. 46430/99, 05 October 2004.
Bilgin v. Turkey, no. 23819/94, 16 November 2000.
Campbell and Cosans v. United Kingdom, judgment of 25 February 1982, Series A, no. 48.
East African Asians v. United Kingdom, Commission Report of 14 December 1973, Decisions and Reports 31.
Farbtuhs v. Latvia, no. 4672/02, 02 December 2004.
Greek Case, Commission Report, 5 November 1969, Yearbook of the European Convention on Human Rights XII (1969), Chapter IV, Section A(2).
Ireland v. United Kingdom. Commission Report of 25 January 1976, Decisions and Reports 31.
Ireland v. United Kingdom, judgment of 18 January 1978, Series A, no. 25.
Iwanczuk v. Poland, no. 25196/94, 15 November 2001.
Kalashnikov v. Russia, no. 47095/99, ECHR 2002-VI.
Keenan v. United Kingdom, no. 27229/95, ECHR 2001-III.
López Ostra v. Spain, judgment of 09 December 1994, Series A, no. 303-C.
Nevmerzhitsky v. Ukraine, no. 54825/00, 05 April 2005.
Peers v. Greece, no. 28525/95, ECHR 2001-III.
Raninen v. Finland, no. 20972/92, Commission Report of 24 October 1996.
Raninen v. Finland, no. 20972/92, 16 December 1997, *Reports* 1997-VIII.
Smith and Grady v. United Kingdom, no. 33985/96; 33986/96, ECHR 1999-VI.
T. v. United Kingdom, no. 24724/94, 16 December 1999.
Tyrer v. United Kingdom, judgment of 25 April 1978, Series A, no. 26.
Valasinas v. Lithuania, no. 44558/98, ECHR 2001-VIII.
Yankov v. Bulgaria, no. 39084/97, 11 December 2003.
Allport, Gordon W. 1937. *Personality: A psychological interpretation.* New York, NY: Henry Holt and Company.
Berlin, Isaiah. 1969. *Four essays on liberty.* Oxford: Oxford University Press.
Cane, Peter. 2002. *Responsibility in law and morality.* Oxford: Hart.
Duff, R. Anthony. 2005. Punishment, dignity and degradation. *Oxford Journal of Legal Studies* 25(1): 141–155.
Dworkin, Gerald. 1988. *The theory and practice of autonomy.* Cambridge: Cambridge University Press.
Dworkin, Ronald. 1977. *Taking rights seriously.* London: Duckworth.
Dworkin, Ronald. 2003. The secular papacy. In *Judges in contemporary democracy: An international conversation*, eds. Robert Badinter and Stephen G. Breyer, 67–111. New York, NY: NYU Press.
Dworkin, Ronald. 2006. *Justice in robes.* Cambridge: The Belknap Press.
Evans, Malcolm and Rod Morgan. 1998. *Preventing torture: A study of the European convention for the prevention of torture and inhuman or degrading treatment or punishment.* Oxford: Oxford University Press.
Jayawickrama, Nihal. 2002. *The judicial application of human rights law: National, regional and international jurisprudence.* Cambridge: Cambridge University Press.

Lawson, Anna and Amrita Mukherjee. 2004. Slopping out in Scotland: The limits of degradation and respect. *European Human Rights Law Review* 6: 645–659.

Margalit, Avishai. 1996. *The decent society*. Cambridge, MA: Harvard University Press.

McCrudden, Christopher. 2008. Human dignity and judicial interpretation of human rights. In *European Journal of International Law* 19(4): 655–724.

Miller, William Ian. 1993. *Humiliation – And other essays on honor, social discomfort and violence*. Ithaca, NY: Cornell University Press.

Millns, Susan. 2002. Death, dignity and discrimination: The case of Pretty v. United Kingdom. *German Law Journal* 3(10). http://www.germanlawjournal.com/article.php?id=197. Accessed 19 May 2009.

Nowak, Manfred. 2005. *U.N. Covenant on Civil and Political Rights – CCPR Commentary*, 2nd edition. Kehl: NP Engel.

Nussbaum, Martha C. 2004. *Hiding from humanity: Disgust, shame and the law*. Princeton, NJ: Princeton University Press.

Rawls, John. 1993. *Political liberalism*. New York, NY: Columbia University Press.

Raz, Joseph. 1986. *The morality of freedom*. Oxford: Clarendon.

Silver, Maury et al. 1986. Humiliation: Feeling, social control and construction of identity. *Journal for the Theory of Social Behaviour* 16(3): 269–283.

Waldron, Jeremy. 1995. On humiliation. *Michigan Law Review* 93(6): 1787–1804.

Waldron, Jeremy. 2007. Dignity and rank. *European Journal of Sociology* 48(2): 201–237.

Waldron, Jeremy. 2008. Cruel, inhuman and degrading treatment: The words themselves. New York University public law and legal theory research paper series. Working paper 08-36. http://ssrn.com/abstract=1278604. Accessed 15 May 2009.

Chapter 7
Dehumanization: Perceiving the Body as (In)Human

Sophie Oliver

Abstract Dehumanization – the designation of the unlivable, the unintelligible, the ungrievable inhuman – is that almost unimaginable process by which human beings are rendered so radically other that their lives count for nothing. In this chapter, the author considers how victims, perpetrators and bystanders of atrocity come to perceive the loss of humanity and, in particular, the extent to which this (mis)perception is linked both physically and discursively to the figure of the human body. Paying attention to the concrete corporeality of dehumanization as it is described in testimonial texts, the author suggests that to think of "human dignity" as an abstract and disembodied quality becomes problematic in its failure to recognize the embodied, lived experience of suffering human beings. By focusing on testimonial accounts of dehumanizing atrocity, this chapter points to the significance of our role as receivers of testimony, also potentially guilty of dehumanizing perception, and emphasizes the possibility within the testimonial encounter both to repeat and to resist the logic of dehumanization and the unmaking, self-destroying power of bodily pain.

7.1 Introduction

It is customary when seeking to understand the somewhat elusive concept of "dehumanization" to refer in the first instance to that which it works against, in other words, to begin by defining what we understand as *human*. Standard definitions of dehumanization define the concept in terms of a negation of such positive "human" qualities as individuality, autonomy, personality, civility, and dignity. While this approach may provide us with relative conceptual clarity, it can lead one to pay too little attention to what I shall call the "lived experience" of dehumanization. Attending to the concrete corporeality of dehumanization as it is described in personal narratives of atrocity, and offering in this way a phenomenology of dehumanizing atrocities, this chapter seeks to present a more holistic view of

S. Oliver (✉)
University of Konstanz, Germany
e-mail: Sophie-Anne.Oliver@uni-konstanz.de

P. Kaufmann et al. (eds.), *Humiliation, Degradation, Dehumanization*, Library of Ethics and Applied Philosophy 24, DOI 10.1007/978-90-481-9661-6_7,

dehumanization, while at the same time reflecting upon our understanding of what it means to be human or inhuman. If testimonial accounts of dehumanizing processes such as genocide, torture, and rape warfare demonstrate anything, it is the precariousness of such abstractly formulated concepts as human dignity. By embodying, and thus demystifying the concept of human dignity, it is argued, we may begin to think new ways to resist the logic of dehumanization.

Drawing on a range of theory and testimony, then, I hope to demonstrate just how closely the physical and discursive violation of the flesh is bound up in the minds of victims and perpetrators with processes of dehumanization and subjective destitution. If the link between sub-humanity and embodiment is so intricately made in the perception of victims and perpetrators, I will later go on to ask, to what extent are bystanders' perceptions also colored by negative symbolisms of the body in everyday dehumanization? The first section of the chapter is dedicated to presenting an overview of the theory of dehumanization as moral exclusion, while thinking also about the reasons why and methods by which individuals and groups are excluded from the human community: this demonstrates the perspective of the perpetrator. As the chapter progresses, the methods and processes of moral exclusion will be examined more closely and with reference to the lived experience of dehumanization as it has been described in testimonial texts; this should provide the reader with a better understanding of the meaning of dehumanization from the perspective of its victims, and not merely that of its theorists. The final section of the chapter will consider dehumanization from the perspective of the bystander or observer, pointing to the significance of our role as receivers of testimony, also potentially guilty of dehumanizing perception, and emphasizing the possibility within the testimonial encounter both to repeat and to resist the logic of dehumanization and the unmaking, self-destroying power of bodily pain.

7.1.1 A Truly Vicious Circle: Dehumanization as Moral Exclusion

> At various periods in history and in different societies, groups and individuals have been treated inhumanly by other humans: slaves by their masters, natives by colonialists, blacks by whites, Jews by Nazis, women by men, children by adults, the physically disabled by those who are not, homosexuals by heterosexuals, political dissidents by political authorities, and one ethnic or religious group by another [. . .]. Who is and who is not entitled to fair outcomes and fair treatment by inclusion or lack of inclusion in one's moral community? (Deutsch 2000: 49–50)

Let us begin with some general clarifications. The term "dehumanization" refers in the most basic terms to the denial, in part or whole, of the humanity of a person or group of persons. It is possible to think of degrees of dehumanization; we might speak of extreme or "mild" forms of dehumanization, the former occurring in instances of, for example, genocide and torture, and the latter in the everyday structures of social, political and economic marginalization, where ambiguities about what might constitute inhuman or dehumanizing treatment are most likely to arise.

There will be times when the threshold for that which we consider a violation of our humanity is historically and culturally dependent. Is it, for example, dehumanizing to deny a particular race or gender the right to vote, as was the case not so long ago in Europe and is still the case within some other cultures today? Is it dehumanizing to deny the very old and very sick autonomy of choice regarding their care or the time and manner of their death? The limits of dehumanizing behavior are often controversial. And yet, even as it is possible to speak of degrees of dehumanization, a general principle is constant: to perceive of or treat someone as less human, not fully human, or subhuman is an act of dehumanization, just as is the total denial of the humanity of an individual or group in genocide or torture. For what these have in common is their foundation in attitudes of exclusion, of which the psychological processes are alike, no matter the severity of the consequences.

Herbert C. Kelman (1973) explains dehumanization as a violation of the two qualities that he suggests we must accord to a person in order to perceive him as fully human: identity and community. To accord a person identity, he writes, "is to perceive him as an individual, independent and distinguishable from others, capable of making choices" (Kelman 1973: 48). This identity (which we might also call agency) is, as we shall see later, among the most affectively devastating losses suffered by victims of dehumanization. But let us focus for now on the loss of community, which is also at the crux of what dehumanization means in *effect*. Kelman's concept of community imagines humanity as "an interconnected network of individuals who care for each other, who recognize each other's individuality and who respect each other's rights" (Kelman 1973: 48). To be dehumanized is to be excluded from this community. It is to be perceived by the "in-group" as outside the moral kinship or scope of justice, and thus as a legitimate target for more active oppressions and exclusions. This, claims Kelman, is what makes sanctioned massacres and mass human atrocities possible. By excluding a person or persons from our moral community, it becomes possible to act inhumanly towards them, or else to allow harm to be done to them by others, without invoking any sense of moral inhibition or self-reproach. Psychological studies have demonstrated the extent to which perceiving others as less human than ourselves increases the opportunities for moral disengagement or indifference (Bandura et al. 1975, 1996). Susan Opotow explains further:

> We perceive those outside [our scope of justice] as nonentities, undeserving, or expendable. Harm that befalls them does not prompt the concern, remorse, or outrage that occurs when those inside the scope of justice are harmed. (Opotow 1995: 347–348)

Morton Deutsch (2000) outlines a number of social and psychological conditions that may serve to propagate excluding attitudes. Moral exclusion of particular groups, he suggests, is often a means of providing a scapegoat upon whom to place the responsibility for economic hardship or political strife. The excluded group may be perceived as a threat (thus during the Rwandan genocide it was claimed that Hutus should kill their Tutsi neighbors in pre-emptive self-defense), or as inferior in terms of race, ethnicity, gender, or class, and thus persecuted because of a fear of contamination, or because of a perceived deviance from normalized standards of appearance or behavior. Moral exclusion and dehumanization may also represent a form of displacement or projection: in psychological terms, the projection of disapproved aspects of the self onto others, through whom the unwanted elements are attacked or expelled (Deutsch 2000: 51). In his essay "Dehumanisation: An Integrative Review," psychologist Nick Haslam points to this phenomenon of placing onto the other that which cannot be accepted in the self; negative and excluding attitudes towards others, he suggests, are a means of confirming in our imagination our own humanity, contrasted with the perceived inhumanity of those seen as exhibiting "undesired" attributes, such as the "animality" of embodiment:

> Disgust enables us to avoid evidence of our animality, so representing others as animal-like may elicit the emotion. Contempt, a kindred emotion, plays a similar role, locating the other as below the self or in-group. (Haslam 2006: 258)

As William Gamson points out in his analysis of the politics of exclusion, the "*other-creating* process" is not limited to its extreme manifestations, but rather it has "certain tendencies and sub-processes that apply across the whole continuum [of exclusion]" (Gamson 1995: 17). Klaus Günther concurs, drawing our attention to dehumanization in the undramatic episodes of the day-to-day: in our attitudes towards certain criminals, or towards asylum seekers, or towards whomever the media chooses to present as "non-members of the community of human beings" (Günther 1999). While such systematic exclusion is in most cases a gradual process by which "over time, harms and dissimilarities eclipse benefits and similarities, gradually moving marginal groups outside the scope of justice" (Opotow 1995: 365), it is possible to identify active strategies of dehumanization, such as labeling, which occur not only in extreme cases but also in the everyday. As Kelman notes, the "traditions, the habits, the images and the vocabularies for dehumanization are already well established through everyday prejudice and labeling, and can thus be drawn upon when groups are selected for massacre" (Kelman 1973: 50). Haslam identifies two "metaphors of inhumanity" which often form part of active dehumanization processes: animalistic metaphor and mechanistic metaphor. These, in turn, correspond to two conceptual models of the human: "unique human" and "human nature". Animalistic metaphor, Haslam suggests, is a process of dehumanization whereby people perceived to be lacking in uniquely human characteristics such as rationality, civility, refinement, and moral sensibility are "seen implicitly or explicitly to be animal-like" (Haslam 2006: 257). Thus during the genocide in Rwanda the ethnic category of "Tutsi" was replaced in the discourse of the perpetrators with the signifier "cockroach", and survivors of Nazi persecution recall the daily insults of which they were the target: "blöde Schweine!", "blöde Hunde!" ("stupid pigs!", "stupid dogs!"). Images of prisoners at Abu Graib being lead naked on a leash, or of medical experiments in concentration camps, or of slaves held in cages, all serve as examples of the use of *physical* metaphor in dehumanizing practices: by treating the bodies of their victims as if they were animals, perpetrators reinforce the belief in their non-humanity. For Haslam, animalizing dehumanization – the denial and destruction of a person's sense of rationality, autonomy, and moral self – is a highly embodied process, not only in the victim's experience but also in the emotional and psychological perceptions of the perpetrators:

> Being divested of [uniquely human] characteristics is a source of shame for the target – often with a prominent bodily component, as in the nakedness of the Abu Graib prisoners [. . .]. Disgust and revulsion feature prominently in images of animalistically dehumanized others: Represented as apes with bestial appetites or filthy vermin who contaminate or corrupt, they are often *viscerally* despised. (Haslam 2006: 258, my emphasis)

Haslam's second term, "human nature", is associated with qualities such as emotional responsiveness, interpersonal warmth, individuality, and agency, and corresponds to mechanistic dehumanization or objectification, whereby people are perceived as "object- or automaton-like" (Haslam 2006: 258). Again, the figure of the slave or the concentration camp victim serves to illustrate this metaphor in action: deprived of autonomous agency and choice, existing as an object of forced labor, as the Foucauldian "docile" body, these individuals are perceived by others and at times by themselves as mere machines, marching "like automatons" with "no words of defiance, not even a look of judgment" by which to assert their agency (Levi 1987: 156).

Dehumanization as moral exclusion functions in a circular, self-reflexive motion by which the perceived in/sub-humanity of the victim(s) is both the effect of and the justification for acts of humiliation, degradation and instrumentalization. The abject status of those degraded by exclusion serves in turn to justify the violence enacted upon them within a vicious circle characterized by what Opotow has called a "bidirectional causal relationship" (Opotow 1995: 350). As Kelman puts it: the process of dehumanization feeds upon itself (Kelman 1973: 50). Thus, as Primo Levi describes in his book "The Drowned and the Saved," former SS Officer and Commandant of Solibor and Treblinka concentration camps Franz Stangl explains the reason for the dehumanizing cruelties of Nazi persecutions:

> "Considering that you were going to kill them all . . . what was the point of the humiliation, the cruelties?" the writer asks Stangl, imprisoned for life in the Dusseldorf gaol, and he replies: "To condition those who were to be the material executors of the operations. To make it possible for them to do what they were doing." In other words: before dying the victim must be degraded, so that the murderer will be less burdened by guilt. This is an explanation not devoid of logic but which shouts to heaven: it is the sole usefulness of useless violence. (Levi 1989: 100–101)[1]

Dehumanization, then, is the process by which human beings are rendered so radically other that it becomes possible for their persecutors to commit murder on a mass scale, and for bystanders to stand by without objection or remorse. For this all the humiliations, defamations, starvations, degradations: the provision of a "false motive" (Scarry 1985) to the perpetrators of genocide, torture, and other gross atrocities. Like Agamben's "Homo Sacer," the dehumanized, the misrecognised, is one who can be killed with impunity because, already in exile from the moral community, his life counts for nothing (Agamben 1998: 71–115).

---

[1] The interview cited by Levi appears in Gitta Sereny's "In Quelle Tenebre" (Sereny 1975).

7.1.2 The Lived Experience of Dehumanization or **This Is Not My Body***: Autonomy, Identity, and Dignity*

> I'm not human anymore. I have no name and even less soul. I'm a thing, not even a dog that gets stroked or a goat that gets protected and then eaten with gusto. I'm a vagina. I'm a hole. (Courtemanche 2003: 244)

This statement made by Gentille, the female protagonist of Gil Courtemanche's novel "A Sunday by the Pool in Kigali," provides readers with a sense of what dehumanization might mean for its victims. For this young Rwandan woman, dehumanization means the loss of identity and spirit. *I have no name and even less soul.* It is the loss of agency and recognition. *I'm a thing, not even a dog that gets stroked.* It is the loss of physical health, strength and beauty, and with that the presentiment of total dissolution. As Gentille comments later in the novel: *I'm a body that's decomposing.* It is also the loss of autonomy and voice: Rather than tell her own story, Gentille recites the narrative imposed upon her body by the authors of the crime to which she has fallen victim. Gentille's semi-fictional story recalls countless testimonial narratives of dehumanization in which victims are all too often reduced, through acts of physical and discursive or symbolic violence, to the status of objectified, fragmented, and abject bodies emptied of "human" subjectivity. What I would like to demonstrate by a reading of testimonial texts is the extent to which violations of human dignity and autonomy are so often inextricably linked to violations – both literal and symbolic – of corporeal integrity, which in turn impacts upon other core concepts such as identity, voice, and recognition. As Courtemanche most crucially portrays here, for its victims dehumanization involves a fragmentation of the self *and* of the body: In Gentille's own eyes, she is no longer whole, no more a unified person; she is a vagina, a body part; she is a hole, an *absence*. The *génocidaires* have not only made her into an object, they have also violated her sense of integrity, and the image of her decomposing, falling apart body-in-pieces mirrors that of her fragmented subjectivity.

Perhaps one of the best-known survivor writers to testify to the horror of the Nazi concentration camps is the Italian born chemist Primo Levi. In February 1944, Levi was deported and interned at Auschwitz, where he remained until the camp was liberated 11 months later. Levi's testimonial writing is so remarkable because, as Judith Kelly notes, it "concentrates upon the moment, the particular episode, the instant that epitomizes for him the nature of the concentration camp experience, the dehumanization of his state" (Kelly 2000: 6). One such moment takes place on the prisoners' arrival at the camp and demonstrates the devastating effect that the loss of personal and physical autonomy can exert upon victims. Having been taken from their homes and separated from their families and their possessions, Levi and his fellow prisoners are ordered to strip naked before their heads are shaved and their bodies "disinfected". For Levi, this violation of the prisoners' intimate, physical being instills in them the first knowledge that they have reached "the bottom" of human experience. The imposed ritual of physical transformation represents for Levi a kind of theft or expropriation of all that belongs to the prisoners, including their own corporeality. As in slavery, the deportees are denied autonomy over their own bodies and deprived of their sense of self-ownership, reinforced by a loss of voice and lack of recognition from the guards: "they will not listen [. . .] they will not understand" (Levi 1987: 33). Dehumanization in the camps begins here and is forever marked by the loss of autonomy symbolized by acts of physical control. For Heinz Wollmann, survivor of Sachsenhausen concentration camp, the initiation constituted both a physical and a symbolic humiliation, and, combined with months or even years of starvation, disease, forced labor, and other horrors, it came to deprive victims of their personality, reducing them to a state of mute infancy, powerless to alter or even lament their situation. His testimony demonstrates how even apparently minor violations of physical integrity – the shaving of the head – can be felt as humiliating and dehumanizing because of what they come to represent, namely, the loss of personal and public autonomy:

> Then something I personally found really demeaning happened, they took away our personality. I was shaved completely bald, and I cried like a baby and just as naked, I was nothing anymore. At least babies can scream and kick. (Wollmann, Sachsenhausen Memorial Museum Audio Tour)

In these accounts of the lived experience of atrocity, in which both animalistic and mechanistic dehumanization are discerned, the victims' sense of individuality and self is jeopardized by forced acts of corporeal control and humiliation, indicating the extent to which corporeal integrity is connected with the concepts of autonomy, identity, and dignity upon which theories of modern subjectivity are based. For the torture victim, too, dehumanization is a process enacted on and through the body of the victim – a body that suffers, starves, and trembles in stark contrast to the strength and power of the torturer's body. For the victim of torture, physical pain and degradation carry with them intense psychological effect. As in the concentration camp, dehumanization of torture victims is to a large degree achieved through the denial of autonomy and the objectification of victims, but also, as Elaine Scarry describes in her enduring study "The Body in Pain," through the alienation of those victims from their own bodies. According to Scarry, physical pain is in itself a weapon of exclusion. A vital aspect of the loss of physical and psychical integrity in dehumanization processes lies in "the unseen sense of self-betrayal in pain." In moments of extreme physical suffering and humiliation, Scarry explains, the body comes to be felt more and more as the source of suffering, as an "active agent" of pain:

> The ceaseless, self-announcing signal of the body in pain [. . .] contains not only the feeling "my body hurts," but the feeling "my body hurts me." (Scarry 1985: 47)

In such instances, the victim's sense of self becomes fragmented: The persecuted body becomes persecutory, alien, other. The body, once a source of pleasure, becomes the source of torment, something to be feared, avoided, fled from. All good in the body, all solidarity in the flesh, is transformed into betrayal, and the prisoner is left in a paradoxical predicament, both detached from and consumed by his body, which "is made a weapon against him, made to betray him on behalf of the enemy, made to be the enemy" (Scarry 1985: 48).

A further dehumanizing effect of physical pain, Scarry suggests, lies in its language destroying capacity. Intense physical suffering is an unshareable and thus isolating experience, cutting its victims off from all forms of worldly extension including this most fundamental symbol of human community. Intense pain is inexpressible; resisting objectification in language, it cannot be spoken. Argentinean survivor Jacobo Timerman describes the pain of torture as "a pain without points of reference, revelatory symbols, or clues to serve as indicators" (Timerman 2002: 32). As Scarry writes:

> Physical pain does not simply resist language but actively destroys it, bringing about an immediate reversion to a state anterior to language, to the sounds and cries a human being makes before language is learned. (Scarry 1985: 4)

An episode from Alicia Partnoy's testimonial "The Little School" illustrates Scarry's observation. A survivor of torture under the Argentine military dictatorship, Partnoy recalls listening to another woman's desperate cries from within the prison. The effects of pain, fear, and humiliation upon this woman are so devastating that she appears disconnected from her own humanity, a condition communicated in her broken and distorted speech:

> But when they come for me . . . to kill me next time . . . No, please don't come . . . I'm not an animal . . . don't make me believe I'm an animal . . . but that's not my scream . . . That's an animal's scream . . . Leave my body in peace. (Partnoy 1988: 96)

If in psychoanalytic theory the birth of the subject coincides with the birth of language, then, here, linguistic paralysis is simultaneous with subjective destitution. Alienation from language, Scarry argues, is devastating for the victims, depriving them of the "final source of self-extension" (Scarry 1985: 33). In being refused access to the speech community and to the possibility of interlocution except with the torturer/interrogator, the torture victim – like the deportee – is denied the possibility of narrating his or her own life story. The act of confession represents the culmination of this loss and constitutes, in this sense, a moment of tragic resignation and self-abandonment in the victim; confession is "a way of saying, yes, all is almost gone, there is almost nothing left now, even this voice, the sounds I am making, no longer form my words but the words of another" (Scarry 1985: 33).

The destruction of language is linked to other "world-destroying" tactics evident in dehumanizing practices, in particular the use of symbolism and metaphor. Traditionally comforting or nurturing objects are "unmade" or transformed into agents of pain, with apparently benign names and expressions such as the "submarine" or "tea party for two" used to indicate even the most brutal acts of torture.[2] This corruption of everyday speech further unmakes the civilizing function of language, closing yet more rapidly the prisoner's space and means for worldly self-extension. The "circle of negation" produced by "the designation of an intensely painful form of bodily contortion with a word usually reserved for an instance of civilization"

[2]The "submarine", for example, refers to the torture method during which the prisoner is immersed to the point of drowning in water that is often dirtied with feces.

ends in a black hole of denial in which the humanity of the victim appears to be irretrievably lost:

> [T]here is no human being in excruciating pain; that's only a telephone; there is no telephone; that is merely a means of destroying a human being who is not a human being, who is only a telephone, who is not a telephone but a means of destroying a telephone. (Scarry 1985: 44)

This in turn enacts what Scarry calls the "double negation of humanity" – a denial both of the specific humanity of the victim and of the collective human present in the objects and language of civilization. The denial of voice, through the apparent reduction of the victim to the status of suffering body, devoid of metaphysical "human" characteristics, can be read both as a cause and an effect of the losses of dignity, autonomy, and identity – concepts which are themselves brought into question through their violation.

7.1.3 *Perceptions of the (In)Human Body: Recognition as Resistance*

Dehumanization, I suggest, is first and foremost a problem of (mis)perception. In order to murder, rape, and torture their victims, perpetrators must perceive those victims as sub- or inhuman, as outside the scope of moral responsibility. The violences enacted upon the body and person of the victim reinforce this (mis)perception in the perpetrator's mind, while all too often leading the victim him or herself to feel as if they were no longer part of the human community. The role of the bystander, who we have not yet discussed, also figures in this dynamic of perception. Let us try to think about this with the aid of the well-known visual trope: the atrocity triangle. In one corner of the triangle, the victim, to whom wrongs are done; in another corner, the perpetrator, who does harm to the victim; and in the third corner, the bystander or observer, who sees or knows what is happening. The role of each is crucial to the logic of dehumanization, for if all three perceive the victim as somehow in- or subhuman, then any possibility of an alternative narrative is excluded. The bystander is thus a decisive actor in the resistance of dehumanization, and the way in which he or she receives images or testimony of atrocity is a vital ethical concern; as Stanley Cohen has pointed out, the corners of the triangle are not fixed and the boundary between observer and perpetrator of dehumanization is often a fluid one (Cohen 2000: 14). The failure of the bystander, witness, or receiver of testimony to acknowledge the victim's experience, to listen to her story, and to recognize as human the traumatized body of atrocity is itself a reiteration of the logic of dehumanization encountered in magnified form in torture: Voice, recognition, and worldly self-extension are obscured behind the totality of the body in pain. Conversely, the observer's recognition of the victim as a member of the human community can provide the basis for a resistance or rejection of dehumanization: As in the brief moments of communication and solidarity between prisoners in the clandestine prison or the concentration camp, it offers victims (and survivors) a corridor to identity, language, and voice. In this light, failing to *witness* the body in pain as integral to the subjective and psychological experience of suffering works to allow for oppression and the abuse of power, not only in the torture chamber, as Scarry describes, but also in the dehumanizing perceptions of the everyday. If dehumanization is an embodied process, then recognition must also take into account the corporeal aspects of human (and inhuman) experience. How to give voice to the traumatized body is a question wracked with complications and controversy. Any attempt to "lift the interior facts of bodily sentience out of the inarticulate pre-language of 'cries and whispers' into the realm of shared objectification" (Scarry 1985: 11) will depend upon the prefigured perceptions of that body's interlocutor(s). Let us consider then what the roots of our prefigured perceptions of the body may be.

In dominant modern philosophical discourse, the body has figured as an abject entity, secondary or even irrelevant to the construction of a human subject that is posited as rational, autonomous, and largely disembodied. Thus, it is claimed, historically oppressed groups such as women, slaves, non-white, and disabled people have been categorized in dominant discourse as "too fully embodied" and somehow less than human, uncivilized or irrational. One of the major contributions of feminist scholarship has been to highlight (and contest), firstly, the ways in which "woman" has been culturally and politically designated as less than fully human and, secondly, the extent to which this dehumanization depends upon negative discourses of the body, as well as philosophical constructions of the human subject as disembodied. Feminist theorist Elisabeth Grosz makes the connection clear:

> Patriarchal oppression [. . .] justifies itself, at least in part, by connecting women much more closely than men to the body [. . .]. [W]omen are somehow *more* biological, *more* corporeal, *more* natural than men. The coding of femininity with corporeality in effect leaves men free to inhabit what they (falsely) believe is a purely conceptual order. (Grosz 1994: 14)

The feminist argument draws attention to mind/body dualism as the basis upon which modern notions of human subjectivity have been built. The construction of embodied female otherness, it is suggested, is precisely that which allows man to regard himself – the universal "self" – as a stable, thinking being. Such binaristic devaluing of the body, of course, has implications not only for women, but for various groups and individuals historically and culturally associated with symbols of abject embodiment. This includes victims of dehumanizing atrocity, whose traumatized bodies, in their failure to conform to the norm of the stable, bounded subject, threaten to disrupt the ontological and epistemological matrices to the margins of which they have been so violently thrust. This presents as a fundamental paradox in human rights discourse, for while any practical endeavor of human rights to protect human beings will nearly always, in some form, work to protect the *bodies* of human beings, in discursive terms the "subject" of human rights is almost always articulated as disembodied – the universal declaration stating the human condition in the most abstract terms as "equal in rights and dignity" and "endowed with reason and conscience," but without a single reference to corporeality. Our moral relation to the suffering other is thus rarely, if ever, phrased in terms of embodied inter-subjectivity. And yet what is ethics if it is not embodied? However hard it tries, ethical theory cannot sustain itself purely in the realm of the metaphysical; it must always return in the end to the lived experience of human beings. In the same way, any attempt to resist dehumanization, whether materially or conceptually, must recognize the embodiment of the human subject. Holocaust survivor Robert Antelme draws attention in his testimony to the impossibility of resisting dehumanization simply by "re-humanizing" victims of atrocity – re-attributing to them abstract qualities such as autonomy, personality or dignity. For Antelme, the only viable resistance to dehumanization is to alter our understanding of the human, since "to locate humanity in positive qualities or capacities is to repeat the logic of the camps, by excluding from this humanity those stripped of such qualities or capacities" (qtd. in Crowley 2003: 10).

Human dignity is a particularly significant concept in this regard. Highly abstract, it has taken on an almost mystical nature within modern moral discourse. A key ideological concept in what Elie Wiesel has called the secular religion of human rights, human dignity is difficult to define, seeming somehow to encapsulate any number of moral and ontological propositions, from Kant's categorical imperative to the ideals of liberal autonomy and moral agency. Rarely is it expressed in relation to embodied subjectivity, however. Posited as an innate or universal human quality, dignity has been shown through historical experience to be a fragile ideal. To return to our atrocity triangle: if victim, perpetrator, and bystander each perceive an absence or loss of human dignity in the victim, does it still exist? Of course, we would like to answer yes. And yet, we can and do perceive or treat people as if it were absent. The violations of human dignity already described in this volume exist on a continuum with dehumanization; if I degrade, humiliate, or instrumentalize another person, I am also to some extent denying or belittling their status as a human being. While an individual violation of human dignity is always also potentially dehumanizing, purposive acts of dehumanization enact a double negation of human dignity, both in the particular and in the universal: The very possibility of dehumanization threatens to destabilize the *ideal* of human dignity as we currently understand it. But what happens when we think dignity as embodied? We may speak about the dignity of the body, which is violated through acts of torture, humiliation, or coercion, as illustrated in the testimonials discussed. From here we may establish the imperative to recognize the position of the body within processes and narratives of dehumanization. To truly think dignity as embodied, however, implies more than this: it involves a re-imagining of the human so as to include within its category that which was hitherto excluded. It involves bearing witness to the body as part of human as well as inhuman experience, thereby refusing to accept bodily suffering and abjection as dehumanizing. If dignity is embodied, then it is inclusive of pleasure and suffering, beauty and disease, strength and vulnerability, life and death. If dignity is embodied then it is local as well as universal; always situated, it cannot be understood as distinct from the individual who carries it, and any defense of dignity must acknowledge and recognize the specificity of its circumstance. To respect the embodied dignity of a human being, therefore, is first and foremost an act of recognition: to recognize as human every aspect of their experience, however abject and foreign it may seem, to acknowledge the specificity of their person, and by doing so to affirm the place of the other alongside the self within the human community.

7.2 Conclusion

As this necessarily limited reading of a vast resource of testimonial and theoretical texts should help us to understand, dehumanization – whether enacted through processes of active or indirect exclusion, metaphorical objectification, or physical violence – depends to some extent upon experiences and/or perceptions of the body and embodiment. Metaphors of inhumanity are, as we have seen, frequently constructed in relation to the corporeal status of the targets of dehumanizing processes. The concentration camp victim is reduced through violences and humiliations to the status of an empty body or walking corpse; the torture victim is alienated from language as well as from her own body as a result of intense unshareable pain. This state of embodied suffering is perceived as confirmation of that which perpetrators claim as vindication for the injustices: It is "proof" of their victim's inhumanity. And yet, if dehumanization depends upon our perceptions of what it is to be human, then we may all play a role in resisting – or at the very least not repeating – its logic of exclusion. This requires a rethinking of the human that demystifies and embodies those abstract concepts that can be denied in our perception, including human dignity. As Giorgio Agamben writes in "Remnants of Auschwitz," the Muselmann's destitution from such positive "human" qualities as "dignity" must be seen not as proof of the victims' inhumanity, but as evidence of the inadequacy of ethical concepts of the human:

> If there is a zone of the human in which these concepts make no sense, then they are not genuine ethical concepts, for no ethics can claim to exclude a part of humanity, no matter how unpleasant or difficult that humanity is to see. (Agamben 2002: 64)

Thinking dignity as embodied calls for a politics or ethics of witnessing that acknowledges and listens to the lived experience of those who have been excluded and dehumanized both past and present; it calls for us all, as bystanders and spectators of suffering, to attend to the concrete and individual humanity of the one who suffers and to reclaim, through recognition, their status as member of the human community. To be human, as those who have suffered the effects of dehumanization will testify, is first and foremost to be included within the community of human beings, to be recognized and accepted as part of this community and thus deserving of its protection. This recognition must occur on the concrete as well as the metaphysical level; our own humanity – always embodied, always situated, and at times suffering – depends upon it.

References

Agamben, Giorgio. 1998. *Homo Sacer: Sovereign power and bare life*. Stanford, CA: Stanford University Press.

Agamben, Giorgio. 2002. *Remnants of Auschwitz: The witness and the archive*. New York, NY: Zone Books.

Bandura, Albert, Bill Underwood, and Michael E. Fromson. 1975. Disinhibition of aggression through diffusion of responsibility and dehumanisation of victims. *Journal of Research in Personality* 9: 253–269.

Bandura, Albert et al. 1996. Mechanisms of Moral disengagement in the exercise of moral agency. *Journal of Personality and Social Psychology* 71(2): 364–374.

Cohen, Stanley. 2000. *States of denial: Knowing about atrocities and suffering*. Cambridge: Polity.

Courtemanche, Gil. 2003. *A Sunday by the pool in kigali*. Edinburgh: Canongate.

Crowley, Martin. 2003. *Robert Antelme: Humanity, community, testimony*. Oxford: Legenda.

Deutsch, Morton. 2000. Justice and conflict. In *The handbook of conflict resolution: Theory and practice*, eds. Morton Deutsch and Peter T. Coleman, 43–68. San Francisco, CA: Jossey Bass.

Gamson, William A. 1995. Hiroshima, the holocaust and the politics of exclusion: 1994 Presidential address. *American Sociological Review* 60: 1–20.

Grosz, Elizabeth A. 1994. *Volatile bodies: Toward a corporeal feminism*. Bloomington, IN: Indiana University Press.

Günther, Klaus. 1999. The Legacies of injustice and fear: A european approach to human rights and their effects on political culture. In *The EU and human rights*, eds. Philip Alston, Mara R. Bustelo, and James Heenan, 117–144. Oxford: Oxford University Press.

Haslam, Nick. 2006. Dehumanization: An integrative review. *Personality and social psychology review* 10(3): 252–264.

Homer, Frederic D. 2001. *Primo Levi and the politics of survival*. Columbia, MI: University of Missouri Press.

Kelly, Judith. 2000. *Primo Levi: Recording and reconstruction in the testimonial literature*. Market Harborough: Troubador in association with Hull Italian Texts.

Kelman, Herbert C. 1973. Violence without moral restraint: Reflections on the dehumanization of victims and victimizers. *Journal of Social Issues* 29(4): 25–61.

Levi, Primo. 1987. *If this is a man*. London: Abacus.

Levi, Primo. 1989. *The drowned and the saved*. London: Abacus.

Opotow, Susan. 1995. Drawing the line: Social categorizations, moral exclusion and the scope of justice. In *Conflict, cooperation and justice: Essays inspired by the work of Morton Deutsch*, eds. Barbara Benedic Bunker and Jeffrey Z. Rubin, 347–369. San Francisco, CA: Jossey Bass.

Partnoy, Alicia. 1988. *The little school: Tales of disappearance and survival in Argentina*. London: Virago.

Scarry, Elaine. 1985. *The body in pain: The making and unmaking of the world*. New York, NY: Oxford University Press.

Scarry, Elaine 2002. The difficulty of imagining other persons. In *The handbook of interethnic coexistence*, ed. Eugene Weiner, 40–62. New York, NY: Continuum.

Sereny, Gitta. 1975. *In Quelle Tenebre*. Milan: Adelphi.

Timerman, Jacobo. 2002. *Prisoner without a name, cell without a number*. Madison, WI: University of Wisconsin Press.

Wollmann, Heinz. Survivor testimony, Memorial and Museum Sachsenhausen Audio Tour.

Part II
Practices of Violating Human Dignity

Chapter 8
Torture

How Denying Moral Standing Violates Human Dignity

Andreas Maier

Abstract In this chapter I try to elucidate the concept of human dignity by taking a closer look at the features of a paradigmatic torture situation. After identifying the salient aspects of torture, I discuss various accounts for the moral wrongness of such acts and argue that what makes torture a violation of human dignity is the perverted moral relationship between torturer and victim. This idea is subsequently being substantiated and defended against important objections. In the final part of the chapter I give a (qualified) defense of the methodology employed in the previous sections.

8.1 Introduction

In a survey conducted by the BBC,[1] respondents in 25 countries were asked which of the following positions came closer to their own views about torture: Should clear rules against torture be maintained because "any use of torture is immoral and will weaken international human rights standards against torture" or do terrorists "pose such an extreme threat that governments should now be allowed to use some degree of torture if it may gain information that saves innocent lives?"

The results were somewhat disillusioning: Almost one-third of the respondents declared to support torture in cases where this may be an inevitable means to avert terrorist threats and, thereby, set themselves in opposition to the prevailing view in

A. Maier (✉)
Centre for Ethics, University of Zurich, Switzerland
e-mail: andreas.maier75@gmail.com

[1]For the complete results see BBC/Globescan/PIPA (2006); in a more recent survey conducted by WorldPublicOpinion, 35% of the respondents opted for exceptions to the prohibition to torture in cases where innocent lives are at risk, and 9% held that the government should be able to use torture in general (Kull et al. 2008).

P. Kaufmann et al. (eds.), *Humiliation, Degradation, Dehumanization*, Library of Ethics and Applied Philosophy 24, DOI 10.1007/978-90-481-9661-6_8,

international law which prohibits torture under any circumstances whatsoever.[2] As disturbing as these results may seem, they are in perfect accordance with the better part of philosophical theorizing about torture. There seems to be a wide consensus that although torture is a horrible thing there are realistic (or even real-world) scenarios which can be used to establish exceptions to the moral prohibition to torture.[3] In the following discussion, I will try to show that despite the possibility and, admittedly, intuitive force of such scenarios, torture can never be morally justified – whatever the circumstances may be.

One very common way of substantiating such an absolutist position is the idea that torture constitutes a *violation of the victim's dignity*.[4] But as sensible as such a contention might look at first sight, it is, at second glance, far from clear what calling torture a violation of human dignity exactly means. This is due to the fact that human dignity is, despite its intuitive appeal, a highly contested concept and, moreover, subject to serious philosophical criticism (Frankena 1986, Macklin 2003, Pinker 2008).

In what follows, I will sidestep this debate for the most part and completely ignore the profound critique of the concept of human dignity. This will result in a somewhat unorthodox approach (which might look like an attempt to discuss a highly controversial issue with an unclear concept): Instead of first arguing for a conception of dignity and then employing it to criticize the practice of torture, I will simply take for granted the assumption that torture is a violation of human dignity and subsequently take a closer look at the reasons why torture is a serious moral wrong. The underlying idea is that a grasp of the very reasons for the wrongness of torture will improve our understanding of the concept of human dignity.[5]

I will proceed as follows: I will start with a look at the practice of torture and identify the central elements of a paradigmatic torture situation (Section 8.2). To maintain an absolutist position towards torture, it has to be shown that the reasons for the moral wrongness of this practice hold good under all conceivable conditions. My corresponding argument comes in three steps: *Firstly*, I will discuss other approaches and try to show that they fall short of identifying the specific moral wrong inflicted on the victims of torture. *Secondly*, I argue that the reasons for the moral wrongness of torture can be found in the asymmetric structure of the relationship between torturer and victim; this relational account will subsequently be

---

[2]See, for e.g., the UN *Convention against Torture and Other Cruel, Inhuman or Degrading Treatment or Punishment* Art.2(2): "No exceptional circumstances whatsoever, whether a state of war or a threat of war, internal political instability or any other public emergency, may be invoked as a justification of torture."

[3]Amongst many others: Dershowitz (2002), Miller (2005), Žižek (2002: 103–104); for a thorough and critical discussion of such scenarios see Brecher (2007).

[4]Cf., for e.g., the aforementioned *Convention against Torture* which bases the protection from torture in the "inherent dignity of the human person."

[5]This is in accordance with Ernst Bloch's insight that the meaning of human dignity becomes most visible when we look at *violations* of human dignity (Bloch 1961).

substantiated and defended (Section 8.4). *Finally*, I will show that the reasons identified by the relational account do not admit of exceptions and therefore support an absolutist position towards torture (Section 8.5). In the last section, I will briefly discuss the limits of my methodological approach adopted in the previous parts and thereby qualify the scope of my results (Section 8.6).

8.2 What Is Torture?

Finding a definition of torture is a notoriously difficult task. This is due to various reasons. On the one hand, there is a wide variety of practices coming under the heading of "torture": Severe beatings, putting persons into stress positions, extended sleep or food deprivation, the use of special devices like the rack or thumbscrews, performing mock executions, or prolonged exposition to noise, and many more count as torture. It is not clear at first sight what might be the common element(s) in these acts. On the other hand, it is hard to draw a clear line between torture and related practices like degrading treatment, harsh punishment or coercion. The need for a clear distinction of these practices becomes evident, for instance, in the dispute about the Bush administration's attempt (manifested in the infamous *Bybee-Memo*) to explore the limits on how far it could go in aggressively interrogating suspected terrorists without having to call such treatment "torture".[6]

These problems, which have received due attention in recent discussions on torture,[7] can safely be ignored in what follows. Since I am not concerned so much with the practice of torture per se but with torture *as a violation of dignity*, I will simply sidestep the problem of marginal, ambiguous or unclear cases and instead focus on the features of a *paradigmatic* torture situation. This should be sufficient to identify the main elements of a typical act of torture we would most likely describe as a violation of human dignity.

I take it that the following report of the torturing of Bangladeshi journalist Tasneem Khalil[8] is paradigmatic in this regard and therefore a suitable starting point for my investigation:

> *At around 1 a.m. on the morning of May 11, 2007, 26-year old critical Bangladeshi journalist Tasneem Khalil is blindfolded, hand-cuffed and taken away from his apartment by a joint military and police task-force; on his enquiry, Khalil is given neither reasons nor a legal warrant for his arrest. After the arrival at what looks like a military camp, a doctor checks Khalil's state-of-health. Then he is taken to a room, still blindfolded and hand-cuffed.*

---

[6]For a thorough discussion see the contributions in Greenberg (2006); another prominent example is the *European Court of Human Right*'s decision in *Ireland vs Great Britain* that the treatment of a prisoner who was interrogated while standing blindfolded in a stress position and, additionally, deprived of food, water and sleep was a case of "maltreatment", but not "torture".

[7]Cf., amongst others, Sussman (2005:1–3) and Miller (2008).

[8]As reported in Human Rights Watch (2008); italics represent my synopsis.

> A voice suddenly yelled, "[expletive deleted, A.M.]! Where is salam?" I then said, "Salam-alekum," which in Arabic means "peace be upon you." The man screamed, "Louder!" I cried out "salam" once again [. . .]. Then he told me to sit down and not to raise my hands off the table at any point. [. . .] Then another voice asked me to give examples of my recent reports. I could not remember anything at that moment. And then the second voice said, "[expletive deleted, A.M.], you have only reported on negative things. And you have [expletive deleted, A.M.] Bangladesh by your bloody anti-state reports [. . .]."
>
> Someone started punching the side and back of my head. I started crying out in pain. Then someone cried out an order, "Bring in salt and nails!"
>
> [. . .] They asked me what things I had reported for The Daily Star. I said I had reported on human rights issues [. . .]. Suddenly people on both sides of me started brutally beating me with batons on the lower back, just below and next to my kidneys. The pain was excruciating. In that instant I assessed my situation. I could be a tough guy and get more of this, or I could cooperate. I quickly decided that it was time to cooperate with these people and do my best to dodge more beatings. I said I was sorry for whatever I had done. [. . .]. I started begging for mercy. The beating continued for some time. Then another person said, "We will think about giving you a chance, but you have to do as we say." He said I had to write a confession [. . .], saying what they wanted me to say. Then I had to beg for his mercy. [. . .] They instructed some junior level staff to give me a pen and paper and take my statement after they had left. They also instructed them not to allow me to go to the toilet or eat anything.
>
> *Although he is willing to do everything his tormentors demand, Khalil is interrogated, shouted at, and severely beaten for a total of 22 h, without knowing if he will get away with his life.*

Perhaps the most salient feature in the report above is the severe physical suffering Khalil is subjected to: He is repeatedly beaten with batons and bare fists, on his kidneys, on his back, and on his head. This infliction of pain is obviously goal-oriented: On the one hand, it is used as a form of punishment for the critical articles Khalil has written in the past ("you have only reported on negative things"), and, on the other, it is a means to enforce a "confession" ("We will think about giving you a chance, but you have to do as we say"). On a more speculative basis, we can assume that another purpose is to terrorize Khalil into renouncing his critical attitude towards the state.

Furthermore, there are various aspects in Khalil's torture that contribute to his suffering without being targeted at his body. The fear for his life and the anticipation of what his torturers might do next add another dimension of suffering over and above mere physical pain; this kind of suffering, which is due to the sequential character of acts of torture, is usually characterized as *mental suffering*.[9]

---

[9]The significance of mental suffering in torture situations is already noticed by Beccaria in his "Essay on Crimes and Punishment," (1995: Chapter. XVI). Expanding the concept of torture toward psychological effects is, also beyond Khalil's case, very plausible since many modern torture methods, like mock executions or extended solitary confinement, put emphasis on the infliction of mental, not physical, harm. For a denial of the necessity of mental suffering as a *sui generis* element of torture see Davis (2005).

The sequential character of torture brings in an important structural element of torture, namely, the victim's inability to influence the course of events.[10] This is significant in two respects: First of all, Khalil cannot react to what happens *presently* and guard himself against the beatings; his torturers can do whatever they want without having to fear any kind of resistance. And, secondly, there is no chance for the victim to have an impact on *future* events: The fact that Khalil is compliant and willing to fulfill the demands of his tormentors has no bearing on the course of events in any way – the torture nevertheless continues for another 22 h. To sum up, Khalil's fate is completely in the grip of other persons: While he is not even able to exercise basic defensive reactions, his torturers can determine every detail of the situation unhindered. Expressive of this disparity of power are the forced demonstrations of respect ("Where is salam?") and the torturers' denial to disclose the legal basis of their actions, on the one hand, and the insults Khalil has to face, on the other.

The fact that his powerlessness is constitutive for the kind of situation Khalil finds himself in points to an important difference between torture and other situations where a person is subjected to violence: While in the latter cases violence against the victim is used as a means to *create* a setting where the aggressor is in full control of the situation, in cases of torture the victim *already finds* himself in a situation where another person has the absolute power to determine what happens without the slightest possibility to evade or resist the situation.

In the last paragraphs, various salient elements present in the depiction of Khalil's torture have been identified. The first, and most obvious, aspect concerns *the act-level*: Torture situations consist of the sequential infliction of physical and mental suffering on the victims. Additionally, since pain is inflicted for a purpose which is determined by the torturers, there are conditions referring to the *attitude* of the torturer. In Khalil's case we identified various goals which might have been pursued, namely, to get a confession or to punish him; this observation points to a more general point, since whatever specific goal the torturer might pursue, it is a goal he himself determined against the will of the victim. So, on a very general level we can say that the main intention of the torturer is to enforce his will on the victim. And, finally, there are *contextual* conditions specifying the setting in which torture acts take place. These conditions fix the unequal distribution of power and thereby ensure that the torturers can act unrestrictedly.

With act-level, attitudinal, and contextual elements put together, we get the following definition of torture:

> *Torture* is the sequential infliction of physical and/or mental suffering on a person P1 by another person P2 (or other persons P2–Pn) *[act-level conditions]* with the intention to enforce P2's (or P2–Pn's) will(s) on P1 *[attitudinal conditions]* performed in a social setting in which P2 (or P2–Pn) can fully determine everything that happens while P1 is completely helpless and fully exposed to P2 (or P2–Pn) *[contextual conditions]*

---

[10] Since at the present stage of the argument I am solely concerned with a description of torture, this is not meant in an evaluative sense.

In the next section, I will consider what is specifically morally wrong with acts fitting this description.

8.3 What Makes Torture Wrong?

Cases of torture, like Tasneem Khalil's, are obviously morally wrong in almost every respect. In what follows, the focus will be on reasons why torture *as a practice* is morally wrong, not reasons for the wrongness of elements of particular acts of torture. These reasons do not necessarily have to coincide: While it might be correct to maintain that Khalil's torture was morally wrong because he was insulted and verbally humiliated, this might not be the reason for the wrongness of another torture case where symbolic humiliation does not play a central role. What are needed are reasons why cases of torture *qua* cases of torture are morally wrong, and the analysis of Khalil's case in the last section made evident what elements of a typical torture situation might provide such reasons.

In the following, I will discuss three accounts for the moral wrongness of torture: first, William Twining's idea that torture is morally wrong since the rights of the victim are violated; second, David Sussman's influential account according to which torture is morally wrong since the will of the victim is turned against the victim herself; and, finally, Henry Shue's idea that torture is wrong since the victim is completely exposed to the torturer. As I will argue, although each account identifies important reasons why torture is morally wrong, they all fail to grasp the *specific* moral wrong torture constitutes.

8.3.1 Twining's Account

William Twining's account for the moral wrongness of torture focuses on the quality of the *acts* carried out. The central idea is that the conditions for torture are independent of the mental attitudes of the participants and that the reasons for the moral wrongness of torture can only be found on the act-level, not on the attitudinal or contextual levels. Accordingly, Twining holds that what makes torture wrong is *solely* the fact that practices comprising torture restrain certain capabilities of the victim.

The starting point of Twining's argument is the thought that we do not have to refer to the mental attitudes of the participants in a torture situation to label such a situation a form of dehumanizing treatment.[11] Twining suggests that thinking otherwise would amount to a confusion of conceptual questions and questions of blameworthiness: Although knowledge about the intention of the torturer might be

[11] Although Twining at first grants that the intention to inflict pain is a necessary condition for torture, he (somewhat paradoxically) later argues for the insignificance of this feature (Twining 1978: 154).

necessary to determine if he is morally or legally *responsible* for his act, the pursuit of a specific goal is not part of the concept and, a fortiori, of the reasons for the wrongness of torture.[12] Twining supports this position with an analogy: When we look at other forms of dehumanizing treatment, say putting a person in a "bad jail," it would seem inadequate to make the question whether he has suffered inhuman treatment dependent on the intention of the judge who sentenced him, since "if the results were due to [...] lack of resources (for example, inadequate heating in a particularly harsh winter) has he not suffered inhuman treatment?" Accordingly, "words like inhuman and degrading, and, more important, the kinds of concern that lie behind them, *refer directly to the situation*, and the rights, of the victim [...]" (Twining 1978: 155).[13]

Twining's main point seems to be that the moral wrongness of torture as a form of inhuman treatment is in no way dependent on the intention of another person: That the victim suffers morally wrong treatment does not presuppose that there is someone deliberately *wronging* the victim but is due to features of the situation. This makes clear that the concept of right employed in the quotation above is *non-relational*: If the violation of the victim's rights is independent of the acts of other persons, these rights must be grounded in relation-independent properties, like, for example, basic human needs or capabilities.[14]

Accepting this account will have two important consequences: Firstly, the decoupling of the concept of torture from references to the intentions of the participants allows for acts of "accidental torture" where someone is being tortured without anybody intending to do so; secondly, and relatedly, in Twining's eyes it does not make a difference if the inhuman and degrading conditions a person finds herself in were intentionally brought about by other agents or are, for instance, simply the effect of some natural disaster. Thus, Twining denies the significance of the attitudinal conditions elaborated in the discussion of Khalil's case above.

But this misses an important point about the nature of torture, namely that torture is something *persons* do to persons: There seems to be an essential difference between someone's losing a fingernail because his hand was hit by a brick and someone's fingernails being torn out to force him to disclose information.[15]

To transform this intuition into an argument, it has to be shown in a first step that an agent's having an intention can, *contra* Twining, be a necessary conceptual

---

[12]Twining (1978: 156): "It may well be the case that in legal and other contexts the term torture will be confined to situations where direct intention to inflict pain is attributable to the front-line torturer; but an adequate theory of torture and related phenomena must confront the conceptual, moral, legal and other practical problems of attributing responsibility to persons higher up the hierarchy."

[13]My emphasis.

[14]For a discussion of non-relational approaches to human rights cf. Powers and Faden (2008: 47–49).

[15]Though I won't argue this point, relation-dependence seems to be an essential feature of the moral wrongness of other forms of inhuman treatment as well.

condition and not significant with respect to blameworthiness only. This can easily be seen when we think about, for example, the practice of lying: Since lying is defined as an act of intentionally deceiving another person about what the liar believes to be true, there simply cannot be an act of lying without the agent pursuing the goal to deceive another person; for this reason, Twining's point cannot be a general truth. The case of lying is relevant in another respect as well: While it is true that the specific content of the liar's intention is not germane to the definition of the concept of lying, there is one intention all liars share, namely the intention to deceive. The same holds true for torture: While the torturer's *specific* intention is certainly not a necessary condition for his act's being a case of torture,[16] every act of torture is characterized by the torturer's intention to break the victim's will. In other words, whatever the purpose of breaking the victim's will might be, the prime purpose of torture is the breaking of the victim's will.[17] And this seems to be an element that accounts for the special moral quality of torture over and above the mere restriction of capabilities or non-fulfillment of basic human needs grounded in certain properties.

These shortcomings in Twining's analysis show that for an adequate account of the moral wrongness of torture reference to the violation of non-relational rights – which is without any doubt an important element – is not sufficient. While it is certainly true that in acts of torture victims cannot exercise their wills, the significance of the fact that there is a second person *using* the will of the victim for her own purposes cannot be underestimated; this insight is the starting point of David Sussman's approach.

8.3.2 Sussman's Account

According to Sussman, what makes torture essentially morally wrong is the fact that the victim's autonomy is used against itself and the tortured person, thereby, forced to play an *active role* in his own suffering. This entails that the victim is, despite his complete submission to the will of the torturer, made an accomplice in the torturer's efforts:

> [. . .] Torture forces its victim into the position of colluding against himself through his own affects and emotions, so that he experiences himself as simultaneously powerless and yet actively complicit in his own violation. So construed, torture turns out to be not just an extreme form of cruelty, but the pre-eminent instance of a kind of forced self-betrayal [. . .] (Sussman 2005: 4).

[16]This is what Twining's bureaucracy-example shows (Twining 1978: 156).

[17]Specific purposes, by means of which various types of torture can be distinguished, include the obtaining of intelligence (interrogation torture); the punishment or the intimidation of the victim (punishment/terroristic torture); or, simply, the sadistic gratification of the torturer (an element present, at least as a side-effect, in most torture cases).

Sussman's argument has obvious merits: If the tortured person is made an instrument of her own violation and insofar forced to become an accomplice of the torturer, it is utterly clear what makes torture morally wrong: It is not only the fact that the torturer does not respect the victim's autonomy but the victim's autonomy is being turned against herself and it is, at least in part, her own doing that constitutes her suffering.[18]

With this criterion it is possible to explain what makes torture especially morally objectionable: Torture does not just amount to an infringement of the victim's autonomy but to an utilization of the victim's autonomy against herself.[19] The victim of torture is forced to use her own rational agency for means pre-determined by the torturer and thus experiences the act as "something I do to myself, as a kind of self-betrayal worked through my body and feelings" (Sussman 2005: 21).

But as plausible as this may seem, this account has various disadvantages. To begin with, it seems to be tailored for one special kind of torture, namely *interrogation torture*. The aim of interrogation torture is to extract intelligence from the victim that she is not willing to give voluntarily and, therefore, to make the victim do something she would not do without being tortured. The success of this form of torture is dependent on finding a balance between impairing the victim's autonomy and leaving her enough autonomy to be able to do what her torturer wants (for example, giving information or a confession); if the torturer administers too much suffering, the victim cannot give what the torturer wants; if he administers too little torture, the victim may not be willing to give it. In this sense, Sussman's claim that the victim's autonomy is used against itself is correct in such cases.

But as a general analysis of the wrongness of torture Sussman's account is insufficient for the following reasons: On the one hand, it is *too wide*. This becomes clear if we look at non-torturing ways of extracting intelligence from a person without her cooperation; in these cases where interrogation experts gain information with non-coercive methods, the interviewee's autonomy is turned against itself in very much the same way, though without violent means. This shows that Sussman's account cannot capture the *distinct* moral wrong that torture constitutes.

On the other hand, and this is the more serious problem, Sussman's account is *too narrow*, since it does not capture other forms of torture where the torturer does not have to be considerate of allowing the victim a residue of autonomy. For example, Tasneem Khalil's case seems in some respects to be what is usually called "terroristic torture", aiming at the intimidation of the victim and others; in such cases the torturer does not have to be considerate of the victim's autonomy, since in this kind of torture no direct response is aimed at. The same holds true for cases solely aimed at the sadistic gratification of the torturer. If this is correct, Sussman's account, though plausible for interrogation torture, does not apply to torture per se.

---

[18]Sussman (2005: 30): "[Torture] is not just an assault on the victim's autonomy, but also a perversion of it [. . .]."

[19]This is an element emphasized by Elaine Scarry whose account Sussman uses as an important empirical source (Scarry 1985).

This is due to the fact that Sussman treats the act-level and contextual conditions as two sides of the same coin[20] and thereby misses the special normative significance of the asymmetric relationship between torturer and victim: It is the very fact that torturer and victim are placed in a social context where the former is in a position of absolute power and the latter is without any power which allows the torturer to employ whatever means he thinks necessary to reach whatever end he pursues with the act of torture.

Put like this, the perversion of the victim's autonomy is not the specific wrong-making feature of torture but only one possible expression of the asymmetric relationship between torturer and victim. Accordingly, an adequate and encompassing account of the wrongness of torture has to take serious the structure of the relationship between the participants. Such an approach is advanced by Henry Shue.

8.3.3 Shue's Account

In trying to find specific reasons for the moral wrongness of torture, Henry Shue starts with the *structure* of a typical torture situation. Accordingly, the focus is not so much on what the torturer does to the victim but what kind of situation allows the torturer to do what he does. Shue holds that what makes torture morally wrong is the fact that the victim is put in a situation where he is completely exposed to the torturer; accordingly, "[torture] is a cruel assault upon the defenseless" (Shue 1978: 130).

By concentrating on the victim's helplessness, Shue performs a change of perspective which allows him to take the contextual conditions of torture into account. According to Shue, an understanding of the specific wrong torture constitutes can only be gained by understanding the helplessness of the victim. But what exactly does "helplessness" mean in this context? This becomes clear when we focus on Shue's argument for cases meeting the definition of torture without being morally wrong. In such cases, Shue holds, "[t]he victim of torture must have available an act of compliance which, if performed, will end the torture" (Shue 1978: 131). Since the availability of an act of compliance shows, according to Shue, that the victim can freely choose a path that will lead to an end of the torture act, we cannot say any more that the victim is helplessly exposed to the torturer; hence, in such cases torture would not be morally wrong. The cases Shue has in mind are cases of interrogation torture where it is up to the victim to disclose the wanted information.[21]

This line of argument elucidates the meaning of "helplessness" in the context of Shue's argument: Only in cases where victims do not have means to interfere in

---

[20]Sussman (2005: 30): "[Torture] is not just an assault on or violation of the victim's autonomy, but also a perversion of it, a kind of systematic mockery of the basic moral relations that an individual bears both to others and to herself."

[21]It is important to note that, if Shue's argument is correct, it would not be necessary that we already *know* that the victim is in possession of the information; it would (in analogy to cases of self-defense) be enough if the torturer would be *justified in believing* that this is the case.

the sequence of events they are "helpless" in Shue's sense and, hence, such acts of torture morally wrong. This can, without residue, be expressed in terms of a violation of the victim's autonomy: What makes morally wrong cases of torture morally wrong is the fact that the victim is deprived of the ability to actively interfere in the course of events, for example, by disclosing the wanted information and thereby bringing the torture to an end. So, what at first glance looked like an account of the moral wrongness of torture based on the contextual conditions of this practice is just a variant of accounts based on act/attitudinal-level conditions.

But this comes as no surprise, since, in his search for wrong-making properties, Shue is solely focusing on the position of the victim in a torture situation and, therefore, misses what is peculiar about the whole relationship between torturer and victim. Once we give up this limited perspective, Shue's argument for exceptions loses whatever initial plausibility it might have had, since, when we take into view the whole relationship between torturer and victim, it becomes clear that the victim's ability to end the torture does not just "exist". This ability must be *granted* by another person, namely the torturer. This means that the kind of autonomy Shue talks about is just sham autonomy, since, even if the victim is willing to do what the torturer wants, it is still the *torturer* who is in the position to determine what happens. This is exactly what happened in Khalil's case where, despite his willingness to do what his torturers wanted, the decision to end the torture nonetheless remained in their power (and Khalil was tortured for almost another day). Once it is seen that the possibility of ending the torture is not "floating free" but inextricably tied to the torturer, it loses its force as a reason for justifying cases of torture but turns out to be a reason why torture is morally wrong.

If these considerations are taken seriously they point in the direction of an approach which takes into account not only the position of the victim but the relationship between torturer and victim as a whole.

8.4 The Moral Wrongness of Torture – A Relational Account

In the context of my discussion of other approaches in the previous section, I have suggested that the specific reason for the moral wrongness of torture lies in the asymmetric structure of the relationship between torturer and victim. This line of argument presupposes that we can make sense of the idea of a basic moral relationship which can be employed as a normative standard, against which we can judge practices like torture. To give this idea more substance we have to specify what it means exactly to stand in a moral relationship and what moral demands are grounded in our standing in moral relations. Thus, *firstly*, more has to be said about what constitutes the basic moral relationship and how it is distinguished from other forms of relationships; and, *secondly*, it has to be shown which moral norms we can justify with reference to our standing in basic moral relationships with each other and how these are violated through practices like torture.

It is an undeniable fact that some moral norms are generated through the relationships we stand in[22]. Friendship-relations, for example, are mainly constituted by mutual (normative) expectations of the participating persons, such as the expectation that our friends are willing to give help and support when we need them, and so on. These expectations, which are directed only at those persons we stand in the respective relation to, provide a normative standard relative to which an agent's act can be evaluated and, where appropriate, judged as constituting a violation of the friendship-norms. The important (and trivial) point is that such an evaluation presupposes an existing friendship-relation: Only when an agent A is friends with another person B can she aptly be criticized for violating the norms of friendship with respect to B. So, in the case of special relationships like friendships, it is an obvious fact that the participants have certain mutual obligations solely in virtue of standing in the respective relation to each other. But why should we think that there is, in analogy to the case of friendship, a *general* reciprocal relationship persons stand in *qua* being persons? What surplus value does a theory of morality have when it incorporates the idea of (some) norms grounded in a moral relationship between all persons?

As Joel Feinberg has pointed out,[23] our moral practice does not solely consist of impersonal norms that moral agents have to follow, but there is an irreducible intersubjective dimension with respect to the duties we have towards other persons: There is an important difference between, on the one hand, thinking that I am not allowed to hurt you because this would violate a demand of morality and, on the other, thinking that *you* as a fellow moral being can *demand* from me that I refrain from hurting you.[24] This means that if we want to do justice to the intuition that within the moral sphere we are confronted with other human beings and not only with abstract rules we have to follow, we have to provide conceptual room for the moral consideration we owe our fellow moral beings.

As the example above made clear, the moral consideration we owe other moral beings should not be confused with mere compliance with the moral norms in play but amounts to giving these others a special standing in our deliberations about what we should do: Treating you as a fellow moral being means to view me as owing you a justification[25] for what I do concerning you; or, vice versa, to give you the moral consideration I owe you means to view you as being entitled to demand a

[22]The following paragraphs have benefitted enormously from Scanlon's account of moral relationships (Scanlon 2008: Chapter 4); the account I propose in this section is modeled very closely to recognition based theories of morality (Honneth 1992).

[23]Cf. the "Nowheresville"-scenario in Feinberg (1970).

[24]This difference corresponds to Stephen Darwall's distinction between third- and second-personal reasons (Darwall 2006: Chapter 3).

[25]"Justification" is meant in a weak sense, i.e. as giving you an account of the reasons I acted for, *not* as being able to show that what I did was not blameworthy.

justification from me for my acts affecting you.[26] This moral standing will in the following be called *human dignity*.[27]

A closer look at the (de facto, not *de jure*) distribution of power in a torture situation allows us to see more clearly why the relationship between torturer and victim is the prime reason for the moral wrongness of torture: What the torturer denies the victim is not merely her exercise of autonomy or respect for her right not to be violated but her very *standing as a moral being* with the right to be given a justification for what is done to her; by putting himself into a position with the absolute power to determine the victim's fate without having to justify his acts to the victim, the torturer places his victim outside of the game of giving and asking for (moral) reasons.[28] An outward sign for this kind of relationship is the frequent use of derogative language and other ways of symbolically humiliating the victim, since such behavior is expressive of the inferior position the victim is assigned in a torture situation. This kind of asymmetric relationship, where one person denies another person her very standing as a moral being, is the specific reason why torture is a violation of the victim's dignity.

8.5 Why Is Torture *Always* Wrong?

In the last section I argued that the moral wrongness of torture consists in the deprivation of the victim's standing as a moral being and that this is the very feature which makes torture a practice which violates the dignity of the victim. The opposition between my intersubjective account and other accounts tying dignity to the properties of human beings was already implicit in my argument against Twining.[29] According to such property-based accounts, a violation of dignity consists in the violation of claims we have as beings with certain characteristics[30]; the question *who* or *what* violates these claims is completely irrelevant for the moral assessment of such acts. In my account, however, the distinctiveness of practices violating human dignity stems from the fact that there is something profoundly morally wrong about the way persons *relate* to each other when engaging in such practices; as terrible as it might be to be harmed in an accident or in consequence of a natural disaster,

[26]This is similar to Feinberg's idea that dignity is the "capacity to claim rights" (Feinberg 1970). Recent renewals and elaborations of this idea can be found in Stephen Darwall's theory of a "second-personal dignity" (Darwall 2006: Chapter 6) and Rainer Forst's conception of dignity as the right to justification (Forst 2007).

[27]Despite the rich tradition of intersubjective accounts of the concept of human dignity (see fn. 26 above) this move might seem quite arbitrary. For a (qualified) defense see Section 5.

[28]This puts torture into a category with other morally wrong practices like rape or slavery where exactly the same asymmetry is a dominant feature.

[29]See Section 8.3.1 above.

[30]For example, the capacity for self-respect (Margalit 1996) or rational agency (Gewirth 1992).

what makes practices like torture especially horrifying is the fact that it is something *persons* do to persons.

So far, it is still an open question if it is always and without exception morally wrong to put another person in a situation where her moral standing is completely denied. Can't we easily imagine scenarios where we have a perfect justification for torture and, hence, can give the victim valid moral reasons for what we do to him? In such cases, torturing a person and respecting her standing as a moral being would be perfectly compatible. A much discussed example in this fashion is the so-called "Dirty Harry" scenario where a kidnapper has hidden his victim in a place where she will suffocate within hours if she cannot be rescued. A police officer arrests the criminal, but since he refuses to cooperate the only means to save the victim is to torture the kidnapper; so the officer inflicts pain on the criminal until he is willing to give up the wanted information.[31]

In this case it seems undeniable that there are good reasons to torture the kidnapper: In analogy to defense of others, the police officer could claim that torture was the only means to avoid the killing of an innocent person and thus give a perfect justification for what he does.[32]

But this objection misses a fundamental point about the role of the justifying reasons: Even if *there is* a justification for torturing, the torturer cannot justify what he does *to* the torture victim himself since the social context in which torture takes place establishes an asymmetric relationship incompatible with viewing the victim as an addressee for moral reasons. When we take seriously the idea that reasons are relational and that in moral discourse the persons affected by our actions are the prime addressees when we have to justify our conduct, then it is incoherent to maintain that we can simultaneously deprive a person of her standing as a moral being *and* engage in a game of giving and asking for (moral) reasons with her.[33] This explains why violations of dignity are, on the one hand, a distinct type of moral wrong and, on the other, especially abominable: Practices like torture do not merely constitute a breach of rules *within* the moral practice but undermine the presuppositions of the moral practice itself and, hence, can never be morally justified.[34]

But, even if this picture is accepted, there is another pressing objection: If the moral relationship between persons is so central, what about the fact that the evil kidnapper in the example above has *himself* cut the ties between him and the moral community? Are there any moral obligations toward a person who refuses to enter into a moral relationship with others? Supposing so might look counter-intuitive on

---

[31] Seumas Miller mentions a real case with these features (Miller 2008).

[32] For a defense of torture along these lines cf. Steinhoff (2006).

[33] The foundation of this account is the idea that the basic elements of morality are concrete others, not ideal and abstract moral agents. Benhabib presents a strong argument against the validity of moral theories not taking the moral identity of concrete persons into view (Benhabib (1987: 88–90).

[34] Jeremy Waldron has a similar argument with respect to the legal wrongness of torture. He contends that with giving up the legal prohibition of torture we would not merely lose a single legal norm but change the shape of the whole legal system (Waldron 2005: 1728–1734).

first glance, since to uphold the absolute prohibition to torture, it seems, we have to force the terrorist to benefit from something he explicitly denies, namely being part of a moral relationship.

But this objection overlooks two important points: Firstly, the moral community is not an association everybody can opt out of at will but a robust social fact which cannot just be denied; otherwise, everybody could just opt out when moral pressure becomes too high. Secondly, we cannot hold a person morally accountable for her actions without entering into a moral relationship with her in which she is accorded the standing of an equal moral being (Darwall 2006: 67–70). Viewing another person as morally responsible and blameworthy already presupposes that we view her as a part of the moral language game; hence, whatever reasons there might be to torture a person, these reasons cannot be *moral* reasons.

This result seems to amount to a cold-hearted and rigorous brand of absolutism which completely blanks out the perspective of the kidnapped person. Furthermore, when moral relationships matter in the way suggested above, it seems incoherent to worry only about our relationship with the kidnapper and neglect the fact that we also stand in a moral relationship with the victim.[35] Once we take into account that we owe *her* a justification for what we do, too, we seem to be stuck in a genuine dilemmatic situation: We cannot justify the decision to torture to the kidnapper and we cannot justify the decision to refrain from torture to the victim.

I take it that this result does not present an objection to my account but captures a common intuition: Even if we grant that the best decision in the "Dirty Harry" scenario is to try to save the victim and to torture the kidnapper, it would seem strange to hold that the police officer has done nothing wrong and has no reason to regret what he did at all; torturing the kidnapper is – even in the face of the horrible alternative – still morally abominable. In situations of this kind, there is just no way out *without* dirtying one's hands.[36]

8.6 The Scope of My Argument

Even if the argument presented in the last sections is sound, there might be some worries about the method employed to arrive at a relational view of dignity. First of all, the results gained by looking at a practice to elucidate a concept C are subject to variation depending on the examples taken as raw data: When certain aspects of C are elaborated by looking at particular instances of C, there is no guarantee that the results represent C as a whole. This can be shown by a simple example: When we want to clarify the concept "bird" we can look at entities typically regarded

[35]Thanks to Susanne Boshammer for this objection.

[36]The same holds true for so-called "catastrophic" scenarios where a morally wrong action (e.g. killing an innocent person) has to be committed to "save the world" (Fried 1994: 76).

as birds, for instance, blackbirds, thrushes, finches, and starlings. The conditions for the concept "bird" that we will end up with will most probably include "can fly," "lays eggs," and so on. But this would only represent a (considerable) subset of birds, since there are of course birds which *cannot* fly (for example, penguins or ostriches). From these considerations, it becomes clear that the results to be expected from looking at torture as *one* practice commonly considered a violation of dignity may be limited in their significance since a look at other such practices might yield very different results – possibly not fully congruent with those presented here.

Secondly, calling a practice like torture a violation of human dignity obviously begs the question for those skeptical about this concept. Skeptics might argue that whatever is morally wrong about practices like rape, slavery, or torture, it is not the fact that they are violations of dignity – since there is no such thing as human dignity. An ornithologist thinking he can do without the concept of oscines will not be impressed when you point at a nightingale and say, "But there is one!" In a way, this objection is justified, since the skeptic is right in pointing out that there is no guarantee that the features identified as those making torture morally wrong really are features of violations of dignity. But, on the other hand, such a proof can never be provided anyway. The only way of establishing a connection between these features and the concept of dignity is to look at the usage of the concept with respect to certain practices; if there is a pattern in the application of the concept of human dignity, and we can give an analysis of this pattern, this is all the proof that can be given.

Both objections point to the same problem: Giving an analysis of one isolated practice, as was conducted here with respect to torture, is not sufficient to bring into view every aspect related with the notion of dignity and the conditions for its application. Understanding why we call torture a violation of dignity can only be a first step towards a clarification of the concept of human dignity.[37]

References

BBC/Globescan/PIPA. 2006. One-third support 'some torture'. http://news.bbc.co.uk/2/hi/6063386.stm. Accessed 3 Aug 2009.

Beccaria, Cesare. 1995. On crimes and punishments. In *On crimes and punishments and other writings*, ed. Richard Bellamy, 111–113. Cambridge: Cambridge University Press.

Benhabib, Seyla. 1987. The generalized and the concrete other. In *Feminism as critique*, eds. Seyla Benhabib and Drucilla Cornell, 77–95. Oxford: Blackwell.

Bloch, Ernst. 1961. *Naturrecht und menschliche Würde*. Frankfurt/Main: Suhrkamp.

Brecher, Bob. 2007. *Torture and the ticking bomb*. Oxford: Blackwell.

Darwall, Stephen. 2006. *The second-personal standpoint*. Cambridge, MA: Harvard University Press.

[37] I would like to thank Holger Baumann, Susanne Boshammer, Paulus Kaufmann, and Elaine Webster for helpful comments on an earlier draft of this paper, and the editors of this volume for many valuable suggestions.

Davis, Michael. 2005. The moral justification of torture and other cruel, inhuman, or degrading treatment. *International Journal of Applied Philosophy* 19(2): 161–178.
Dershowitz, Alan. 2002. *Why terrorism works: Understanding the threat, responding to the challenge.* New Haven, CT: Yale University Press.
Feinberg, Joel. 1970. The nature and value of rights. *The Journal of Value Inquiry* 4: 243–257, Dec 1970.
Forst, Rainer. 2007. *Das Recht auf Rechtfertigung.* Frankfurt/Main: Suhrkamp.
Frankena, William. 1986. The ethics of respect for persons. *Philosophical Topics* 14: 149–167.
Fried, Charles. 1994. Right and wrong as absolute. In *absolutism and its consequentialist critics*, ed. Joram Graf Haber, 73–92. Lanham, MD: Rowman & Littlefield.
Gewirth, Alan. 1992. Human dignity as the basis of rights. In *The constitution of rights. Human dignity and american values*, ed. Michael J. Meyer and William A Parent, 10–28. Ithaca, NY: Cornell University Press.
Greenberg, Karen, ed. 2006. *The torture debate in America.* Cambridge, NY: Cambridge University Press.
Honneth, Axel. 1992. Integrity and disrespect: Principles of a conception of morality based on the theory of recognition. *Political Theory* 20(2): 187–201.
Human Rights Watch. 2008. *The torture of Tasneem Khalil.* http://www.hrw.org/sites/default/files/reports/bangladesh0208_1.pdf. Accessed 3 Aug 2009.
Kull, Steven et al. 2008. *World public opinion on torture.* http://www.worldpublicopinion.org/pipa/pdf/jun08/WPO_Torture_Jun08_packet.pdf. Accessed 3 Aug 2009.
Macklin, Ruth. 2003. Dignity is a useless concept. *BMJ* 327: 1419–1420.
Margalit, Avishai. 1996. *The decent society.* Cambridge, MA: Harvard University Press.
Miller, Seumas. 2005. Is torture ever morally justified? *International Journal of Applied Philosophy* 19(2): 179–192.
Miller, Seumas. 2008. Torture. In *The Stanford encyclopedia of philosophy* (Fall 2008 edn), ed. Edward N. Zalta. http://plato.stanford.edu/archives/fall2008/entries/torture/. Accessed 3 Aug 2009.
Pinker, Stephen. 2008. The stupidity of dignity. *The New Republic* May 28, 2008.
Powers, Madison and Ruth Faden. 2008. *Social justice: The moral foundations of public health and health policy.* Oxford: Oxford University Press.
Scanlon, Thomas, and Rainer Forst. 2007. *Das Recht auf Rechtfertigung.* Frankfurt/Main: Suhrkamp.
Scanlon, Thomas, and Rainer Forst. 2008. *Moral dimensions. Permissibility, meaning, blame.* Cambridge, MA: Harvard University Press.
Scarry, Elaine. 1985. *The body in pain: The making and unmaking of the world.* Oxford: Oxford University Press.
Shue, Henry. 1978. Torture. *Philosophy and Public Affairs* 7(1): 124–143.
Steinhoff, Uwe. 2006. Torture – The case for dirty harry and against Alan Dershowitz. *Journal of Applied Philosophy* 23(3): 337–353.
Sussman, David. 2005. What's wrong with torture? *Philosophy and Public Affairs* 33(1): 1–33.
Twining, William. 1978. Torture and philosophy. *Proceedings of the Aristotelian Society* 52(Suppl): 143–194.
Waldron, Jeremy. 2005. Torture and positive law. Jurisprudence for the white house. *Columbia Law Review* 105(6): 1681–1750.
Žižek, Slavoj. 2002. *Welcome to the desert of the real.* London: Verso.

Chapter 9
Rape

Does International Human Rights Law Adequately Protect the Dignity of Women?

Ivana Radačić

Abstract While rape has long been thought of as a prime example of a violation of human dignity, it has only recently started to be conceptualized as a human rights violation. This chapter analyzes international human rights jurisprudence on rape, assessing whether it adequately protects the human dignity of women. In particular, it examines how rape has been classified in international human rights jurisprudence and what obligations have been imposed on states to ensure respect for the dignity of women. While acknowledging significant contributions in setting the standard of protection of women's dignity, the chapter criticizes the failure of the mainstream human rights bodies to conceptualize rape as a form of sex discrimination, as well as their gendered application of the public/private divide and occasional reference to family integrity and morals. The chapter argues that rape is a severe violation of human dignity regardless of whether it has been committed by a private individual or a state actor, and violates the right to be free from torture, the right to private life and the right to equality and freedom from discrimination.

9.1 Introduction

Rape has long been thought of as one of the prime examples of a violation of human dignity. While throughout history the concept of dignity in rape discourse has primarily reflected the notion of sexual morals, as rape was seen as an attack on honor (first of the man and family, and then of the woman), with the rise of the human rights movement, dignity violated by rape is conceived primarily in terms of equality and autonomy of women (Radačić 2005).[1]

I. Radačić (✉)
Ivo Pilar Institute of Social Sciences, Centre for Croatian Studies, University of Zagreb, Croatia
e-mail: ivana_radacic@yahoo.com

[1] Thus, the notion of dignity in rape discourse has developed from the communitarian understanding of dignity to an individualistic conceptualization of dignity, and from the concept of dignity as connoting a certain quality of an individual to expressing the inherent and (equal) value of a human being.

P. Kaufmann et al. (eds.), *Humiliation, Degradation, Dehumanization*, Library of Ethics and Applied Philosophy 24, DOI 10.1007/978-90-481-9661-6_9,

However, it was not before the late 1980s that rape started to be conceptualized as a human rights violation. When rape entered human rights discourse, it was first understood as a violation of private life. Later on, with the growth of the global women's rights movement, rape was also considered to constitute a violation of the right to be free from torture and inhuman and degrading treatment or punishment, its precise characterization depending on whether it was committed by a state agent or a private individual. The concept of human dignity has had a prominent role in the conceptualization and interpretation of both of these rights (Feldman 1999, McCrudden 2008). Finally, in women's rights instruments, which have been developed since the mid 1990s, rape has been defined as a form of gender-based violence and thus gender-based discrimination.[2] Discrimination has also been linked with a negative conception of human dignity (Grant 2007).

In this chapter, I analyze the international human rights jurisprudence on rape, assessing whether it adequately protects the human dignity of women, and propose a way forward. I call for a conceptualization of rape not only as a form of inhuman treatment but also as a violation of the right to private life, as well as a form of sex discrimination, as only then are all aspects of a violation of dignity acknowledged. Moreover, I argue that the circumstances external to the victim should not be relevant for assessing the level of severity of rape, as rape is a severe violation of human dignity in any circumstances of its commission. Finally, I argue that no reference should be made to any notion of sexual morals.

9.2 Dignity in International Human Rights Law

Human dignity plays a central role in human rights discourse: It has been a source from which the validity and universal authority of human rights is derived (Schultziner 2003). The whole international human rights movement arose from the need to protect the inherent human dignity and equality of all people. All major human rights conventions contain references to dignity in their preambles, asserting the centrality of dignity to human rights in general, and in specific articles, asserting the relevance of dignity to specific areas of human rights law in particular.[3]

[2]Gender-based violence is defined as violence that is directed against a woman because she is a woman or that affects women disproportionately. Committee on Elimination of All Forms of Discrimination against Women (1992), General Recommendation No. 19, para. 6.

[3]See, for example, Universal Declaration of Human Rights (adopted 10 December 1948) UNGA Res 217 A (III) (UDHR), Preamble and Articles 1, 23, 24; International Covenant on Civil and Political Rights (entered into force 23 March 1976) 999 UNTS 171 (ICCPR), Preamble, Article 10; International Covenant on Economic, Social and Cultural Rights (entered into force 3 January 1976) 993 UNTS 3 (ICESCR), Preamble and Article 13; Convention against Torture and Other Cruel, Inhuman or Degrading Treatment or Punishment (entered into force 26 June 1987) 1465 UNTS 85 (CAT) Preamble; Convention on the Elimination of All Forms of Discrimination against Women (entered into force 3 September 1981) 1249 UNTS 13 (CEDAW), Preamble.

However, the meaning of dignity is not defined. As an underlying principle of international human rights law, human dignity is linked to the values of autonomy (freedom) and equality. Thus, for example, the Universal Declaration of Human Rights, International Covenant on Civil and Political Rights and International Covenant on Economic, Social and Cultural Rights (in their preambulary paragraphs) stipulate that the recognition of dignity and equality (equal rights) is a foundation for freedom.

The interrelated nature of dignity, freedom and equality is further seen in the use of dignity language in certain areas of human rights: protection from ill-treatment, self-determination, equality and non-discrimination, and socio-economic rights. For example, the Vienna Declaration and Platform for Action refers to dignity not only as a foundation of human rights but also in provisions dealing with the treatment of indigenous people, the prohibition of torture, the prohibition of gender based violence, the abolition of extreme poverty and the issue of medical bioethics.[4] While human rights conventions differ in their use of dignity language, in international human rights jurisprudence dignity has been employed specifically in interpretation of freedom from torture, inhuman and degrading treatment and punishment, the right to private life, the right to equality and freedom from discrimination, as well as the right to social security and work (McCrudden 2008).

In sum, in international human rights law – the central aim of which is to protect human dignity – inhuman treatment, violations of private life, discrimination and severe denials of social and economic rights have all been seen as attacks on human dignity. The concept of human dignity in international law thus seems to have, as Clapham (2006: 545–546) writes, at least four aspects: (1) the prohibition of all types of inhuman treatment, humiliation, degradation by one person over another; (2) the assurance of the possibility of individual choice and the conditions for "each individual's self-fulfilment," autonomy, or self-realization; (3) the recognition that the protection of group identity and culture may be essential for the protection of personal dignity; (4) the creation of the necessary conditions for each individual to have their essential needs satisfied. Not all of these aspects of dignity are, however, fully recognized in international human rights law jurisprudence on rape.

9.3 Rape in International Human Rights Law

Rape is not specifically mentioned in any of the main human rights conventions. Moreover, until the 1990s, rape, together with other forms of gender-based violence, was marginalized in international human rights law. It was only under the pressure of grass-root women's rights activists, who have vigorously documented the extent of sexual violence against women in different countries and the inadequacy of states' responses to the problem, that violence against women became a topic

[4]Vienna Declaration and Programme for Action (12 July 1993) UN Doc A/CONF.157/23, the second preambulary paragraph and paragraphs 11, 18, 20, 25, 55.

of international human rights law. The wide media coverage and documentation of the unprecedented scope of sexual violence in the wars of the former Yugoslavia and Rwanda and the developments in international criminal law that these events prompted also contributed to placing gender-based violence on the human rights agenda (Radačić 2005).

The major change in the treatment of sexual violence in international human rights law occurred at the Vienna Conference on Human Rights as this was the first time that violence against women was a major topic of an important human rights conference. Since then many regional and global instruments addressing violence against women have been adopted and mechanisms set up.[5] Moreover, as the Beijing Declaration and the Platform for Action promoted the strategy of gender mainstreaming,[6] the UN treaty monitoring bodies and regional courts have also started addressing sexual violence against women in their mandate, realizing the fact that gender-based violence violates a number of civil and political as well as economic, social and cultural rights (Center for Reproductive Rights 2002).

Within international human rights law, two approaches to rape have been developed. Jurisprudence of the mainstream international human rights bodies defines rape primarily as a form of inhuman treatment. The focus is on physical and psychological abuse of a woman in a particular case at issue rather than on discriminatory effects of rape on women in general. The importance of the protection of the group identity, of achieving equality of women, for the dignity of any singular woman is neglected. Women-specific instruments conceptualize rape primarily as a form of gender-based discrimination. The focus is thus on the group identity, and dignity is conceived of in more collective terms: dignity owed to women as women.[7]

9.4 Rape Jurisprudence

Rape cases until now have been adjudicated both within the European and Inter-American systems for the protection of human rights. In addition, there was a number of individual complaints adjudicated by the Committee against Torture (CAT) in which women, members of opposition parties, who were raped in their country of origin, argued that their expulsion to these countries would violate Article 3 of the Convention against Torture on account of the risk of being subjected to

[5] For example, UN Declaration on Elimination of Violence against Women, UNGA Res 48/104 (20 December 1993) UN Doc A/RES/48/104; Inter-American Convention on the Prevention, Punishment and Eradication of Violence against Women (entered into force 5 March 1995) (1994) 33 ILM 1534. In 1994 the position of the Special Rapporteur on Violence against Women, Its Causes and Consequences was instituted.

[6] Beijing Platform for Action (15 September 1995) UN Doc A/CONF.177/20/Add.1, paras. 37–42.

[7] For an account of the collective dimension of human dignity see Neuhäuser (Chapter 3, this volume).

torture.[8] Due to lack of space, CAT jurisprudence will not be analyzed here. It is important to mention, though, that CAT only analyzes on merits the cases in which a woman was raped by a state agent, as it holds that "the issue whether the State party has an obligation to refrain from expelling a person who might risk pain or suffering inflicted by a non-governmental entity, without the consent or acquiescence of the Government, falls outside the scope of article 3 of the Convention."[9]

9.4.1 Cases of the Inter-American Commission[10]

The Inter-American Commission has dealt with two rape cases: *Raquel Martin de Mejia v. Peru*; and *Celia, Ana and Beatriz Gonzalez Perez v. Mexico.*[11] Inter-American Court also examined cases in which (some of) the applicant(s) alleged that they were, inter alia, raped: *María Elena Loayza-Tamayo v. Mexico; Plan de Sanchez Massacre v. Guatemala; and Castro-Castro Prison v. Peru.*[12] However, rape complaints ware not the only allegations, nor were they at the centre of the submissions; and therefore, for the lack of space these cases will not be analysed here.[13]

---

[8] Article 3(1): No State Party shall expel, return ("refouler") or extradite a person to another State where there are substantial grounds for believing that he would be in danger of being subjected to torture. Supra n. 2.

[9] CAT "Views on Communication no 87/1997 (*GRB v Sweden*)" (15 May 1998) UN Doc CAT/C/20/D/83/1997, para 6.5.

[10] The Inter-American Court also examined cases in which (some of) the applicant(s) alleged that they were, inter alia, raped: *María Elena Loayza-Tamayo v. Mexico; Plan de Sanchez Massacre v. Guatemala*; and *Castro-Castro Prison v. Peru.* However, rape complaints ware not the only allegations, nor were they at the centre of the submissions; in the *Loayaza-Tamayo* case the applicant alleged that rape was one of the acts of torture she suffered while being illegally detained; in the *Plan de Sanchez Massacre* twenty of the hundreds of victims were raped before they were killed in the context of an attack on the village by the government's agents; and in the *Castro-Castro Prison* one of the detainees was submitted to "finger vaginal inspection" in the context of the attack on the prison (mainly women's wing) by the government's agents. In the first case, the Court simply stated that the allegation was not substantiated, even though other allegations of torture were no more substantiated but were considered proven; in the second case, the Government accepted the facts of the case and its responsibility; and in the third case, the Court held that the treatment in question constituted rape in violation of the right to humane treatment. It also held the state responsible for the failure to investigate these acts and punish those responsible. Due to lack of space, these cases will not be analyzed here. For the analysis of these cases, see Quintana Osuna (2008).

[11] Case 10.970, Report No. 5/96, Inter-Am.C.H.R., OEA/Ser.L/V/II.91 Doc. 7 at 157 (1996); Case 11.565, Report No. 129/99, Inter-Am.C.H.R., OEA/Ser.L/V/II.106 Doc. 3 rev. at 232 (1999).

[12] Case of Loayza-Tamayo v. Peru (Merits), Inter-Am. Ct. H.R. (ser. C) No. 33 (Sept. 17, 1997). Case of the Plan de Sanchez Massacre v. Guatemala (Merits), Inter-Amer. Ct. H.R. (ser. C) No. 105, at 36 (April 29, 2004). Case of the Miguel Castro-Castro Prison v. Peru (Merits, Reparations and Costs), Inter-Amer. Ct. H.R. (ser. C.) No. 160 (Nov. 25, 2006).

[13] In the *Loayaza-Tamayo* case the applicant alleged that rape was one of the acts of torture she suffered while being illegally detained; in the *Plan de Sanchez Massacre* twenty of the hundreds of victims were raped before they were killed in the context of an attack on the village by the government's agents; and in the *Castro-Castro Prison* one of the detainees was submitted to "finger

The cases of the Inter-American Commission both concerned rape by a state agent (members of the military). While the Gonzalez Perez sisters reported rape to the prosecutor and submitted a gynecological report, Raquel Mejia did not report rape to the domestic authorities. In both cases the applicants argued a violation of their right to be free from torture, their right to privacy, and the right to have access to domestic recourse for remedying violations they suffered.

9.4.1.1 Implicated Rights

One of the issues in these cases was how rape (by a state agent) is to be defined under the American Convention on Human Rights.[14] In both cases, the Commission found a violation of both the right to be free from torture and the right to a private life (Articles 5 and 11 of the Convention).[15] In the *Raquel Mejia* case, the Commission, defining torture as an intentional act through which physical and mental pain and suffering are inflicted on a person with a purpose (such as punishment, intimidation or discrimination of any kind) by a public official or by a private person acting at the instigation of the former, looked at whether rape could be so classified. Finding that the rape in question was committed by a state agent for the purpose of punishing the victim, it focused on the first element. Considering rape as "physical and mental abuse that is perpetrated as a result of the act of violence," the Commission defined the rape of Raquel Mejia as an act of torture. Discussing the effects of rape, the Commission noted the condemnation of the victims by the community, stating that the integrity of the family was at stake in the case of rape and that "no woman wants to publicly announce that she was raped, as she does not know how her husband would react."

In the *Gonzalez Perez* case, the Commission referred to its statements in *Mejia*, the case-law of the European Court of Human Rights, and the ICTY[16] and held that "abuses targeting the physical, mental and *moral* integrity of the three Tzeltal sisters committed by the agents of Mexican state constitute torture" (para. 22).

In both cases, the Commission also found a violation of the right to privacy. In the *Rachel Mejia* case it referred to the statement of the Special Rapporteur on

---

vaginal inspection" in the context of the attack on the prison (mainly women's wing) by the government's agents. In the first case, the Court simply stated that the allegation was not substantiated, even though other allegations of torture were no more substantiated but were considered proven; in the second case, the Government accepted the facts of the case and its responsibility; and in the third case, the Court held that the treatment in question constituted rape in violation of the right to humane treatment. It also held the state responsible for the failure to investigate these acts and punish those responsible. For the analysis of these cases, see Quintana Osuna (2008).

[14] American Convention on Human Rights (entered into force 18 July 1978).O.A.S. Treaty Series No. 36, 1144 U.N.T.S. 123.

[15] Article 5 contains an express reference to dignity in the first paragraph.

[16] *Aydin v. Turkey* (App no 23178/94) ECHR 1997–VI; *Anto Furundžija* (judgment) IT–95–17/1–T (10 December 1998).

Torture that rape is a particularly base attack against human dignity, and stated further that women are affected in the most sensitive part of their personality. Thus, the Commission concluded that "besides being a violation of the victim's physical and mental integrity [rape] implies a deliberate outrage to [the victim's] dignity, and thus constitutes a violation of the victim's private life." Similarly, in the *Gonzalez Perez* case, the Commission (in para. 52) found that events at issue "represent a violation of the private lives of the four women and their families and an illegal attack on their privacy which led them to flee their community in a situation of fear, shame and humiliation."

The Commission's classification of rape as both a violation of the right to be free from torture and other forms of ill-treatment, and the right to privacy (which is in the American Convention explicitly linked to the protection of dignity) is to be welcomed, as it recognizes that rape violates both physical and mental integrity, and autonomy. However, the problem is that according to the Commission, only rape by a state agent can be classified as torture, since its definition of torture requires a direct involvement of a state official. This is, however, problematic as rape by a private individual is not qualitatively different from rape by a state agent: In both instances, it causes severe mental and physical pain and suffering, and constitutes a denial of sexual autonomy and a form of discrimination, and thus a serious violation of human dignity.

Further, while the ostracization often suffered by the rape victims is acknowledged, the Commission's concern with the integrity of the family and the husbands' reactions does not do much to challenge views about sexual honor which lead to the stigmatization of victims. Moreover, the pronunciation that rape is an attack on the moral integrity of the victim might imply that victims become morally diminished once they are raped and thus goes against the understanding of dignity as inherent in humans, which can be violated but not lost or diminished.

9.4.1.2 Scope of Positive Obligations

Another question raised in these cases was the scope of the state's positive obligations to investigate and prosecute rape. In both cases, the Commission found a violation of the right to a fair trial and to judicial protection (Articles 8 and 25 of the American Convention in relation to Article 1). In *Rachel Mejia*, it concluded that there was no access to a domestic recourse for determining a violation of Mejia's rights, as the practice in Peru was that these types of acts involving state agents were not investigated while those who reported them ran the risk of reprisal.

In the *Gonzalez Perez* case, the Commission criticized the fact that the complaint filed by the sisters to the prosecutor was transferred from ordinary courts to military courts, which lacked both competence and impartiality. It also critiqued the fact that at the time of its submission before the Commission, the case was pending for 8 years without results. Addressing the state's argument that the inactivity of the authorities was due to the failure of the applicants to subject themselves to another gynecological exam, the Commission held:

> Rape is an aberrant act, which, because of its very nature, requires evidence that is different from other crimes. Subjecting the victim to another episode of humiliation or one that causes that person to relive the events involving the most private parts of the person's body in the form of review proceedings should be avoided. Consequently, [. . .] the investigating authorities should analyze the circumstances surrounding the case and all available elements such as statements, circumstantial evidence, presumption, and other legal elements. In the absence of evidence, the medical examination must provide all the guarantees for fully respecting the dignity of the person and for considering that individual's mental and psychological condition.

The recognition of the humiliation caused by subjecting the victims to repeated gynecological examinations, directing the states to use other means of evidence and imposing an obligation on states to institute guarantees for respecting the dignity of a victim when conducting medical examinations, goes a long way in protecting the dignity of the victims. The need to examine victims with sensitivity was also emphasized in the jurisprudence of the European Court of Human Rights, which further clarified the scope of positive obligations to effectively investigate rape crimes.

9.4.2 Cases of the European Court of Human Rights

The European Court has dealt with three rape cases. *X and Y v. the Netherlands* concerned a rape of a mentally disabled girl by a private individual; *Aydin v. Turkey* concerned a rape of a 17 years old Kurdish girl in police custody by a state agent; and *M.C. v. Bulgaria* concerned a rape of a young woman by her acquaintances.[17]

9.4.2.1 Implicated Rights

As in the jurisprudence of the Inter-America Commission, one of the issues raised was how to classify rape under the Convention. In *X and Y v. the Netherlands* and *MC v. Bulgaria*, the applicants claimed a violation of the right to respect for private life (Article 8) and the right to be free from torture and inhuman and degrading treatment or punishment (Article 3), without specifying what kind of treatment under Article 3 was at issue.[18] In *Aydin v. Turkey*, the applicant claimed that the rape she had suffered constituted torture.

Rape was classified as torture only in *Aydin v. Turkey*. The Court explained that the concept of torture, as distinct from "inhuman and degrading treatment and punishment," referred only to "deliberate inhuman treatment causing very serious and

[17] *X and Y v Netherlands* (App no 8978/80) (1985) Series A no 91; *Aydin v Turkey* (App no 23178/94) ECHR 1997–VI; *MC v Bulgaria* (App no 39272/98) ECHR 2003–VII.

[18] In the Court's jurisprudence, dignity discourse is most present in its interpretation of Article 3.

cruel suffering" on account of the severity and special stigma attached to torture.[19] Assessing whether rape could be so classified, the Court held that:

> Rape of a detainee by an official of the State must be considered to be an especially grave and abhorrent form of ill-treatment given the ease with which the offender can exploit the vulnerability and weakened resistance of his victim. Furthermore, rape leaves deep psychological scars on the victim which do not respond to the passage of time as quickly as other forms of physical and mental violence. The applicant also experienced the acute physical pain of forced penetration, which must have left her feeling debased and violated both physically and emotionally.

The Court's conceptualization of rape in custody as an "especially grave and abhorrent form of ill-treatment" and its recognition of the vulnerable position of detainees in respect of sexual abuse is to be greeted as a gender-sensitive judicial pronunciation that acknowledges rape as a severe violation of human dignity. However, the focus on the vulnerability of the detainee in determining the severity of treatment is problematic, as it leaves unclear whether a rape by a private individual also reaches the level of severity of torture (Dembour 2006: 204–205).

This question was not answered in either of the remaining cases: in *X and Y*, the Court refused even to consider the Article 3 complaint, and in *MC v. Bulgaria*, it failed to state what kind of Article 3 treatment was at issue. Rape, however, should always be assessed as a grave and abhorrent form of ill-treatment constituting torture, regardless of whether it was committed by a state or a non-state actor, provided that the state responsibility is established. As noted by the Appeals Chamber of the International Criminal Tribunal for the Former Yugoslavia (ICTY) in the *Kunarac* judgment:

> [S]ome acts establish *per se* the suffering of those upon whom they were inflicted. Rape is [. . .] such an act. [. . .] Sexual violence necessarily gives rise to severe pain or suffering, whether physical or mental, and in this way justifies its characterisation as an act of torture. Severe pain or suffering, as required by the definition of the crime of torture, can thus be said to be established once rape has been proved, since the act of rape necessarily implies such pain or suffering.[20]

---

[19] *Aydin v Turkey,* para 82. Article 3 does not explicitly require the Court to draw a distinction between the forms of ill-treatment it prohibits, but the Court has tended to state the nature of ill-treatment suffered by a given applicant. The distinction between various forms of ill-treatment prohibited by Article 3 derives principally from the intensity of suffering inflicted. For the treatment to constitute torture under the Convention, it has to be intentional, it has to cause severe suffering, and it has to be committed with a purpose, such as: obtaining from the victim or a third person information or a confession, punishing the victim for an act s/he or a third person has committed or is suspected of having committed, or intimidating or coercing the victim or a third person for any reason based on discrimination of any kind. The level of severity is assessed according to the facts at issue (duration of treatment, physical and mental effects on the victim, and, in some cases, personal characteristics of the victim, such as sex and age) and in light of "social developments". See, e.g., *Tyrer v UK* (App no 5856/72) (1978) Series A no 26.

[20] *Kunarac, Kovač and Vuković* (Appeals Chamber Judgment) ICTY–96–23 (2 June 2002), paras. 149–151.

Whether an individual was raped by a state agent or by a private individual should not be relevant for determining the severity of treatment but only for establishing the responsibility of the state. State responsibility is under the European Court's jurisprudence and, unlike in the jurisprudence of CAT or the Inter-American Commission, is not limited to a direct state action (or instigation or acquiescence), but includes responsibility to prevent and investigate human rights violations by private individuals (Mowbray 2004). Thus, where responsibility of the state is found, rape should always be conceptualized as torture, regardless of the implicated sphere.

9.4.2.2 Scope and Content of Positive Obligation

The content and scope of a state's obligations in respect of securing effective protection from rape was another question addressed in the cases. In *X and Y v. the Netherlands*, at issue was the adequacy of legislation, as the applicant challenged the prosecutor's refusal to institute proceedings due to the fact that the criminal provision prohibiting indecent assault, which he found applicable in the case at issue, required a victim herself to institute proceedings (which she was not able to do due to her disability).[21]

The Court, clarifying first that states have positive obligations even in the sphere of the relationship between individuals, analyzed whether civil remedies were sufficient, as the government argued. It concluded (in para. 27):

> [...] This is a case where fundamental values and essential aspects of private life are at stake. Effective deterrence is indispensable in this area and it can be achieved only by criminal-law provisions; indeed, it is by such provisions that the matter is normally regulated.

It then looked at the compatibility of the Dutch criminal law provision with Article 8. It found a violation of Article 8, concluding that it left the applicant unprotected because of its requirement that the victim file a criminal report.

Recognizing rape as implicating fundamental aspects of a private life and imposing on states a positive obligation to provide criminal law remedies in respect of forceful intercourse with a person with mental disability is a positive development, which affirms the dignity of women with disabilities. However, the Court's analysis of the relevant legislation was too narrow, as the Court only examined the provision that the government argued was applicable, and only in respect of its requirement that the victim herself had to institute proceedings. The fact that the provision offered protection only to the "minor of the blameless conduct" was not criticized. Moreover, it was not questioned whether it was appropriate to define the

[21] The provision prohibits "causing a minor of blameless conduct to commit indecent acts or to suffer acts through gift, promises, abuse of dominant position, or deceit." It required the victim herself to take the action. As she was unable to do so, the father filed a criminal report, but the prosecutor declared it inadmissible, which was affirmed by the courts. While the provision prohibiting rape does not require a victim to institute the proceedings, the authorities found it inapplicable as it required recourse to force.

crime in question as an "indecent act" or whether it would have been more appropriate to define the crime as rape (or criminalize specifically the forceful sexual intercourse with a person with mental disability). The requirement of recourse to physical force as an element of rape was not criticized, despite its apparent incompatibility with human rights standards in respect of protection of women from sexual abuse. This was to be done only later.

In *Aydin v. Turkey*, the question was whether the investigation in the applicant's case was effective. The Court held that the investigation was ineffective and incomplete; the prosecutor had not taken all the measures at his disposal to verify the applicant's statements, and the medical examinations were aimed at establishing whether she had lost her virginity rather than whether she was a rape victim. In this respect the Court noted that doctors did not have experience in examining rape victims, and held (in para. 107):

> The requirement of a thorough and effective investigation into an allegation of rape in custody at the hands of a State official also implies that the victim be examined, with all appropriate sensitivity, by medical professionals with particular competence in this area and whose independence is not circumscribed by instructions given by the prosecuting authority as to the scope of the examination.

Imposing this specific obligation on the state is a progressive step in establishing standards of the protection of women's dignity in the context of rape investigation. Together with the obligation to respect the dignity of women pronounced in the *Gonzalez Perez* case, it sets the standards of protection of the victims from humiliation and re-victimization in the criminal proceedings.

In *MC v. Bulgaria*, at issue was the adequacy of both legislation and prosecution. The applicant argued that the investigation into her case was ineffective and that Bulgarian laws and practices generally leave the victims of sexual abuse unprotected by prosecuting only those cases where the victim resisted violently.[22] The Court, examining the scope of positive obligations, first concluded that "states have a positive obligation inherent in Articles 3 and 8 of the Convention to enact criminal-law provisions effectively punishing rape and to apply them in practice through effective investigation and prosecution" (para. 153).

The Court then went on to discuss what was meant by "effective". Examining the state of the European consensus, documents within the Council of Europe, the standards in international criminal law,[23] and noting the "evolution of societies toward

---

[22]The definition of rape in cases where the victim was not incapable of defending herself required recourse to the use of force or threats by the perpetrator. The applicant claimed that only cases in which there was evidence of physical force and active resistance were prosecuted. She supported her claim by an overview of the reported judgments of the Supreme Court and the Supreme Court of Cassation, which showed that from 21 judgments, 18 involved significant physical force.

[23]The Court looked at the rape laws in Europe, the ICTY case *Prosecutor v Kunarac, Kovač and Vuković* (Appeals Chamber judgment) (12 June 2002), and Recommendation Rec (2002) 5 of the Committee of Ministers of the Council of Europe on the protection of women against violence and Explanatory Memorandum. It also examined Interights' *amicus curiae* brief which argued that the central element of rape is non-consent. See paras. 104–108 of the judgment.

effective equality and respect of each individual's autonomy," the Court (in para. 166) held:

> The Court is persuaded that any rigid approach to the prosecution of sexual offences, such as requiring proof of physical resistance in all circumstances, risks leaving certain types of rape unpunished and thus jeopardising the effective protection of the individual's sexual autonomy. In accordance with contemporary standards and trends in that area, the member States' positive obligations under Articles 3 and 8 of the Convention must be seen as requiring the penalisation and effective prosecution of any non-consensual sexual act, including in the absence of physical resistance by the victim.

The Court finally examined whether Bulgarian legislation and practice on rape and their application in the applicant's case, combined with the alleged shortcomings in the investigation, had such significant flaws to amount to a breach of positive obligations under Articles 3 and 8. Accepting the applicant's submission of restrictive interpretation of "force" as an element of rape, and finding that in the case at issue the authorities had failed to investigate sufficiently all the surrounding circumstances (including consideration of the special psychological factors involved in cases of rape concerning minors)[24] while putting undue emphasis on the "direct" proof of rape, the Court held that there was a violation of positive obligations under Articles 3 and 8.

Imposing the obligation on states to prosecute all forms of rape, regardless of whether the victim actively resisted, is a landmark development from the perspective of protection of women's dignity, achieved by a gender-sensitive methodological approach. In assessing the scope and content of state obligations, the Court asked whose experience the challenged laws and practices reflected and what their effect was on protecting women's sexual autonomy, dignity and equality. The Court looked at the implications for women – in particular, a vulnerable category of young women – of prosecuting only those cases where victims actively resist. In this respect, the Court took seriously the experiences of women and acknowledged and challenged the discriminatory social and legal attitudes in respect of the victims of sexual violence, especially present in date rape scenarios (McColgan 1996).

Furthermore, by acknowledging that sex might be non-consensual even when there is no active force or active resistance, due to many factors connected to inequalities in relationships (MacKinnon 2005), the Court opened a way for a re-conceptualization of consent from investigating when "no means no" to investigating when "yes means yes", when consent is given freely and voluntarily (Little 2005, Munro 2005). This "affirmative consent" approach, which requires the parties of sexual acts to take steps to ascertain whether there is a free and genuine agreement, has greater potential to challenge gender subordination and stereotypical

---

[24]The applicant submitted research by a Bulgarian psychologist and psychiatrist on the response of young women to rape, which concluded that most young women displayed a passive psychological reaction to panic (known as "frozen fright").

norms of sexuality (according to which men propose sexual advances and women passively accept them) and of prompting the establishment of norms of sexuality that see women and men as equal parties.[25] Only such norms can adequately protect the dignity of both women and men.

9.5 Conclusion

In this chapter I have examined the international human rights law on rape, assessing how it protects women's human dignity. While in international human rights law dignity has four interrelated aspects – physical and moral integrity, autonomy, non-discrimination, and enjoyment of social conditions in which a person can strive – international human rights jurisprudence has not yet recognized all of these elements as implicated in rape, since the mainstream human rights bodies have failed to conceptualize rape as a gender-based discrimination. Moreover, it has only been recently that the European Court of Human Rights has defined rape as a violation of both the right to respect for a private life and the right to be free from torture and other forms of ill-treatment. On the other hand, in the jurisprudence of the Inter-American Commission on Human Rights we can still see a conceptualization of dignity connected with sexual morality and a focus on the integrity of family. Such conceptualization of dignity does nothing to challenge the stigmatization of rape victims and runs against the understanding of dignity as inherent in human beings and owed to an individual.

Another problematic aspect of the jurisprudence is the operation of the public/private divide. Thus, CAT has refused to examine expulsion cases in which victims had been raped by non-state actors; the Inter-American Commission requires direct involvement of a state actor (through action or instigation) for rape to be classified as torture; and the European Court has defined rape as torture only when committed by a state agent, even though direct involvement of the state agent is not an element of torture in its jurisprudence. These applications of the public/private divide are, however, harmful to women as they create hierarchies of rape and its victims. In international criminal law no such boundaries are found, as any rape is seen as constituting torture.

While the failure to conceptualize rape as torture – regardless of whether it is committed by a public or a private actor, provided that the state responsibility is engaged – and as an act of gender-based violence fails to reflect all aspects of the dignity of women. The following features of the human rights

---

[25] Under this approach mere submission would not indicate consent; only free and genuine agreement would suffice. Certain circumstances – such as where force, threats, fraud or abuse of power was used – would entail a presumption of a lack of consent as well as a reasonable belief in the lack of consent. Only reasonable mistaken belief of consent, where the accused took steps to ascertain whether the other party agreed to the sexual act, would negate criminal responsibility (see Radačić and Turković 2010).

jurisprudence represent significant steps forward in setting the standard of protection of women's dignity:

1. Imposing on states the obligation to criminalise all forms of sexual abuse;
2. Imposing on states the obligation to effectively prosecute all forms of sexual abuse, regardless of whether the perpetrator used force and whether the victim resisted, and thus identifying non-consent rather than force or resistance as the central element of rape;
3. Imposing on states the obligation to secure respect for dignity of women in investigation of rape, particularly in respect of conducting gynaecological examinations.

References

Center for Reproductive Rights. 2002. *Bringing rights to bear: An analysis of work of the treaty monitoring bodies on reproductive and sexual rights.* New York, NY: Center for Reproductive Rights.

Clapham, Andrew. 2006. *Human rights obligations of non-state actors.* Oxford: Oxford University Press.

Dembour, Marie-Bénédicte. 2006. *Who believes in human rights? Reflections on the European convention.* Cambridge: Cambridge University Press.

Feldman, David. 1999. Human dignity as a legal value – Part I. *Public Law* 682–702.

Grant, Evandé. 2007. Dignity and equality. *Human Rights Law Review* 7(2): 299–329.

Little, Nicholas J. 2005. From no means no to only yes means yes: The rational results of an affirmative consent standard in rape law. *Vanderbilt Law Review* 58: 1321–1365.

MacKinnon, Catharine A. 2005. Unequal sex: A sex equality approach to sexual assault. In *Women's lives – Men's laws*, ed. Catharine A. MacKinnon, 240–248. Cambridge, MA: Harvard University Press.

McColgan, Aileen. 1996. *The case for taking the date out of rape.* London: Pandora.

McCrudden, Christopher. 2008. Human dignity and judicial interpretation of human rights. *European Journal of International Law* 18(9): 656–724.

Mowbray, Andrew W. 2004. *Development of positive obligations under the European convention on human rights.* Oxford: Hart.

Munro, Vanessa. 2005. Concerning consent: Standards of permissibility in sexual relations. *Oxford Journal of Legal Studies* 25(2): 335–352.

Quintana Osuna, Karla. 2008. Recognition of women's rights before the Inter-American court of human rights. *Harvard Human Rights Journal* 21(2): 301–312.

Radačić, Ivana. 2005. Status of women and treatment of gender-specific violence in international humanitarian and international criminal law. *Zbornik Pravnog fakulteta Sveučilišta u Rijeci* 26(1): 1041–1062.

Radačić, Ivana, and Ksenija Turković. 2010. Rethinking Croatian rape laws: Force, consent and the contribution of the victim. In *Rethinking rape law: international and comparative perspectivesl*, eds. Clare McGlynn and Vanessa Munro, 169–183. Oxon: Routledge.

Schultziner, Doron. 2003. Human dignity – Function and meaning. *Global Jurist Topics* 3(3), Article 3.

Chapter 10
Social Exclusion

Practices of Misrecognition

Steffen K. Herrmann

Abstract Social Exclusion can be mainly understood in three different ways: as a form of spatial separation, a lack of participation, or as emanating from *practices of misrecognition.* One of the approaches based on the latter understanding was proposed by the Israeli social philosopher Avishai Margalit. For him, social exclusion by practices of misrecognition is one way to harm human dignity. Margalit frequently referred to the persecution of Jews during National Socialism in order to substantiate this thought. In my chapter, I take up this thought and demonstrate that in national socialist Germany various practices of misrecognition played an important role within anti-Semitism, a fact which can be clearly shown in the politics of the *personal name*. This is because the personal name is a unique symbol of human dignity. The giving of a name is not only a performative act by which we become singular and distinctive; first and foremost, it inaugurates us as social beings. I would like to distinguish four stages within which Jewish names were targets of social exclusion during National Socialism: *insult*, *degradation*, *debasement* and *humiliation*. What began as a seemingly harmless and ordinary practice of teasing, displayed in nicknames such as "*Itzig*", gradually developed into a system of utmost cruelty, embodied in a state-run policy of debasement and exclusion of a whole section of the population, which was initiated by the declaration of the names "Sarah" and "Israel" as obligatory for Jews. This system culminated in the concentration camps where the number replaced the human name. As the paradigmatic figure of the nameless, I will examine the so called "Muselmann" more closely. He marks the transitional point where social exclusion turns into *social death*, and the loss of human dignity becomes absolute.

S.K. Herrmann (✉)
Department of Philosophy, Freie Universität Berlin, Germany
e-mail: s.k.herrmann@fu-berlin.de

P. Kaufmann et al. (eds.), *Humiliation, Degradation, Dehumanization*, 133
Library of Ethics and Applied Philosophy 24, DOI 10.1007/978-90-481-9661-6_10,

10.1 Introduction

When the idea of "social exclusion" entered into academic debates as a theoretical concept around the end of the twentieth century, it was meant to reflect the situation of those people who no longer experience themselves as fully participating members of society, but instead as part of a merely dispensable human mass. In contrast to members of the underprivileged lower classes, who at least experience having a positive social identity within a system of social inequality, these individuals find themselves in a state of social isolation providing no positive identification at all. The sociologist Zygmunt Bauman coined the expression "wasted life" to describe this condition (Bauman 2004).

The concept of social exclusion, resulting from the need to conceptualize this condition, was principally influenced by two basic approaches. One of the latter takes the concept literally and examines the phenomenon of social exclusion mainly in regard to practices of *spatial separation*. Seminal contributions to this position were provided by the works of Erving Goffman (1961) and Michel Foucault (2003), which investigated the shutting away of mentally-ill patients into psychiatric institutions. While their work focused mainly on the fate of those stigmatized as "abnormal" from a hegemonic point of view, the subsequent research widened the focus on other socially marginalized groups – for example, the marginalization of economically disadvantaged classes who live largely separated from society in socially deprived areas, ghettos, or favelas. Based on this perspective, social exclusion is understood as a process of setting up spatial zones in which the socially disadvantaged are segregated from the rest of society. On the other hand, there is a second tradition which considers social exclusion in regard to the lack of possibilities for social groups to participate politically and socially. In the Anglo-Saxon context, these inquiries focused on the concept of the "underclass" to examine to what extent poverty, unemployment, or social origin make it impossible to participate in what is commonly considered to be a good life (Dahrendorf 1988). In similar ways, close attention has been paid to this potential for a lack of participation with the concept of "*les exclus*" in France. However, more socially proven factors were at play here, such as, for example, lack of education, cultural habitus or a minority lifestyle (Castel 2002). In contrast to the first perspective, these approaches do not consider social exclusion within a context of spatial segregation, but rather as a *lack of participation* as a result of political, economic, and social barriers. Consequently, this theoretical tradition therefore regards social exclusion as being the systematic discrimination of socially disadvantaged groups to whom participation in society's good life is denied.

A third theoretical tradition recently became available as a research resource. Here, exclusion processes are not traced back to local separation or a lack of participation but rather understood as emanating from *practices of misrecognition* (Honneth 1995, Taylor 1994). Central to this theory is the exclusion from social belonging. In analogy to the approach first introduced, the concept of social exclusion here is also understood literally, with the crucial difference, however, that it is not the concept of exclusion which is taken literally, but rather that of "the social".

Social rather than spatial positionings are now the central focus of interest. Based on this perspective, exclusion is understood as a lack of recognition of certain social groups through which individuals are driven into a state of social isolation, where any positive identification with their own identity is no longer possible. One of the approaches based on the latter theoretical tradition was proposed by the Israeli social philosopher Avishai Margalit. His reflections are of particular importance in that, for him, in acts of humiliation social exclusion can be increased to the extent that a human being is excluded from "the family of man" (Margalit 1996: 108). In this case it is not only questioned whether the excluded are full-fledged members of society, but rather it is their basic human dignity which is at stake. In what follows, I would like to show that, based on this notion, it is not only possible to adequately describe the state of "wasted life" in theoretical terms, but also to work out an entire set of symbolic practices of misrecognition through which social exclusion processes are executed.

Margalit frequently exemplified his reflections on exclusion through the example of the persecution of Jews during National Socialism. For him, the misrecognition of the Jewish community is a paradigmatic case which serves to demonstrate how social exclusion can escalate into dehumanization. In the following, I would like to take up Margalit's basic thought and apply it to a specific matter: the human personal name. I would like to concentrate on the personal name because it is especially useful in clearly depicting the transformation and increase of practices of misrecognition – and this, indeed, not by showing how exclusion expands quantitatively but rather how it increases qualitatively. Therefore, first of all, I would like to demonstrate how our human existence is inimitably expressed by the personal name (10.2). Based on this, I would like to succinctly reconstruct how the politics of personal names became a fundamental component of the persecution of the Jews in National Socialism (10.3). Subsequently, the third section will reveal how processes of the social exclusion of Jews were implemented with the help of the misrecognition of the personal name (10.4). In the fourth section, it will ultimately become clear how, through the humiliation of the personal name, social exclusion could reach so far that the affected individuals' humanity was put into question (10.5). In conclusion, I will summarize the continuum of practices of misrecognition and their relevance for social exclusion processes (10.6).

10.2 The Personal Name as a Sign of Humanity

"No mortal remains nameless," stated Homer in the Odyssey – and it seems that he was indeed right when he alleged that no human being was without a name. For, not only is it so that, according to current knowledge, the personal name is a solid component of all natural languages, it is also the case that we know of no culture in which people are not bestowed with a name. It appears as though the personal name plays a decisive role for our human existence. For this reason, in the Anglo-Saxon as well as the continental philosophical tradition, relevant studies have continuously been devoted to personal names. Although I am not able to reproduce the entire controversial debate surrounding the functionality of personal names here, I would like to point out two important characteristics.

First of all, the personal name is special in that it names an individual object without defining it conceptually. In this way, it is contrasted to definite descriptions which name an individual object by means of a specification. An example of this distinction is the personal name "Aristotle" compared to the description "Alexander the Great's teacher." While the latter does attempt to name a person by particular characteristics, the former names an individual without any specifications about the one named. The fact that the proper name can't be understood as a description was first pointed out by John Stuart Mill (Mill 1843: book 1, ch. 2, §§ 1–5) with his realist theory and then subsequently by Saul Kripke (Kripke 1980) who developed it into a pragmatic theory of the personal name. This means that it makes no conceptual declaration about the named person and that the person is named omitting any concrete characteristics. Therefore, the name is not in fact the word with the most abstract meaning but rather the most concrete: It names a unique social being. The personal name *individuates* its bearer as no other verbal expression can. We do not have to make any particular effort in order to complete the name, it just names us: at all times. Even if our characteristics change with time, the personal name names the same person when she/he is a child, an adult or in old age. Independent of all changes, it guarantees that "I" was the same yesterday as "I" am today and that "I" will be tomorrow. In this way, the personal name notably endows "selfsameness" as it was termed by Paul Ricœur (1992: 27–40). As a result, the personal name uniquely stabilizes our individual existence. This also becomes clear when we consider the basic difference between addressing someone with "you" versus addressing someone by name: The "you" address has no continuous reference: "You" retains its continuity only for the duration of the act of addressing, for in the moment where another addressee is spoken to, the "you" is someone different. "You", according to Benveniste, is a "mobile sign" whose reference is constituted in each case based on the performance of the utterance – due to its indexicality, the appellative power of the pronoun is rooted within the context (Benveniste 1971: 220). By contrast, the use of the personal name is stable across contexts; its naming does not only make reference to the addressed person in completely varied situations, but also in their absence – and it is for exactly this reason that it is unique. In contrast to "you", personal names constitute a "fixed sign" to which its reference adheres.[1] Thus, at all times, and even in the absence of the concerned person, the existence of a concrete "you" can be referred to and with that the situation-specific game of presence and absence can be transcended. For this reason, our individual existence is anchored in our personal names as it is in no other form of address. The personal name accords individuality throughout time and different contexts. Not least because of this does it serve as an identificatory sign in the signature: It is the identification of an unmistakable singularity.

[1] Cf. also Saul Kripke's concept of the *rigid designators* (Kripke 1980: 48–71).

We must, however, differentiate between this analytical meaning of the name and the social meaning, which only comes to the fore if we address the naming process. The latter will demonstrate to us that not only is it true that singularity is imparted upon individuals through names in what concerns space and time, but that *social belongings* are also endowed through them. The act of baptism is one social ritual which represents a clear example of this. The baptism ritual belongs to the "original performatives", referred to as such by John L. Austin; in other words, those classes of utterances which name and produce something in the same breath. However, the endowing power of naming is not only of interest here in that the priest dictates a name to the newborn before the eyes of the community and in doing so creates a singular societal being, but rather is representative of the child's belonging to the Christian community. In this case, the act of immersion into holy water can be read as the symbolization of immersion into the human community.[2] This social importance of the naming process, the endowment of belonging, is also apparent in other rites of passage. The transition into, for example, marriage, a monastery, or the priesthood is sealed with a new name. Here, naming represents a kind of social rebirth which is meant to make it clear that the individual now belongs to a new social group. This effect is also evidenced in very different cultural contexts: For example, in Borneo, the Kayan only grant their newborns a personal name after 8 months. If the child dies before the naming ritual, it is mourned with the same rituals as if it had been stillborn (Bering 1992: 186). There is thus a direct connection between the granting of a name and being treated as a social being with the corresponding burial ceremonies. What this and the previous examples demonstrate is that the name granting which occurs in our social practices does not only serve to create a clearly identifiable reference for someone from the very beginning, but rather also to mark her/his belonging. While the context of belonging can differ from case to case, all personal names do have one thing in common: The personal name vouches for the fact that we recognize someone to be a member of the human community. The name itself conveys a fundamental belonging to this species; in other words, having a name means that one is recognized as human.[3]

---

[2]Subsequently, Judith Butler emphatically referenced Austin regarding the constitutive power of the name. She writes that to obtain a name means "to have the very term conferred by which the recognition of existence becomes possible" (Butler 1997: 5). While Butler focuses on the subject-constituting power of the name, in the following context I am more concerned with the social belonging which accompanies the name.

[3]The much discussed question of what status we accord animals when we grant them a name naturally comes up in this case. Although I am not able to debate this in detail here, I would like to point out two important considerations concerning how this problem could be solved: First of all, for the most part, we grant animals with just one first name and not with a personal name which includes a first and last name. One could conclude from this that we follow a different practice in the naming of animals as compared to the naming of humans. And, indeed, I think we should keep in mind that the naming of a human being makes a different normative claim then does the naming of an animal. However, we should also be aware of the fact that the naming of animals causes the

The analytical and social research concerning the meaning of the personal name shows us that two extremes are condensed within it. On one hand, it names a *unique* being: an individual; on the other hand, a *general* being: a human. Individuality and sociality create the inseparable double-sided nature of the name granting process through which we are simultaneously produced as individuals and as members of the human community. However, the personal name's inimitable endowment power has a consequence: Its misrecognition has the ability to not only injure our individuality but also our very humanity.

10.3 The Politics of the Personal Name

The misrecognition of the personal name played an influential role in the German history of antisemitism. In this case, the Jewish name was used in a unique way as a means of enforcing the politics of social exclusion. The initial use of nicknames or derogatory names, which can be regarded as seemingly harmless and belonging to ordinary teasing practices, gradually developed into a systematically controlled policy which culminated in the complete disappropriation of the name. In order to understand this process, we must first return to the point of origin which enabled the naming politics in German-Jewish relations to attain such decisive importance in the first place.[4]

(i) The "baptism" of the German Jews: The decisive starting point of personal name policy is the year 1812. Up until this year, Jews were almost completely excluded from social life in the German States. During the Age of Enlightenment, however, the emancipation of the Jews was promoted: The forced segregation was to be repealed in favor of assimilation. The Jews were to leave behind their old identity and become a part of the "German community" as citizens. This social rebirth of the "German Jew" was directly tied to a naming law: Jews, who traditionally up until that point often only had a first name, were supposed to take on a last name. This new social belonging was meant to be confirmed through the names by a kind of collective baptism – the choice of name was consequently not subject to restrictions. On the contrary, Jews were even encouraged to take on Germanic names in order to be able to completely identify with German society. In this way, one was well and truly abiding by *Wilhelm v. Humboldt*'s quintessentially progressive inspired opinion about the Law of Emancipation which stated "that each individual who has no reason to ask about it for religious reasons, shall remain uncertain whether someone is Jewish or not" (Bering 1989: 198).

---

line of separation between animals and humans sometimes to become indistinct. For, to the degree to which we give animals names, we surprisingly often begin to treat them as social beings.

[4]The onomast Dietz Bering has done an excellent job of tracing the various stages of antisemitic political strategies in Germany regarding the personal name in several publications. His research, upon which I will draw below, is to this day unrivalled in the field (Cf. above all Bering 1992, 1989).

(ii) Restoration and incipient regulation: No later than the emergence of modern antisemitism in the late nineteenth century (representative of this is the time between the publication date of the antisemitic "founding works" by Gobineau in 1853 and Chamberlain in 1899) (Gobineau 1983, Chamberlain 1912), it was attempted to limit and reverse the emancipation process begun at the beginning of the century. The antisemitic movement demanded that clear measures concerning names must be established once again. This demand was doomed to failure, however, for in the same way that there were Christians with Old Testament names, there were now Jews with Germanic names. In order to stop anymore "misclarifications", the adoption of German names was therefore subjected by degree to strict regulations. Thus, in 1898, the right which had been given to Jews to freely choose their first names was retracted, and in turn, five years later the right to take on a name at baptism which had less of a Jewish background was revoked. At the same time that it was attempted to make it difficult for Jews to take on German names through such restrictions, Germans were supposed to be motivated to take on Germanic names. The following is a citation from the weekly newspaper *Schlesische Landwacht* in a 1924 issue: "He who loves Germany, should risk everything! A German man must have a German name."[5]

(iii) Marking and Segregation in NS: After the transfer of power, the National Socialists continued with already existing efforts: Not only should it be made easier for Germans with apparently Jewish names to take on Germanic names, but also, as was proposed in 1933 by the German Bar Association [*Deutscher Anwaltsverein*], all Jewish name changes were to be reversed. Consequently, on January 5, 1938, the law concerning the "changing of surnames and first names" did indeed come to pass. According to §7, a compulsory reversal of every Jewish name change before 1933 could be initiated. This process ended up being more difficult and less applicable than initially assumed by the Nazis, so that while the compulsory reversal process was in progress, an ordinance was released on January 1, 1939 which stated that the additional name of "Israel" or "Sarah" would be attached to every Jewish name which was not easily recognized as such. This enforced naming act was nearly the exact opposite to the 1812 emancipation edict: In that case it aimed at integrating the Jews into German society and making them indiscernible as Jews, whereas with this second "baptism act", the intention was to make the Jews visible in society so that their exclusion could be implemented all the more easily. This stigmatization process was intensified once again just two years later. Jews were subject to permanent visibility after the introduction of the Yellow Star on which the word "Jew" was resplendent in large letters: This visual stigma guaranteed their separation prior to any personal contact. The last chapter in the National Socialists' naming policy was finally begun with the incarceration of Jews into concentration camps and the beginning of the extermination policy: Upon arrival at the camp, names were

---

[5]"*Wer Deutschland liebt, soll auch das Letzte wagen! Ein deutscher Mann muß deutschen Namen tragen.*" Exemplar in "Geheimes Staatsarchiv Berlin/Dahlem" Justizministerium Rep. 84a, Nr. 2365, p. 91.

replaced with numbers. The sign of social existence was replaced with the number; the sign of serial death.

10.4 Insult, Degradation, and Debasement

After this short summary of the antisemitic personal name policy, I would like to examine the various naming practices used in this context with regard to their power to implement social exclusion. At this point I'd like to take up Margalit's distinction between insult and humiliation (Margalit 1996: 119). What Margalit means by this is that, where the former questions the reputation of a human being, the latter questions the human being as such. Therefore, the meaning of social exclusion differs in both cases: Where the insult tries to exclude its addressee from a social context *within* the social sphere, the humiliation tries to totally exclude a human being from all social contexts and, therefore, to situate it *beyond* the social sphere. While in his studies Margalit argues that the forms of misrecognition, that a "decent society" should care for, are primarily acts of humiliation, social philosopher Axel Honneth (1997) has tried to show that the insult can exert a dramatic form of misrecognition too. Following this latter argument, I would like to deepen Margalit's concept of insult by distinguishing between three different practices.[6]

(i) Transforming names into an insult: One of the most obvious forms of name misrecognition is the nickname. However, unlike an insult such as "Jewish Pig" [*Judensau*], which comes across as coarse and violent, nicknames always make use of a certain kind of linguistic wit in their transformation of the name. On a very basic rhetoric level, one example is the linking of a personal name and an attribute through a rhyme, such as in the nickname "*Itzig-Witzig*" [ger. "*witzig*" means "funny"]. The creativity used in this simple play on words can develop into elaborate metaphors. The following passage from Wilhelm Marr's 1873 appeal "Don't vote for Jews" can serve as an example here, where seemingly typical Jewish names are transferred into a Darwinist scenario: "If you open the cages in a zoological garden and set free the beasts of prey, shall the *fox* then not devour the chicken, shall the *wolf* not tear up the sheep, shall the *lion* not break into the herds, shall the *bear* not steal the honey? Yes, shall even the *deer* and the *stag* not graze to their hearts' content wherever they can?" (Bering 1989: 200)[7] Marr here takes up the semanticity of particular names and transfers them from their purely signifying use through a method of both decontextualization and recontextualization into a setting where they seem to reflect their bearers' social roles. Here, Marr makes use of the iterability of language – in other words, of the fact that no linguistic sign is permanently fixed in its meaning,

[6] A profound analysis of the relationship between the works of Margalit and Honneth is given by Jonathan Allen (1998). My distinction between the following three forms of insults is inspired by the different discrimination mechanisms that were pointed out by Carl Graumann and Margret Wintermantel in their research on discriminating speech acts (1989).

[7] Translator's note: The German names of these animals [*Fuchs*, *Wolf*, *Löwe*, *Bär*, *Reh*, *Hirsch*] were perceived as typical Jewish surnames.

but is able to take on new meanings in new contexts through grafting (Derrida 1982). Marr uses this openness of linguistic signs to incorporate seemingly Jewish names into a context where these names suddenly seem to unveil the characteristics of their addressee.

However, it would hardly occur to anyone to take these insults literally, for nicknaming is not primarily about the semantic meaning but about the creative transformation of names. This transformation is the reason why nicknames are laughed at. Consequently, the crucial point of the insult is not what they denote on a semantic level, but which social relationships they construct. The nickname produces a solidarity community in that those who laugh are included in this community while those who are laughed at are excluded from it. On this note, what is most insulting of all is the distinction which is made between those who belong and those who must remain on the outside. The nickname does not only indicate to the addressed Jews that they are not a part of the laughing German community, but at the same time claims the otherness of their existence. In this way, the insult reveals itself to be merely an act of *rejection* which marks its addressees as social outsiders.

(ii) Ascription of names as degradation: The "*Weiß vs. Goebbels* case is a well-known example of name ascription" (Bering 1983). When the future NSDAP minister of propaganda Joseph Goebbels came to Berlin in 1926 and was in search of a protagonist for his anti-Jewish propaganda, he chose Bernhard Weiß: a Jew from an assimilated family and a bearer of the "Iron Cross" [*Eisernes Kreuz*]. In the 1920s, Weiß was Berlin's vice police president and therefore presided over the largest Prussian administrative body of 20,000 men. This important public figure served Goebbels as a symbol for the "infiltration" of the most prestigious and highest positions in Germany by "Eastern Jews" ["*Ostjuden*"]. In his periodical *Der Angriff* – German for *The Attack* – Goebbels tried to unmask Weiß as the paradigmatic case of the Jews' dangerous mimicking nature. Goebbels used the practice of name ascription to support his claim that the reassuring mask of the police president was only a façade used to hide the "eternal Jew" lurking behind it. From this moment on, he would claim in his anti-police-column, "Watch out for rubber truncheons" [*Vorsicht Gummiknüppel*], that Bernhard Weiß' actual name was "Isidor."[8] Let us now take a closer look at what the ascription of this name means: For the anti-Semites, "Isidor" represented not only a typical Jewish name, but moreover was a description for a "typical Jew". Therefore in its manner of use regarding Weiß, the name did not serve as a proper noun for a person anymore but rather as a declaration about his character – a declaration that Goebbels would make explicit on many other occasions (ugly, stinky, obsessed with power, devious) and which condenses into a conglomeration of prejudices in the form of the name Isidor. In this case, the name becomes merely an ascription; in other words, it no longer refers to a person independent of his or her characteristics but rather makes a declaration about this

---

[8] "Yes, Isidor! I dare. I am breaking the spell. Under the cowardly protection of immunity, I call the child by its name. Isidor! The 'O' must be stretched to real length, and the 'R' must be rolled, and then the name will once again resound with unspeakable sweetness and strength. The gift of the East." Goebbels quoted in Bering (1989: 194) (unofficial translation).

person on a connotative level. This has the effect that the addressee is not named anymore as an individual, but is rather ascribed certain characteristics – in this case, this results in the typical array of contemporary antisemitic stereotypes.

In contrast to the insult, which attempts to label its addressees as social outsiders through the marking of their non-belonging, the degradation achieved by the use of the name "Isidor" works precisely because it ascribes devalorizing characteristics to Weiß and thus questions his authority and integrity. The decisive analytic difference between the insult and the degradation therefore lies in the fact that, while the former serves first and foremost to mark those concerned as social outsiders, the latter aims primarily at claiming their social inferiority. The rejecting dissociation is in this case, first and foremost, an ascribed devalorization. The degradation therefore consists in a twofold step of *devalorizing* and *ascribing*.

(iii) De-individuating names as debasement: It has been reported that acts of debasement were already occurring within the context of the 1812 Jewish Emancipation Bill. While this edict allowed the Jews in Prussia to freely choose their surnames, Jews in Western Galicia had to "receive" their new name – and this name was often full of scorn and disdain: "Trumpet Slime", "Banister" or "Garlic Smell"; such were the names that were conferred at this time. In contrast to the degradation which gives names a conceptual character, those acts of debasement rely exactly on the opposite mechanism: A concept is used as a personal name. This mechanism is also similarly deployed more than a 100 years later in the National Socialist "Jew Policy": Starting on September 19, 1941, all Jews had to wear the Yellow Star in a clearly-visible manner on their clothes; the Star featured the word "Jew" in letters which were supposed to look like Hebrew characters. This act corresponds precisely to the paradigmatic naming moment which Wittgenstein describes as the act of "attaching a label to a thing" (Wittgenstein 2001 [1953]: 6). The six-pointed Yellow Star was not only literally pinned on, it simultaneously served as a name. However, in this case it was not a true personal name, but rather a term for a particular class: From now on, the name of a Jew would be "Jew". Therefore, the power of the name to establish individuality increasingly disappeared. The Yellow Star instead transformed its bearer into part of an anonymous mass. This was exactly the effect intended by the Nazis. They were no longer interested in the power of naming to establish identity but, conversely, in subsuming individuals into one class. The Yellow Star was a visible sign of belonging at all times, and its concealment was severely punished. Its permanent visibility was the precondition for a comprehensive exclusion of Jews from public life: sitting on park benches, going to the theatre, using the tramway, and other forms of social participation were made impossible through the Star. In this way, the imposed name became a key element in the exclusion of Jews from everyday social life.

The debasement exerted through the Yellow Star differs from degradation in several ways: First, through state policy, the devalorizing power of the degradation was increased to general invalidation. To the same extent that the Jews were increasingly deprived of their rights, they were consequently treated as second-class citizens. Secondly, the degrading power of naming is increased through its legal anchoring.

It no longer solely depends on individual or collective acts of misrecognition, but is decreed by the state's sovereignty. Thus, ascription becomes an imposition. Thirdly, with the introduction of the Yellow Star, the name lost its function of establishing individuality. The individual became part of the masses where he or she no longer enjoyed any individual esteem. The decisive mechanisms underlying debasement thus consist of a threefold step of *invalidating*, *imposing,* and *de-individuating*.

10.5 Humiliation

Forcing individuals to wear the Yellow Star was not the end of the National Socialist policy of misrecognition. It was not until the concentration camps that a last, drastic step was implemented. Those who upon arrival were not sent directly from the platform to the gas chamber were subjected to extermination through labor under inhumane conditions. In her autobiographical records, Ruth Klüger describes the predominant communication structure as follows:

> During the following weeks I was to hear this hate-drenched tone all the time, and every time I cringed. It was a tone which stripped the person it addressed of her or his personhood, and at the same time held her like a lifeless thing; it was a tone no one should ever get used to, designed to intimidate and thereby deaden the sense of self. [. . .] Authority in Auschwitz meant disrespect for the prisoners to the point of rejecting their existence, their right simply to be (Klüger 2001: 94–95).

The aporia to which this kind of speech leads is noticed by Klüger herself shortly afterwards when she writes:

> This relentless need to insult those discriminated against, at their expense: It can only mean that it actually wasn't so easy for the 'master race' to deal with the death camps. One had to prove to oneself by exercising such flippant cruelty that these subhumans weren't human. And by proving it to oneself, they would actually become humans again, because they counted on them having a reaction to the insult. The insult would have been meaningless without the mortification that it was meant to produce.[9]

The address situation in the camp thus presents itself as follows: On the one hand, it denies its counterpart's humanity, but on the other hand, the act of denial itself is in turn an acknowledgment of this very humanity. As inhumane as the address may be, it always retains some remains of humanity. This leads to a state of contradiction between the recognition and the misrecognition of the addressee. Avishai Margalit called this problem the "paradox of dehumanization," and considers it to be representative of the unique nature of the National Socialist humiliation during the Shoah (Margalit and Motzkin 1996). The fact that this contradiction can increase to such an extremely critical degree becomes apparent not only in the fact that the camp SS

---

[9]This passage was not included in the English translation of the German original, due to some minor deviations from the German edition. It can be found in Klüger (1994: 143, unofficial translation).

reduced their speaking to the prisoners to a minimum, but above all in the way they dealt with the prisoners' names.

The rite of passage for those who were not murdered immediately upon their arrival at the Auschwitz camp was the tattooing of the number. In his autobiographical record "Survival in Auschwitz," Primo Levi describes this scene as a baptismal rite which assigns him a "new name." He remembers: "My name was 174, 517" (Levi 2008: 18). Now, *prima facie*, Levi seems to be right in thinking of the number as a name, because the number can in fact assume the individuating function of the personal name. It even seems to fulfill this task better than the name, since no overlapping of numbers can occur, as can happen with conventional personal names – and the associated administrative advantage is certainly one of the reasons why the Nazis decided to number the camp prisoners. However, the number does not seem to be a better name for those concerned. Only shortly after his description of the assignment of the number, Levi proclaims a particular uneasiness when he writes that the bluish number engraved under his skin seems "taunting" to him. What Levi depicts with such a moderate tone was experienced as a particularly forceful act of injury by many other prisoners. This is apparent in Ilse Stephan's record. She writes: "In the concentration camp, we were not humans, but only numbers! My camp number was 45,708" (Henneberg 1996: 82). As opposed to Levi, Stephan does not experience the number assignment as an act of naming but as the revocation of one's name. In her eyes, it is precisely a number which cannot be a name. However, if we want to understand this experience, we cannot inquire about the analytical meaning of names and numbers; we instead need to refer to their social meaning. The dehumanization experience linked to the assignment of the number is rooted in our way of dealing with it. We already saw that the human personal name fundamentally expresses belonging to the community of human beings. It is precisely this meaning that is undermined by the number, in that its function is not to name people but to name an object. The number is a unit, it is used for quantification, counting and charging; it is an element within a universal series of all possible objects. Through the number, a person is appropriated as an object and holds a functional value within a defined context. She or he becomes an element in an equation in which different values are calculated according to one another. Even if the number is therefore similar to the personal name when it comes to its identifying function, its social meaning is an entirely different one. Where the name humanizes, the number dehumanizes, because while the former indicates a belonging to the community of human beings, the latter stands for the marking of the non-human. This experience of dehumanization was reinforced by the fact that human beings who were reduced to numbers were actually treated as objects. This becomes apparent in what kind of death people died in the camps. For instance, in Claude Lanzmann's *Shoah* documentary, survivors recount how the Germans had prohibited them to refer to murdered prisoners as "the dead" or "victims." Instead, they had to talk about "figures," "dolls" or "marionettes" and refer to the murdered as "things." In the camps, no human beings were supposed to be carried to their graves; instead, things were to be destroyed. Giorgio Agamben sums up this process when he states: "In Auschwitz, people did not die, rather, corpses were produced. Corpses without death, non-humans whose decease is debased into a matter of serial production" (Agamben 1999: 72). Death was entirely devoid of any social ritual of human expression of grief; no ceremony whatsoever testified to the demise of a human being – the individual burial was replaced by the mass extermination of individual units.[10] This reifying function can be seen as an additional reason why the Nazis resorted to using numbers. The expropriation of the name was supposed to be a means for depriving the victims of their human visage. This was meant to facilitate the executioner's ability to annihilate humans like things without feeling any emotions.

Now, it is subject to discussion whether or not the number was introduced as a technical-administrative aid in order to allow for a smoother mass extermination procedure, or if it was supposed to be a morality disinhibiting tool for the perpetrators. In any case, for the victims it was undoubtedly linked to experiencing the revoking of their humanity.[11] At precisely this point, the expropriation of the name changes from being a form of debasement to becoming a form of *humiliation*. Regardless of what entitlements and rights we perceive as founded in human dignity, they are all based on the fact that we treat human beings as human beings. Now the humiliation does precisely the opposite: It treats human beings as if they were *things*. Or, as Margalit puts it: "The key concept for humiliation is rejection from the human commonwealth. But such rejection is not based on a belief or attitude that the rejected person is merely an object or an animal. The rejection consists of behaving *as if* the person were an object or an animal" (Margalit 1996: 112). So even if humiliation works in a very similar manner to debasement, it goes one decisive step further: It denies the very humanity of a human being by treating it as an object. In the erasure of the name, this step becomes completely apparent.

The loss of belonging to the community of human beings often implied that those concerned were no longer able to positively identify with their own self. Through this loss of self-esteem, the prisoners entered that very state of "wasted life" that represents the outmost vanishing point of social exclusion procedures. In the context of the camp, this incarnation of the wasted life is embodied in the character of the Muselmann, who is also often referred to as a "nameless hulk".[12] This expression was used to characterize those prisoners whose physical appearance was marked by extreme emaciation. Their physical decline became obvious due to skin discoloration, loss of hair, development of edema all over the body and the vulnerability to

---

[10]This also explains the importance of the struggle to turn the numbers back into names, as, for instance, Hans-Joachim Lang succeeded in achieving with 86 victims. For the families' grieving rituals, the knowledge about the time and place of their relatives' death is crucial (Lang 2004).

[11]Although I mainly focus in this paper on the fate of the persecuted Jews, in remembrance of all Shoah victims, I would like to point out that all other camp prisoners – Sinti and Roma, homosexuals, the mentally disabled, political opponents, or so-called asocials – were of course affected by dehumanization too.

[12]Margalit mentions the Muselmann as the paradigmatic figure of dehumanization: "Sometimes directed efforts were made to bring the victims of aggression to a state where they can be seen as non-human, as in the case of the Muselmann in the concentration camps" (Margalit 1996: 104). For a closer analysis of the figure of the Muselmann, see also the seminal contributions by Sofsky (1997: 200) and Agamben (1999).

all sorts of infections. In the course of their immiseration, they lost up to two thirds of their normal body weight. As Zdzislaw Ryn and Stanislaw Klodziński write in their study, unique up until today, the Muselmanns were avoided by all persons in the camp due to their physical infirmity: "No one felt compassion for the Muselmann, and no one felt sympathy for him either. The other inmates, who continually feared for their lives, did not even judge him worthy being looked at. For the prisoners, who collaborated, the Muselmann was a source of anger and worry; for the SS, he was merely useless garbage" (Ryn and Klodzińksi 1987: 127, unofficial translation). The Muselmann represented the figure who was excluded from nearly all social circles and who found him/herself at the point of utmost social isolation. This figure represented a fate which threatened all camp prisoners: *social death*. For, when the others had stopped addressing the Muselmann as a human being, he would lapse into total social apathy. His face became apathetic, his eyes became dull, and his voice grew increasingly faint. His speech, which could no longer hope for any kind of response, changed into mere muttering. But it was not only the social capacities to express oneself which were incrementally lost, it was also the basic social practices such as washing oneself or using the toilet; investment in social relations gradually faded away, only to finally disappear entirely. The Muselmann is therefore merely depicted as a "bundle of physical functions" (Améry 1980: 9), as a "living dead" (Carpi 1993: 17) who vegetates on the "threshold between life and death" (Agamben 1999: 47). In this state of social isolation, in most cases he inevitably progressed towards his own physical expiration. It is, however, significant to note that if the Muselmann was addressed once again by someone, he could sometimes be saved from his fate. This could be in the form of a letter from the outside, an arousing speech by a comrade, or through some human gesture.[13] The minimal amount of human recognition contained in such gestures created the beginning of a social bond which could provide the broken-down bodies with the strength they needed to survive.

10.6 Practices of Misrecognition

The history of the antisemitic personal name policy is one possible way to understand the social exclusion of Jews from the community of human beings in National Socialism. However, this is certainly not sufficient to comprehend the National Socialist politics of exclusion in its entirety. Apart from symbolic practices of exclusion, acts of physical violence also played an essential role: In the form of physical abuse, of pogroms and of forced deportations, they contributed to the Jews' exclusion from the social sphere. But just as it is important to emphasize that the Jews' exclusion cannot be understood solely by looking into the symbolic practices, it is just as crucial not to overlook the symbolic dimension contained in the acts

[13] See the testimonies collected in Ryn/Klozińksi (1987).

of physical violence (Margalit 1996: 88). It would be wrong to assume that practices of misrecognition only take place in a symbolic domain. In many cases, they are intimately linked to acts of physical violence. For instance, people were forced, under threat of violence, to abase themselves in numerous instances. Let me cite a particularly stirring example from Vienna in the 1930s, where anti-Semites coerced the local Jews to clean a cobbled street with toothbrushes (Stoecker 2003). This scenario plainly shows that the threat of physical violence was often simply a means for a symbolic purpose – the humiliation of those concerned. For, not only the threat, but also the actual execution of physical violence can have humiliation as its goal. For instance, the torture which was often conducted in the concentration camps did not only aim at inflicting pain upon the tortured. This act of violence was also used in order to remind them of their defenselessness and inferiority. Torture was not only a cruel ordeal, but also a *mise-en-scène* of misrecognition (Scarry 1985). It is precisely those traumata of misrecognition which are so difficult to overcome for many survivors. The wounds of the abuse may be scarred over, but the experience of humiliation remains and cannot be coped with: the fact that a human being could have done this to another human being. With torture, it becomes apparent in an exemplary way that symbolic misrecognition is a part of even the most brutal acts of violence. Nevertheless, the often lethal consequences of torture refer us to a decisive characteristic of National Socialism: As of 1939 at the latest, it was no longer about the social exclusion of Jews but their extermination. The goal of the persecution of the Jews was mass murder. However, being aware of this goal must not lead us to try and decipher the entire National Socialist persecution politics solely by considering its physical brutality. It had been prepared and supported to a large extent by a policy of social exclusion which operated through practices of misrecognition. By using the example of the history of the personal name, I attempted to outline a typology of such practices in this paper and will now resume them conclusively. I would like to mention at this point that these practices cannot always be clearly distinguished from one another, but that they appear as a continuum whose intensity gradually increases, and in which transitions are often not easily discernable.

(1) The *insult* is the most basic form of misrecognition, consisting mainly in a *rejection*. It aims to create a dissociation between the individuals involved. A negative social relationship is thereby created which marks the addressee as a social outsider.

(2) The *degradation* is a more powerful form of misrecognition than the insult in that it transforms the rejection into the twofold step of *devalorizing* and *ascribing*. In claiming to reveal certain negative characteristics or types of behavior of the addressee, it not only aims to create a dissociation between the individuals involved, but also to emphasize the social inferiority of the addressed person.

(3) The *debasement* consists of a threefold step of *invalidating*, *imposing*, and *de-individuating*. The addressed person is treated as an interchangeable member of a declassed group and not perceived anymore in his or her individuality. This aims at codifying the person as belonging to a worthless social class.

(4) The *humiliation* contains the three steps of *invalidating*, *imposing*, and *dehumanizing* in which an individual is treated *as if* she or he were a thing. Practices of

humiliation do not recognize their addressee anymore as a social being. They represent the utmost margin of social exclusion, in the sense that what is questioned is no longer the social value of a person, but her or his human existence in its entirety.

Translated by Jess Ring and Katharina Voss

References

Agamben, Giorgio. 1999. *Remnants of auschwitz: The witness and the archive*. New York, NY: Zone.

Allen, Jonathan. 1998. Decency and the struggle for recognition. *Social Theory and Practice* 24: 449–469.

Améry, Jean. 1980. *At the mind's limits: Contemplations by a survivor of Auschwitz and its realities*. Bloomington, IN: Indiana University Press.

Bauman, Zygmunt. 2004. *Wasted lives: Modernity and its outcasts*. Cambridge: Polity.

Benveniste, Emile. 1971. The nature of the linguistic sign. In *Problems in general linguistics*, ed. Emile Benveniste, 217–222. Miami, FL: Miami University Press.

Bering, Dietz. 1983. Der Kampf um den Namen Isidor. Polizeivizepräsident Bernhard Weiß gegen Gauleiter Joseph Goebbels. *Beiträge zur Namensforschung* 18: 121–153.

Bering, Dietz. 1989. Gewalt gegen Namen. Ein sprachwissenschaftlicher Beitrag zur Geschichte und Wirkung des Alltagsantisemitismus. *Muttersprache. Zeitschrift zur Pflege und Erforschung der deutschen Sprache* 99: 193–212.

Bering, Dietz. 1992. *The stigma of names: Antisemitism in German daily life*, 1812–1933. Michigan: Michigan University Press.

Butler, Judith. 1997. *Excitable speech*. New York, NY: Routledge.

Carpi, Aldo. 1993. *Diario di Gusen*. Turin: Einaudi.

Castel, Robert. 2002. *From manual workers to wage laborers: Transformation of the social question*. London: Transaction.

Goffman, Erving. 1961. *Asylums: Essays on the social situation of mental patients and other inmates*. New York, NY: Anchor.

Chamberlain, Houston S. 1912 [1899]. *The foundations of the nineteenth century*. London: The Bodley Head.

Dahrendorf, Ralf. 1988. *The modern social conflict: An essay on the politics of liberty*. New York, NY: Weidenfeld & Nicolson.

Derrida, Jacques. 1982. Signature event context. In *Margins of philosophy*, ed. Jacques Derrida, 307–330. Chicago, IL: Chicago University Press.

Foucault, Michel. 2003. *Abnormal: Lectures at the college de France*, 1974–1975. New York, NY: Picador.

Gobineau, Arthur. 1983 [1853–55]. *An essay on the inequality of the human races*. Los Angeles, CA: Noontide.

Graumann, Carl, and Margret Wintermantel. 1989. Discriminatory speech acts: A functional approach. In *Stereotyping and prejudice. Changing conceptions*, eds. Daniel Bar-Tal et al., 184–204. New York, NY: Springer.

Henneberg, Ilse. 1996. *Vom Namen zur Nummer. Einlieferungsritual in Konzentrationslager*. Bremen: Donat.

Honneth, Axel. 1995. *The struggle for recognition: The grammar of social conflicts*. Cambridge: MIT Press.

Honneth, Axel. 1997. A society without humiliation? On Avishai Margalit's draft of a 'decent society'. *European Journal of Philosophy* 5(3): 306–324.

Klüger, Ruth. 1994. *Weiter leben. Eine Jugend*. München: DTV.

Klüger, Ruth. 2001. *Still alive: A holocaust girlhood remembered.* New York, NY: The Feminist Press.
Kripke, Saul A. 1980. *Naming and necessity.* Cambridge, MA: Harvard University Press.
Lang, Hans-Joachim. 2004. *Die Namen der Nummern. Wie es gelang, die 86 Opfer eines NS-Verbrechens zu identifizieren.* Hamburg: Hoffmann und Campe.
Levi, Primo. 2008. *Survival in Auschwitz.* New York, NY: Classic House.
Margalit, Avishai. 1996. *The decent society.* London: Harvard University Press.
Margalit, Avishai, and Gabriel Motzkin. 1996. The uniqueness of the holocaust. *Philosophy and Public Affair* 25(1): 65–83.
Mill, John Stuart. 1843. *A system of logic.* London: Elibron.
Ricœur, Paul. 1992. *Oneself as another.* Chicago, IL: Chicago University Press.
Ryn, Zdzislaw, and Stanislaw Klodzińksi. 1987. An der Grenze zwischen Leben und Tod. Eine Studie über die Erscheinung des Muselmanns im Konzentrationslager. *Auschwitz-Hefte* 1: 89–154.
Scarry, Elaine. 1985. *The body in pain: The making and unmaking of the world.* Oxford: Oxford University Press.
Sofsky, Wolfgang. 1997. *The order of terror: Concentration camp.* Princeton, NJ: Princeton University Press.
Stoecker, Ralf. 2003. Menschenwürde und das Paradox der Entwürdigung. In *Menschenwürde – Annäherung an einen Begriff,* ed. Ralf Stoecker, 133–151. Wien: Öbv & Hpt.
Taylor, Charles. 1994. *Multiculturalism: Examining the politics of recognition.* Princeton, NJ: Princeton University Press.
Wittgenstein, Ludwig. 2001 [1953]. *Philosophical investigations.* Oxford: Blackwell.

Chapter 11
Absolute Poverty

Human Dignity, Self-Respect, and Dependency

Peter Schaber

Abstract The paper deals with the question of whether poverty as such violates the dignity of persons. It is argued that it does. This is, it is argued, not due to a lack of basic goods, nor to the fact that poverty prevents persons from enjoying the rights they have, particularly the right to bodily integrity. Poverty does violate dignity, so it is argued, insofar as poor people are dependent on others in a degrading way.

11.1 Introduction

Is the dignity of all people living in poverty violated? Does poverty as such violate dignity? Or does this apply only to severe forms of it? One reason why it is unclear whether poverty can be considered a violation of human dignity is at least partly due to the fact that poverty, in contrast to other violations of dignity, is normally not intentionally brought about by third persons. It is a state of affairs that is – if at all – only indirectly caused by others. In most cases, poverty is an unintended side-effect of the acts of many. Often, it does not result from acts at all but from omissions. When we talk about violations of dignity, however, we are normally concerned with what individuals do to each other. For example, we hold it to be a violation of human dignity if one person humiliates another. The former individual's acts violate the latter's dignity. In the case of poverty, others do not do anything comparable to the poor. Therefore, it is unclear in what way poverty might violate human dignity. In what follows, I will try to remedy this lack of clarity.

Some preliminary remarks are in order on the notion of poverty: Scholars as well as practitioners commonly distinguish between relative and severe (absolute?) poverty (Spicker 1998). Relative poverty is measured as a standard of basic needs

P. Schaber (✉)
Centre for Ethics, University of Zürich, Switzerland
e-mail: schaber@philos.uzh.ch

P. Kaufmann et al. (eds.), *Humiliation, Degradation, Dehumanization*, Library of Ethics and Applied Philosophy 24, DOI 10.1007/978-90-481-9661-6_11,

acknowledged by a certain society. The notion of basic needs may be irritating, as it normally refers to claims a human being has *qua* human being. Relative poverty, however, refers to society-specific basic claims. In wealthy societies, the catalogue of basic needs will be more comprehensive than in poor societies. According to the standard definition by the World Bank, individuals live in severe poverty if they have less than 1.25 dollars a day. These persons, it could be said, lack goods essential for any form of a good life in any imaginable society in the world. This notion of poverty presented in this brief discussion will be applied in what follows.

11.2 Dignity as a Claim to Be Respected

The following description of severe poverty by Robert McNamara, former director of the World Bank, indicates that severe poverty at least could constitute a violation of human dignity:

> [Absolute poverty] as a condition of life so characterized by malnutrition, illiteracy, disease, squalid surroundings, high infant mortality and low life expectancy as to be beneath any reasonable definition of human decency. (Singer 1993: 219)

In order to be able to determine why and in what way severe or relative poverty violates dignity, we first of all have to establish what it means to have dignity. What is it that is violated when human dignity is violated?

The dignity I will be concerned with is *inherent dignity*, a form of dignity that must be distinguished from forms of contingent dignity (Balzer et al. 1998: 17–20). This inherent dignity is what the German Constitution refers to in stating that, "Human dignity shall be inviolable." It is also addressed in the preamble of the United Nations' Universal Declaration of Human Rights that talks about the "inherent dignity of all members of the human family." Inherent dignity is characterized by the fact that it cannot be acquired, lost, or regained. What I call contingent dignity, on the contrary, can be acquired, lost or regained. Different forms of contingent dignity can be distinguished: There is social dignity, which is related to social functions. It is the dignity of a bishop or a judge, for example, who have dignity *qua* office holders. There is expressive dignity, which refers to a person's behavior. This form of dignity is what we talk about when we say that a person bears her defeat with dignity.

One important aspect of the inherent dignity of a person, distinguishing it from forms of contingent dignity, is that it can be violated. It can be violated because it is something normative. We can act in a way that is right or wrong in regard to it. That inherent dignity is something normative does not mean that it is a normatively- or morally-relevant property, like, for example, the capability to feel pain. For, unlike dignity, morally-relevant properties of this kind cannot be violated. Dignity, however, can be violated. This is expressed, for example, in Article 1 of the Constitution, stating that "human dignity *shall* be inviolable" – therefore implying that dignity is something that can be violated. Normatively-relevant properties like the capability to feel pain, in contrast, cannot be violated. Even if I inflict pain on another human being – which, of course, is possible – I do not violate this person's capability to feel pain but rather I violate a right or a claim he or she has. And this is what someone does who violates another person's dignity: He or she violates a *claim* that this person can legitimately assert.

What claim does the term "human dignity" refer to? If we assume that the humiliation of a person violates their dignity, we could say: The dignity of a person relates to the claim to be acknowledged as a being that is allowed to live his or her life according to his or her own ideas – in other words, to live a life with self-respect. This is the claim against which humiliation is directed. Accordingly, one could say: The *claim to self-respect* is inherent to dignity (Schaber 2007a). To be sure, what is meant here should not be mistaken for self-esteem.[1] Rather, self-respect must be understood under the rubric of the right to live one's *own* life. Self-respect consists in realizing this right; it is not a claim to self-esteem, i.e. to believe in, or think much of, oneself.

The claim to self-respect, and as such human dignity, is paradigmatically violated, for example, in the case of torture. This is not due to the pain inflicted on the victims but to the fact that torture humiliates them. Torture is humiliating because it is used to make it clear to the victims that they do not count, that they are fully dominated. The victims are no longer accepted as independent beings. Torture is a violation of dignity regardless of whether or not the victim *feels* humiliated. Although torture often causes feelings of humiliation, it does not necessarily and inevitably provoke such feelings. Regardless of whether a person survives torture psychologically unharmed or not, he or she has been humiliated. He or she has been treated as someone whose interests do not count. When the Nazis, during their takeover of power in Vienna in 1938, forced Jewish citizens to clean the pavement with tooth brushes, they intended to show to the world that these persons did not count (Margalit 1996: 127, Stoecker 2003: 135). They treated them like things, and as such like something that cannot plausibly be regarded as having any claims.

Slaves are also fully dominated. To enslave human beings is humiliating, as the concerned individuals are denied any right to assert claims. It would be humiliating, and as such constitute a violation of human dignity, even if the slaveholders cared for the slaves and provided for their wellbeing. Given that slaves would then still not be acknowledged as independent beings, their treatment would still be humiliating. They would live under degrading conditions, regardless of whether or not they would feel humiliated or whether or not they were in a bad physical condition.

[1] See also Margalit (1996: 44): "[S]elf-respect and self-esteem [. . .] can and should be distinguished [. . .]."; and Margalit (1996: 24): "Self-respect, in contrast to self-esteem, is the honour a person grants herself solely on the basis of the awareness that she is a human." However, it is not clear whether Margalit is really able to distinguish between self-respect and self-esteem. His paradox of humiliation consists in the fact that we have no reason to feel humiliated when being treated in a humiliating way. What is affected is self-esteem. Humiliation gives us a reason to esteem ourselves less. Either way, it is a violation of rights.

11.3 Lack of Basic Goods

What is it then that is humiliating about a life in poverty? One obvious answer refers to the lack of basic goods: The dignity of a person is violated by the fact that he or she lacks goods essential for a good life. This is the case when one lives in severe poverty. A poor person does not have at his or her disposal the goods that are essential for any form of a good life in any imaginable society, and this, one may argue, is humiliating.

I do not think this suggestion is correct. Let us consider the following example: For religious reasons, Paul has decided to live an extremely ascetic life. Secluded from society, he lives a religious life, and the goods he has at his disposal are scarcely sufficient for his survival. He does not have access to the goods that are essential for a good life. With a view to material goods he is as bad off as many people living on less than 1.25 dollars a day. That is all he wants; it is other things he cares about.

Do the conditions under which Paul lives violate his dignity? One reason against this conclusion is the fact that he has chosen this form of life and the lack of vitally important goods that goes with it. A lack of vitally important goods can only be a violation of human dignity if it is forced upon the person concerned. Hence, one could say: Poverty violates human dignity only insofar as the lack of goods essential for any form of a good life is forced upon the victims.

This suggestion, however, is not plausible either. The following example makes this clear: A castaway finds himself on an uninhabited island with water, but no food. Nobody knows about the fate of our castaway who has no possibility of getting in touch with anybody. He will die a slow and cruel death from starvation.

This, no doubt, is horrible for him. Death from starvation involves great suffering and pain. But is our castaway's dignity violated? What happens to him is bad, very bad indeed, but it is not humiliating. His self-respect is not affected. Within the limits of what nature allows him to do, he remains an independent being. I will come back to this point later in the chapter.

11.4 No Rights (Shue)

Following Henry Shue, one could argue that poverty is degrading because it deprives poor persons of the ability to realize their rights:

> No one can, if at all, enjoy any right that is supposedly protected by society if he or she lacks the essentials for a reasonable healthy and active life. Deficiencies in the means of subsistence can be just as fatal, incapacitating, or painful as violations of physical security. The resulting damage or death can at least as decisively prevent the enjoyment of any right as can the effects of security violations. (Shue 1996: 24–25)

Whoever lacks vitally important goods, so Shue's idea goes, is unable to realize any other rights like property rights, the right to political participation, the right to education, etc. This, however, is true also for our ascetic. Although he could do things that would enable him to realize rights in the future, in his isolated asceticism he is not able to do so. If poverty were a violation of dignity because it disables individuals from realizing their rights, the dignity of our ascetic would be violated. This, however, is not what makes poverty a violation of human dignity. It is not the fact that an individual is unable to realize his or her right to property or education that violates dignity. As we will see later on, it is rather the fact that poverty disables individuals to assert claims altogether.

Furthermore, it is unclear whether the inability to realize rights is limited to individuals who live in absolute deprivation. Shue writes: "[E]veryone has a basic right not to be allowed to die or to be seriously ill" (Shue 1996: 25).

If we make sure that people survive and are not severely ill (as far as that is possible), we enable people to realize their rights. And if dignity is only violated if these absolutely minimal provisions are no longer provided, then the dignity of many to whose situation McNamara's description of severe poverty applies would not be violated.

11.5 The Right to Bodily Integrity

One could also argue that poverty constitutes a violation of human dignity because it very often involves a violation of the right to bodily integrity. Persons who live in poverty are often the victims of physical violence; women, for example, are often the victims of rape. This particularly applies to individuals who live in severe poverty – in slums, for example. These violations of the right to bodily integrity are no doubt violations of human dignity. Poverty, or at least severe poverty, can thus lead to violations of dignity.

If this is what violates the dignity of individuals living in severe poverty, it is, however, not poverty as such that violates human dignity. The violation of dignity, according to the present suggestion, consists in physical violence to which the poor are particularly exposed. The factor that violates human dignity, then, is not an aspect that is necessarily part of poverty. That it is not is implied in the fact that people could be protected against physical violence without their poverty being decreased. Empirically this may be unlikely, yet it is not impossible. Physical violence is not part of what it means to be poor. Accordingly, with a view to the current suggestion, it is not poverty itself that violates dignity.

11.6 What is Degrading About Poverty?

Poverty, I have argued, does not violate the dignity of human beings because poor people lack vitally important goods. Neither does it violate dignity because poor people, due to poverty, are unable to realize their rights. Poverty violates human dignity, because, and insofar as, poor people are *dependent* on others in a specific way. It violates dignity when it is responsible for the fact that a person's survival and her way of survival are placed at the mercy of others. Individuals who have to live in poverty are not able to stand up to others when it comes to securing their own survival. This does not have to be the case with every form of poverty. There may be forms of relative poverty that allow individuals to live independent lives and stand their ground. Yet even individuals living in relative poverty may depend on others in a degrading way. If a person needs a pair of shoes and, in order to get them, has to file an application at the social security office, she may rightly see this as degrading. The more severe the poverty, the stronger this special form of dependence becomes, for the dependence concerned here rests upon a lack of options from which one can choose. And, given that the options decrease with the severity of poverty, the dependence grows as the poverty becomes more severe.

The dependence of the poor is not necessarily always exploited by others. However, it exists even if the better-off mean well towards the poor and – to take our example – donate the shoes they need. The situation is degrading for the solicitant, even if help is granted. The humiliating dependence on others consists in the lack of options. Of course, others can use this dependence for their own ends and exploit the (emergency) situation of poor people, which in fact happens often enough. This is a violation of dignity in itself, but poverty is a violation of dignity even in the absence of such reactions – at least when, as a consequence of poverty, individuals cannot stand up to others, as independent beings.

This does not apply to our castaway. He does not depend on others, simply because there are no others in his situation. He experiences great suffering. His fate, however, is not at the mercy of others, but at the mercy of (impersonal) nature. And this allows him to live a life according to his own ideas and convictions, until his physical forces will cease. The aforementioned ascetic does not live in dependence on others either. On the contrary, he lives an independent life that resembles a life in poverty only insofar as he lacks goods that are essential for any form of a good life in any imaginable society. This, however, does not constitute a violation of dignity. For the ascetic lives a life according to his own convictions.

The dependence on others and the inability to stand up to them violates a person's self-respect, for in order to respect oneself, one must be able to live a life of one's own choice and to interact with others as an independent being. Yet this is possible only if one has options and one's survival is not entirely at the mercy of others.[2] And this, in turn, presupposes that one has access to the goods and capabilities essential for a good life. This requires not only material goods but also abilities to enable the realization of options. The claim to self-respect therefore relates not only to a

[2]This is a phenomenon that we can also find in the context of torture. The victim is at the mercy of the torturer, evident in Jean Améry's descriptions of his experiences (Améry 1977: 55).

right to subsistence[3] but also a right to basic education.[4] Only when these rights are fulfilled is one able to lead a life in self-respect. The rights to subsistence and basic education must not be equated with the right to self-respect. These rights protect goods that enable individuals to stand up to others. The claim to self-respect entails them as means necessary to its realization.

At this point, some will note that we all depend on one another in many ways. Children, for example, depend on their parents. At least during the first years of their lives, they are placed at the mercy of their parents or educators. This dependence of children, however, does not constitute a violation of dignity; this is, I would argue, because infants do not yet have a claim to self-respect. This claim comes with the ability to lead one's own life; for one's dignity is violated only if one has this ability but is hindered from using it by others or by circumstances. Of course, children must be treated in a way that enables them to realize the claim to self-respect in the future.[5] Yet this does not imply that their dependence constitutes a violation of dignity.

But we are all, many will nevertheless object, dependent on each another in many ways. How can dependence on others be considered a violation of dignity if it is a part of the *conditio humana*? The dependence I am concerned with here is a special form of dependence. It applies when, in order to acquire vitally important goods, I have to rely on others without having any choice. It is the lack of reasonable options that makes dependence on others degrading. Of course, everyone depends on others' willingness to, say, sell food. Nevertheless, as long as one can choose between different ways of obtaining basic goods, and as such has options, this form of dependence is not degrading.

If it is this special form of dependence that makes poverty a violation of dignity, it is clear that poverty violates dignity regardless of whether or not it is self-induced. And accordingly, if it is the case that recognition of the dignity of other persons places upon us an obligation of respect (Schaber 2007b), then it is also the case that those who are able to prevent poverty have a moral duty to do so, no matter whether or not they have contributed to it.[6] The dependence on others that poor people experience violates their dignity. To abolish poverty is the moral duty of those who have the ability to do so.

---

[3]As Henry Shue has in mind when he writes: "By minimal economic security, or subsistence, I mean unpolluted water, adequate food, adequate clothing, adequate shelter, and minimal preventive health care" (Shue 1996: 23).

[4]See Nickel (2007: 141): "The right to basic education focuses on literacy, numeracy, and preparation for social participation, citizenship, and economic activity. It helps orient social rights towards action, choice, self-help, mutual aid."

[5]See Scanlon (1998: 185): "Infants and young children are not separate kinds of creatures. Rather, infancy and childhood are, in normal cases, stages in the life of a being who will have the capacity for judgement-sensitive attitudes."

[6]If one has contributed to the poverty of others, it is, of course, one's duty to fight this poverty as well, and in this case it is a duty of compensation.

References

Améry, Jean. 1977. *Jenseits von Schuld und Sühne*. Stuttgart: Klett-Cotta.
Balzer, Philipp et al. 1998. *Menschenwürde vs. Würde der Kreatur*. Freiburg: Alber.
Margalit, Avishai. 1996. *The decent society*. Cambridge, MA: Harvard University Press.
Nickel, James. 2007. *Making sense of human rights*. Malden, MA: Blackwell.
Scanlon, Thomas. 1998. *What we owe to each other*. Cambridge, MA: Harvard University Press.
Schaber, Peter. 2007a. Achtung vor Personen. *Zeitschrift für philosophische Forschung* 4: 423–438.
Schaber, Peter. 2007b. Globale Hilfspflichten. In *Weltarmut und Ethik*, eds. Barbara Bleisch and Peter Schaber, 139–152. Paderborn: Mentis.
Shue, Henry. 1996. *Basic rights. Subsistence, affluence, and US foreign policy*. Princeton, NJ: Princeton University Press.
Singer, Peter. 1993. *Practical ethics*. Cambridge: Cambridge University Press.
Spicker, Paul. 1998. Poverty. In *Encyclopedia of applied ethics* (3), ed. Ruth Chadwick, 1625–1632. San Diego, CA: Academic Press.
Stoecker, Ralf. 2003. Menschenwürde und das Paradox der Entwürdigung. In *Menschenwürde. Annäherungen an einen Begriff*, ed. Ralf Stoecker, 133–151. Wien: Öbv & Hpt.

Chapter 12
Relative Poverty

On a Social Dimension of Dignity

Julia Müller and Christian Neuhäuser

Abstract Consumption and material wealth are important values for most people living in affluent societies. Unless we opt for an ascetic life, caring about material goods is rather inescapable; we all need to consume at least basic goods like food and shelter, and most of us desire to have at least some material belongings. This said, there seems to be nothing wrong with this state of affairs, it is just how things are. But there are two facts that turn the whole issue of consumption and possession into a moral question of great importance. One major issue is that there are many people in the world who are so very poor compared to the people living in affluent societies. That in one part of the world people are struggling for survival while in another people dwell in the palaces of consumption is a major question of global justice, a question political philosophy is putting more and more attention to, and rightfully so (Pogge 2001, 2007), but this is not the question we are concerned with in this paper. We want to look at the second issue, which is the wealth differences within affluent societies and the high income gaps there, a moral problem totally different from the global situation.

12.1 Introduction

On the one hand, there are rich people in our affluent societies who care a lot about, what we call, luxurious goods, like fancy dresses and nice cars, and they seem to suffer a great deal if they can't afford the newest and most hip items. On the other hand, we can observe in the same affluent societies how people collect returnable bottles from garbage bins or offer to clean windscreens at red traffic lights for a few cents. Obviously these people don't do these things for fun, but they desperately need to earn some money in order to be able to purchase their basic goods. Something seems to be seriously wrong with the concurrence of those two extremes within affluent societies. But what exactly is so irritating about this clearly visible

C. Neuhäuser (✉)
Department of Philosophy, Ruhr-University Bochum, Germany
e-mail: Christian.neuhaeuser@rub.de

P. Kaufmann et al. (eds.), *Humiliation, Degradation, Dehumanization*,
Library of Ethics and Applied Philosophy 24, DOI 10.1007/978-90-481-9661-6_12,

concurrence of relative poverty and the opulence of the rich? Why is it that we think collecting bottles from garbage bins is humiliating while being in a fret about the newest designer dress somehow appears to be a luxurious problem? Why – as we want to argue – is the first scenario an issue of self-respect, while the latter is just a prestige problem? There are different possible answers to the question why that is so.

One first answer would point at the fact that poor people just have too little. They cannot afford to buy the essentials that are really needed in order to live a decent life. When someone has to collect bottles out of garbage bins, she is engaging in an activity that is seen to be humiliating exactly because she has no choice, but must do something degrading and embarrassing – something dirty so to speak – in order to be able to have access to those basic goods. This answer points to the fact that absolute poverty is humiliating and therefore a state of affairs that should be abolished for ethical reasons. An open question is how narrow the definition of absolute poverty should be. One very narrow definition would only see extreme life-endangering poverty as absolute poverty, where only the most basic goods need to be provided. A broader definition would include more goods like the ability to play, to take part in political life, or to access information. Such a broader definition would have the advantage that what goods are needed is somehow relative to the conditions of a society. If information is mostly provided by television then a TV becomes a basic good in this given society.

But is this society-relative concept of absolute poverty really all we care about, when we think that someone is humiliated through her poverty? Imagine a different situation: Think of a school class where almost all of the kids have lots of different nice dresses because their parents are fairly well off. Among these youngsters, there is just one poor boy, whose mom is a single mother with three children. This woman obviously can't go to work because she has lots of important work to do at home. Therefore, she has to rely on welfare aid. Her boy has one pair of cheap shoes, two pairs of jeans and a couple of not very fancy t-shirts and sweaters; more she cannot afford. Still, this boy has much more than many people in this world have, and his basic needs are surely taken care of. He is not, therefore, suffering from absolute poverty in the strict sense, because he is not starving. He is also not suffering from absolute poverty in the wider sense, because he has access to basic goods. But is he not still a poor boy? He in fact is humiliated every day, because he clearly sees the gross difference between himself and his classmates, and if those kids are not a nice bunch, they might even ridicule him because of his poverty, and actively show disrespect and diminish his self-respect in doing so.

Imagine another example: A young woman grew up in a very rich neighbourhood. Her family owns a middle-sized company and some real-estate. Now the company suddenly doesn't run so well anymore, and there is some trouble with the structure of their buildings. The family is still very well off; they just have to cut down on some things most people would deem as unimportant. One of the things they cannot afford in this troublesome time is buying their daughter the newest Gucci dress for the annual ball of her tennis club. She has to wear one of the dresses of the previous years. To the young woman, this feels very humiliating, as would be not attending the ball without a good reason. She seriously considers hurting herself in order to have a good excuse for not going to the ball.

Now what is strange about these two cases is that both, the boy and the young woman, feel humiliated, because they have less than others, but it is only the boy most people would think of as poor. We might even want to say that the boy is justified in feeling humiliated, while the young woman is not. But why is this so, and what marks the difference? One prominent answer would identify equality as the core value which is at issue here. Considering the standard in this given affluent society, the young woman is still living high above average while the boy is living far below. So it is this social equality problem that explains why the boy is poor and the woman is not, and it also gives appeal to a moral demand for the boy to better his social condition, exactly because equality is the core principle of distributive justice (Rawls 1971, Sen 1980, Cohen 1993).

This is an important insight, and we agree that equality is a fundamental value, but in this paper we want to argue that the issue of equality is not the only consideration here in relation to relative poverty as a phenomenon distinct from absolute poverty. Describing the situation of the poor boy as humiliating and not only unjust hints at the point we are concerned about. We want to argue that relative poverty is a kind of violation of human dignity, because it is humiliating and destructive to the agent's self-respect. One important insight of this description should be that it not only explains why relative poverty is a serious problem for the humiliated poor, but for all of us. The reason is that we all take part in social interaction that constitutes the degrading situation for the poor.

We cannot escape the fact that most of us – the doing-well middle class, living between the extreme poles of poverty and opulence – are part of the reason why the poor are justified in feeling humiliated. It is our relative wealth and the advantages that go hand in hand with it that are the cause for their humiliation. Remember the situation of a person collecting returnable bottles from a garbage bin. If we stand by and observe what she is doing and she notices us, we will be the cause for her humiliation. We surely don't want to, but can't help it, because the situation alone – regardless of our behaviour, if we look away or not, or if we are even actually there or not – will scream into her face that what she is doing is highly embarrassing and a serious threat to her self-respect.[1] The only thing we can do is try to act as decently as possible and work for a society where all kinds of shameful poverty are abolished.

With this in mind, in this article we want to explore the relation between relative poverty and human dignity in three steps. First, we will have a closer look at what relative poverty is about and what distinguishes it from absolute poverty. Second, we will analyze why describing relative poverty as unjust inequality is, while neglecting its humiliating dimension, nonetheless important. Finally, we will try to elaborate

[1]It is, of course, possible that someone decides freely to make a living by collecting returnable bottles and even accept that this means to live in relative poverty. But here, like with all other important goods, it should be clear that it is before all else the involuntary deprivation that is morally problematic.

the argument why relative poverty is a violation of human dignity by pointing to the social dimension of self-respect. In doing so we want to clarify that relative poverty is distinct from absolute poverty, but still an all-too-common phenomenon which could reasonably be expected to provoke moral concern.

12.2 Applied Absolute Poverty

One prominent way of understanding relative poverty construes it as a concept not very distinct from absolute poverty (Schaber 2007, Schaber, Chapter 11, this volume). It describes absolute poverty as sensitive to social circumstances and declares it to be relative in this sense. While in many societies it is not necessary to have shoes, a TV, or even a car in order not to be poor, this may indeed be the case in other societies. It is necessary, therefore, to apply absolute poverty to special social circumstances if we want to find out what counts as poverty and what does not. This rings true, because we can surely think of a society where not having shoes is an indicator of poverty and others where it is not. But does the same count for TVs or cars? Can we really imagine that people are poor just because they do not have a TV or a car? And if not, is that because our imagination is not original enough or because poverty, TVs, and cars just don't have anything to do with each other? An account of relative poverty as applied absolute poverty can provide answers to all these questions, exactly because it starts from the basic idea of abstract absolute poverty and applies it to different socioeconomic contexts.

The central idea of absolute poverty is the claim that poverty is about lacking the most basic goods which are necessary for a good, or at least decent, life (Singer 1993: 218–221). If we can imagine a society where cars are basic goods and needed for having a chance to live a good life, then not having a car is in fact an indicator of being poor. At the core of this concept lies the idea of basic goods. Only when we have understood what those basic goods are does it become clearer how absolute poverty can be relative to social circumstances and maybe even be about not having cars. Moreover, the term "basic goods" establishes the link to decency which in turn can provide the normative groundwork for poverty as a "thick" concept not only describing certain situations but also indicating why their existence is morally wrong. But what are these basic goods?

The most prominent and well developed account of basic goods is neo-Aristotelian in spirit and offered by Martha Nussbaum (Nussbaum 1992, 1993). She produces a list of ten (sometimes eleven) goods, which she declares to be basic, because life cannot be decent without them, or at least not decent without having access to them, as Amartya Sen sharpened the account (Sen 1993). Here the decent life is understood as a necessary base for being able to live a good life. In this sense, basic goods are needed to have a chance to live a decent and good life. Among those goods on Nussbaum's list are food, shelter, and medical treatment, but also the possibility to take part in public life, to travel freely and to play. Now we can see how not only shoes but also TVs and cars come into the picture. If we imagine a society where much of public life happens on TV and taking part in public life is a basic good, then having a TV is essential to have one's basic goods fulfilled. This describes the situation in most industrial societies. Likewise, if we imagine a society where people cannot move freely or travel properly without having a car, then cars can indeed be needed to enable access to a basic good. Societies of this kind actually do exist. Think of American suburbs without any public transportation at all and long ways to the next supermarket, medical specialist, or bookstore at the edge of town. Here cars are definitely needed to move freely, because many social institutions of practical relevance, like those mentioned, can only be reached with a car.

One of the great advantages of this account is the widespread agreeability of Nussbaum's list of basic goods. Nobody really questions that the goods she mentions are of fundamental importance to us humans to be able to live a good life. Some might question the order of goods and others might want to add one or two (Wolf and De-Shalit 2007: 57–61). Moreover the meta-ethical justification of the list can be discussed (Antony 2000). Yet these issues don't really raise the question of the idea of basic goods as such; they can be accommodated within the concept. Relating poverty to basic goods therefore provides quite a robust basis for judging what it is really about. It gives us a reasonable argument for identifying which social situations count as circumstances of poverty, because goods appearing to be of contingent character – like shoes, TVs, and cars – can be related to basic goods. Under certain circumstances they can be necessary tools for the access to certain basic goods. Therefore, not having these apparently not so contingent goods constitutes being poor in this concrete social situation.

A second advantage rests on the connection between basic goods and the good life. If we understand a decent life as a life a person can live in dignity, which includes being respected as well as the possibility to exercise self-respect and a fair amount of autonomy, then it becomes clear why basic goods are important for such a life (Nussbaum 2006: 159–160). Only when a person has access to those basic goods can she command autonomy and rightfully respect herself, without seeing her dignity violated. She probably will also need those goods in order to be fully respected by others as a fellow citizen. Basic goods therefore provide her with the tools needed to construct her own good, or at least decent, life in a social context. On the one hand, this explains why basic goods are so important, and on the other hand, it justifies why everybody should have access to them. Moreover, in this picture, basic goods give material content to the ideas of decency and dignity. Thereby a stable framework of mutual support emerges, and both dignity and basic goods obtain a firm foundation.

The third advantage of this account stems from the fact that it needs only one notion of poverty to describe the apparently diverse and dissonant phenomenon of being poor. Accounts which work with the traditional distinction between absolute and relative poverty are confronted with the considerable inconvenience that they have to explain how the two different concepts of poverty can be arranged with each other. Understanding relative poverty as applied absolute poverty does not need to do that. There is only one notion of poverty, which is lack of access to basic goods. The differences on the surface phenomena come from the different composition basic goods can have in different societies. This explains why social circumstances are relevant to whether not having shoes, TVs, or cars counts as lack of basic goods and constitutes poverty or not.

These three advantages of understanding relative poverty as applied absolute poverty seem to build up a strong case for relative poverty perceived as socially applied absolute poverty, but there are also some fundamental flaws that seriously weaken this approach and even make it indefensible, or so we want to argue. This understanding of relative poverty is too broad and too thin and, moreover, in an important sense much too sketchy. It is too sketchy because it fails to draw an important line between different kinds of poverty. The apparent strength of just having one notion of poverty turns into a serious weakness. If there is only applied absolute poverty relative to socioeconomic circumstances, it becomes hard to differentiate between what is normally called absolute and relative poverty. Then those people we normally call absolutely poor are in the same sense poor as those we normally call relatively poor. This is counterintuitive, because the distinction between absolute and relative poverty is designed to indicate that people in absolute poverty live under much worse conditions than those in relative poverty.

A defense of relative poverty as applied absolute poverty could point at the plurality of basic goods. It could be argued that in absolute poverty more important basic goods like food or health are threatened, or simply that, in general, more basic goods are lacking. This is certainly true, but it fails to capture the point of the differentiation between relative and absolute poverty because it cannot establish that we do, indeed, have two different kinds of poverty, only different intensities of poverty. While the first account establishes a categorical difference, the latter can only establish gradual differences. Thereby, an important intuition concerning the dissimilar nature of relative and absolute poverty is lost. Someone who is absolutely poor is endangered in his ability to live any decent life at all, because he is facing an existential threat. Someone who is relatively poor is endangered in his ability to live a decent life in his given society, because he is facing a social threat. An account of relative poverty that can explain while both, relative and absolute poverty, are kinds of poverty, but different kinds of poverty, as we attempt to present in the final section, brings us closer to this intuition.

Another major problem of this understanding of relative poverty as socially applied absolute poverty is that it fails to capture fully what we normally perceive as relative poverty. As said: It is too broad and too thin. Think again of the two examples of the poor boy and the rich young woman. The poor boy has access to all basic goods; he can go to school, has shelter and food, is in good health; he can even play, maybe not with the school kids who ridicule him, but surely with other poor boys in the area he lives in. Yet although he has access to all basic goods he is still poor and humiliated by his classmates for this poverty. Now, the rich young woman, on the other hand, is still rich, but maybe she does not really have access to all basic goods. For her the ball is one of the most important events she can go to and have fun. Now this ball and all the other similar events she used to attend are not options anymore; she cannot do what is needed to be accepted there, which is showing up with a new dress each time. Yet for her it is the only way to go out to party, show herself to others, and have fun.

Of course, one might want to object that the young woman could go to other events to play and have fun there. There are no external obstacles which forestall this option. In fact, she still has many more possibilities than most of the other people in her society. After all, she is a rich girl. Her point of view is indeed very subjective and can be criticized for that, as we will do in the final section. But one should take seriously, at least initially, that there is an inner hindrance, because she cannot go to the events of the society she feels she belongs to. Her society does not consist of all people living in the same state, but only of those very rich people who attend fancy balls. So, in a way, her situation seems to be even worse than that of the poor boy. To be sure, to have access to the basic good of education, the boy needs to endure the humiliating behavior of his classmates, but at least he has access to all basic goods. The young woman, on the other hand, does not – in a way – have access too all basic goods, because she cannot move and play freely anymore in the society she thinks she belongs to. Yet we would still say that the boy is relatively poor and the young woman is not.

One way to solve this paradox could be to introduce the concept of social inequality, wherever the borders of the relevant society are identical with the borders of a sovereign state.[2] This could be related to poverty by understanding equality as a basic good itself, which could help to explain why the poor boy is poor and the rich girl is not. We, therefore, want to explore and finally reject this idea – not the idea of inequality as such, but as a substitute for relative poverty.

12.3 Unfair Inequality

The last section indicated that it is not possible to reduce the troublesome concept of relative poverty to a form of socially applied absolute poverty, but another reductive strategy might do the job. The idea is simply to drop the talk of relative poverty altogether and replace it by talking about inequality instead. In this perspective, the moral problem in regard of those people who have been called relatively poor is not that they are poor, but that they have to suffer from unjustified inequality. The schoolboy and the woman collecting garbage are not really poor; instead, they are treated harshly by society and unfairly so. The young rich woman, on the other hand, is not treated unfairly. Although her situation might seem to be harsh to her, she will have to learn to live with it, because no right is infringed and no moral problem at stake.

---

[2]This is not to imply that there is some kind of strange collective entity that has a value in itself, something like a nation. A society identical with a state should rather be understood in the terms of an encompassing group as Margalit and Raz (1990) phrase it. It is a constructed group with no direct value of its own, but, nonetheless, the identity of the individual members is dependent on it, which makes the group very valuable in an instrumental way.

This perspective on the issue of relative poverty as unjustified inequality goes well with our intuitions about what is morally acceptable and what is not. It seems to get the difference between the schoolboy and the young rich woman right. Moreover, it rests on the powerful ideas of justice and equality. The idea that all humans are equal by birth has a long history, and the idea that justice, therefore, includes a fair distribution of wealth and goods among those equal beings was brought to prominence (again) by John Rawls and his groundbreaking theory of justice as fairness (Rawls 1971, 2001). In this tradition, much work has been done to clarify the concept of justice as fairness and to establish what kind of inequality is acceptable (Barry 1973, Beitz 1979, Cohen and Rogers 1983, Pogge 1989, Daniels 1996, Freeman 2006). The basic idea is simple: All inequality that stems from contingent causes needs to be counterbalanced. Only inequality that stems from the achievements of the agents themselves is justified. There is some discussion about what qualifies as given and what as earned – for instance, when it comes to intelligence – but, apart from these secondary problems, the approach is clear and compelling.

There is a further complexity within the liberal theory of justice that makes it even more attractive as a basis for replacing the idea of relative poverty by the idea of unjust inequality. Rawls establishes a second principle of justice which leads to redistribution independent of the idea of equal starting conditions. He calls it the "difference principle", because it states that those in the worst condition need to benefit most from the socioeconomic structure (Rawls 1971: §§ 11, 12, Rawls 2001: §§ 13, 14). One might imagine that this could lead to a society where taxing is so penetrating that in the end all individuals have roughly the same amount of money. Rawls rejects this solution because he thinks that money is an important incentive for skilful people to work harder and thereby increase the overall level of welfare. A rather high inequality of income can be justified in this way, because it increases the overall amount of goods that can be distributed (Rawls 2001: § 20, Cohen 2000: 117–120, Cohen 2008: 68–86). Compared to other liberal theories of justice, the Rawlsian difference principle still sets a relatively harsh limit on the acceptable inequality that stems from unequal merits of individuals (Gosepath 2004: 425–433).

The idea of individuals who cooperate fairly combined with the difference principle produces a formidable argument for initial equality, and a robust notion of egalitarian justice can be constructed on this account. Nonetheless, the approach of justice as fairness still fails to capture the whole problem of relative poverty. It fails, because it is unable to grasp that relative poverty is humiliating and a threat to decency regardless of being unfair or not. At this point, it is rather unclear if decency itself is best understood as a part of justice next to fairness or a separate idea of social morality besides justice. We do not want to take a stance on this issue, but for matters of clarity we will present decency as an idea different from justice, especially justice as fairness. Margalit understands his concept of decency as somehow weaker than the concept of justice. In his view a society can be decent but still unjust. He thereby implies that a society cannot be just and still be indecent (Margalit 1996: 3, 271–281, Honneth 1997).

But that is exactly the point of view we want to defend. A society can be just but indecent; at least, if justice is understood as fairness alone and not also including decency. Now it becomes clear why the concept of relative poverty cannot simply be replaced by the concept of unjust inequality. The point simply is that the idea of justice as fairness fails to establish that nobody has to live in relative poverty, because people might come to this state of relative poverty without any unfairness involved in the process. Maybe it is the fault of the mother of the poor boy that she is poor. Maybe she left school early on her own free will; maybe she freely decided never to go for any secondary qualification; maybe she used to spend money on expensive, but useless, things before she had children, and never made any savings. In this situation, her poverty might be justified from the point of view of fairness, but it is, nonetheless, indecent.

A defender of justice as fairness can insist that such a state of relative poverty is impossible under conditions of fairness, because a cooperating society of free and equal citizens will always produce a basic structure that excludes relative poverty. These are high hopes that do not follow from the difference principle alone, because it is possible that the weakest group of society will benefit most in a situation of high inequality, where the strongest group benefits even more. One might even want to argue that this describes the situation of contemporary societies where managers and other professionals in key positions make lots of money and where the overall welfare of society is high. In this view, such a situation is justified because the good performance of the professionals benefits the whole society. Rawls and his followers would probably question the empirical validity of these claims, and rightfully so. Be that as it may, the theoretical point that such a situation might be possible in his approach is still a valid complaint.

But as indicated above, Rawls understands the difference principle as an additional principle of justice different from equality of opportunity. This principle rests on the idea that inequality cannot be so high that some people have cause to see themselves as secondary citizens. This follows from his idea of society as cooperation among free and equal citizens (Rawls 2001: § 7). We do not question this principle, yet we want to clarify that in our perspective it introduces the idea of decency next to fairness and therefore rests on the notion of relative poverty and not inequality. The reason why citizens loathe huge differences in income is not, or not only, because it is unfair, and certainly not out of envy, but because it is indecent (Anderson 1999: 314). This is not part of the idea that true cooperation is fair but part of the idea that citizenship as a normative ideal entails decency. It doesn't matter why the poor boy is poor, or why someone has to collect cans from the garbage bin or beg for money, or why she cannot afford a TV. These situations are instantiations of relative poverty in any case and, therefore, humiliating. In the next section, we will defend why relative poverty is humiliating and, therefore, contradictory to the idea of a decent society.

According to this understanding of humiliation and decency, the proper relation between inequality and relative poverty can be expressed thus: Relative poverty is the result of indecent cooperation while unjustified inequality is the result of unfair cooperation. In many situations the relative poverty of people is also an instantiation of unjustified cooperation. But while it is often unfair, it is always indecent. Aside from this, it is still possible, of course, that someone's economic situation is unfair, without constituting relative poverty. This is the case when women with good qualifications are not paid the same amount of money for the same kind of work or when someone abuses his oligarchic bargaining power to cut exploiting deals with weaker companies. Unjust inequality can go far beyond relative poverty, and in this sense it might be true that most forms of relative poverty are also cases of unfair inequality, but this does not take the normative power from the additional and universally valid argument that relative poverty is always indecent because it is humiliating.

12.4 Humiliation and Relative Poverty

Relative poverty can neither be reduced to absolute poverty nor to unjust inequality. Instead, the idea of relative poverty functions to describe a genuine moral problem of its own. But what exactly is so problematic about relative poverty, and why can this moral problem only be described in terms of relative poverty? Those are the questions we want to address in this final section. Our answer will very much rely on Margalit's account of humiliation and decency (Margalit 1996). The idea is basically this: Relative poverty is humiliating, because relatively poor people have reason to see themselves as second class citizens, which gives them a reason to see their self-respect undermined (Margalit 1996: 225–231). This is a violation of their human dignity, which a decent society has to avoid; therefore, we should put great effort into trying to end relative poverty.

But why does relative poverty humiliate and diminish self-respect? The answer does not lie so much in a conceptual link between human dignity and material wealth. It, indeed, is possible to live a dignified life without too many material goods. The answer lies in the significance material wealth has in a real society and the consequences this fact has for those people who lack the needed goods to be seen as equal fellow citizens in this society. Relatively poor people are marginalized, rejected, and humiliated in many subtle ways (Bourdieu et al. 1999). Single incidents or situations often do not seem to be humiliating as such, but taken together they give a reason to see one's self-respect and human dignity violated. Examples of this are the inability to be as mobile as others, to dress in a proper way, to attend ordinary social events, or to spend money on goods for entertainment in general. These examples reveal the hidden mechanisms of humiliation that are in place when it comes to relative poverty. Not being able to dress properly might be acceptable in a single event or at a certain situation, but when someone realizes that he is never dressed in a proper way compared to the majority of his fellow citizens, he realizes that he is somehow left behind on an overall social level. Not being able to purchase one special, trendy good of entertainment is not humiliating at all, but realizing time and again that one is not able to purchase for oneself or one's family some of those goods that the others play and have fun with makes it quite obvious that one is some kind of social outsider.

The problem becomes even more visible, and surely more pressing, when relatively poor people have only very limited healthcare or no healthcare at all, while others can afford the fanciest kinds of plastic surgery. The same counts for having very different and fewer education opportunities or having to live in segregated housing areas because everything else is far too expensive. The availability of all these things, from clothing and entertainment goods to healthcare and housing, very much depends on a person's income. The problem here is not that relatively poor people do not have access to basic goods at all, but that they have much less access to those goods compared to their fellow citizens. But why should that be a problem? To understand the humiliating character of relative poverty, it is necessary to see the social character of self-respect. Self-respect is not something totally individualistic, but dependent on how others see and treat us. Moreover, we see ourselves as part of certain groups, and our identity is very much dependent on our membership in those groups (Sen 2006, Young 1990, 2000). If we are rejected by one of the groups we identify with, this can be humiliating, because it harms our identity on which our self-respect is built (Margalit 1996: 134–137). A very special group that we belong to, and our identity and self-respect is dependent on, is the society we live in. We see ourselves as citizens, who belong to the same group as our fellow citizens. Relative poverty seriously undermines this self-perception and is, therefore, humiliating.

To be sure, not every rejection by a group someone identifies with is humiliating, but rejection by the society she lives in does constitute a violation of human dignity. What marks the difference? This can be seen when we once more stress the differences between the two cases of the poor boy and the young rich woman. Both are rejected by their groups because of their improper dressing. In the case of the young woman, the group can be described as the local upper class. In the case of the boy, the group can be described as his schoolmates. The obvious difference between these two groups is that the first consists of especially privileged people within society, while the latter group consists of an arbitrary assembly of members of this society. This second group can be seen as representative for society, while the first cannot. The boy gets the message that he is not seen as an equal member of this group, and, because this group stands for society, he gets the message that he is not seen as an equal member of society. The young woman only gets the message that she is not seen as an equal member of this privileged group within society. As Margalit says, the first is a threat to the boy's self-respect, while the latter is only a threat to the woman's self-esteem (Margalit 1996: 44–48).

One could object to this and claim that, according to our own account presented here, the situation of the young woman is humiliating as well. There is a group within society that is very exclusive and only very few privileged people have access to. This, the objection would claim, is humiliating to all others, including the young woman, because they are seen as inferior by this privileged group. The difference is only that the young woman is aware of this humiliating fact while most other people are not. They simply do not know that there is a social group that sees them as inferior, but they still have a reason to see themselves humiliated by this group. This objection is not sustainable but touches upon an important point. Some institutions, indeed, indicate the existence of a two-class society. Examples are different areas in trains for rich and not so rich people, or even more seriously, the already mentioned two-class system in healthcare due to different insurances. A very serious problem of growing concern is the difference between professionals and mere workers (Young 1990: 214–222). These institutionalized differences ought to be seen very critically, and if their number, or the intensity of difference, becomes too high, they can, indeed, be seen as humiliating for the lower class. However, this cannot be transferred to the example of the young woman and her tennis club just like that.

The reason is simply that the tennis club does not form an institution standing for society as such. It can rather be seen as a snobbish social group with a limited capacity to undermine a sense of equal citizenship. This club simply does not stand for society as a whole, and its attempt to humiliate non-members by exclusion therefore does not work, but rather leaves an impression of an establishment folly. This is why it is only a threat to one's self-esteem but not to ones self-respect. The young woman could, therefore, just walk away and reflect on the new opportunities she has gained by opening herself up to a much richer and more interesting society. But if the differentiation between those who can attend tennis club balls and those who cannot becomes a crucial symbol of belonging in a society, it can indeed be humiliating not to be able to attend those balls.

This shows how fragile the concept of human dignity is. It very much depends on the constitution of a society and how the different groups within this society relate to each other and manage not to dominate or oppress each other (Miller 2007: 111–134). This actually opens up a second objection against the idea that relative poverty undermines the self-respect of those who are poor and, therefore, humiliated. We can imagine a society where people can have great differences in income and possessions and where this does not lead to a two-class society, because material wealth does not play an important role at all. The connection between equal citizenship and relative poverty, which leads to humiliation, is not a conceptual one but, in a way, contingent. But we still doubt that a decent society with great difference in income can exist. The reason is simply that in a society where income does not play a crucial role for the construction of the self and where public life is seriously de-commercialized, nobody will care very much about material goods. So either relative poverty should not occur, because it is humiliating, or it will not occur, because everyone will share their goods willingly.

There is a third objection to the thesis that relative poverty is humiliating and should therefore be eradicated. It is a common enough argument that some people deserve their poverty because it is their own fault that they are poor (Rakowski 1991). They may have spent too much money in the past or are just a lazy lot. This criticism often neglects the importance of structural factors influencing the opportunities individual agents have. But even if it is true that some people are relatively poor due to their own fault, society still has reason to end their poverty. This is because relative poverty is not a problem of fairness but a problem of decency. A decent society does not tolerate that its members are humiliated. Relative poverty is humiliating because relatively poor people are seen as second-class citizens and have reason to see themselves in their self-respect violated. It does not matter why they are poor; it only matters that they have a right to be seen and treated as equal citizens. Their human dignity is fragile and can be violated, but they can never fully lose their human dignity and the rights that come with it. A decent society, therefore, has to end relative poverty no matter why it exists.

References

Anderson, Elizabeth. 1999. What is the point of equality? *Ethics* 109(2): 287–337.

Antony, Louise. 2000. Natures and norms. *Ethics* 111(1): 8–36.

Barry, Brian. 1973. *The liberal theory of justice*. Oxford: Clarendon.

Beitz, Charles R. 1979. *Political theory and international relations*. Princeton, NJ: Princeton University Press.

Bourdieu, Pierre et al. 1999. *The weight of the world: Social suffering in contemporary society*. Stanford, CA: Stanford University Press.

Cohen, Gerald A. 1993. Equality of what? On welfare, goods and capabilities. In *The quality of life*, ed. Martha Nussbaum and Amartya Sen, 9–29. Oxford: Clarendon.

Cohen, Gerald A. 2000. *If you're an Egalitarian, how come you're so rich?* Cambridge, MA: Harvard University Press.

Cohen, Gerald A. 2008. *Rescuing justice and equality*. Cambridge, MA: Harvard University Press.

Cohen, Joshua, and Joel Rogers. 1983. *On democracy*. New York, NY: Penguin.

Daniels, Norman. 1996. *Justice and justification: Reflective equilibrium in theory and practice*. Cambridge: Cambridge University Press.

Freeman, Samuel. 2006. *Justice and the social contract*. Oxford: Oxford University Press.

Gosepath, Stefan. 2004. *Gleiche Gerechtigkeit. Grundlagen eines liberalen Egalitarismus*. Frankfurt a. M.: Suhrkamp.

Honneth, Axel. 1997. A society without humiliation? *European Journal of Philosophy* 5(3): 306–324.

Margalit, Avishai. 1996. *The decent society*. Cambridge, MA: Harvard University Press.

Margalit, Avishai and Joseph Raz. 1990. National self-determination. *Journal of Philosophy* 87(9): 439–461.

Miller, David. 2007. *National responsibility and global justice*. Oxford: Oxford University Press.

Nussbaum, Martha. 1992. Human functioning and social justice. *Political Theory* 20(2): 202–246.

Nussbaum, Martha. 1993. Non-relative virtues: An aristotelian approach. In *The quality of life*, eds. Martha Nussbaum and Amartya Sen, 242–269. Oxford: Clarendon.

Nussbaum, Martha. 2006. *Frontiers of justice. Disability, nationality, species membership*. Cambridge, MA: Harvard University Press.

Pogge, Thomas. 1989. *Realizing rawls*. Ithaca: Cornell University Press.

Pogge, Thomas, ed. 2001. *Global justice*. Oxford: Blackwell.

Pogge, Thomas. 2007. *Freedom from poverty as a human right: Who owes what to the very poor*. New York, NY: Oxford University Press.

Rakowski, Eric. 1991. *Equal justice*. Oxford, NY: Clarendon Press.

Rawls, John. 1971. *A theory of justice*. Cambridge, MA: Harvard University Press.

Rawls, John. 2001. *Justice as fairness. A restatement*. Cambridge, MA: Harvard University Press.

Schaber, Peter. 2007. Globale Hilfspflichten. In *Weltarmut und Ethik*, eds. Barbara Bleisch and Peter Schaber, 139–153. Paderborn: Mentis.

Sen, Amartya. 1980. Equality of what? In *Tanner lectures on human values*, ed. Sterling M. McMurrin, 197–220. Cambridge: Cambridge University Press.

Sen, Amartya. 1993. Capability and well-being. In *The quality of life*, eds. Martha Nussbaum and Amartya Sen, 30–53. Oxford, NY: Clarendon.
Sen, Amartya. 2006. *Identity and violence: The illusion of destiny*. New York, NY: Norton.
Singer, Peter. 1993. *Practical ethics*. Cambridge: Cambridge University Press.
Wolf, Jonathan, and Avner De-Shalit. 2007. *Disadvantage*. Oxford: Oxford University Press.
Young, Iris M. 1990. *Justice and the politics of difference*. Princeton, NJ: Princeton University Press.
Young, Iris M. 2000. *Inclusion and democracy*. Oxford: Oxford University Press.

Chapter 13
Labor Exploitation

Crossing the Threshold Between Acceptable and Unacceptable Labor Conditions

Kirsteen Shields

Abstract "Dignity" is often evoked in the pursuit of better labor standards, and labor exploitation is often found to entail a loss of human dignity. In a bid to understand what dignity means in the context of labor, this chapter examines and compares the threshold between acceptable labor conditions and labor exploitation from the perspectives of the International Labour Organization (ILO) as international standard-setter, of selected NGOs as international monitors, and of a field-study of Fairtrade laborers as subjects of international labor standards. The distinction between the material and the immaterial elements of the labor relationship emerges as a key to all three perspectives, with the ILO demonstrating a prevailing tendency to link dignity with the immaterial elements of the labor relationship. In response, this chapter asks whether it is enough to consider dignity as contingent on the immaterial elements of the employment relationship or whether dignity in labor does not also require the satisfaction of certain material needs of the laborer.

13.1 Introduction

The concept of "labor exploitation" comes loaded with ideology. For Kant, one wrongfully exploited when one treated another instrumentally or merely as a means. For Marx, exploitation was making use of some vulnerability in another person in order to use him or her to attain one's own ends at his or her expense. Whilst divided on the causes of exploitation (for Liberals, it is organizational; for Marxists, it is structural), Liberals and Marxists agree that the involuntary nature of the labor relationship is key to any situation of labor exploitation. Nowadays the term "exploitation" is often evoked in a way that is detached from its ideological origins as a corollary of capitalist society, if not as a symptom (see, for example, Kymlicka 1989).

According to the estimates of Kevin Bales, one of the world's leading experts on contemporary slavery, there are 27 million slaves in the world today (Bales

K. Shields (✉)
London School of Economics and Political Science, Centre for the Study of Human Rights, UK
e-mail: k.shields@lse.ac.uk

P. Kaufmann et al. (eds.), *Humiliation, Degradation, Dehumanization*,
Library of Ethics and Applied Philosophy 24, DOI 10.1007/978-90-481-9661-6_13,

1999). The International Labour Organization's (ILO) first global estimate on forced labor is more modest at 12.3 million. This prevalence has not gone unnoticed, and, in response, civil society and the "international community" have mobilized to condemn labor exploitation through legislation, social movements and consumer protest. Yet as chains of production grow longer and as labor mutates into increasingly unrecognizable forms, is it plausible that these organs are fighting for a common cause under the banner of labor exploitation? If so, what is that common cause? Is it something we could call human rights? Fairness? Or dignity? In fact, all of these paradigms are evoked in the pursuit of improved labor standards.

In respect of this anthology, this chapter attempts to understand what is meant by "dignity" when it is evoked in relation to labor exploitation. In a bid to understand what dignity means in this context, this chapter seeks to identify the triggers that drive diverse organs to act on the grounds of dignity in labor. These triggers may be considered to operate on the threshold between "acceptable" labor conditions and labor exploitation. This chapter seeks to examine and compare the thresholds set for labor exploitation from the perspectives of the ILO as international standard-setter and of selected NGOs as international monitors, before considering the relevance of these triggers from the perspective of a field-study of laborers.

13.2 Labor Exploitation According to the ILO

Labor legislation comes from overlapping sources: national labor laws; human rights law at the national and regional level; UN human rights law; and international trade law. At the centre of all of this, the International Labour Organization, as a UN specialized agency, is charged with drafting and directing the universal minimum labor standards to be implemented at the national level. As the institutional leader in the campaign against labor exploitation, the ILO has been developing standards for the protection of the individual from exploitative labor practices since its creation in 1919. As with exploitation, it is difficult to talk of the ILO's labor standards regime without acknowledging its ideological origins. Perhaps more than any other set of norms, the ILO's labor standards regime embodies the clash of ideologies inherent in the UN and everything emanating from it. At once utilitarian and deontological, individualist and collectivist, the ILO's labor standards regime is a complex creature.

The rationales for the adoption of the ILO's labor standards in its formative period varied between the ethical and the economic. In many ways it is this duality that has made their existence possible; worker's organizations, as members of the ILO, campaigned for and supported the ILO's labor standards as minimum rights; equally, business enterprises, as members of the ILO, accepted the standards on the basis of economic efficiency (and states swung between the two). Increasingly, however, in recent decades we have witnessed the domination of the economic rationalization of labor standards over ethical rationalization. This is reflected in trends whereby labor standards are treated as a bargaining tool in bilateral and regional free trade agreements or relegated to the form of voluntary commitments in multilateral codes of conduct.

Despite these trends, it is important to recall that whilst the economic function of labor standards is often recognized as being of equal relevance to the ethical function, it is no more than that (see Ghebali 1989, Engerman 2003, Davies 2004). Reference to the ILO's constitutional documents reveal that the ILO's labor standards originated from a quest for "social justice"[1] *a priori*, and, more generally, the moral consensus set by the Abolitionist Movement cannot be overlooked as the deontological predecessor of universal labor standards. Subsequently, the International Bill of Human Rights has unfolded to comprise many of the ILO labor standards, and much of the ILO's labor standards regime now constitutes codified international human rights obligations.[2] On this basis it is arguable that labor standards should be valued as rights and awarded that status (see Alston 2005b, Dworkin 1985).[3]

This marriage with international human rights law is of immense importance when we come to consider the relationship between labor exploitation and dignity, as reference to the functions and roles of labor standards helps identify what is at

---

[1]Preamble ILO Constitution 1919.

[2]To be precise: (i) *Freedom of Association* features in Article 23(4) Universal Declaration of Human Rights (UDHR) and Article 22 International Covenant of Civil and Political Rights (ICCPR) (and also included as an economic and social right, the right to form and join trade unions is included in Article 8 International Covenant of Economic Social and Cultural Rights (ICESCR)); (ii) *The right to be free from forced or compulsory labor* can be interpreted from Article 4 UDHR: "the right not to be held in slavery or servitude" and Article 23 UDHR: "everyone has the right to work, to free choice of employment [. . .]"; also Article 8 ICCPR: "No one shall be held in slavery; slavery and the slave-trade in all their forms shall be prohibited; No one shall be held in servitude; No one shall be required to perform forced or compulsory labour (except in the conditions of imprisonment)"; (iii) *The effective abolition of child labor* is contained in Article 3 Convention on the Rights of the Child (CRC) (1989): "the right of the child to be protected from economic exploitation"; (iv) is provided by Article 7 UDHR, Article 26 ICCPR and features in almost every human rights document (although some instruments contain a right not to be discriminated against which applies only to the human rights contained in the instrument itself). Beyond this, just and favorable conditions of work are included under Article 7 ICESCR and Article 24 UDHR. The right to work is included in UDHR (Article 23(1)) and ICESCR (Article 6); Article 23 states that everyone who works has the right to just and favorable remuneration ensuring for himself and his family an existence worthy of human dignity, and supplemented, if necessary, by other means of social protection. EU provisions go farther regarding protection of dignity: Article 26 EU Charter protects the right to dignity at work, and applies both to sexual harassment and to other forms of bullying. The EU Charter contains a general reference to working conditions which protect a workers dignity (Article 31). (See generally Davies 2004).

[3]For a good summary of the opposing viewpoint see Hepple (2005: 22), the principal argument being that much of the labor rights agenda are desirable social goals but to call them human rights is to devalue the importance of basic civil and political rights. Hepple also makes the points that: "Rights to decent working conditions and fair pay depend upon the level of socio-economic development in a particular country and they generally presuppose economic growth and expanding social welfare. Secondly there is a contradiction between the inequality of class in the market place and the democratic element of citizenship and equal rights in the political sphere" (Hepple 2005: 265).

risk when these standards are not upheld. More specifically, the question *what is the purpose of labor standards*? leads us to the more acute question of *what, and indeed whom, are labor standards intended to protect*? Adopting a human rights perspective when answering this question implicates the rationales behind the human rights movement; that human rights seek to preserve individual liberty or autonomy (Hart 1973); and, similarly, that they seek to protect human dignity (Dworkin 1985). Therefore, if we consider labor standards in their human rights cloak, the link between labor standards and the protection of dignity becomes clearer.

Indeed, it is not necessary to look far to find glimmers of human rights threads within the ILO's normative tapestry. The Declaration of Philadelphia 1944 (an amendment to the original ILO's constitution of 1919) includes a blend of material and non-material values as encapsulated in this provision from Article II *(a):* "All human beings, irrespective of race, creed or sex, have the right to pursue both their material well-being and their spiritual development in conditions of freedom and dignity, of economic security and equal opportunity." From the outset, therefore, dignity is described as a requisite element of labor conditions detached from the material gains of labor.

The next logical question is how does the international labor standards regime go about protecting dignity (setting aside for the moment the question of whether this is effectively achieved in practice)? The ILO pertains to do this in two ways: (i) by legislating against labor exploitation, and (ii) by promoting "acceptable" labor conditions under the "Decent Work" agenda.

13.2.1 Legislating Against Labor Exploitation

The ILO seeks to legislate against labor exploitation under the broad ambit of "forced labor", within which forms of labor exploitation such as slavery and trafficking are included. The ILO's "A Global Alliance Against Forced Labour" 2005 report (hereinafter "ILO report 2005b") aimed to develop an initial typology on forced labor. This typology referred to the sector in which forced labor situations could occur and included as forms of forced labor: slavery and abductions; compulsory participation in public work; forced labor in agriculture and remote rural areas; domestic workers in forced labor situations; bonded labor; forced labor exacted by the military (with particular reference to Myanmar); forced labor related to trafficking in persons; and prison-linked forced labor (ILO Report 2005b: para. 39).

The ILO's original convention on forced labor, the Forced Labour Convention 1930 (ILO Convention No 29), provides the starting point for the ILO's definition of forced labor. Therein, the ILO defines forced labor as "all work or service which is exacted from any person under the menace of any penalty and for which the said person has not offered himself voluntarily".[4] This is reiterated in the ILO's only other convention on forced labor, the Abolition of Forced Labour Convention 1957 (No 105), where it is specified that forced labor can never be used for the purpose

[4]ILO Forced Labour Convention, 1930 (No 29) Article 2(1).

of economic development or as a means of political education, discrimination, labor discipline, or punishment for having participated in strikes.[5]

Over a period of 75 years, the ILO has developed its definition of forced labor to detail aspects of the penalty imposed, the nature of consent and the significance of the relationship between employer and employee, thereby sketching with greater detail the boundaries whereby the employment relationship may become exploitative. At each stage, the material conditions of the labor relationship are presented as secondary to the ILO's focus on the immaterial conditions of the relationship.

As regards the penalty that constitutes the first element of the ILO's legal definition of forced labor, the ILO has expressed that the penalty does not need to be in the form of penal sanction, but may also take the form of a loss of rights and privilege (ILO Report 2005b: para. 13). The menace of a penalty can take multiple different forms; the ILO suggests six indictors of a menace or penalty (see ILO Report 2005a: 20):

(i) Threats or actual physical harm to the worker.
(ii) Restriction of movement and confinement to the workplace or to a limited area.
(iii) Debt bondage: where the worker works to pay off a debt or loan, and is not paid for his or her services. The employer may provide food and accommodation at such inflated prices that the worker cannot escape the debt.
(iv) Withholding of wages or excessive wage reductions that violate previously made agreements.
(v) Retention of passports and identity documents, so that the worker cannot leave or prove his/her identity and status.
(vi) Threat of denunciation to the authorities where the worker is in an irregular immigration status.

The significance of the immaterial elements of the labor situation is made yet clearer by the ILO's description of instances where forced labor cannot be invoked as situations where material conditions are poor but there is no evidence of immaterial harm to the person:

> Forced labour cannot be equated simply with low wages or poor working conditions. Nor does it cover situations of pure economic necessity, as when a worker feels unable to leave a job because of the real or perceived absence of employment alternatives. Forced labour represents a severe violation of human rights and restriction of human freedom, as defined in the ILO conventions on the subject and in other related international instruments on slavery, practices similar to slavery, debt bondage or serfdom.

According to the ILO, therefore, there must be immaterial harm to the person for conditions to be deemed to amount to forced labor.

The "voluntariness" of the labor relation forms the second element of the ILO's legal definition of forced labor. In this respect the ILO considers the form and subject matter of consent, in particular the role of external constraints or indirect coercion

[5]ILO Abolition of Forced Labour Convention 1957 (No 105).

and the possibility of revoking freely given consent. The ILO report 2005b makes the following point relating to the durability of consent:

> Many victims enter forced labour situations initially of their own accord, albeit through fraud and deception, only to discover later that they are not free to withdraw their labour. They are subsequently unable to leave their work owing to legal, physical or psychological coercion. Initial consent may be considered irrelevant when deception or fraud has been used to obtain it. (ILO Report 2005b: para. 15)

Both of these conditions, penalty and "voluntariness", impact upon the relationship between employer and employee, and this is perhaps the most illuminating aspect of the ILO's theorization on forced labor. According to the ILO, a forced labor situation is determined by the nature of the relationship between employee and employer, "and not by the type of activity performed, however hard or hazardous the conditions of work may be" (ILO Report 2005b: para. 16). In summary, in crossing the threshold between the acceptable labor conditions and exploitative labor conditions, according to the ILO, the key factor is the nature of the relationship between employee and employer, and that relationship is defined by the extent to which it may be considered to be voluntary in nature and by the non-material harm or penalty (actual or threatened) experienced by the employee.

13.2.2 Promotion of "Decent Work" Agenda

Ancillary to the ILO's work on forced labor, an equally important aspect of the ILO's approach to prevention of labor exploitation is its promotion of "core labour standards" and the Decent Work Agenda. Through the promotion of core labor standards, the ILO has sought to establish a "minimum floor of labour conditions". The ILO's Declaration on Fundamental Principles and Rights at Work 1998 (hereinafter the 1998 Declaration) is often misrepresented as the *definitive* statement of the ILO's core labor standards agenda. It is perhaps better described as the ILO's most *general* statement of its international labor standards regime. It consists of the following four standards:

(i) Freedom of association and the effective recognition of the right to collective bargaining;
(ii) The elimination of all forms of forced or compulsory labour;
(iii) The effective abolition of child labour;
(iv) The elimination of discrimination in respect of employment.[6]

The value of the 1998 Declaration's contribution is doubtful; it is difficult to perceive the presentation of a limited group of labor rights in non-binding declaratory form as the *definitive* core labor standards to be in any way progressive. As Alston puts it:

[6]Article 2, ILO Declaration on Fundamental Principles and Rights at Work 1998. The introduction of core labor standards has been surrounded by debate as to the impact of these norms (see Alston 2005a, Langille 2005).

"The bottom line is that the Declaration proclaims as 'principles' a range of values which had already been recognized as rights exactly 50 years earlier in the Universal Declaration of Human Rights" (Alston 2004: 483).

The impact of the promotion of these four labor rights as core labor standards on the wider labor standards regime cannot be underestimated. It has essentially codified a hierarchy among labor standards, as Alston puts it, "those rights which did not make it into the premier league were inevitably relegated to second-class status" (Alston 2004: 488). Those rights left out include: the right to a safe and healthy workplace; the right to some limits on working hours; the right to reasonable rest periods; and protection against abusive treatment in the workplace. Compa describes the core labor standards as taking "no account of the essential economic and social component of rights at work (which legitimizes matters such as maternity provisions, pensions and holidays)" (Compa 2000: 15).

Shortly after the adoption of the Declaration on core labor standards, the ILO's Decent Work Agenda was launched in order to address some of the labor standards that had been left out of the core group in a non-binding form. Of considerable significance for the purpose of this study is the fact that "dignity" is freely invoked in the Decent Work Agenda. The ILO describes "decent work" as:

> Productive work under conditions of freedom, equity, security and dignity, in which rights are protected and adequate remuneration and social coverage are provided. (ILO Decent Work 1999 Report: 15)

Furthermore, the ILO adopts the following as its working definition of "decent work":

> [Decent work] involves opportunities for work that is productive and delivers a fair income; provides security in the workplace and social protection for families, better prospects for personal development and social integration, freedom for people to express their concerns, organize and participate in the decisions that affect their lives and equality of opportunity and treatment for all women and men.[7]

Pursuant to the promotion of "decent work" (described by ILO Director General Juan Somavia as the ILO's primary goal[8]), the ILO is in the process of establishing a global template for measuring decent work conditions composed of qualitative indicators for labor standards. The proposal includes the following main indicators[9] of decent work standards: access to employment opportunities; work that should be eliminated or abolished; adequate earnings and productive work; decent hours; stability and security of work; combining work and family life; equal opportunity and treatment in employment; safe work environment; social security; social dialogue; and worker's representation (ILO Report 2008: Table 1).

---

[7]See www.ilo.org/global/Themes/Decentwork/lang–en/index.htm

[8]See: www.ilo.org/global/about_the_ILO/Mainpillars/WhatisDecentWork/lang–en/index.htm

[9]Besides main indicators, the ILO report also considers additional indicators, context indicators, indicators which are candidates for future inclusion, indicators which are candidates for exclusion, and indicators of a legal nature (ILO Report 2008).

By promoting the "essential economic and social component" of labor standards under the Decent Work Agenda, with its reliance on the rhetoric of dignity, the ILO has established the social and economic component of labor standards as integral to dignity. However, by promoting these labor standards, integral to dignity, under the non-binding and voluntarist Decent Work Agenda, the ILO throws them into the ambiguous territory of "second-class standards", – i.e. below the set of rights that the ILO calls the "minimum floor of labour standards." On the basis that the minimum floor of acceptable standards does not include components of labor standards which are elsewhere asserted by the ILO as integral to dignity in labor, it would seem that the ILO's minimum floor of labor standards is set below conditions of labor which respect *dignity*. Whether this represents acquiescence by the ILO, or merely an oversight, is impossible to say; more fundamentally, it would seem to demonstrate that efforts to protect dignity are not necessarily synonymous with efforts to prevent violations of dignity.

13.3 Civil Society Organizations

While the ILO standards attempt to set boundaries between acceptable and unacceptable labor practices, these decisions largely remain at the standard-setting level. As the malpractice of multinational corporations has become a subject of international notoriety, social movements and consumer campaigns have assumed the traditional battleground of trade unions. In general, both trade unions and civil society organizations alike refer to the ILO's core labor standards as the minimum level of acceptable labor standards, but to what extent may their activities further inform the discussion as to the threshold between acceptable and unacceptable labor conditions? Campaigns by Anti-Slavery International, Oxfam, and International Labor Rights Forum offer insights into the meaning of labor exploitation from the perspective of civil society.[10]

13.3.1 Anti-Slavery International

Anti-Slavery International, founded in 1839, was at the forefront of movements to abolish the transatlantic slave trade and slavery throughout the British colonies. In 1975, it worked for the creation of a group of experts within the United Nations dedicated to the elimination of slavery, now called the UN Working Group on Contemporary Forms of Slavery. The organization's activities have moved beyond

---

[10]For the purpose of this study only campaigns that are specifically concerned with the improvement of labor conditions are presented, as opposed to those campaigns which advocate alternatives to trade liberalization. Moreover, it is worth noting that many major international NGOs, Human Rights Watch and Amnesty International amongst them, have often explained their hesitancy to include economic and social rights in their mandate due to the absence of specific international standards of measurement, amongst other reasons.

the transatlantic slave trade to campaign against labor exploitation in its modern forms.[11]

Besides awareness-raising and lobbying, Anti-Slavery International has engaged in groundbreaking research that builds and extends a modern concept of labor exploitation under its terminology of "modern slavery". Within its definition of modern slavery, Anti-Slavery International includes forced labor, bonded labor, child labor, and trafficking. According to Anti-Slavery International, common characteristics of modern slavery are:

- Forced to work – through mental or physical threat;
- Owned or controlled by an "employer", usually through mental or physical abuse or threatened abuse;
- Dehumanised, treated as a commodity or bought and sold as "property";
- Physically constrained or having restrictions placed on one's freedom of movement.[12]

Further to this, a recent report by Anti-Slavery International addresses the implications of ILO's six indicators of forced labor; "cases where at least one of the ILO indicators is identified should at the very minimum merit a thorough investigation, and where two or more elements of coercion are identified then the case should be identified as forced labour" (Guichon and van den Anker 2006: 8).

The report highlights the absence of consent in labor exploitation by illustrating the difference between trafficking and smuggling. According to the report, in the case of smuggling, even though it often happens under "dangerous and undignified conditions", it is a contract with consent; "Trafficking involves ongoing exploitation and even if the person might have consented at some stage, this consent is meaningless, because of the deception and coercion involved" (Guichon and van den Anker 2006: 8).

Beyond the ILO's indicators, Anti-Slavery International has identified common factors experienced by exploited workers from its research cases on trafficking for forced labor in the UK, Ireland, the Czech Republic and Portugal. The first set of common factors identified in the cases of trafficking for forced labor relates to the vulnerable situation of migrant workers. These are: "isolation, lack of knowledge of their rights and multiple dependency" (Guichon and van den Anker 2006: 10). In addition, the report goes on to identify the following factors; "subject to complex and confusing labour laws" (Guichon and van den Anker 2006: 11); "living under the threat of violence" (Guichon and van den Anker 2006: 15); and part of a demand for cheap labor often linked to supply chains for cheap products (Guichon and van den Anker 2006: 18). Significantly these are factors that qualify consent.

---

[11] Recent successful campaigns include a campaign for the introduction of new laws against slavery in Niger in 2003 and against bonded labor in Nepal in 2002 following Anti-Slavery International reporting and lobbying.

[12] http://www.antislavery.org/homepage/antislavery/modern.html

Secondly, the report identifies "a complexity of labour and migration laws" and a related difficulty of knowing one's legal rights as common factors faced by the subjects of trafficking for forced labor (Guichon and van den Anker 2006: 11).

13.3.2 Oxfam's "Make Trade Fair" Campaign

Oxfam's "Make Trade Fair" campaign seeks to "press decision-makers and governments for new trade rules – fair rules to make a real and positive difference in the fight against poverty".[13] As part of this campaign, Oxfam conducted research with partners in 12 countries involving interviews with hundreds of women workers and many farm and factory managers, supply chain agents, retail and brand company staff, unions and government officials. The report sought to illustrate "how retailers (supermarkets and department stores) and clothing brands are using their power in supply chains systematically to push many costs and risks of business on to producers, who in turn pass them on to working women" (Raworth, Oxfam 2004: 5). Chapter 1 of the report sets out the impacts of this trend on women workers and their families as workers being "permanently temporary"; "with no formal contracts"; "no support for families such as maternity pay"; "little or no job progression"; "low pay for high pressure jobs"; "long overtime at short notice"; "violence and sexual harassment"; and "prevention from joining a union" (Oxfam 2004: chap. 1).

The report gives the following examples of unacceptable labor conditions:

- In Chile, 75% of women in the agricultural sector are hired on temporary contracts picking fruit, and put in more than 60 h a week during the season. But one in three still earns below the minimum wage.
- Fewer than half of the women employed in Bangladesh's textile and garment export sector have a contract, and the vast majority gets no maternity or health coverage – but 80% fear dismissal if they complain.
- In China's Guangdong province, one of the world's fastest growing industrial areas, young women face 150 h of overtime each month in the garment factories – but 60% have no written contract and 90% have no access to social insurance. (Oxfam 2004: 5).

The issue of contract is of central importance to Oxfam's definition of unacceptable labor standards:

> Commonly hired on short-term contracts – or with no contract at all – women are working at high speed for low wages in unhealthy conditions. They are forced to put in long hours to earn enough to get by. Most have no sick leave or maternity leave, few are enrolled in health or unemployment schemes, and fewer still have savings for the future. Instead of supporting long-term development, trade is reinforcing insecurity and vulnerability for millions of women workers. (Oxfam 2004: 4)

---

[13] See http://www.oxfam.org/en/campaigns/trade/about

The report identifies the importance of workers being recognized by law in the labor relationship:

> When workers are not formally recognized as employees, they fall outside the protection of labour law. In some countries, having no written contract means having no legal recognition. (Oxfam 2004: 20)

Examples from Oxfam's "Make Trade Fair" campaign demonstrate a focus on the non-material dimensions of labor, and more specifically on the legal recognition created by contract. This reinforces the issue of consent at the heart of labor exploitation; the nature of the activity is not as significant as the means by which it is carried out, i.e. whether the activity is voluntary or involuntary.

13.3.3 The International Labor Rights Forum

The International Labor Rights Forum (ILRF) describes itself as "an advocacy organization dedicated to achieving just and humane treatment for workers worldwide". It was established in 1986 as the International Labor Rights Education and Research Fund.[14] Its mission statement reads:

> We believe that all workers have the right to a safe working environment where they are treated with dignity and respect, and where they can organize freely to defend and promote their rights and interests. We are committed to ending the problems of child labor, forced labor, and other abusive practices.

The ILFR has had considerable success with organized campaigns against Nike and other firms (see Cavanaugh 1997). The ILFR's current campaign against Wal-Mart's labor practices provides an example of the kinds of conditions the ILRF considers unacceptable. In its report "Wal-Mart in China: Rolling Back Labour Rights" the ILRF raised the following concerns:

(i) Many workers did not possess any copy of the labor contract, most of them do not know the precise stipulations regarding their work hours or wage and benefits.
(ii) Wages at the Winbo factory were below the national minimum.
(iii) Overtime was not compensated appropriately.
(iv) No paid days of rest.
(v) No holidays.
(vi) No sick pay.
(vii) Factory frequently withholds workers' salaries for at least one and a half months (sometimes 2 months).
(viii) Excessive working hours (11 h per day).
(ix) Inadequate health and safety provision such as failure to provide protective clothing where necessary.

---

[14] Subsequently shortened to the "The International Labor Rights Fund" and in 2007 changed again to the "International Labor Rights Forum".

(x) Inadequate safety training.
(xi) No social security, including pensions, injury insurance or medical insurance.
(xii) Inappropriate fining and punishments.
(xiii) Prevention of union activities (through fining for involvement and through terminating the employment of union leaders).

ILRF identifies the absence of a contract of employment as a key element of the unacceptable labor conditions. The labor contract is considered to codify consent, thereby ensuring that the activity is not undertaken involuntarily.[15]

13.4 The Laborers: Views from South African Vineyards[16]

The ILO sets the framework for international labor standards and builds international consensus on these conditions. Meanwhile, civil society fleshes out these standards with application to specific situations and often demands "economic justice" beyond the ILO's core labor standards. But what relevance do these boundaries have at the local level to the subjects of these standards, the laborers?[17] This section attempts to draw a sense of what amounts to labor exploitation from the perspective of landless farm-workers in Rawsonville, South Africa.

The information presented was collected during a field study carried out in South Africa in July 2008 as part of a research project on the Fairtrade Movement funded by the Art and Humanities Research Council at Queen Mary, University of London.[18] In 2005, the Fairhills Rawsonville Fairtrade Project was set up in the Rawsonville region. In its most recent report, the South African Human Rights Commission Farming Inquiry Report 2008 identified Rawsonville as "an alleged human rights abuse hotspot" (South African Human Rights Commission Report 2008: 61). The report also noted that the underlying causes of human rights abuses appeared to be rooted in the paternalistic relationship between farm-owner and farm-dweller.

The Fairtrade cooperative in Rawsonville is currently the largest Fairtrade cooperative in the world, whereby over 800 people (farm-workers and their families) benefit from the premiums generated. In order to qualify for Fairtrade status from the Fairtrade Labelling Organization, the farms are obliged to organize themselves as a cooperative, with group representatives from the farms making decisions as to changes on the farms. Through the cooperative, the farm-workers receive a

---

[15] The extent to which perceptions of consent in employment contracts may be inaccurate is the subject of on-going research by the author.

[16] These findings are intended to be anecdotal in nature and are limited to this unique case study Further conclusive findings would require further field trips.

[17] In the context of South Africa, "farm-workers" on wine estates in the Western Cape are almost without exception landless and of black or "Coloured" descent. The South African Human Rights Commission uses the term "farm-dwellers" to describe the workers and their families.

[18] http://www.qmul-fairtradeproject.org/index.htm

community payment into the Fairhills joint body account, alongside their wage payments. The joint account is used to finance crèches and community centers and vocational training. The Fairtrade Labelling Organization obliges the provision of training courses (on topics such as health and safety, and IT skills) and daycare for infants, but there is no obligation as to the provision of social security benefits such as sick pay, holiday pay or pensions.

Previous studies in different geographical contexts have found that the benefits to individual producers participating in Fairtrade are significant, with many benefits occurring in forms far more complex than simply increasing income. Benefits occurring at other levels are subtle but significant. These can be tangible benefits such as the provision of crèches and adult education programs, or they can be more subtle changes in organizational structure which enable greater participation and transparency in decision making and impact on the relationship between employee and employer. Several studies on Fairtrade employers have reported a "marked increase in self-esteem" of Fairtrade employees (Murray et al. 2003: 8).

In light of the introduction of Fairtrade in Rawsonville in 2005, the information presented below comes from anecdotal evidence collected during interviews with the farm-workers in Rawsonville and consists of the farm-worker's reflections on the changes that had been brought by the introduction of Fairtrade. In assessing the value of these changes, farm-worker's comments have been grouped under two questions – *Are the principal benefits material or are the immaterial changes equally important to the farm-workers? And have the Fairtrade changes had any impact on the relationship between farm-owner (employer) and farm-worker (employee)*?

13.4.1 Hierarchy of Benefits: Are Material Benefits More Significant than Immaterial Benefits or Vice Versa?

In order to assess the contribution of the Fairtrade changes to the farm, the farm-workers were asked: (i) What was the greatest change that the Fairtrade system had introduced? (ii) Would the farm-workers remain on the farm should their income drop? In response to the first question, the farm-workers almost unanimously responded that the introduction of childcare had been the greatest change on the farm – the Fairtrade organization had built crèches for infants on every Fairtrade farm we visited, which were maintained by financing from the Fairtrade joint body's account. According to the farm-workers, the second greatest change had been improvements to the farm-worker's houses (situated on the farm), although many stressed that there should be more improvements made in this regard.

Secondly, regarding a decrease in income, the majority of farm-workers interviewed commented that should their income decrease below the minimum wage they would remain as farm-workers on the farm. Many farm-workers said that they would stay attached to the farm because they were unaware of any other employment options and because they believed that "a good year would follow a bad one" and many explicitly mentioned that they would remain on the farm because of the community benefits.

As regards social security benefits such as pension, incapacity for work due to sickness, and incapacity for work due to invalidity, these varied between farms in Rawsonville, as the Fairtrade Labelling Organization does not place obligations on the provision of social security. However, on one farm the provision of an unconventional pension scheme had clearly generated goodwill, if not pride, amongst farm-workers there. The farm-owner had offered a plot of arid land, which they planned to use to graze sheep, as an ongoing project for their pension scheme. As regards sick pay and maternity leave, these rights did not even seem to be envisaged by the farm-workers. Rather, their concern in this respect was that they should not be prevented from working (and thereby earning) when they were sick or pregnant (as some farm-owners had forced farm-workers to take unpaid leave when sick or pregnant).

13.4.2 Relationship: Did the Farm-Workers Feel Greater Choice or Control Over Their Labor Conditions?

One farm-owner commented that he felt that there had been a change of attitudes of farm-workers since the Fairtrade changes had taken places. He told us that there had been increased motivation to work well on the farm, that the farm-workers took greater pride in their crop, and that they knew that the quality was important for Fairtrade.

Very few farm-workers were aware of alternative employment; however, it is worth recalling that according to the ILO, "forced labour" does not "cover situations of pure economic necessity, as when a worker feels unable to leave a job because of the real or perceived absence of employment alternatives" (ILO Report 2005b: para. 13). Several farm-workers were unsure of the content of their contract but said that they had signed the contract because it meant guaranteed work and the benefits of remaining in the community.

The Fairtrade Labelling Organization seeks to improve "social dialogue and worker's representation" by obliging cooperatives to increase worker's participation through collective decision-making. These criteria have led to the creation of a joint body composed of farm-workers and farm-owners who take decisions regarding how the joint-body account is used to finance improvements in working and living conditions on the farm. In the farms we visited, the group communicates with the farm-owner informally once a week or once every 2 weeks. Some farm-workers reported that this gave them greater bargaining power with the farm-owner. However, one farm-worker admitted, "we attend the meetings because the farm-owner tells us to".

In general farm-workers use collective bargaining to regulate what they considered to be unfair conditions imposed by the farm-owner; from the farm-worker's point of view, their most effective way to improve a situation is to visit the farm-owner as a group. Yet demands on the farm-owners in Rawsonville were generally tempered with either realism or submission; one farm-worker commented, "it's not the farm-owner's fault if there is not enough money". Similar apathy was expressed by one farm-owner when he explained that he saw limits as to what he could offer the farm-workers on his farm: "Everyone talks about 'upliftment', but 'upliftment' to where? We cannot all be running the farm; someone has to do the manual labor. I believe we can improve living conditions but not labor conditions".

On several occasions, the farm-workers and farm-owners listed the following as milestones towards decent living conditions: first electricity, then running water, then toilet and shower, then gardens. They did not have a similar list related to decent labor conditions (however, childcare seemed to be a shared priority over higher wages). The ILO and the NGOs would suggest such a list starts with contract, includes the core labor standards, and then social security benefits such as sick pay and holiday pay. The farm-workers I met did seem to value the established stages of decent work (of contracts, core labor standards and social security benefits), but, more intrinsically, what seemed to matter most was their relationship with their employer, the farm-owner (and on occasion this extended to the wider world of buyers and consumers). With the lingering of the master-servant relationship, there was a prevailing sense that the employer had the power to remove the improved living and labor standards, and, as a result, their sense of empowerment seemed to rest precariously on this relationship. Certainly the farm-owner's cooperation was not to be taken for granted, attitudes amongst farm-owners varied, but in this region at least, progress was apparent. One farm-owner explained: "It's not only the world that wants improved labor conditions, we [the farm-owners] also want them for our men [the farm-workers]".

13.5 Conclusion

In seeking to understand the relationship between dignity and labor exploitation, this paper has examined associations made between labor exploitation and a loss of human dignity from the perspectives of the ILO, a selection of NGOs, and a case-study of laborers. It has been shown that the ILO, as international standard-setter, identifies the nature of the employment relationship as key to labor exploitation and, at the same time, acknowledges that the essential economic and social components of labor standards are integral to "work in conditions of freedom, equality, security and dignity" (otherwise known as "Decent Work"). Yet the ILO fails to formalize the economic and social components of labor standards through a binding legal framework. Instead, the essential economic and social components of labor standards, concerning as they do questions of distribution, are now, in light of the disintegration of trade unions, the concern of civil society organizations. NGO campaigns against labor exploitation advance the ILO's political rights agenda whilst demanding "economic justice" beyond the ILO's limited regime. On the ground, my case-study in South Africa suggests that for this group of laborers, improvements in labor conditions are changes which improve their relationship with their employer whilst strengthening the communities they go home to.

According to the three perspectives examined, both the immaterial and the material have an impact on the dignity of any labor situation. Whilst NGOs and laborers appear to place the material and immaterial benefits of labor on an equal footing, the ILO prioritizes the immaterial, and this bears significant consequences. With little incentive or legal obligation for states to implement the ILO's Decent Work Agenda (which I see as constituting the material branch of dignified labor standards), ultimately it is left to ethical consumerism, through initiatives such as the Fairtrade Movement, to deliver the economic and social components of labor standards. The rights to a safe and healthy workplace, to a decent wage, to reasonable working hours, to security in the work place and social protection for workers and their families, and to prospects for personal development and social integration are now the concern of ethical trade initiatives. These are labor standards that are recognized as human rights and have been internationally recognized as integral to dignity in labor – the dignity of laborers is thereby made subject to the altruism of consumers. This would appear to represent an enormous failure of the International Labour Organization and the machinery of international economic law in general.

On the other hand, the interaction of the actors examined here may itself be considered a finely tuned mechanism of international economic law. These actors converge on what constitutes dignity but diverge on when to act on that cause, generating what Sen describes as a combination of rights-based reasoning and goal-based programming (Sen 2000). Yet, regardless of the angle from which it is viewed, the international labor rights regime would appear to be manifestly failing in its "pursuit of social justice" as millions fall through the cracks somewhere between the promotion and the protection of dignity. The task of drawing a line in the sand between acceptable and unacceptable labor conditions becomes all the more difficult when, upon examination, the ILO's allusion to dignity evaporates like a mirage.

References

Alston, Philip. 2004. Core labour standards and the transformation of the international labour rights regime. *EJIL* 15(3): 457–521.

Alston, Philip. 2005a. Facing up to the complexities of the ILO's core labour standards Agenda. *EJIL* 16(3): 467–480.

Alston, Philip. 2005b. *Labour rights as human rights*. Oxford: Oxford University Press.

Bales, Kevin. 1999. *Disposable people: New slavery in the global economy*. Berkeley, CA: University of California Press.

Cavanaugh, John. 1997. The global resistance to sweatshops. In *No sweat: Fashion, free trade and the rights of garment workers*, ed. Andrew Ross, 39–51. New York, NY: Verso.

Compa, Lance. 2000. The promise and perils of "Core" labour rights in global trade and investment. Paper for CUNY conference January 17, 2000, cited in Alston 2004.

Davies, Anne C.L. 2004. *Perspectives on labour law*. Cambridge: Cambridge University Press.

Dworkin, Ronald. 1985. *A matter of principle*. Cambridge, MA: Harvard University Press.

Engerman, Stanley L. 2003. The history and political economy of international labour standards. In *International labour standards: History, theory and policy options*, eds. Kaushik Basu et al., 9–83. Malden, MA: Blackwell.

Ghebali, Victor Yves. 1989. *The international labour organisation: A case study of the evolution of the UN specialised agencies*. Dordrecht: Nijhoff.

Guichon, Audrey, and Christien van den Anker. 2006. Trafficking for forced labour in Europe: Report on a study in the UK, Ireland, the Czech Republic and Portugal, November 2006. Anti-slavery international with La Strada Czech Republic, Dublin City University, Migrants Rights Centre Ireland, APAV Portugal, November 2006.

Hart, Herbert L.A. 1973. Bentham on legal rights. In *Oxford essays in jurisprudence* (second series), ed. Alfred W.B. Simpson, 171–201. Oxford: Oxford University Press.

Hepple, Bob. 2005. *Global trade and labour laws*. Oxford: Hart.

ILO Report. 1999. Decent work. Report of the Director General to the 87th meeting of the international labour conference, Geneva, 1999.

ILO Report. 2005a. Human trafficking and forced labour exploitation: Guidelines for legislation and law enforcement. Geneva: ILO Publications, 2005.

ILO Report. 2005b. A global alliance against forced labour. Global report under the follow-up to the ILO declaration on fundamental principles and rights at work. Geneva: ILO Publications, 2005.

ILO Report. 2008. Measurement of decent work. Discussion paper for the tripartite meeting of experts on the measurement of decent work. Geneva: ILO Publications, September 2008.

Kymlicka, Will. 1989. *Liberalism, community and culture*. Oxford: Clarendon Press.

Langille, Brian. 2005. Core labour rights – The true story (reply to Alston). *EJIL* 16(3): 409–437.

Murray, Douglas, Laura T. Raynolds, and Peter L. Taylor. 2003. *One cup at a time: Poverty alleviation and fair trade coffee in Latin America*. Fort Collins: Colorado State University Press.

Oxfam. 2004. *Trading away our rights: Women working in global supply chains*. Oxford: Oxfam International Publications.

Sen, Amartya. 2000. Work and rights. *International Labour Review* 139(2): 119–128.

South African Human Rights Commission Report. 2008. Progress made in terms of land tenure security, safety and labour relations in Farming Communities Since 2003.

Chapter 14
Bonded Labor

Dynamics Between Bondage, Identity, and Dignity

Tamara Enhuber

Abstract Bonded labor relations in India have commonly and primarily been understood in terms of economic exploitation and manifestations of local power structures. While their frequent concomitant conditions such as impoverishment, denial of freedom, physical stress, adverse health effects, practices of social degradation, and, not rarely, also physical violence are reported in almost all studies on bonded labor, these factors have rarely been looked at from the perspective of human dignity. However, the link between conditions of labor bondage and violations of dignity has yet to be established and respective dynamics to be discovered. This essay is intended as a first attempt to systematically interrogate various acts and conditions of subjugation within bonded labor relations with regard to the laborers' experiences of deprivation, degradation, and annihilation, and the violations of dignity that may result. It is argued that seemingly comparable humiliating conditions may be processed and dealt with differently by different bonded laborers. While it is certain that, within bonded labor relations, human dignity is violated every day on a massive scale, there is also evidence that bonded laborers may, under certain conditions, yet be able to maintain their dignity. Once we stop reducing bonded laborers to their bondage and pay attention to their collective and individual identities, their social practices and social spaces, we may not only be in a position to grasp the extent of violations suffered individually but also to identify the resources that may allow for the limiting, negating or negotiating of those violations.

14.1 Introduction

While bonded labor is to be found in various regions of the world, this chapter will – for methodological reasons – focus on the Indian context only. The advantage is two-fold: On the one hand, this choice limits the scope of research to *one* polity that offers a reasonable number of commonalities and that allows for the

T. Enhuber (✉)
Department of Anthropology, University of Trier, Germany
e-mail: tamaraenhuber@yahoo.com

P. Kaufmann et al. (eds.), *Humiliation, Degradation, Dehumanization*,
Library of Ethics and Applied Philosophy 24, DOI 10.1007/978-90-481-9661-6_14,

development of a "thick analysis" of the complex dynamics between relations of bondage and the experience of (violations of) dignity. On the other hand, the situation in India provides in itself a considerable level of heterogeneity in regard to distinctive systems of bonded labor and their respective contexts, which does not only enable us to cover a broad empirical spectrum but also to develop an analysis that might be applicable beyond the particularities of a single system of labor bondage.

Setting out to identify the conditions under which bonded labor may affect human dignity, this contribution pursues two main questions. The first aims at determining those consequences of various acts of subjugation within relationships of bondage that are apt to violate the dignity of bonded laborers. The second question investigates the circumstances that may influence how a bonded laborer may process and respond to those acts. That is, whether he will suffer a violation of his dignity and to what extent, and whether he will be able to restore it, or whether he may succeed in maintaining it in the first place. While violations of dignity are generally conceived of in their intersubjective-social dimension, often discussed under the heading of human rights (violations), the explicit focus here is on the *subjective-psychological* processing[1] by those whose dignity is offended. This approach is accounted for by an understanding that does not wish to reiterate the reduction of bonded laborers to their bondage but rather to recognize them in their entirety and complexity as human beings who are not only victims but also agents of their lives. The room to manoeuvre may, in many cases, be small but it *might* allow the laborers, under certain conditions and to varying extents, to defend their dignity.

The structure of the discussion is the following. Section 14.2 starts with a definition of bonded labor and a brief introduction to this phenomenon in India. The third section deals with the social status, and its theological and institutional foundations, of the communities from which bonded laborers are drawn. The following section offers a glimpse of the everyday experience of subjugation which these communities are confronted with. A few case studies illustrating two central aspects of bondage – loss of freedom and self-alienation – open up initial questions concerning the relationship between acts of subordination and the experience of deprivation, degradation and dehumanization. In Section 14.5 an attempt is made to conceptualize those acts in terms of their potential to violate dignity. The final section then avails itself of socio-psychological theories and of research on the impact of, and responses to, slavery and further relationships of subordination in order to identify the conditions that determine whether a bonded laborer may either *actually* experience those acts as violations of his dignity or, in contrast, be able to negate or negotiate such effect.

[1]These two terms are the result of an ongoing discussion during the process of writing this essay; their authorship belongs to Christian Neuhäuser.

14.2 Bonded Labor

India's *Bonded Labor System (Abolition) Act* of 1976 acknowledges bonded labor as a kaleidoscope of distinctive features and realities. Here the *bonded labor system* is defined as any system of forced labor under which someone agrees, first, to work for someone else either due to some *advance* given by that person (usually credit or land), *or* some *customary or social obligation* (e.g., the involvement of family members), or any *economic consideration* (accepting certain conditions of bondage in order to secure at least one meal per day), or simply due to his or her *birth in any particular caste or community* (i.e., a low-caste or non-caste group that is expected to render certain services to the caste-Hindu community). And secondly, thereby to forfeit the freedom of employment or other means of livelihood, or the right to move freely, or the right to appropriate or sell at market-value any of his property or product of his labor. In practice, these conditions commonly do not occur individually; their boundaries are blurred and mutually reinforcing.

Despite its legal abolition, bonded labor is still prevalent and also found to be emerging in new forms throughout the country and in a wide range of economic sectors. Its extent is difficult to assess and a matter of dispute; Indian and international NGOs speak of several million people in bondage.

A closer look at the roots of bonded labor renders a complex picture of various converging factors: First, bonded labor is to be found in an *economic environment* that is marked by a huge informal labor market, high rates of unemployment/underemployment, and an extremely low livelihood potential in agriculture (the largest economic sector). It is, furthermore, favoured by *socio-cultural structures and processes* that have culminated in a highly stratified society with its hierarchy based on a religious belief system and on a set of concepts justifying and stabilizing the status quo, and on remnants of feudal relations in rural areas. The alienation of certain communities from their land and, in the case of tribal communities, from their traditional livelihood systems, are aspects that illustrate how inextricably interwoven economic and societal influences may be. Finally, it is also an issue of *state formation*: where we find local state agents frequently not implementing the respective laws, judgments and programs; that, in conjunction with the previous factors, leads to and perpetuates non-compliance with regulations on minimum wages in the informal sector, unequal distribution of land, and unequal access to education and credit facilities. This inevitably results in, and increases already existing poverty and forces laborers who are predominantly assetless to either take up credit from a private money lender, thus agreeing to work for him or pledge their children, or to accept traditions such as the *Devadasi* system,[2] or render compulsory services/labor for the upper castes. The purpose of

[2]*Devadasis* are girls that are dedicated and "married" to a deity without their consent. Once they enter puberty they are considered available to sexual use by higher caste men, sometimes also by their own communities (Antislavery 2007).

credit may generally range from medical expenses to seeds for cultivation and to social ceremonies; in India's poorest districts the major impulse, however, is hunger (Sainath 1996: 216, CEC 2004: 67, 70). Laborers therefore endure exploitative terms of employment rather than suffer starvation (Pandit 2000: 5). Having entered bondage, poverty is bound to increase and with it the probability of remaining in bondage. Given meagre wages, sometimes in-kind wages, and high compound interest, there is little chance of ever paying back the loan (Srivastava 2005: 13–14). This process creates dependency and servility on the part of the laborers: because of the "sanctity of repayment" among the poor (Sainath 1996: 200), and also since laborers feel forced to remain loyal towards their employers as poverty may bring future situations in which they will rely upon the latter's financial support.

This situation allows for particularly harsh and degrading working conditions, including the presence of physical violence, grossly undermining minimum labor standards and human rights.[3] The degree of dependency of the bonded laborer upon the employer varies: The extent of control may be partial or total, ranging from surveillance limited to the labor process to domination of the entire conduct of life by the master; the duration in bondage may span from relatively short and one-time occurrences to repeated, permanent or even inter-generational bondage. The fact that bonded labor continues to be practised despite its legal abolition may allude to the low social ascription and perception of rightlessness of its "victims" (Srivastava 2005: 9) and the "cumulative domination" they are subjected to (Oommen 1990: 254–255): almost all bonded laborers are assetless, functionally illiterate (CEC 2004: 67), and predominantly members of the Scheduled Castes and Scheduled Tribes (Srivastava 2005). While the Scheduled Castes comprise those communities who have, in the past, been considered the Untouchables, the Scheduled Tribes are commonly understood as India's indigenous population. Both groups are known under various names with different connotations. I have chosen to refer to them as *Dalits* and *Adivasis* respectively[4]; however, where authors employ different designations or if the context requires, other terms will be applied accordingly. References to bonded laborers and their communities in this chapter refer to the *Dalit* and *Adivasi* communities.

---

[3]Bonded labor conditions characteristically entail wages below the subsistence level (up to 90% less than the statutory minimum; with far-ranging consequences such as malnutrition, no access to proper medical treatment, no or little access to formal education, etc.), long working hours (up to 18–22 h per day as well as few or no holidays), above-average exposure to hazardous substances, frequent accidents, and various occupational diseases, and not seldom also subjection to sexual exploitation.

[4]*Dalits* and *Adivasis* appear to be the terms by which members of the respective communities seem to self-identify most (Mendelsohn and Vicziany 1998: 3–4; Appadurai 1988: 36–40; Barnes et al. 1995: 286; Ghurye 1980: 362–364; Waite 2006: 8; Isaacs 1964: 41; Zelliot 1996: 1).

14.3 Below the Lowest

14.3.1 Social Status and Its Foundations

Among various factors that determine the *social* position of an individual and his community within Indian (Hindu) society, caste, with endogamy as its essence, and the notion of purity-impurity appear to be the prevalent organizing principles of society. According to classical texts of Hinduism, the population is divided into four ranked *varnas* (generally translated as castes), with the *Brahmans* at the top. Below those four categories there are the Untouchables, who are supposedly outside the system but who are, if we take economic, social and even ritual relations into account, an integral part of it (Srinivas 1966: 4, Milner 1994: 46). Today's *Adivasis*, in contrast, have generally remained outside the Hindu order (Oommen 1990: 255). This construction around ritual status and along an axis of purity-pollution, which presumably has been developed to support Brahmin supremacy (Srinivas 1966: 3–4), attributes the Brahmin with the highest level of purity, while the Untouchables allegorise the "embodiment of ultimate ritual defilement" (Gokhale 1993: 3) at the opposite and complementary pole (Thapar 2002: 63–64, 279). To a certain extent integral to the *varna* system is the institution of *jati* (frequently translated as sub-castes), i.e. hereditary, endogamous units, commonly associated with one or a few particular occupation(s). However, the ranking of *jati* varies regionally and temporally (Thapar 2002: 63, Srinivas 1966: 4–5). Within this degree of leeway for different interpretations and for mobility may lie a central stabilising factor of the system, as it always allows every *jati* to feel superior to at least one other *jati* (Srinivas 1992: 50, Pandit 2000: 4). Nevertheless, those groups that *are* attributed with pollution are always "[s]et apart to perform needed but ritually impure functions" (Isaacs 1964: 27), which automatically puts the lowest *varna*, the *Sudras*, but also everyone else up the line on a higher footing; "[The] humiliations [of the *Dalits*] are a matter of pride with others." (Ambedkar, in Keer 1962: 233) Even many of the *Dalit jatis* practice untouchability among themselves and against each other.[5]

While it has to be acknowledged that Hinduism has to be thought of as a diversity of distinct traditions (Flood 2005: 1) and that one needs to be careful not to totalize or essentialize the hierarchical component (Appadurai 1988: 41), it is established that caste, whether someone believes in its legitimacy or not, *has been* a dominating factor in Indian life, "influencing if not determining [one's] choice of occupation, diet and spouse, [. . .] collective rank in relation to other caste groups, and numerous other matters" (Srinivas 1992: 59). This implies "institutionalized inequality [and] differential access to the valued things in life" (Berreman 1979: 159). This is

[5]The motivation appears to be the same as for the caste Hindus: the pursuit of status enhancement by maintaining distance from the subsequently inferior caste and by adopting "clean" occupations and habits (Isaacs 1964: 29, Ram 1995: 156).

still valid, particularly in rural areas "where caste looms large", and even for non-Hindu groups that, to some extent, "took on [. . .] the colour of caste" (Srinivas 1992: 59–60).

Obviously there are also various other forces besides those Brahmanic doctrines discussed – be it economic, political, or administrative structures, or the general state of the educational system – that add to the perpetuation of the status quo (as far as the situation of *Dalits* and *Adivasis* is concerned) and that frequently touch upon issues of dignity. Yet one could imagine that the indignities the latter carry may be experienced as rather impersonal; it is, presumably, "the domination [. . .] that particularly leaves its mark on personal dignity" (Scott 1990: 112–113), a domination that is based on perceptions of "the other and the self" on the grounds of caste and of the notion of pollution. This chapter will primarily focus on the consequences of the *Dalits*' and *Adivasis*' *social status* in its narrow sense.

14.3.2 Social Practice: Everyday Indignities and (the Threat of) Atrocities

The blatant untouchability, where even the footprints, the shadow and the voice of *Dalits* were considered contaminating (Isaacs 1964: 27–28), is generally not found anymore, yet it may be suspected that its impact on the self-identity of former Untouchable communities may well have extended to succeeding generations. Besides, untouchability as such has not altogether disappeared but rather has frequently assumed a disguise. Despite its abolition and a policy of affirmative action with reservations for Scheduled Castes and Scheduled Tribes in public sector/government jobs, in educational institutions, in parliament and in local governing bodies, various forms of discrimination, marginalization, and ostracism continue. In many rural places even today *Dalits* are expected to perform *begar* (a traditional form of unpaid community service) and/or polluting jobs (e.g., ploughing, carrying night soil, removing carcasses). They are expected to live in separate hamlets outside the "real" village or in "Dalit only" housing in the cities, with lack of drinking water, sanitation facilities, roads, street lights, and denial of access to common taps or wells or to public sites such as streets, temples, and burial and cremation grounds (Ram 1995: 225, Gatade 2009, Varadarajan 1993, Human Rights Watch 1999). Most common yet seems to be that *Dalits* generally continue to be avoided by caste Hindus in domestic or "private" situations surrounding food and general social life (Mendelsohn and Vicziany 1998: 13).

Furthermore, new kinds of atrocities have emerged exceeding previous levels of intensity. The *Scheduled Castes/Scheduled Tribes (Prevention of Atrocities) Act* of 1989 lists 22 types of atrocities that are committed towards *Dalits* and *Adivasi*. These include murder, rape, false and vexatious litigation, forcing people to leave their homes and areas of residence, polluting sources of water, exerting pressure during elections, grabbing land, parading people naked in public, forcing people to eat or drink inedible or obnoxious substances, dumping excreta or carcasses on their premises, and so forth. It can be assumed that the commission of those atrocities is a direct reaction by the higher castes to the rising self-consciousness of the *Dalits* and the *Adivasis* and to the challenge this entails to the status quo. It is mostly the latter's defiance of age-old caste customs and boundaries, accompanied by the rising economic and social status of *some* sections among them, that result in atrocities (Ram 1995: 224, 278, 323–324, Mendelsohn and Vicziany 1998: 12, 47). Any refusal by bonded laborers and their communities to continue performing tasks that are considered polluting leaves the higher castes with a dilemma – if they had to take on these jobs themselves they would become ritually polluted themselves and the rationale of their claim to superiority would be lost (Mendelsohn and Vicziany 1998: 48–49). What is at stake on the part of the caste Hindus is thus not just the convenience of having others to do the menial work or the material benefit of cheap labor but, maybe even more important, the status that is derived from these privileges as well as the access to various resources such as land, higher education, jobs, and political power (Srinivas 1992: 2).

This is the context within which *Dalits* and *Adivasis* generally have to manoeuvre. Those who *have had* access to education and/or who have been able to benefit from governmental programs or from India's reservation policy are affected to a (sometimes considerably) lesser extent, but for the majority – particularly those living in remote rural areas, and definitely the communities of bonded laborers – the constant threat of everyday indignities and occasional atrocities is the ever-looming scenario (Freeman 1986: 160). Even sporadic occurrences of such treatment towards individuals within a certain area may suffice to instill enough fear and feelings of helplessness among the members of those communities to perpetuate or reinstall compliance. This is even more so if it is considered that the police and other local authorities, for various reasons, frequently side with the caste Hindus, commonly hampering the efforts by *Dalits* and *Adivasis* to assert their rights or even violently obstructing any attempt at defiance.[6] The following incident in which a female *Dalit* agricultural laborer who had been sexually harassed by a superintendent of police (SP) and who then complained to the subcollector may illustrate the situation:

> The next morning the police broke all the doors and arrested all the men in the village. [...] The SP came looking for me. My husband hid under the cot. [...] The police started [...] beating me. The SP dragged me naked on the road for one hundred feet. I was four months pregnant at the time. [...] They brought me to the police station naked. [...] I spent 25 days in jail. I miscarried my baby after 10 days. Nothing has happened to the officers who did this to me. (Guruswamy Guruammal, Tamil Nadu: Human Rights Watch 1999)

These experiences and those within bondage may not always be distinguishable, yet it can be safely said that increased dependency through bondage generally creates an aggravated basis for humiliating structures and interactions.

[6]Unpublished interviews with various social activists, conducted between January and July 2004 by the present author.

14.4 Living in Bondage

Bonded labor, embedded in the overall scenario just described, is marked by (various degrees of) constant structural degradation as well as occasional or frequent interpersonal humiliations. In the following, two central aspects of labor bondage – the deprivation of freedom and self-alienation – shall be interrogated in regard to their potential to affect the laborers' dignity. It goes without saying that both are interrelated and frequently reinforce each other.

14.4.1 Deprivation of Freedom: Chains, Taints, and Boycotts

Bonded labor relations are characterized by a high asymmetry of power which is manifested in the ability of the employer to execute any decision against the will of the laborers. The dominant's means "to make the weak perform" and thus to deprive them of their basic freedoms can take on physical, social or economic force (Pandit 2000: 3) as the cases below illustrate:

In July 2001, Bachhan Singh, a 37-year-old laborer was found in Fatehabad district, Haryana, working in the fields with his hands and legs chained to a tractor-trailer.[7] *He had been severely beaten up by the owner of the farm for whom he had worked as a bonded laborer for the last 20 years. His wife was working as a maid in the same house.* (CEC 2004: 38)

Shoba Gasti, a Dalit girl, was 12 when she was married to a Hindu goddess and became a Devadasi. *She thought that the ceremony was just a religious ritual but soon she found out that her job was to sexually serve any man who would ask for her. There was no option to reject any of them. The chances are small that she will ever be able to marry and lead a normal life. The fact that someone else can turn her into an object is still very painful to her* (Roy 2006).

Pushpaben, like many other manual scavengers, used to ask for vadvu *as a part of fulfilling her caste duties.* Vadvu *is the act of going door-to-door and begging for leftover scraps of food from others' homes. Malnutrition is one, increasing dependence on their employers as well as the reinforcement of the scavengers' low status are further implications of this custom* (Navsarjan). *It is difficult for Pushpaben to find alternative employment as "the ascribed link between occupation and jati" traps her community into that work, "[b]earing the taint of being sweepers in perpetuum".* (Prashad 2000: xvi–xviii, 45)

Once bonded laborers attempt to assert their rights, "the whole landowning community blocks access to local roads and the village well, would not let [the bonded laborers] use the fields to go for toilet, pass orders to shop keepers, milkmen, and grain mill owners, not to sell anything to them, and to [the laborers'] own community not to cooperate with them, no landowner in the area would employ them."[8]

---

[7] Although it is not the rule, there are repeated reports of bonded laborers found in chains (Srivastava 2005: 13, 24, CEC 2004: 46, 54).

[8] Unpublished Interview with Jai Singh, Director of "Volunteers for Social Justice", Punjab, conducted by the author in 2004.

How may Bachhan Singh have felt, having forcibly been deprived of his physical freedom to that extent, knowing that he would also be seen in this state by his wife and his children? Considering that "manhood" and fatherhood are attributed with the ablity to control, can Bachhan Singh today still feel himself to be a "real" man and father? What effect may it have had on Shoba Gasti's self-respect and identity to realize that she could be forced by any man to have sex with him, and that it was her parents that had pushed her into that situation; to live as a single woman in a society where unmarried women are considered shameful and inauspicious; to be asked by her daughter about her job? Is it possible *not* to internalize a sense of inferiority if one is forced to carry out the most stigmatized profession, to remove human excreta (often with bare hands and an odor that follows everywhere), if one's children avoid any physical contact, if one is expected to beg for leftovers? What impact may it have on a person's feeling of self-reliance, one's pride, if he is forced to contribute to his own subjugation as happens in the case of socio-economic boycotts?

14.4.2 Self-alienation: "You Forgot Who You Were"

> [The landlords] have bought our body, life and soul, and we have sold ourselves to them as we have no other way to live. (Bonded laborer at Pendravan, in Kumar 1986: 1)

Self-alienation can take on various shapes. While, on the face of it, the following cases appear to cover a wide range of unrelated experiences, they share one significant commonality: the deprivation of human beings of their past, their present and their future; the alienation from "who they were or, rather, who they could have been".

Dala Ram, a twenty five-year old Bhil was sold to a Stone Crusher Company at the age of 4 years. Hari Ram, working in a quarry for more than 5 years, has received no payment nor does he remember how he came there. The laborers there did not know their exact place of origin as most of them were bonded from an early age (CEC 2004: 40).

"Listless eyes, sunken belly and unable to speak above a whisper – that is Ramdeen [. . .]. He was born in bondage, labored all his life for a pittance. Ramdeen had to pay dearly for the Rs 550 and three mounds of rice taken by his father from the landlord." (Sharma 1999: 14)

A kamiya[9] *at times has to work for 24 h a day without any rest* (Kumar 1994: 4). *Shiv Narain of Singhanpur village in Chhattisgarh had got so used to this kind of life "that he hardly ever had the time or reason to visualise a different life for himself"* (Dogra 1998: 6). *To be at the master's beck and call around-the-clock is a quite general feature of bonded labor. "Even if we were eating our food or sleeping and the master sent for us, we had to leave immediately", released laborers recall with resentment.* (Dogra 1998: 2)[10]

---

[9] "Kamiya" is a regional term for an agricultural laborer who enters bondage as a result of a loan for his marriage.

[10] A study on workers in the US has found that people greatly resent being ordered around and "being treated like nothing, [. . .] like you was dirt, [. . .] like you are part of the woodwork", that

Repeatedly one finds statements by bonded laborers expressing the notion of living the life of an animal or worse than that (Pandit 2000: 60, 62). *"Look at my shoulders, the skin calloused like the back of a buffalo carrying earth for 40 years now. Am I in any way different from those animals?"* (Bonded laborer at Pendravan, in Kumar 1986: 1)

These statements and observations strongly suggest that Dala and Hari Ram, Shiv Narain, Ramdeen and the bonded laborer at Pendravan have been left with little opportunity to design, live and become agents of their *own* lives, to nurture their relationships, to cultivate their roots, to develop and live their potentials, and to build up assertive community identities.

Yet, while one might still argue that, in the cases just mentioned, it is the conditions that *keep* people low, there are other forms of domination that bluntly tell the subordinate that they *are* low, inferior, subhuman, or dirt:

> That anybody white could take your whole self for anything that came to mind. Not just work, kill, or maim you, but dirty you. Dirty you so bad you couldn't like yourself anymore. Dirty you so bad you forgot who you were and couldn't think it up. (Sethe, a former slave, one of the central characters in the novel *Beloved*; Morrison 1988: 251)[11]

Dirtying can also be found in the context of bondage where it is used as a device to put the laborers and their communities in their place; we only need to remember those instances such as being paraded naked, being (gang-)raped, etc. The second aspect of Sethe's experience, "forgetting who one was" may, however, also be triggered by everyday forms of degradation. In some localities, *Dalits* are still not supposed to dress decently (Sainath 1996: 211) as they are expected to position themselves physically lower than caste Hindus when in the same place (Mendelsohn and Vicziany 1998: 52). In several cases the name of the *jati* has become a "common term of contempt and shame whenever it [is] used by others and [can] hardly avoid carrying this freight with it whenever one use[s] it to identify oneself" (Isaacs 1964: 43). Some tribes such as the (often bonded) Katkaris are labelled by the government as "Primitive Tribes" and enlisted by the police as "Criminal Tribes" (Datar). *Dalits* and *Adivasis* are habitually called by their first name or by derogative terms indicating their membership in a "polluting" caste, or are addressed like children or with insults (Freeman 1979: 416; 1986: 156; Zelliot 2005: 35). Occasionally, they and their ancestors have even been given names by their overlords that express their menial or subhuman position:

> Puchchi, a man from Tamil Nadu, is in his sixties. He has lived all his life with that name which means insect. Another person is called Adimayee, slave. These names have even been internalized by them. (Sainath 1996: 209)

---

is as if "you almost cease to exist". (Sennet and Cobb 1973: 94, 97, 114–115, 139) In contrast to those wageworkers in the US who can regularly call it a day after all, most bonded laborers have to endure this lot without any break in which they had a chance to pursue their lives.

[11] While the characters of *Beloved* are fictional, their statements may be understood as the essence of the experience of former slaves upon whose testimonies Morrison based the novel.

It is how bonded laborers and their communities are being addressed or referred to, the demonstrations of powerlessness they are confronted with, the way they are supposed to perform in public, the fact that their individualities are simply not seen by customarily being reduced to their profession or their *jati*, the general understanding that the laborers' sentiments do not count (if *Dalits* are at all perceived as beings equipped with feelings), that constantly suggests the subordinates' lowness and that culminates in the perfidy to expect them to comply and to even self-identify with their ascribed inferiority. It seems highly probable that those steady acts of categorization, outright degradation and dehumanization, of destruction of their social roots and bonds, and of frustration of a positive self-identification and of personal visions of a different life gradually result in the laborers' alienation from themselves.

14.5 Indications of Violations of Dignity

How may these various acts of subjugation that bonded laborers and their communities face be interpreted within a framework of violations of dignity? In order to determine *violations* of dignity it would, at first sight, seem appropriate to start with a definition of *dignity*. For two reasons, however, I propose to approach the subject from the other perspective. One consideration lies in the common experience of dignity as something that is usually only felt in its absence or in any threat to it. The second is to be sought in the objective of this chapter, namely to identify violations of dignity by letting the material speak for itself; material in which, for obvious reasons, positive references to dignity, or to *garima*,[12] do not figure prominently.

Extracting from the previous discussion and from research on similar relationships of domination the essence of those acts and conditions that are *apt* to provoke a *violation of dignity*, one can say that these acts and conditions involve a person or a group:

(i) being forced to act or being "acted upon" in a way that is perceived as degrading, humiliating, defiling, embarrassing, dishonouring, shaming, be it by society as a whole, by the dominating group or a dominating individual within a relationship, by one's primary community or any significant other or by oneself; and/or
(ii) being deprived of the freedom of designing and determining one's own life: being cut off from one's roots and one's relationships; being prevented from living one's own potentials and one's identity according to one's values, from developing oneself the way one would long to; being prevented from enjoying some space for withdrawal and rest where one can simply *be*; being prevented from expressing oneself; and/or

---

[12] While there are various "Indic" terms for dignity, the one that has recently come into abundant usage among *Dalit* politicians, writers and scholars is *garima*.

(iii) being denied any recognition, acknowledgment, value, or rights, possibly even being made to feel subhuman, as dirt, as an object or a means, or as non-existent; as if nothing of what one *is*, feels, thinks, and does were of any worth; and, thus, consequently, losing one's self-reliance and self-esteem and experiencing self-alienation.

While the second condition, denial of self-determination, may require the first and/or the third, to possibly result in violated dignity, any degrading treatment or forced self-humiliation or structural depreciation could, in contrast, suffice in itself. To be sure, at this point of the discussion we can only speak of these manifestations of subordination within the context of bonded labor as indications of *potential* violations of dignity; no more, no less.

From these observations we may now infer an understanding of *dignity* as an (alterable) condition and capacity of an individual or a collective that touches upon issues of self-identity, self-value, authenticity, integrity, humanity and civility, and of belonging to (an existing or imagined) community, as well as on notions of honour, grace, and pride; which results from an enjoyment of choice, freedom, and agency. I would claim that someone may maintain his dignity as long as he is able to maintain his self, that is, an internal sense of personal worth, a positive self-identity, a certain measure of self-reliance and responsibility, his values and his humanity, a sphere of privacy, etc. Dignity can be described as the ability to exert agency, to control, hold onto, determine at least *one* aspect of life that cannot be manipulated by someone else, or, to put it differently, one aspect that one is able to resist against, "warding off capitulation, [. . .] insisting upon the observance of a boundary between self [possibly also one's community, *added by T. E.*] and world" (Des Pres 1976: 202).

14.6 Dignity Defended, Violated, Regained, or Lost? *Or* the Role of Identity

A variety of sources on bonded laborers and their communities but also findings from other empirical fields indicate that it is, generally speaking, not an act or condition of subjugation alone but rather its conjuncture with other factors that may result in a person experiencing a violation or even a long-lasting loss of his dignity. How could it otherwise be explained that, within seemingly comparable situations, some people feel stripped of their dignity, while others (or the same persons at some other time) are able to maintain it? For example, whereas manual scavenging today commonly evokes a feeling of shame by those cleaning the latrines, historical documents of the Mehtars, a sweepers' community, reveal that at a certain point in time the latter "[took] pride in their [. . .] occupation" in a way that allowed them to "fashion some dignity for themselves", which appears to have been due to their ability at that time to partly control the labor process (Prashad 2000: 5, 123). Remarkably, even in a place where the most extreme and most systematic attempts were made to dehumanize and de-individualize human beings, that is, in Nazi concentration camps, we may find support for this claim of contextuality. While the reports by former inmates bear testimony to an extent and severity of violations of human dignity experienced that is beyond imagination, at the same time they give evidence that, in certain instances, people were yet able to, at least temporarily and occasionally, uphold or regain their dignity. From Maja Suderland's analysis of the "debate" between Jean Améry and Primo Levi, both camp survivors, as well as well-known writers and intellectuals, we learn that both could, rarely enough but nevertheless, draw on resources that served that very purpose; resources that had their origin in their respective pasts and which carried great personal significance for them. For Levi it was his education and his humanistic identity respectively, and in Améry's case his political identity, that they were able to revert to and thus resume a "personal continuity" that allowed them, momentarily, to experience dignity (Suderland 2004: 105–111, 131).

The previous findings make obvious that it might be difficult to grasp from the outside whether – in a *particular* situation – a person has been deprived of his dignity. Returning to the context of bonded labor, the intention of the present contribution is, as emphasized before, to come as close as possible to an understanding of the perception held by the respective *bonded laborers* themselves. For that purpose, the ultimate authority to determine whether a given act of degradation amounts to a violation or even loss of dignity, and to what extent, lies with them as the bearers of that dignity. Unfortunately, for a number of reasons *the* authentic voice of bonded laborers on that matter cannot easily be captured. Nevertheless, here and there the literature on bonded labor does reveal authentic statements of bonded laborers, indicating notions of dignity by references to experiences of "shame–pride/honour", "inferiority–superiority", or "humiliation–self-respect". Alas, these are just scattered instances, unlikely to convey the multifariousness of how bonded labor conditions are experienced and even less to shed much light on the particular contexts of the respective laborers. Yet these original expressions, located within the general social scenario that has been depicted at the beginning of this chapter, may serve as a starting point, complemented by observations by social activists working closely with bonded laborers and by statements by other subordinates in similar power-laden contexts.

The following discussion will also draw on the theory of psychological reactance and learned helplessness theory, James Scott's concept of the hidden transcript, and Toni Morrison's novel *Beloved* and the extensive literature that has developed around it, both of the latter offering powerful findings on the long-lasting implications of slavery. They all provide valuable keys to an understanding of how human beings deal with threats to, or loss of, their freedom – freedom broadly understood as the capacity for control over one's life. Having already identified the loss of freedom as a central indicator for potential violations of dignity, we may thus also be able to derive from those theories and concepts how people may respond to threats to their dignity. In particular, this chapter aims to analyze, first, under what conditions acts of subordination are likely, or less likely, to be experienced as violations of dignity and to what extent, and second, to identify resources that bonded laborers may be (un)able to tap in order to keep or regain their dignity.

While it seems to be common sense "that those who must routinely knuckle under to insults or physical beatings they consider unjust pay a heavy psychological price", findings in the area of social psychology draw a more differentiated picture (Scott 1990: 108–109). Shared by several theories is the assumption that human beings like to view themselves as causal agents; they strive to maintain control over their lives and to avoid any dependence as much as possible (Wortman and Brehm 1975: 280–283). Once this behavioral freedom is threatened or taken away, a person will, according to reactance theory, experience some motivational arousal, or reactance, i.e., an initiative to restore his freedom as long as he expects to have control over the situation and does not consider the cost of resistance higher than the value he ascribes to freedom (Wortman and Brehm 1975: 283, 327).

In *some* cases – usually where initiative has been taken and support given by social movements, NGOs or state officials, and/or where bonded laborers or their communities *have had* an experience of agency, self-assertion, and self-value[13] – the bonded laborers have resisted their oppression. One example is the sweepers of Delhi before they were forcibly incorporated into the municipal authorities. When they were mistreated or withheld wages by the householders, the collective of sweepers refused to work in the neighbourhood; none of the filth got removed until the offended sweeper got pacified by the householder (Prashad 2000: 3–10). It can be assumed that it was that "ordinary luxury of negative reciprocity: trading a slap for a slap, an insult for an insult" (Scott 1990: 22) that played a crucial role in maintaining the sweepers' dignity. Another case in point is that of the bonded agricultural laborers in Maharasthra among whom, in the process of organizing, an expectation to win control over their lives was generated, nourished by being told that their freedom was guaranteed by the law, by learning that other struggles for freedom – in other places and successively in their own circle – had been successful, by developing a sense of community and experiencing mutual support and thus empowerment in their "individual" conflicts with their employers and with dominant caste communities. A social activist describes the release of the first bonded Adivasi by his trade union as:

[13]This experience may be grounded in a collective history of a dignified and glorious past or an imagination of, and justification for, a positive future: a tradition of resistance, myths of an originally higher social status (and thus some claim for a higher morality), a symbolic figure, counter-ideologies, counter-beliefs to the Brahmanic tradition, or conversions to religions that emphasize the equality of the believers. Some accounts of the latter may exemplify the dignifying effect that all of these sources of self-identification might carry. Where conversions have been accompanied by a change of mind, they appear to have generated "a new sense of dignity and self-worth" among the converts. *Mahars* who converted along with Ambedkar to Buddhism experienced that "the [prior] sense of shame, inferiority and degradation was washed away". A prominent Buddhist intellectual said, "I have become a human being. [...] I am not lowborn or inferior now. [...] The chains of Untouchability which shackled my feet have now been shattered. [...] I am no longer the slave and menial servant of high-caste Hindus. I will never again accept servile labor from the high-caste Hindus. [...] I have become a free citizen [...]." (Gokhale 1993: 182, Scott 1990: 117–118).

> [. . .] a sudden eruption of a volcano; [the] relative outer calm had masked generations of rage. From village after village tribal people started approaching us [. . .]. It was like the force of dammed water breaking out and flooding everything in its way. I have always found anger seething just below the surface of silence. People organise when they are convinced that any alternative which includes death also is better than the present oppression. (Pandit 2000: 62)

In this sense, people who participated in this struggle decided to bear starvation and physical violence rather than to continue complying with their own subordination; "We will eat bitter roots and crabs but we will no more bow before the landlords." (A released bonded woman, cited in Pandit 2000: 61) This decision to take charge of their lives regardless of the costs involved eventually helped them to regain their dignity.

Obviously, in the context of bondage this kind of development is the exception. In general, a bonded laborer would *not* expect to be able to control the situation due to lack of social support (e.g., as a result of migration, of *jati* divisions, possibly also of physical confinement) and to barred access to those valued goods (material and immaterial) and relations with which he can positively self-identify and from which he can derive self-esteem. Furthermore, and partly consequently, he would also dread the consequences of any attempt at freedom since any form of defiance would usually carry negative implications for himself and for his family, if not for the entire community. In most cases the laborer's fear of starvation (possibly of the entire family), the loss of livelihood (through socio-economic boycotts) and of housing, of physical violence, maybe even death, is greater than his urge for freedom. Particularly when considering that he would also have to interact with the "powerful freedom threatener" in future, he would generally avoid any overt rebellion (Wortman and Brehm 1975: 327, Miron and Brehm 2006: 11). As Scott puts it, "[the] cruellest result of human bondage is that it transforms the assertion of personal dignity into a mortal risk". (Scott 1990: 37)

Yet, reactance theory tells us that even if this first option of open and direct reactance is not available, or perceived not to be, bonded laborers may attempt to restore their freedom by implication, i.e., by showing resistance in some other way, which is called covert reactance (Wortman and Brehm 1975: 286). Scott's "hidden transcript" can give us an idea of what that might look like:

> Providing the threat is sufficiently imposing, overt agreement and compliance [in the 'public transcript'] may prevail [as it is] often secured [. . .] by close surveillance to detect and punish deviance, [. . .] but *covert reactance* will increase [emphasis added, T. E.], attempting to neutralize and negate the public version. (Scott 1990: 109, 111)

While the public transcript may be understood as the sphere of open interaction between subordinates and the dominant, its complement, the hidden transcript, rather characterizes the discourse that takes place "offstage", the responses and rejoinders to that public transcript that escape direct observation by power-holders (Scott 1990: 2, 4). The hidden transcript is nurtured by the "systematic frustration of reciprocal action in relations of domination". In its social sites "the unspoken riposte, stifled anger, and bitten tongues created by relations of domination [can] find a vehement, full-throated expression", a "safe articulation of the assertion [and] aggression [. . .] that is thwarted by the onstage power of the dominant". (Scott 1990: 37, 111, 114, 120)

There are various dynamics by which the indignities of subordination may be counterbalanced or even be fended off. For one, Scott suggests that the greater the extrinsic reasons compelling the performance, the less the subordinate may consider it representative of his "true self". It is rather like *a mask that he wears*, having little or no bearing on his self-conception (Scott 1990: 110) and thus, one could assume, on his dignity. A further way to counteract humiliations is to *put oneself above the dominant*, either in the sense of considering oneself morally superior, or by denigrating the threatener through jokes, bad talk, etc. (Miron and Brehm 2006: 10). Yet another device is *tricking the dominant*, e.g., by using attributions as a weapon: if the dominant think that the subordinates are stupid the latter might just decide to use it to their own advantage and play stupid. According to a proverb of Jamaican slaves, "Play fool, to catch wise" (Scott 1990: 3), this might not only minimise their work load but also give them deep satisfaction having been able to curtail the power of the dominant over them, having made the dominant experience the limits of their power, and, possibly, even having let them subtly know they hit back. Other variations pursuing the same aim are spitting into the master's food, ruining the expensive *saree* (traditional cloth) in the laundry, or torturing the favourite pet of the mistress as in Robert Darnton's "The Great Cat Massacre".

However, in order for an individual or a community to be able to sustain a hidden transcript, the subordinates need spaces outside the domains of the dominant (Scott 1990: 123) in order to offset the latter's constant attempts to keep them, individually and as a group, at an inferior level, leaving long-lasting imprints on their self-esteem and identities, and their relationships and their community fabric. These spaces may be any kind of physical or symbolic sites (Scott 1990: 121) where community – or collective identity, for that matter – can be felt. These must be spaces where the subordinates can live their lives, at least some part of the day or the year, where they find some refuge that provides emotional and physical sustenance, where they can join, rest, separate themselves from the values they have inculcated from the dominant, nurture their "true self", create a discourse of dignity and justice, abandon those norms and concepts they have adopted "to ensure an equality of suffering" (Jesser 2004: 82), overcome their traumata, heal each other, nurture a collective memory and identity, gather strength, formulate strategies necessary for emancipative struggles[14]; in sum, a space where dignity can be lived. Eventually, the experience here may also embolden the laborers to seek dignity even onstage as happened in Maharashtra.

To be sure, within the context of bonded labor social spaces of that kind are scarce which is due to extremely *long working hours* that leave little or no energy and time for social interaction; a *high level of surveillance* (e.g., restricted mobility by being confined to, or prohibited to leave, the workplace, or by attempts to inhibit

[14]For the discussion on space see also Bloom (2004: 26, 117), Harris (2004: 60), Jesser (2004: 75).

any meeting among the laborers); the *absence of any secluded site* where the laborers can meet, or some device through which they could communicate unobserved by the dominant; the possible situation of *working isolated from each other* (in remote rural areas it is sometimes just one or two laborers working for a smallholder, similarly in domestic services); or a *lack of efforts* to create and fight for a social space. This last aspect might assume a central role, particularly if it has to be put down to *lack of social cohesion* among the bonded laborers and/or between their communities and other subordinate communities. A frequent reason for that is the observance of strict caste divisions (be it between distinctive *jati* or, in the case of an encounter of local and migrant labor, the perception of distinctive, separate entities even within the same *jati*/profession), to the extent that the practice of untouchability is even followed among the *Dalit* communities against those at the very bottom of the casteist order (Sainath 1996: 208). Various prohibitions such as of inter-dining and intermarriage constantly renew and perpetuate this "centuries-old divide, deeply rooted as it is in the [collective] conscious", impeding any socializing, and acting "as a formidable barrier preventing the building of solidarity" (Mukherjee 2004: 460). Within the logic of caste ranking and mobility, the advancement of others may, furthermore, be seen as at one's own expense (Prashad 2000: xiv). Beyond that, and definitely not to be underestimated, may also be the fear of consequences as well as the experience of shame that may hinder community members from reaching out to each other. This overall scenario makes obvious that social space needs to be fought for on different fronts, and has to be constantly created, built, and defended.

We do not know whether the negotiations and negations within the hidden transcript and the existence of social spaces uncontrolled by the employers may help the bonded laborers to actually maintain their dignity at the time of concrete acts of degradation or whether they can "only" reconstitute their dignity some time afterwards. One could assume that it may vary, depending on the particular context. However, it seems that the more a subordinate has access to these kinds of spaces the more he may succeed in coping with the indignities inflicted by the dominant.

However, when a person has had the previous experience of not being able to control a certain kind of situation, he would have no expectation to be in a position to restore his freedom in any similar situation (Wortman and Brehm 1975: 309, Miron and Brehm 2006: 12). Once a comparable situation arises the person who experienced defeat in the past would now not show any reactance but rather remain passive (Wortman and Brehm 1975: 307–309). The theory of learned helplessness even claims that the person may generalize his expectancy of powerlessness to other situations (Hiroto and Seligman 1975: 327). This happens particularly if the individual attributes some global cause (in the case of bonded laborers that could, for example, be domination by higher castes, poverty, or one's karma) to some negative experience that is perceived as significant; equally if this experience had negative consequences (e.g., miscarriage after a beating, ostracism after having been raped, starvation due to a socio-economic boycott by the high caste employers and shopkeepers). Or, if this negative experience has prompted the individual to attribute his self with negative traits (e.g., having lost one's womanhood or manhood, not being a good parent, being a coward) or if the person lacks social support (Petermann 1999: 229). It thus seems that it is not the aversive situation per se but its conjuncture with further factors that may render a person in a state of helplessness (Wortman and Brehm 1975: 289); factors that, to be sure, may have their origin in the context of bondage itself and that may leave long-lasting imprints on the self-perception and the dignity of the individual.

Various social activists stress that not few oppressed have internalized a sense of inferiority, after having been patronised, despised, discriminated against and shamed since childhood, and, for that matter, for generations. For them, the "very thought of challenging the oppressor, asking a question, saying 'no' to injustice opens a sense of intense insecurity" (Pandit 2000: 7). The more important the stake, the greater is the degree of a person's helplessness (Wortman and Brehm 1975: 309) and, I would claim, of the damage that is done to his dignity. The situation of the husband hiding under the bed, not daring to protect his wife and the baby she carries, epitomizes this kind of helplessness. What this man may have lost in that very moment is his role as the head of the family, the role of the protector, his manliness, and the trust of his family and community. Particularly when a child is violated, Scott claims that,

> [. . .] the parents suffer [. . .] a devastating public display of their powerlessness to keep their child from harm. They lose [. . .] the public claim to be parents, above all in the eyes of their child and also in those of any onlookers. It is difficult to conceive a more damaging loss of standing as a person. The impact seems to be seared in the memory of those who suffer it. (Scott 1990: 113–114)

This appears to be generally valid when the audience is composed of those "before whom one's dignity, one's standing as a person, is most important because [they form] the social source for one's sense of self-esteem." (Scott 1990: 113–114, Bouson 2004: 97).

It has been found that the higher the level of powerlessness, the stronger the anger and shame that a person will develop. Anger (Wortman and Brehm 1975: 317), presumably particularly in its combination with shame (Bouson speaks of "shame-rage"), may develop energy towards "outhurting the hurter" (Bouson 2002: 148), which *might* find some outlet in the hidden transcript through which some dignity might be recuperated. It can be assumed, however, that extremely intense experiences of shame offer no option of denial or negotiation and result in helplessness and a severe damage to one's dignity as the following might indicate. In the discourse on Morrison's *Beloved*, Janoff-Bulman observes that persons "overpowered by another" feel not only helpless but also "sullied and tarnished" in the process (Janoff-Bulman 1992: 80). Bouson emphasizes that "deliberate infliction of injury can induce unbearable and chronic feelings of shame" (Bouson 2004: 91); according to Langer, humiliations suffered are often felt "worse than death", indicating a "toxicity"[15] of the "humiliated memory [. . .] reanimating the governing impotence of the worst moments" of a debilitating past (Langer 1991: 83–84). Herman argues

[15] The term "toxicity" in this context was coined by Bouson (2004: 91).

that this may eventually even lead to a "contaminated identity", preoccupied with "shame, self-loathing, and a sense of failure". (Herman 1992: 94)

In sum, the discussion makes obvious that violations of dignity feature regularly within relations of bonded labor. The laborers would usually not consider it an option to openly challenge any act of subjugation, and they would also, particularly in cases of accumulated deprivation and degradation, not easily have access to those resources that would allow them to negate or negotiate those violations. However, the extent of the damage may vary considerably, depending upon whether a violation inflicted by the dominant may spill over to other relationships and thus infect the experience of dignity in other spheres of the person's life, possibly also his future, or whether it may remain limited to that specific situation within which it occurred. The outcome is contingent on the particular collective and individual identities, social practices, and social spaces a person and his community have developed. Where the interplay of those factors renders a supportive environment, bonded laborers may be able to partly, temporarily, and occasionally keep or restore their dignity.

At an abstract level, the material suggests that dignity is not monolithic and static, but complex and multi-dimensional. It may be comprehended, firstly, as a continuum running from "intact" to "lost"; secondly as an array of various spatial as well as temporal compartments. While dignity may be violated and lost in some compartments and/or at a certain point in time, it may be defended and upheld, nurtured and enjoyed in others, and also restored later on.

14.7 Conclusion

This discussion has endeavoured to investigate how bonded labor, from a subjective-psychological perspective, may impact upon human dignity. Studies and reports on bonded labor indicate that everyday oppression, deprivation, and degradation factor centrally in the lives of bonded laborers and their communities, from time to time complemented by outright atrocities. It can be safely assumed that, in this process, the dignity of large numbers of bonded laborers is violated everyday throughout India. Yet, we cannot be absolutely sure in which *particular* situation a *particular* bonded laborer may actually experience a violation of his dignity and to what extent. I have argued that it is, generally, *not the act of abasement* per se but the concurrence of several conditions that determines whether a bonded laborer will suffer, *or* be in a position to ward off, violations of his dignity or, at least, limit the damage in terms of time and reach: One important factor appears to be the "thickness" of deprivation, degradation and annihilation that the laborer has been subjected to. What may tip the scales, however, is the person's prior experience of powerlessness in similar situations, the significance the person attributes to the particular humiliation suffered and the level of shame inflicted, the audience witnessing, the person's access to any social sites where a "life-beyond-control-by-the-dominant" can be lived, the fabric and historicity of the person's own and his community's self-identity (and the extent to which these are a result of the power structures that have been constructed by the dominant in the first place), the person's ability to maintain a personal continuity, and the identity of the person that is at the forefront in a particular moment – the shamed, dehumanized, objectified one, or a self-conscious and proud identity.

To be *possibly* able to hold on to one's dignity in the face of repression does not insinuate that human rights have not been violated. What needs to be acknowledged, however, is that any person, in principle, is endowed with agency and with an identity that encompasses more than the experience of subordination, no matter how distant some aspects of that identity and how restricted that agency might be within relations of bondage. To deny agency where it *does* exist, similarly as to assert it where it *does not*, would deprive that person, once again, of his dignity.

Yet, in order to develop a genuine and differentiated understanding of, first, the *actual* meaning of dignity for those in bondage, and second, of the circumstances under which dignity within varied conditions of labor bondage may be violated or upheld, we need to listen to many more stories bonded laborers have yet to tell. While each of them may reveal a particular set of experiences, all of them together should give us a clue to the socio-psychological dynamics that construct, nourish, violate, sometimes sustainably destroy, and restore human dignity.

References

Antislavery International. 2007. Ritual slavery practices in India – Devadasi, Jogini and Mathamma. http://www.antislavery.org/includes/documents/cm_docs/2008/r/ritual_slavery_briefing_paper_1_august_2007.pdf. Accessed 3 Apr 2009.

Appadurai, Arjun. 1988. Putting hierarchy in its place. *Cultural Anthropology* 3(1): 36–49.

Barnes, Robert Harrison, Andrew Gray, and Benedict Kingsbury, eds. 1995. *Indigenous peoples of Asia*. Ann Arbor: Association for Asian Studies Inc.

Berreman, Gerald D. 1979. *Caste and other inequities essays on inequality.* Meerut: Folklore Institute.

Bloom, Harold. 2004. Summary and analysis. In *Blooms guides. Toni Morrison's beloved*, ed. Harold Bloom, 16–48. Philadelphia, PA: Chelsea House Publishers.

Brooks Bouson, J. 2002. *Quiet as it's kept: shame, trauma, and race in the novels of Toni Morrison*. Albany, NY: State University of New York Press.

Brooks Bouson, J. 2004. Sethe's best thing. In *Blooms guides. Toni Morrisons beloved*, ed. Harold Bloom. Philadelphia, PA: Chelsea House Publishers.

Center for Education and Communication (CEC). 2004. *Debt bondage in India.* New Delhi: CEC.

Datar, Chhaya. Integrating Tribals in the Mainstream. Emerging Dissimilarities in the Status of Tribal Women in Maharashtra. http://www.winaindia.com/chhaya.htm. Accessed 22 Aug 2009.

Des Pres, Terrence. 1976. *The Survivor*. New York: Oxford University Press.

Dogra, Bharat. 1998. *Land and freedom struggle of released bonded laborers to obtain land in Chattisgarh*. Delhi.

Flood, Gavin. 2005. Introduction: Establishing the boundaries. In *The Blackwell companion to Hinduism*, ed. Gavin Flood, 1–19. Malden: Blackwell Publishing.

Freeman, James M. 1979. *Untouchable an Indian life history*. London: George Allen and Unwin.

Freeman, James M. 1986. The consciousness of freedom among India's untouchables. In *Social and economic development in India a reassessment*, ed. Dilip K. Basu, 153–171. New Delhi: Sage Publications.

Gatade, Subash. 2009. Dalits in a Hindu Rashtra. http://www.countercurrents.org/gatade040309.htm. Accessed 24 Jun 2009.

Ghurye, Govind Sadashiv. 1980. *The scheduled tribes of India*. New Brunswick: Transaction Publishers.

Gokhale, Jayashree. 1993. *From concessions to confrontation.* Bombay: Popular Prakashan.
Harris, Trudier. 2004. Images of slavery. In *Blooms guides Toni Morrisons beloved*, ed. Harold Bloom, 59–70. Philadelphia, PA: Chelsea House Publishers.
Herman, Judith Lewis. 1992. *Trauma and recovery.* New York, NY: HarperCollins/Basic Books.
Hiroto, Donald S., and Martin E.P. Seligman. 1975. Generality of learned helplessness in man. *Journal of Personality and Social Psychology* 31: 311–327.
Human Rights Watch. 1999. *Broken people.* http://www.hrw.org/reports/1999/india/India994.htm. Accessed 19 Jun 1999.
Isaacs, Harold R. 1964. *Indias ex-untouchables.* New York, NY: Harper and Row.
Janoff-Bulman, Ronnie. 1992. *Shattered assumptions: Towards a new psychology of trauma.* New York, NY: Free/Macmillan.
Jesser, N. 2004. Violence, home and community. In *Blooms guides. Toni Morrisons beloved*, ed. Harold Bloom, 74–90. Philadelphia, PA: Chelsea House Publishers.
Keer, Dhananjay. 1962. *Dr. Ambedkar, life and mission.* Bombay: Popular Prakashan.
Kumar, Ajoy. 1994. From slavery to freedom. In *Struggle for justice*, ed. Mathew, P.D. Delhi: Indian Social Institute.
Langer, Lawrence. 1991. *Holocaust testimonies: The ruins of memory.* New Haven, CT: Yale University Press.
Mendelsohn, Oliver, and Marika Vicziany. 1998. *The untouchables.* Cambridge: Cambridge University Press.
Milner, Murray Jr. 1994. *Status and sacredness.* New York, NY: Oxford University Press.
Miron, Anca M., and Jack W. Brehm. 2006. Reactance theory – 40 years later. *Zeitschrift für Sozialpsychologie* 37(1): 9–18.
Morrison, Toni. 1988. *Beloved.* London: Picador/Macmillan Publishers.
Mukherjee, Mridula. 2004. *Peasants in Indians non-violent revolution.* New Delhi: Sage Publications.
Navsarjan. I am not my Caste: Pushpaben. http://navsarjan.wordpress.com/stories-main/nadiad/. Accessed 13 Aug 2009.
Oommen, T. K. 1990. *Protest and change: Studies in social movements.* New Delhi: Sage Publications.
Pandit, Vivek. 2000. *Fearless minds.* Bombay: National Centre for Advocacy Studies.
Petermann, Franz. 1999. Nachwort. In *Erlernte Hilflosigkeit*, 3rd edn, Martin E.P. Seligman. Weinheim: Beltz.
Prashad, Vijay. 2000. *Untouchable freedom.* New Delhi: Oxford University Press.
Ram, Nandu. 1995. *Beyond Ambedkar. Essays on dalits in India.* Delhi: Har-Anand Publications.
Roy, Kaushik G. 2006. Eyes wide open. Film and Television Institute of India. http://creativecontent.unesco.org/media-library/product?usca_p=t&product_id=36856. Accessed 17 Aug 2009.
Sainath, P. 1996. *Everybody loves a good drought. Stories from India's poorest districts.* Delhi: Penguin Books.
Scott, James C. 1990. *Domination and the arts of resistance.* New Haven, CT: Yale University Press.
Sennett, Richard, and Jonathan, Cobb. 1993. *The hidden injuries of class.* New York, NY: Norton.
Sharma, Anita. 1999. Freed bonded labor: From flying pan into the fire. *The Times of India*, 9 Nov: 14.
Srinivas, M. N. 1966. *Social change in Modern India.* Berkeley, CA: University of California Press.
Srinivas, M. N. 1992. *On living in a revolution and other essays.* Delhi: Oxford University Press.
Srivastava, Ravi S. 2005. Bonded labor in India: Its incidence and pattern. In *ILO special action program to combat forced labor, working paper 43.* Geneva: ILO Publications Bureau.
Suderland, Maja. 2004. *Territorien des Selbst.* Frankfurt: Campus.
Thapar, Romila. 2002. *Early India: From the origins to AD 1300.* Berkeley, CA: University of California Press.

Varadarajan, A., and Ambedkar, Prakash. 1993. Atrocities on Dalits, A plea for remedial action. PUCL Bull. http://www.pucl.org/from-archives/Dalit-tribal/atrocities.htm. Accessed 2 Jul 2009.

Waite, Louise. 2006. *Embodied working lives: Work and life in Maharashtra, India.* Lanham: Lexington Books.

Wortman, Camille B., and Jack W. Brehm. 1975. Responses to uncontrollable outcomes: An integration of reactance theory and the learned helplessness model. In *Advances in experimental social psychology*, vol. 8, ed. Leonard Berkowitz. New York, NY: Academic Press.

Zelliot, Eleanor. 1996. The Dalit movement. *Dalit International Newsletter*, 1(1): 1, 4.

Zelliot, Eleanor. 2005. *From untouchable to Dalit.* New Delhi: Manohar Publishers.

Part III
Conclusions for a Positive Account of Human Dignity

Chapter 15
Human Dignity and Human Rights

Marcus Düwell

Abstract An analysis of violations of human dignity seems to offer an inductive pathway to human dignity, that some find more promising than theory-guided elaborations of a positive account. This paper wants to stress the need to develop a positive account of human dignity. It is impossible to determine which kind of actions are violations of human dignity without a positive account. It is furthermore difficult to understand the relevance of those violations for a comprehensive concept of human dignity without a positive approach. The paper aims at developing an understanding of what one could expect from an account of human dignity in two steps. In the first place some general features of a modern concept of human dignity are described, such as the equality of dignity, the other-regarding prescriptivity, the emphasis on the inherent worth of the individual and the overriding normative claim of human dignity. The aim would be to show those elements that distinguish disputes about human dignity from other debates about honour, social standing, ideals of excellence and the like. In a second step the paper formulates a set of questions that each theory of human dignity must answer: Who has human dignity? What is the relationship between human dignity and human rights? What is the normative content of human dignity? What is the ontological status of human dignity? And what kind of justification for human dignity can be expected? The list is not complete but the paper aims to identify those questions to which each account of human dignity should give an answer. Human dignity is the basic concept of our moral and political order. Therefore a comprehensive understanding of human dignity is only possible through the development of a positive account. Perhaps such a positive account can not be developed and justified but that can only be decided after a discussion of the questions raised above; and if those questions cannot be answered then we have reasons to abandon the concept of human dignity altogether. Whether or not human dignity is a meaningful, or meaningless and empty concept, can only be decided through a discussion about success and failure of a positive account.

M. Düwell (✉)
Department of Philosophy, University of Utrecht, Netherlands
e-mail: M.Duwell@uu.nl

P. Kaufmann et al. (eds.), *Humiliation, Degradation, Dehumanization*,
Library of Ethics and Applied Philosophy 24, DOI 10.1007/978-90-481-9661-6_15,

15.1 A Positive and a Negative Account of Human Dignity

The notion "human dignity" has appeared in a variety of discourses in the last decennia. The history of the concept and its political, moral and legal function was disputed in a variety of contexts, perhaps most extensively in bioethical debates. The current volume deals with violations of human dignity. The assumption behind such an approach could be that it would be neither appropriate to start with the contested discussions of human dignity nor with philosophical conceptualizations but that an analysis of concrete violations of human dignity would be the most promising way to develop an understanding of the concept. One could assume that it is very difficult to agree whether or not the use of embryos or the allowance of euthanasia is a violation of human dignity or not but that it is much more likely that we can agree that rape, torture or absolute poverty are violations of human dignity. Therefore it would follow a well established strategy in moral philosophy to start with an analysis of less contested cases in order to develop a concept and to assess more contested cases in the light of the so-developed understanding of the concept. There may be heuristic reasons to use the analysis of those cases of violations as a kind of entrance for an understanding of the concept and there is some historical evidence that the experience of degradation and humiliation has been the reason why "human dignity" became such an important political and legal concept. But there are several reasons to assume that such an analysis is insufficient. And it is a mistake to think that the analysis of violations of human dignity can be used as an inductive strategy for the developing of a concept of dignity (as it is often assumed by followers of Margalit 1996). Here are some arguments for a reservation against such an inductive strategy:

First of all, in our actual understanding of the concept "human dignity" there are a variety of presuppositions that are in various respects contested. It is, for example, contested whether or not all members of the human species and all members of the human species have to be treated as beings with dignity. An analysis of the supposedly uncontested cases will not help to decide about those questions.

Secondly, in order to decide which cases are violations of human dignity, we already presuppose a specific concept. Traditional religious thinkers for example thought that one would compromise one's own dignity by religiously unacceptable behaviour. To exclude those cases from an analysis of dignity is only acceptable if one has already a theoretically developed understanding of the concept.

Thirdly, the use of human dignity in the context of the Universal Declaration of Human Rights is a concept that is deeply interrelated with the development of modernity that emphasized the moral protection of each individual. It is difficult to see how an inductive approach can relate to the historical dimension of the concept.

Fourthly, although a variety of questions are contested about human dignity, there are various legal and ethical traditions that understand human dignity as a very fundamental concept; that means a concept that determines the position of human beings in the world, that should provide a basis for the legal and moral status of human beings in general or should give us a reason why human beings have human rights. It is not clear how this more fundamental relevance of human dignity for the legal and moral framework in general can be disputed in an inductive way.

Fifthly, an inductive approach will tend to have a bias towards a specific kind of injustice. It will focus more easily on injustice that manifests themselves in individual cases, meaning cases that have to do with face-to-face-relationships with individual people instead of structural injustice of the political order. Such an inductive approach will furthermore prioritise injustice that is already manifest and visible instead of injustice that is not yet visible (for example our treatment of future generations). I do not want to speculate at the moment on whether or not such a bias is justified (which is possible) but it is at least necessary to offer a theoretical justification for such a bias.

Sixthly, references to human dignity are contested in terms of the conceptual dimension, of whether or not a non-arbitrary meaning of the concept can be developed, and the justificatory dimension concerning the extent to which the moral, political and legal claim for protection of human dignity can be justified. It is difficult to see how an inductive approach can help to clarify such questions of justification.

These six criticisms are far from complete. Depending on the expectations concerning an inductive approach these criticisms will be more or less fatal. There may be reasons to start a discussion about human dignity with an analysis of those actions that are generally seen as violations of human dignity. But such a starting point could only be a first heuristic step. Therefore a "negative approach" – as proposed in this book – can only offer some heuristic tools and not an "approach" to human dignity. If one would try to develop an "inductive" account of human dignity this would make things even worse: Talking about a negative approach leaves at least room for compatibility with a "positive account" while the notion of an "inductive approach" would deny this possibility.

I have suggested so far that it is necessary to develop a positive account of human dignity and that an inductive approach on the basis of analysing violations of dignity offers no theoretical alternative. The development of a positive account of human dignity is, however, confronted with several obstacles. It is not immediately evident what one could expect from such an account. Would any such account of human dignity not simply reflect the general assumptions made in a specific ethical approach? A debate about human dignity would have to relate to the general plurality of approaches in moral philosophy. Furthermore one can wonder whether the development of a positive account would not already presuppose some kind of prior understanding of human dignity. How should one relate, for example, to the general plurality of historical concepts of dignity?

One could begin by simply proposing a concept of human dignity based on a specific ethical theory. Instead, I will consider some preliminary questions about what one can expect from such a theory of human dignity. This kind of preliminary debate is necessary in order to understand what kind of theories are on the table (which is, at least, not self-evident) and what kind of questions are contested when discussing human dignity. My point of reference for this debate is the understanding of human dignity as it was established in the context of the Universal Declaration of Human Rights and the process that followed from that. I do not assume that what emerged post-World War II was a completely different concept of human dignity (unlike Menke and Pollmann 2007); I assume that "our" concept of human dignity is internally related to various debates in modern moral and political philosophy and that this concept can only be understood against the background of those broader moral and political orientations about the worth and rights of individuals (some important studies concerning the prehistory of the concept are Haakonssen 1996, Tierney 1997, Trinkhaus 1970, Tuck 1979).

To structure the debate the paper will proceed in two steps: In the first step I will identify some common features of those concepts of human dignity that we can find in the context of the human rights framework. In a second step I aim to identify those questions to which all accounts of human dignity would have to find an answer. The assumption would be that if those questions cannot be answered then there are reasons to have doubts that human dignity can be used in moral and political discourses. It is therefore not settled that a positive account of human dignity can be developed and successfully decided upon. But whether or not that is the case can only be decided after either answering the questions raised below or by showing that it is impossible at all to answer the questions. To continue using the notion without trying to answer the relevant questions is just dogmatism. But it is not less dogmatic if philosophers are bashing the notion of dignity never having tried to demonstrate the impossibility of a successful defence of the concept. To develop a common agenda of questions – unavoidable questions – would be a necessary first step for an unprejudiced discussion about human dignity.

15.2 Common Features of Positive Accounts of Human Dignity

15.2.1 Equality of Human Dignity

The Universal Declaration grants human dignity to "all members of the human family" regardless of their other features, like race, gender, intelligence, faith, age, etc. This means that dignity is not based on some contingent features of some human beings (Gewirth 1992, Meyer 1989) relating to honor, rank or status. Even though some authors claim that human dignity is a kind of democratization or universalisation of the contingent dignity of rank (e.g. Waldron 2009), even those authors will agree that the concept at stake is an account of dignity that is not graduated by features that human beings have in different degrees or that are the result of characteristics or accomplishments. That is the fundamental differentiation between the modern concept of human dignity and pre-modern concepts (although it is possible that we find some elements of the modern concept even in pre-modern theories).

Two comments are, however, necessary here. First of all, it might be argued that this concept necessarily rests on a specific prejudice that Peter Singer and others tend to criticize as "speciesistic" (Singer 1993). "Speciecism" is a prejudice that favors the members of one biological species and it is unjustified in a similar way as racism or sexism which favors the members of a specific race or gender. Singer has been criticized (e.g. Steigleder 1991, Düwell 2009) for being very unspecific in his use of the term "speciecism" since he does not distinguish between positions that accept the brute fact that someone is a member of a biological species as a sufficient reason to grant him a specific moral status (which is arguably a flawed argumentation) and those positions that holds that the members of the species homo sapiens are morally special, a position that may be justified by very different arguments. So it can be argued that for the justification of a specific moral status features like communicability, (moral) agency, creativity or the like are of ultimate importance and that those features are – so far – only familiar within the human species. These positions would have to present an argument as to why even those members of the species that do not have those features or only to a limited degree, would participate in the moral protections of this specific status as well. These arguments are perhaps flawed, problematic or wrong, but they are nevertheless not speciesistic in the sense that they are based on a prejudice towards a specific biological species. Nearly all philosophical positions will base human dignity on a feature that is argued to be morally relevant, not on a brute biological fact. In any case, to grant human dignity to all members of the human family is not necessarily a speciecistic position; human dignity is not a speciesistic concept.

This debate leads to a further question. The extension in the protection of human dignity is in some respects not uncontested. Nearly all legislation in the western world makes some distinctions in the way that legal protection is granted to the early stages of human existence; some legal regulations are explicit in this grading of protection whilst others only implicitly treat embryos differently from born human beings. The beginning of protection by human dignity is in fact contested. Furthermore, the extent to which we should grant dignity to some animals is contested, especially to some apes (then it would not be "human" dignity but an extension of equal dignity). This contested borderline in the extension of human dignity is common to nearly all philosophical conceptualizations as well as to various political debates about the topic.

15.2.2 The Other-Regarding Nature of Human Dignity

A second common feature of positive accounts of human dignity is that they aim to regulate the relationship between humans and between humans and political institutions. This is different to the Renaissance account of human dignity for example, which was in the first place interested in the cosmological position of the human being and wanted to determine the place of the human being in relation to God, angels and beasts. It is also different to some religious accounts of human dignity that are concerned with the salvation of a human being, his religious positions or generally his relationship to God. One can relate that to a more general distinction in ethics. Ethical accounts can either be concerned about the excellence of human beings (their perfection), as in perfectionistic theories (Hurka 1993), or they can be primarily concerned with other-regarding obligations. Of course, we can find both aspects in one ethical theory as well: An ethical theory can deal with obligations towards, or harm to other people and deal also with obligations towards, and harm to oneself. Ethical theories can ground obligations towards others in perfectionistic considerations, they can see ethical excellence as a result of a specific form of fulfillment of moral obligations or they can strictly distinguish between both dimensions. In any case both aspects can be distinguished and for this context it is only relevant that a modern account of human dignity is formulating moral prescriptions concerning the way we ought to treat human beings, independently of the specific justification for those prescriptions.

The important point presently is that a positive account of human dignity should deal with other-regarding obligations. In general these other-regarding obligations are spelled out in the form of rights of human beings. That does not mean that a positive account of dignity must only be a theory of rights but at least such an account will provide an answer to the question of how we should treat fellow human beings and, in general, that will have some consequences in terms of the moral requirements of political institutions.

15.2.3 Dignity as Inherent Worth of the Individual

A positive account of human dignity will suppose that each individual has a kind of moral status that implies that he cannot be substituted or replaced by other individuals in a morally relevant sense. This can be described as the inherent worth of the individual, which forbids weighing the value of the individual in an algorithm of goods and values; Kant would call this "absolute value". Various scholars object to talk about "values" here because "inner worth" or "dignity" is opposed to the terminology of "values". There are good reasons to be careful here: If we are committed to an objective value-theory we seem to be committed to some kind of moral realism. A moral realist seems to be committed to objective values that make it especially difficult to understand the specific exclusivity that is ascribed by human dignity. If we are, however, committed to a value-concept that in general assumes that values can be weighed against each other, an idea of "absolute value" seems to be odd in that context. The specific status of the "human" to which we ascribe "worth" or "absolute value" cannot be understood as a value like other values; the human being in its specific moral status must be seen in its capacity to create or to perceive values, to follow moral norms, etc; it is the human being in its specific moral capacities to which we ascribe the specific moral status of "human dignity". To talk about the "value of the individual" seems to neglect this difference between "values" in general and the status of a "subject of valuation" and if the concept of human dignity makes sense it seems to be related in one way or the other to this subject-status. With this in mind, however, it is not principally problematic to talk about the "value of the individual" (as noted above, Kant spoke about an "absolute value") if it is clear that this kind of value is a specific one.

It is worth noting that giving specific worth to the individual must not necessarily be identified with specific forms of social order or it need not necessarily be aligned with the phenomenon that sociologists describe as "individualization". It is not a priori clear that respect for human dignity can only be realized in specific forms of social order or political institutions or what kind of social order or political institutions that would be. It is obvious that the normative content of human dignity will have normative implications for political institutions and for the rights of the individual but it is not conceptually evident that the appropriate institutions to protect and promote "human dignity" are those Western political and social institutions to which the concept "individualization" refers to. A theory of human dignity would have to show which kind of institutions would be appropriate.

To talk about an "inherent worth" or "absolute value" that cannot be weighed against other goods has, however, another problem. It could be understood as suggesting that "human dignity" would be nothing other than a stop-signal in the "weighing of goods". That would mean that in general all goods and values could be weighed against each other as long as human dignity is not infringed. This understanding of human dignity would presuppose that human dignity marks only a specific protected area of worth in relation to which weighing would be morally unacceptable. This presupposes a specific idea of the relevance of human dignity for the whole of our moral regulations and ethical convictions that is highly contested.

15.2.4 Overridingness

Human dignity in the context of the human rights framework is characterized by a claim for overridingness. In one sense or the other an account of dignity will articulate a normative consideration that "trumps" other considerations. To say that an action violates human dignity but it is morally permissible to do it, is odd. One can dispute whether or not an action is a violation of human dignity but if it is a violation, than it will outweigh other possible considerations. In this respect one could wonder whether the normative content of the concept "human dignity" is co-extensive with the content of the concept of "morally right". For some theories that may be the case if those theories include "enabling a life in dignity for all" as the ultimate and exclusive justification for other-regarding moral norms. In this case, "human dignity" would have the same meaning as "morally right actions with regard to others". In that sense human dignity will always demand respect and will trump conflicting prudential, aesthetic and religious considerations. I am not defending the position that it is co-extensive but I think that it seems at least not eo ipso conceptually impossible.

This is different if one sees violations of human dignity as a specific kind of morally forbidden action that is distinct from other morally forbidden actions. In this sense torture, rape, genocide, etc, are violations of human dignity whereas lying or stealing are morally wrong actions towards other people but not violations of human dignity (important here is the conceptual distinction and not the examples as such).

In that case it would be morally obligatory to avoid violations of human dignity first and foremost; in a case of conflict of duties, the respect for human dignity would always be more important than other moral obligations.

15.2.5 To Sum Up

For the time being I would therefore summarize my considerations concerning a modern concept of human dignity as follows: Such an account will ascribe the status of human dignity to all human beings equally (the borderline question has still to be discussed); human dignity will be the source of prescriptions concerning other-regarding behavior (generally formulated in terms of rights) and normally accompanied by prescriptions about morally acceptable political institutions; it will say something about the worth of each individual; and respecting human dignity is seen as more important than other possible considerations. These elements are certainly not sufficient for a positive account of human dignity but they are sufficient to distinguish theories about human dignity from very different theoretical disputes about personal excellence, rank and ideals. To formulate those elements does not mean, however, that a positive account of human dignity can successfully be developed and justified. Up until now I have not argued that it is possible that we can develop a positive account; perhaps it can even be demonstrated that it is impossible to defend such a positive account, which would be fatal for the concept of "human dignity" altogether. But if an account of human dignity could be developed it would include at least these elements.

15.3 Questions for a Positive Account of Human Dignity

In the following section I will pose some questions to which one can assume any account of human dignity would have to give an answer. These questions have to do with the basic content of human dignity and the scope of its application; the questions deal with the basic requirements for a non-arbitrary application of the concept. I assume that these questions are also central questions for scholars who want to argue that human dignity is a meaningless, useless or empty concept. Only if it can be demonstrated that it is impossible to answer these questions in a non-arbitrary way, is it justified to denounce the concept of human dignity as empty or meaningless.

15.3.1 The Subject of Human Dignity

The question of which beings deserve the status ascribed by "human dignity" is strongly contested. This question seems, however, to be odd insofar as the formulation already seems to answer the question: all human beings (This formulation recalls the debate about speciecism mentioned above). Nevertheless, for the applicability and justification of the concept of human dignity, there are at least two further questions to be answered: To whom do we have to ascribe this status? And why do we have to do so? To start with the second question: It is necessary to offer some kind of justification for the selection of beings that deserve a kind of absolute moral protection or respect, after all this respect can imply a possibly strong restriction of one's own liberty. If respecting human dignity is of such high moral importance then there is no alternative but to give justification for this respect. But each kind of justification will refer to some kind of feature of a being that fulfills a role in the justification of why this respect is morally required. If we could not offer a feature that is relevant for the fact that we owe respect to a being, we would not be able to understand to whom we owe respect. In that context different features are on the table, such as rationality, personhood, being in the image of God, vulnerability, sensitivity, etc. It is not impossible that an ethical theory will offer a variety of relevant features (e.g. Nussbaum 2006) for the ascription of human dignity; there is then the need to explain the relationship (equal importance, hierarchical order, lexical order, etc) between those features. It is furthermore possible for theories to differentiate between the reasons why a specific feature is morally relevant and the pragmatic or empirical criteria that are relevant for the practical applicability of human dignity. If, for example, a feature like personhood or being in the image of God is a relevant feature for the status of a being with dignity there remains the problem that we cannot empirically test whether or not a being is a person or an image of God. It would even be a fundamental misunderstanding of personhood if we would assume that personhood would be an empirically testable feature. If, however, respect for human dignity is morally so important, then there are good reasons to have an applicable practical criterion (or criteria) for ensuring the protection of beings with dignity. These criteria could be: membership of the human species, being born a human being, showing some kind of mental activity, etc. Furthermore, it is contested to what extent features like rationality and personhood have actually to be realized in order to grant the status of human dignity (potential personhood could be sufficient as well).

It is highly contested to what extent we have to grant the same moral protection, as follows from human dignity, to (at least some) animals as well. The notion "dignity of the creature" (Balzer et al. 1998, Baranzke 2002) that was introduced in the Swiss Constitution must be mentioned here. This term does not only grant dignity to animals but to plants as well (in the theological tradition "creature" is a term that means everything that is created by God; that is everything beside God). Nussbaum refers as well to dignity of animals (Nussbaum 2006). It is, however, unclear what the normative implications are if a being has dignity. For Nussbaum it is, for example, not forbidden to kill animals or to experiment upon animals (e.g. Nussbaum 2006: 371), and nor did Switzerland forbid the use of animals or plants for all kind of economic and scientific purposes. It seems therefore that the notion "dignity of the creature" means something different. One can, however, expect that scholars who are using this concept clarify the relationship between "dignity of the creature" and "human dignity" otherwise the whole discussion is nothing more than a linguistic confusion.

One distinction could be helpful in this context. Some scholars distinguish between a full moral status and some moral status. A being that has "full moral status" would enjoy the protection of all rights while a being that has "some moral status" would morally be worthy of protection (that is, more than just a "thing") but it would not have the same status as beings that have the entire set of rights. In the context of this distinction "human dignity" would normally imply "full moral status". In the Swiss debate and similar conceptualizations it seems that animals and plants are understood as beings worthy of some kind of moral protection whilst not necessarily having the status of beings with dignity.

15.3.2 The Relationship Between Human Dignity and Human Rights

In the context of the Universal Declaration of Human Rights we find the assumption that there is an internal relationship between having human dignity and having human rights. In several documents we find the idea that human dignity is the basis of human rights, as in Articles 21 and 23 of the Universal Declaration where it is stated that "everyone [...] is entitled to realization [...] of the economic, social and cultural rights indispensable for his dignity", and that these are rights "ensuring [...] an existence worthy of human dignity". In the literature this relationship is often neglected or not explained. We find at least the following concepts:

(1) Human dignity is seen as only another label for "the entire set of human rights"; the difference would just be a linguistic one. This approach makes it impossible to assume that human dignity could be the basis of human rights and a discussion about human dignity would add nothing to the general discussion of human rights.

(2) Human dignity might be understood as a term for the most basic human rights. In this sense human dignity would be violated if the most fundamental liberties and rights were at stake. This approach would additionally leave the relationship between human dignity and the entire concept of human rights unexplained and this concept of human dignity could not be the basis of human rights. Many scholars interpret Kant's formula of humanity in that direction; it is argued that the formula forbids only the complete instrumentalization of a person. It is overlooked in this interpretation that the formula of humanity has a much broader and more fundamental dimension since it prescribes that humanity (rational nature) has to be treated as "end in itself". To see rational nature as "end in itself" is, however, not only relevant as a constraint against severe violations of human beings, but rather it is basic for the understanding of Kant's whole concept of moral philosophy. The whole concept of rational obligations as such, that there is something like a moral ought, has to do with our rational nature. Therefore the formula of humanity has a much broader meaning than is assumed in this interpretation.

(3) Some bioethical scholars see human dignity as a mid-level-principle that has to be weighted against other mid-level principles (Kemp et al. 2000). This

approach is an attempt to use the methodology of Beauchamp/Childress' four-principle-approach with the introduction of four different principles. This approach is far from all traditional conceptualizations of human dignity and has no theoretical tools to explain the relationship to the human rights-framework. This debate is, however, very significant for the use of the notion "human dignity" in bioethics. Very often references to human dignity are made alongside other concepts like "integrity" or "autonomy" without making an attempt to explain the internal relationships. I would see this approach as a symptom of conceptual confusion.

(4) Human dignity is understood as "the right to have rights". This concept of "human dignity" refers to some reflections of Hannah Arendt in her analysis of totalitarianism. In the context of the 2nd World War many refugees lost their citizenship and with it all legal protection. Here, to claim a "right to have rights" is a claim for a right to citizenship for each human being and with this citizenship, the protection that a political and legal community would grant. Of course, the first "right" in the "right to have rights" must be of another kind than the "rights" that come with citizenship. This concept of human dignity emphasizes the rights-orientations of human dignity. But it leaves the content of the human rights unexplained. Hanna Arendt herself had strong reservations about human rights terminology. One can doubt that this approach will offer a full account of human dignity.

(5) Human dignity as the basis of human rights. This idea is formulated in the context of the human rights framework itself. This would imply that human dignity is something other than human rights; it would not just be another name for the entire set of human rights but possessing human rights would be the normative consequence of having human dignity. The foundational function in relation to human rights is central to this concept of human dignity. In this context, the normative consequences of human dignity would have to be explained in terms of human rights. One can doubt whether "human dignity" here has a distinct normative content beyond the human rights. The specificity of human dignity would have to be seen in the foundational function in relation to the rights and not in a specific normative content. If one were to assume that "human dignity" has normative elements that go beyond the human rights themselves, those elements would have to be explained within the whole framework of human rights.

15.3.3 The Normative Content of Human Dignity

In light of this last point, discussion about the normative content of human dignity has to take place in relation to the content of human rights. That content is contested (see, for example, Donnelly 2002, Griffin 2008). Relevant in this context is the distinction between negative and positive rights: negative rights are rights not to be hindered in exercising one's freedom; positive rights are rights to be supported in the exercise or development of one's capacities (in that connection see

Shue 1980, Gewirth 1996: 31–70). While the negative rights protect the negative liberty of human beings, the positive rights support humans in the development of their capacities. It is worth mentioning that the protection of negative rights also presupposes active measures to ensure them (political institutions, etc). So, these two rights are not distinguished along the line of non-interference or active measures. The main debate here is to what extent there are positive duties to support people (welfare rights, cultural rights, etc) and whether or not we can speak about "rights" in this context, since political institutions have only limited power to enforce these "rights". A minimalistic concept would see human dignity violated only if the most basic rights are at stake. For a concept that sees human dignity as the basis of human rights it makes much more sense to see human dignity not only as a concept that refers to a (or the most basic) part of human rights but as a foundation of the concept of human rights as such. It is especially contested to what extent the granting of welfare rights is a consequence of respect for human dignity.

One possibility would be to see the relevance of human dignity, not so much in the protection of specific normative goods, rights or values but in developing an understanding of the content and systematic approach of the human rights framework. There are at least four questions that arise here:

(1) Where are the limits of the further developments of human rights? Many scholars are speaking of a proliferation of human rights, which refers to the tendency to broaden the human rights framework by the introduction of new human rights. Furthermore there are severe demands to broaden the framework even more and to introduce new aspects into the human rights framework that answer new challenges. A notable example is inclusion of an intergenerational dimension in the framework; up until now the debates about human rights and sustainability have hardly been interrelated. If there were no rationale behind this development and no reason for a limitation of this development, than the whole framework of human rights would be compromised.
(2) This broadening of the human rights framework forces us to understand the inner hierarchy between the human rights. It is virtually impossible to give all rights the same importance. But it would compromise the framework if processes of weighing between the rights were just a question of political negotiations.
(3) A central question is whether the normative content of human dignity can be completely spelled out in terms of human rights. There are several dimensions that, at least according to the intuitions of a lot of people, are morally relevant but for which it is difficult to think about in terms of human rights. These dimensions seem, however, to be very prominent examples for the use of human dignity. We can think about examples where human beings are accused of compromising their own dignity (prostitution, dwarf-throwing), or, for example, the status of the cadaver where it is difficult to construct a right but that seems not to be a morally neutral thing. We touch here several aspects that seem to be related to symbolic representations of our dignity where people feel humiliated or disrespected by actions that can hardly be constructed as rights violations.

It seem to be precisely these aspects of human dignity that is part of the reason why the whole concept has become so contested, as being a garbage-notion where everything can be covered as being morally relevant where no reasonable argument is at hand. It is the challenge for a theory of human dignity to discuss whether these symbolic dimensions can be theoretically elaborated and to what extent such symbolic elements can justify limitations in the exercise of rights by other human beings.

(4) The provisions of the Universal Declaration of Human Rights seem in the first place to aim to establish a specific political order that is appropriate to ensure basic liberties and fundamental rights. In the course of Western history the development of the human rights framework was accompanied by the development of specific institutions, like the nation state and democracy. If the human rights framework was, not only in its historical genesis, but also in its justification necessarily intertwined with those institutions then its validity would necessarily depend on the future of those institutions. If in the future, for example, nation states as we know them would be abandoned, then the normative authority of the human rights framework would end as well. In the last decades we have seen a lot of changes of political institutions in the context of globalization. It is very likely that diverse economic and ecological challenges, together with new technological possibilities, will be a reason for fundamental changes in the international political order in the next decades. It is very likely that these changes will affect the concrete formulation of human rights. Nevertheless, it is not evident that the core idea behind human rights will have to be abandoned.

15.3.4 The Ontological Status of Human Dignity

We speak about human dignity as if it were a property of humans like having blue eyes and black hair. That raises the question whether for the ascription of human dignity some kind of specific ontological assumptions are necessary; such as if human beings would have this dignity as a property. Some theological concepts see dignity as a gift that humans have because it is given by God. Others see human dignity as the articulation of a demand for a specific kind of respect that we owe towards human beings. The formulation that we "have" human dignity would then articulate the conviction that this moral demand for respect is not constituted in the act of ascribing human dignity. To "have" human dignity means that we owe this respect to human beings in a categorical sense, which means that the validity of this demand does not depend upon specific laws or specific social practices of respect. Different theories offer different reasons why we have the obligation to respect human dignity. But it seems to be common to all concepts that the ascription of "human dignity" articulates the demand for universal and categorical respect. This seems to be ontologically neutral; in any case each account of human rights will have to give an explanation about ontological presuppositions.

15.3.5 The Justification of Human Dignity

If respect for human dignity is categorically obligatory for us, one can wonder what kind of justification is needed to demonstrate the validity of this demand. The form of the justificatory theory seems to depend on the kind of demand that "human dignity" lays upon us. Pluralistic value-theories will have difficulties with the concept because they only know a plural set of values (something similar would be true for a theory of plural prima facie duties). Human dignity could than not be understood as one of those values that would have to be weighted against other values. A theological approach would either have to give a strong metaphysical argument for our respect for human dignity (for example, in a thomistic tradition of natural law) or would see the moral demand as grounded in a decision of God to just give us this specific moral status. For a thomistic natural law theory it would be necessary to show that the relevant justification would be compatible with the idea that human dignity would have a substantial relation to the human rights framework (against the thomistic tradition). The "divine command theory" (as grounding the moral obligations in a decision of God) would just abandon the justificatory task in a decisionistic manner.

For a contractarian approach it would be necessary to show that the idea of a social contract would be able to justify a categorical obligation. A strategy that relies on the self-interest of the contracting parties would have difficulties in viewing human dignity as a categorical demand. Kantian types of transcendental argumentations ground respect for human dignity, in some way, as rationally necessary; as an obligation that follows from our rational nature or as a result of our agency.

To avoid any justification of human dignity seems to be impossible given the fact that the validity of the claim is factually contested, in the context of concrete applications (like in bioethics) as well as in intercultural contexts. The kind of theory that is necessary for a justification of human dignity would have to provide an answer to the question of why we should see ourselves as obliged to respect human dignity. An appropriate theory would in the first place have to be evaluated in light of a meaning of the concept. If human dignity articulates a categorical claim for respect then the justificatory theory would have to provide us with an argument that is sufficient to show that we owe this kind of respect to other human beings.

15.4 Expectations of a Positive Account of Human Dignity

The list of contested questions is clearly not complete. One could be pessimistic as to whether it is possible at all to develop a positive account given all of these questions that must be answered. I do not share this pessimism. But, first of all, it would be important for the discourse on human dignity that it were accepted that we have to make some effort to develop an understanding of that concept and it is therefore necessary to gain an overview of the relevant questions and the spectrum of possible theoretical solutions. To start with an analysis of "violations of human dignity" presupposes already that most of the conceptual questions have been answered. But if human dignity were to be a principle for the foundation of human rights (as I am tempted to think), then it is not very likely that the analysis of violations will be the appropriate way for conceptual clarification.

Human dignity is such an important concept because it has not only to do with some specific parts of moral demands and the political order. It is much more likely that human dignity has to do with the human rights concept as such. Human dignity is the categorical demand for structuring the social and political order in a way that respects the worth of the individual. To develop such a concept, to discuss its normative implications and to discuss the different possibilities of justification is a central task for moral philosophy. This has aimed only to show what kind of questions each serious philosophical attempt about human dignity would have to answer.

References

Balzer, Philipp, Klaus Peter Rippe, and Peter Schaber. 1998. Menschenwürde vs. Würde der Kreatur. *Begriffsbestimmung Gentechnik Ethikkommissionen*. Freiburg: Alber.

Baranzke, Heike. 2002. *Würde der Kreatur? Die Idee der Würde im Kontext Der Bioethik.* Würzburg: Königshausen und Neumann.

Donnelly, Jack. 2002. *Universal human rights in theory and practice*, 2nd edition. Ithaca: Cornell University Press.

Düwell, Marcus. 2009. Equality speciecism and sanctity of life. On some philosophical presuppositions of Peter Singer's practical ethics. In *Peter singer under fire*, ed. Jeffrey A. Schaler, 395–418. Chicago: Open Court.

Gewirth, Alan. 1992. Human dignity as basis of rights. In *The constitution of rights. Human dignity and American values*, eds. Michael J. Meyer and William A. Parent, 10–28. Ithaca: Cornell University Press.

Gewirth, Alan. 1996. *Community of rights*. Chicago, IL: Chicago University Press.

Griffin, James. 2008. *On human rights*. Oxford: Oxford University Press.

Haakonssen, Knud. 1996. *Natural law and moral philosophy. From Grotius to the Scottish enlightenment*. Cambridge: Cambridge University Press.

Hurka, Thomas. 1993. *Perfectionism*. Oxford: Oxford University Press.

Kemp, Peter, Jacob Rendtorff, and NielsMattson Johansen, eds. 2000. *Bioethics and biolaw, vol. II: Four ethical principles*. Copenhagen, Rhodos: International Science and Art Publishers.

Margalit, Avishai. 1996. *The decent society*. Cambridge: Harvard University Press.

Menke, Christoph, and Arnd Pollmann. 2007. *Philosophie der Menschenrechte zur Einführung*. Hamburg: Junius.

Meyer, Michael J. 1989. Dignity rights and self-control. *Ethics* 99: 520–534.

Nussbaum, Martha C. 2006. *Frontiers of justice disability, nationality species membership*. Cambridge: The Belknap Press of Harvard University Press.

Shue, Henry. 1980. *Basic rights. Subsistence, affluence, and U.S. Foreign Policy*, 2nd edition. Princeton: Princeton University Press.

Singer, Peter. 1993. *Practical ethics*, 2nd edition. Cambridge: Cambridge University Press.

Steigleder, Klaus. 1991. Die Abenteuer der Bioethik – Ein kritischer Vergleich der Ethikkonzeptionen H. Tristram Engelhardts und Peter Singers. In *Ethik ohne Chance? Erkundungen im technologischen Zeitalter*, 2nd edition, eds. Jean-Pierre Wils and Dietmar Mieth, 225–246. Tübingen: Attempto.

Tierney, Brian. 1997. *The idea of natural rights*. Cambridge: William B. Eerdmans Publishing Company.

Trinkaus, Charles. 1970. *In our image and likeness: Humanity and divinity in Italian humanist thought*, 2nd edition. Chicago, IL: Chicago University Press.

Tuck, Richard. 1979. *Natural rights theories: Their origin and development*. Cambridge: Cambridge University Press.

Waldron, Jeremy. 2009. *Dignity rank and rights*. Tanner Lecture on Human Values. http://www.law.nyu.edu/news/waldron_tanner_lectures

Chapter 16
Dignity and Preservation of Personhood

Samuel J. Kerstein

Abstract This paper sketches a partial account of human dignity. The account is Kantian in the loose sense of having been inspired by some of Kant's views. But it contrasts sharply with a traditional Kantian account. The paper tries to isolate some shortcomings of the traditional account – in particular that it condemns as morally impermissible certain actions of heroic self-sacrifice as well as certain actions of privileging the young over the old in the distribution of scarce, life-saving resources. The new account attempts to avoid such implications while preserving some of the traditional account's attractive features. According to the new account, dignity is preeminent and unconditional value, possessed by all and only persons, that is, beings who have certain psychological capacities, including autonomy. An agent's action expresses respect for persons' dignity if, without treating anyone merely as a means, he or she aims in performing it to maximize persons' preservation. The paper distinguishes between two dimensions along which person preservation might be maximized and suggests how to weigh each of these dimensions in decisions about whom to try to preserve.

16.1 Introduction

This paper sketches a partial account of human dignity. According to the account, dignity is preeminent and unconditional value, possessed by all and only persons, that is, beings who have certain psychological capacities, including autonomy. An action respects persons' dignity roughly if it maximizes their preservation without treating anyone merely as a means. The account is Kantian in the loose sense of having been inspired by some of his views. But it contrasts sharply with what we shall call the traditional account – one associated with the historical Kant. The paper begins by setting out the traditional account and trying to isolate some of its

S.J. Kerstein (✉)
Department of Philosophy, University of Maryland, USA
e-mail: kerstein@umd.edu

P. Kaufmann et al. (eds.), *Humiliation, Degradation, Dehumanization*, Library of Ethics and Applied Philosophy 24, DOI 10.1007/978-90-481-9661-6_16,

philosophical shortcomings. The new account sketched here attempts to avoid these while preserving some of the traditional account's attractive features.[1]

16.1.1 The Traditional Account

The traditional account has a basis in Kant's texts, but this paper focuses neither on the extent of that basis nor on whether the account represents the best interpretation of Kant on dignity.[2]

Kant uses "humanity" interchangeably with "rational nature" (Kant 1996a [1785]: 439). He suggests that having humanity involves having certain rational capacities, among them the capacities to set and pursue ends and to conform to self-given moral imperatives purely out of respect for these imperatives (Hill 1992: 38–41). For Kant, rational nature is a threshold concept. If one has the set of capacities that are constitutive of it, one has it, no matter how well- or ill-developed those capacities may be.

According to Kant, all and only beings with rational nature have dignity. Any human being who did not possess rational nature would not have dignity; and any non-human being who did possess rational nature would have dignity.

To say that humanity has dignity is to say that it has a value with three main features. First, it is value that attaches to something that exists rather than to something that needs to be brought about. An appropriate reaction to the value of the sort humanity possesses is to honor, cherish, or preserve it, rather than to produce more of it. Second, humanity has unconditional worth (Kant 1996a [1785]: 428). That means it is good in every possible context in which it exists. It is good no matter how it came to exist or what the effects of its existence may be. Moreover, if something is unconditionally good in this sense, then neither what it affects nor what happens to it can at all diminish its goodness (Kant 1996a [1785]: 393–394).

Finally, to say that humanity has dignity is to say that it has incomparable worth: It has no equivalent for which it can be legitimately exchanged (Kant 1996a [1785]: 434–436, Kant 1996b [1797]: 434–435, 462). Humanity can never be legitimately sacrificed for or replaced by something with mere price. Not even all the riches of Silicon Valley would truly compensate for the killing of one rational agent. Moreover, since humanity possesses incomparable worth, it cannot even be legitimately sacrificed for or replaced by something else with such worth (Hill 1992: 47–49). It makes no sense to say that in some context one or more instances of humanity have more or less value than one or more other instances of humanity. In Kant's view, everything that lacks incomparable worth, including human happiness and well-being, has mere price. In sum, all and only extant beings who have rational nature possess dignity: unconditional and incomparable value.

---

[1]The new account is based on an account of respect for persons originally developed and defended in Bognar and Kerstein (2009).

[2]For rival interpretations, see, for example, Dean (2006) and Sensen (2009).

Kant suggests that the special value of rational nature forms the basis for a version of the categorical imperative, namely the Formula of Humanity (FH): "*So act that you use humanity, whether in your own person or in the person of any other, always at the same time as an end, never merely as a means*" (Kant 1996a [1785]: 429). According to one prominent interpretation of this principle, it amounts to a command always to act in a way that expresses respect for the worth of humanity, in one's own person as well as that of another (Wood 1999). Let us call this principle RFH, since it is a specification of Kant's Formula of Humanity that invokes the notion of expressing respect for humanity's value. Any action that fails to express respect for humanity's value does so at least in part by suggesting an inaccurate message regarding what this value is, according to the interpretation. So, for example, an account of what makes (or purportedly makes) an attempt at suicide wrong would necessarily include the notion that it expresses a false message, namely that some person, presumably the one trying to kill himself, does not have dignity. Moreover, if an action expresses such a message, then it expresses disrespect for the value of humanity and is morally impermissible.

The traditional account, which incorporates RFH and the notion of dignity upon which it is based, has several features many of us find attractive. For example, an individual's dignity does not vary with his wealth, social status, or achievements. Any being who has the capacities requisite for possessing dignity has no less (and no more) dignity than anyone else. Moreover, RFH seems to capture a core of deontology. It would forbid an action that aimed to maximize the preservation of dignity by killing one innocent person in order to preserve the lives of two. For such an action would suggest that the value of persons is not incomparable.

16.1.2 Shortcomings of the Traditional Account

But the traditional account faces some serious difficulties. One well-known problem concerns the status of some beings who seem not to have rational nature, for example, very young children. If they indeed fail to have rational nature, then they have mere price, according to the account. But how, then, is our treatment of them subject to constraints? Instead of pursuing these familiar questions, let me here highlight briefly two less well-known challenges, which I develop at length elsewhere. The challenges emerge from cases of killing oneself to save others and cases of having to choose to whom to distribute a scarce, life-sustaining resource.[3]

Cases of what many of us take to be heroic self-sacrifice pose problems for RFH (Kerstein 2009a). Here is a narrative accompanying the award of a military honor, the Silver Star, to a United States army private killed while on patrol in Northeast Bagdad:

[3]As Kerstein (2009a) tries to show, other sorts of cases also pose difficulties for the traditional account. It seems to condemn as morally impermissible cases of what many of us take to be legitimate killing in self-defense and legitimate withdrawal of life-sustaining treatment.

> PFC [i.e., Private First Class] McGinnis was manning the [machine gun] on the Platoon Sergeant's [vehicle]. His primary responsibility was to protect the rear of the combat patrol from enemy attacks. Moments after PFC McGinnis' vehicle made [a] turn traveling south-west, a fragmentation grenade was thrown at [it] by an unidentified insurgent from an adjacent rooftop. He immediately yelled "grenade" on the vehicle's intercom system to alert the four other members of his crew. PFC McGinnis made an attempt to personally deflect the grenade, but was unable to prevent it from falling through the gunner's hatch. His Platoon Sergeant, the truck commander, was unaware that the grenade physically entered the vehicle and shouted "where?" to PFC McGinnis. When an average man would have leapt out of the gunner's cupola to safety, PFC McGinnis decided to stay with his crew. Unhesitatingly and with complete disregard for his own life he announced "the grenade is in the truck" and threw his back over the grenade to pin it between his body and the truck's radio mount. When the grenade detonated, PFC McGinnis absorbed all lethal fragments and the concussion with his own body killing him instantly. His early warning allowed all four members of his crew to position their bodies in a protective posture to prepare for the grenade's blast. As a result of his quick reflexes and heroic measures, no other members of the vehicle crew were seriously wounded in the attack. His gallant action and total disregard for his personal well-being directly saved four men from certain serious injury or death. (Arlington National Cemetery Website 2008)

Many of us believe that PFC McGinnis' action was not only morally permissible, but also morally admirable. Yet RFH implies that it was wrong. According to the narrative, PFC McGinnis' action of throwing his back over the grenade showed "total disregard for his personal well-being" and "complete disregard for his own life." The narrative implies that McGinnis intentionally allowed himself to be killed in order to save his comrades, or at least that in order to save them, he did something which, as he was aware, would have as a virtually certain consequence the elimination of his own humanity. Either way, his action failed to express respect for the incomparable worth of his humanity. It sent the message that its value was not as great as the value of that of the four other soldiers taken together. So, according to RFH, PFC McGinnis' action was wrong.[4]

A second difficulty with the traditional account of dignity emerges from consideration of the following example (Bognar and Kerstein 2009). We have one indivisible life-saving drug and two patients who desperately want it: a 20 year old and a 70 year old. It is our job to allocate the drug, so our giving it to one person or the other

[4]I consider and try to rebut several objections to this conclusion in Kerstein (2009a). But note that in the "casuistical questions" Kant raises after he discusses the duty not to commit suicide, he asks: "Is it murdering oneself to hurl oneself to certain death (like Curtius) in order to save one's country? – or is deliberate martyrdom, sacrificing oneself for the good of all humanity, also to be considered an act of heroism?" (Kant 1996b [1797]: 423–424). If we take the respect-expression approach to FH, then in my view such a self-sacrificial act does turn out to be "murdering oneself" and thus to be morally impermissible. In the "Notes on the lectures of Mr. Kant on the metaphysics of morals" taken by Johann Friedrich Vigilantius, we read: "It is permissible to venture one's life against the danger of losing it; yet it can never be allowable for me deliberately to yield up my life, or to kill myself in fulfillment of a duty to others; for example, when Curtius plunges into the chasm, in order to preserve the Roman people he is acting contrary to duty [. . .]" (Kant 1997 [1793]: 629).

would not simply be an act of beneficence. Each person has a claim on the drug in the relatively weak sense that it would be wrong for us to refrain from giving it to her on morally arbitrary grounds (for example, because we did not like her skin color or her home town). Finally, neither patient is morally responsible for her need of the drug in any way that would affect her claim on it. The patient who does not get the drug will die. If the younger person gets the drug, she will thrive for decades; if the older person gets the drug, he will thrive for a couple of years but then die of natural causes.

Many of us are convinced that the younger patient should get the drug. One might suggest that she should get it on the grounds that the older patient has already had a full human life, that is, his "fair innings." But giving it to her on that basis would send a message contrary to the notion that humanity has dignity, as it is defined in the traditional account. For it would suggest that an instance of rational nature that has endured long enough to constitute a full life has less value than an instance that has been around for a shorter time. But this suggestion contradicts the notion that the value of humanity is unconditional.

What resource-distributing action in this difficult scenario would accord with RFH? It seems that flipping a fair coin to decide to whom to give the life-saving drug would do so. For this action would send the message that each patient is valuable; each is worthy of having an equal chance to be saved. And this action would also suggest that the longer existence (or, alternatively, the greater quantity of well-being) to be had by the younger patient fails to make her more valuable than the older one. The action does not seem to run afoul of the notion that persons have dignity. But, again, it does run afoul of a widespread view that the younger person should get the drug.

Some might agree with the assessment offered here of what RFH implies in these cases, yet insist that these implications are not implausible. Nothing I can say in this brief paper would be likely to move them from this position. Others might agree with my view that these implications are implausible, and yet claim that we are forced to embrace them. For Kant and/or contemporary Kantians have arguments that rationally compel us, or at least those of us who believe ourselves to have any good ends or any reasons for our actions, to hold all persons to have dignity (Korsgaard 1996). Elsewhere I have defended the view that such arguments fail (Kerstein 2001, Kerstein 2002). Even if a Kantian argument establishes that we must hold persons to be valuable in every possible context in which they exist – and I do not know of one that really does this – how would we arrive at the conclusion that we must hold them to have incomparable value? That a being with rational nature has unconditional value fails to entail that nothing, including no other such beings, however many, have more value than it does.

Rather than relying on questionable a priori arguments, I adopt a much more modest approach to defending an account of dignity. I try to reach a reflective equilibrium between our particular considered judgments of what constitutes respecting or violating dignity and general principles specifying what dignity is, as well as any constraints on our treatment of beings who have it.

16.1.3 Beginnings of a New Account

Let me now try to sketch an account of human dignity, or, more precisely, a sufficient condition for respecting human dignity, that will not fall prey to the difficulties illustrated in the two examples. The account is intended to suggest a fruitful direction for further work, not to be complete in itself.

According to the account, to say that a being has dignity is to say that it has a special worth. A being has this special value or worth in virtue of having certain psychological capacities: the capacity to perceive and understand the world, to form projects, to reflect and deliberate on these projects, and so on. Chief among these capacities is autonomy: the capacity "to direct one's life in accordance with values that one reflectively endorses" (McMahan 2002: 256). Let us call the beings who have these capacities persons. On this account, persons and persons alone have dignity.

The special worth possessed by persons has several main features. Each person who has the capacities just mentioned possesses worth equal to that of every other person, no matter how well- or ill-developed the capacities may be. Echoing the Kantian account described above, this worth is unconditional: Neither what the person affects nor what happens to him can at all diminish it. Moreover, the worth of persons is preeminent: Nothing that is not a person has worth equal to that of a person. But the worth of persons is not incomparable. The account does not rule out the possibility that two persons have greater value than one. That is not to say, however, that the value of persons is a value to be maximized, for example, by taking whatever measures are necessary to bring as many exemplars of it as possible into existence. Dignity attaches only to extant persons. It is a value in virtue of which they are to be *respected*. Respecting this value involves refraining from treating persons merely as means. And respecting it can involve trying to preserve the value. According to this account, an agent's action expresses respect for persons' dignity if, first, in performing it he does not treat anyone merely as a means and, second, the action is of a sort which, it is reasonable for the agent to believe, would maximize persons' preservation. Here "reasonable belief" is, of course, an epistemic rather than a moral notion. It is reasonable for an agent to believe something if, given the facts as he perceives them in light of his education, upbringing, and so forth, he would be justified in believing it.

In order to flesh out the account, let me say more about two things: what treating someone merely as a means amounts to and what it means to aim to maximize the preservation of persons, starting with the latter.

We can preserve persons along two dimensions.[5] First, we can preserve a person by extending the period of time in which a being has the capacities that make up personhood. Let us call preserving persons along this dimension preserving "person years." Second, we can preserve persons by maintaining them in existence. Let us

[5]The account of maximizing person preservation that follows stems from and is defended in greater detail in Bognar and Kerstein (2009).

call doing so preserving persons along the "person numbers" dimension. If we save five people for 3 years, then on the person years dimension we preserve 15 years, while on the person numbers dimension we preserve five people. Reflective common sense values the preservation of persons along these two dimensions, I believe.

But what might it mean to maximally preserve persons? There can, of course, be cases where maximizing preservation along one dimension fails to do so along the other. For instance, suppose we can save one person for 20 years or five persons for 2 years each. Choosing to save the one person would best preserve personhood along the person years dimension; choosing the five people would best preserve personhood along the person numbers dimension. How should we proceed?

Here is a suggestion. We begin by determining the proportion between the values possessed by the two sets of persons on each dimension. The set that contributes the higher value to the proportion on a given dimension is "favored" on that dimension. We then determine which proportion along the person years and person numbers dimensions is greater. We preserve the set of persons that is favored in the proportion that yields that higher number.

Returning to the example above illustrates the procedure. We have to choose between saving one person for 20 years or five persons for 2 years each. The one person has a higher value on the person years dimension, but the group of five has a higher value on the person numbers dimension. On the person years dimension, the proportion between the values is 20/10 (2/1). Thus, the one person is favored. In contrast, the proportion on the person numbers dimension is 5/1. On this dimension, the larger group is favored. The second proportion is equivalent to a number (5) which is greater than that yielded by the first proportion (2). So, according to this method, we should preserve the group of five persons.[6]

This procedure does admittedly yield controversial results in some cases. For example, suppose we could save one person for 20 years or two people for 5 years each. On the person years dimension, the proportion between the values is 20/10 (=2) in favor of the one, while on the person numbers dimension the proportion is 2/1 (=2) in favor of the two. So the procedure would entail that we be indifferent about how to proceed. In order to avoid any unintended bias, we should then presumably decide whom to save on the basis of a coin flip. But some believe that we ought simply to save the two. In general, people seem to value preservation along both dimensions, although they may give somewhat more weight to the person numbers dimension. How much more weight is a question that empirical studies might help to resolve. There is a growing literature on the relative weight people place on extending lives and saving them (Nord 1999). This literature should be considered in the course of formulating a weighting scheme.

According to the account I am sketching, certain actions which, it is reasonable for an agent to believe, will maximize persons' preservation express respect for

[6] A complete weighting scheme would, of course, need to take into account the uncertainty of a choice regarding person year and person number preservation.

persons' dignity, namely those actions that do not treat anyone merely as a means. But what does it mean to treat someone merely as a means?

Here I outline a simple account of treating someone merely as a means. It is meant to be suggestive rather than sufficient as it stands. A person treats someone as a means – or, equivalently, *uses* the person as a means – if she intentionally does something to the person's body or mind in order to realize one of her ends and she intends the person's body or mind to contribute to her end's realization.[7] A person does not treat an individual as a means unless she intends the individual's presence or participation to contribute to the end's realization (Scanlon 2008: 106–107).

An agent treats a person *merely* as a means – or, equivalently, *uses* the person merely as a means – if it is reasonable for her to believe that something she has done or is doing to the person renders that person unable to consent to her treating him as a means to her aim. A person is unable to consent to someone's treating him as a means if he has no opportunity to alter or forestall the action by withholding his agreement to it (O'Neill 1989).

For example, consider the well-known "transplant case" in which a healthy person goes to the hospital for a checkup. By harvesting his organs (and, in the process, killing him) we could save six patients who would otherwise die. If, without giving the healthy person any opportunity to opt out of our using him to save the six, we harvest his organs, we treat him merely as a means. Or consider a terminally ill patient whose remaining life would be very painful. As long as the patient remains a person, she has dignity. However, it would be a mistake to think that respecting this value in her would involve trying, by whatever method, to preserve her personhood. Trying to preserve it by, for example, deceiving or coercing her into taking a drug to help her body fend off infection would violate the mere means constraint.

At this point it is natural to be concerned with two issues.[8] First, should we regard the mere means constraint as absolute? I think not. If the only way to preserve millions of persons were to use one individual merely as a means, doing so would be morally permissible, I believe. But then where should we place the threshold for overriding the mere means constraint? I do not address this difficult question here. Second, in some cases a person is justified in coercing, forcefully defending herself against, or deceiving another person, or so many of us believe. But the simple account I presented implies that in some of these cases the person treats the other merely as a means and thus, presumably, acts wrongly. A more complex account of treating others merely as means would, I believe, enable us to avoid such implications.[9]

---

[7] For a more restrictive account, see Kaufmann (Chapter 5, this volume).

[8] Important challenges to the plausibility of constraints on treating others merely as means are to be found in Parfit (forthcoming), Scanlon (2008), and Schaber (2009). I believe, but obviously cannot here try to establish, that these challenges can be met.

[9] Here is what a more fully specified account of treating others merely as means would look like: Suppose an agent uses another. She uses him merely as a means if it is reasonable for her to believe that something she does to the other renders him unable to consent to her using him, unless it is also reasonable for her to believe either that she is using the other in order to prevent him from

Let us now return to the cases that prompted us to propose that an agent's action expresses respect for persons' dignity if in performing it he does not treat anyone merely as a means and his action is of a type that, it is reasonable for him to believe, would maximize persons' preservation. PFC McGinnis was not using another merely as a means in jumping on the grenade; he was not using another at all. And since he presumably had the opportunity to avert his own use of his body to absorb the impact of the grenade – after all, it was he himself who chose to put his body to this use – he was not using himself merely as a means. Moreover, he did the kind of thing which, it was reasonable for him to believe, would maximize persons' preservation, both on the person numbers and person years dimensions. So, in harmony with the considered moral judgments of many, the account implies that he acted in a morally permissible way.

But let me hasten to make two points. First, some people (although very few, in my experience) tend to have more orthodox Kantian leanings in cases such as this. According to them, PFC McGinnis has failed to respect his own dignity.[10] And I have not here provided any argument that would prompt them to abandon this judgment. Second, let me emphasize that I am proposing a sufficient condition for respecting the dignity of persons, not a necessary condition for doing so. Respect for the dignity of persons does not require the sort of self-sacrificing action PFC McGinnis performs, in my view.

In the case of the life-saving drug that has to be distributed to a 20 year old or a 70 year old, the new account implies that our giving it to the 20 year old would respect the dignity of persons. This allocation is obviously of a type that, it is reasonable for us to believe, would maximize the preservation of persons. On the person numbers dimension, both courses of action would have the same result. But on the person years dimension, saving the 20 year old would be favored by a wide margin. Moreover, in giving the drug to the 20 year old, we would not be using the 70 year old merely as a means. In fact, we would not be using him at all; for his presence or participation would play no role in our effort to distribute the drug to the 20 year old. Of course, someone might object that, in effect, we treat the 70 year old as if he wasn't even there. Does not respect for his dignity require that he get at least some chance at getting the drug? I do not think so. I believe that our refraining from

intentionally doing something that renders someone unable to consent to his (the other's) using him, or that if, before using the other in a particular way in order to attain her end, the agent were able, without rendering her action ineffectual, to inform him of her intention to do so and she did inform him of it, the other would voluntarily consent to her using him in this way. For further discussion, see Kerstein (2009b).

[10]Perhaps they would appeal to Kant's own account of treating *oneself* merely as a means and suggest that since PFC McGinnis did that, he failed to respect his own dignity. It is not easy to discern what treating oneself merely as a means amounts to, according to Kant. For one attempt see Kerstein (2008). Of course, given the account of treating someone merely as a means that I have sketched, it is hard, although not in my view impossible, to think of cases in which a person treats himself merely as a means.

treating him merely as a means as well as our giving his person years just as much weight as those of the 20 year old would exempt us from the charge of failing to respect him.

16.1.4 Some Remaining Issues

The new (but admittedly incipient) account of dignity I have proposed shares some of the advantages of the traditional Kantian account. Just like its predecessor, the new account has an egalitarian bent. It implies that a person's dignity does not rise or fall with his wealth, social status, or accomplishments. And the new account also captures a central feature of deontology by incorporating a constraint against treating persons merely as means.

But let me close by considering a couple of issues that would need to be addressed in order to flesh out the new account. (Of course, it faces many other challenges as well.) The first issue is easy to discern with the help of an example. Suppose that it is a government official's job to distribute healthcare resources. He can either preserve one person's life with the help of a sophisticated and very expensive operation, or he can use the money to help victims of an annoying skin disease – one that has no impact on their length of life, but does cause mild pain and, in many, significant embarrassment. According to the partial account I have sketched, it would be respectful of the dignity of persons if the official saved the one. But the account does not itself entail that it would be wrong to help the thousands instead. A full account would have somehow to come to terms with the question of whether it would be.

It is not obvious how best to answer this question. One might hold that respecting the dignity of persons requires not only performing actions that respect the capacities that give them this value, but also performing ones that promote the successful exercise of these capacities. According to this view, for example, respecting the special value of a person can require not only that we preserve her autonomy (i.e., her capacity to direct her life in accordance with values that she reflectively endorses) by, say, saving her life, but also that we further the projects she autonomously pursues, say, by removing obstacles to their accomplishment. If a person autonomously pursues a career that requires her frequently to perform in public, then a skin ailment that brings her embarrassment might pose a significant obstacle to her success. But it is not obvious how to weigh promoting the successful exercise of autonomy with the bare possession of it. Is there a threshold number of people like the one just described who could be helped by the treatment of the skin disease that, if reached, would render it legitimate for the government official to opt for treating that disease rather than for saving the life of the one?

A further set of questions concerns the status of beings who are not persons in the sense defined above, for example, human embryos, fetuses, infants, and severely disabled adults, as well as non-human mammals. If, as I have suggested, all and only persons have dignity, then these beings lack it. Of course, Kant holds that if beings fail to have the value he calls "dignity" then they have mere price. But that does not compel us to maintain that if beings fail to have the value we call "dignity," they have mere price. It is open to us to insist that they nevertheless have a special value and that their treatment is subject to moral constraints. And we need not conclude that these constraints derive their force from the rights or interests of extant persons, for example, that constraints on the treatment of an infant derive solely from the rights or interests of the infant's parents or other persons who might care about him. The challenge is to make precise just what special value these beings have and just which constraints govern their treatment.

References

Arlington National Cemetery Website. 2008. Ross A. McGinnis: Specialist, United States Army. http://www.arlingtoncemetery.net/ramcginnis.htm. Accessed 19 Mar 2009.

Bognar, Greg, and Samuel J. Kerstein. 2009. Saving lives and respecting persons. Unpublished Manuscript.

Dean, Richard. 2006. *The value of humanity in Kant's moral theory*. Oxford: Clarendon.

Hill, Thomas E., Jr. 1992. *Dignity and practical reason in Kant's moral theory.* Ithaca/NY: Cornell University Press.

Kant, Immanuel. 1996a [1785]. *Groundwork of the metaphysics of morals*, trans. Mary Gregor In *Immanuel Kant: Practical philosophy.* Cambridge: Cambridge University Press.

Kant, Immanuel. 1996b [1797]. *The metaphysics of morals*, trans. Mary Gregor In *Immanuel Kant: Practical philosophy.* Cambridge: Cambridge University Press.

Kant, Immanuel. 1997 [1793]. *Lectures on ethics*, trans. Peter Heath. Cambridge: Cambridge University Press.

Kerstein, Samuel J. 2001. Korsgaard's Kantian arguments for the value of humanity. *Canadian Journal of Philosophy* 31: 23–52.

Kerstein, Samuel J. 2002. Kant's search for the supreme principle of morality. Cambridge: Cambridge University Press.

Kerstein, Samuel J. 2008. Treating oneself merely as a means. In *Kant's ethics of virtue*, ed. Monika Betzler, 197–214. Berlin: de Gruyter.

Kerstein, Samuel J. 2009a. Death, dignity, and respect. *Social Theory and Practice* 35:505–530.

Kerstein, Samuel J. 2009b. Treating others merely as means. *Utilitas* 21: 163–180.

Korsgaard, Christine. 1996. *The sources of normativity*. Cambridge: Cambridge University Press.

McMahan, Jeff. 2002. *The ethics of killing: Problems at the margins of life.* New York, NY: Oxford University Press.

Nord, Erik. 1999. *Cost-value analysis in health care: Making sense out of QALYs.* Cambridge: Cambridge University Press.

O'Neill, Onora. 1989. Between consenting adults. In *Constructions of reason.* Cambridge: Cambridge University Press.

Parfit, Derek. *On what matters*. Oxford: Oxford University Press.

Scanlon, Thomas. 2008. *Moral dimensions: Permissibility, meaning, blame.* Cambridge, MA: Harvard University Press.

Schaber, Peter. 2009. Using people merely as means. Unpublished manuscript.

Sensen, Oliver. 2009 Kant's conception of human dignity. In *Kant-Studien* 100:309–331.

Wood, Allen W. 1999. *Kant's ethical thought.* Cambridge: Cambridge University Press.

Chapter 17
Embodied Self-Respect and the Fragility of Human Dignity: A Human Rights Approach

Arnd Pollmann

Abstract After 1945, we were confronted with the need for a new conception of human dignity, since totalitarian mass destruction had proven the fundamental violability and fragility of dignity. This chapter will argue that human dignity can no longer be seen as an "inalienable value" that we cannot lose, but as a precarious capability for basic human flourishing – and more specifically, as a potential for embodied self-respect that needs to be protected by corresponding human rights. Therefore, dignity is the explicit reason or "purpose" behind the proclamation of human rights today: as necessary legal conditions for living a life in embodied self-respect. And as a consequence, philosophy should not make the mistake of extrapolating from categorical human rights, held by all human beings just by being human, to a likewise categorical possession of dignity. Instead, it is *because* human beings do not have equal human dignity from the start that they all have equal human rights.

17.1 Introduction

A vast number of books and articles have been published on human dignity in the last few years,[1] but only recently has it been *photographed*: Günter Pfannmüller and Wilhelm Klein (2008) have traveled around the world for more than 6 years taking pictures of "threatened life forms" such as warriors, hunters, shepherds, sachems, monks and market-women in Ethiopia, Kenya, India, Tibet, Myanmar and Bhutan. Pfannmüller and Klein avoided producing ethnological "kitsch" by shooting their portraits in front of a color-neutral background, within a transportable studio-box,

A. Pollmann (✉)
Institute of Philosophy, Otto-Von-Guericke-University Magdeburg, Germany
e-mail: arnd.pollmann@ovgu.de

[1] This is just a selection of important contributions: Beyleveld and Brownsword (2001), Kretzmer and Klein (2002), Stoecker (2003), Wetz (2005), Tiedemann (2007), Malpas and Lickiss (2007), President's Council on Bioethics (2008).

P. Kaufmann et al. (eds.), *Humiliation, Degradation, Dehumanization*, Library of Ethics and Applied Philosophy 24, DOI 10.1007/978-90-481-9661-6_17,

in order to transcend the exotic context in which the persons portrayed lead their everyday lives. Looking at those pictures, each reveals the unique and individual but at the same time human and universal "countenance" of the people and faces portrayed, as they were looking into the camera – most of them for the first time – self-confidently and unpretentiously.

The title of the photobook shall remind the viewer of Article 1 of the German *Basic Law*[2] and could be translated as follows: "Untouchable. On human dignity." More than any philosophical paper I have read before, these photographs make a case that I will try to put into words in the following article: Human dignity should not be seen – as it is in the most common view – as an "inherent value" or "inalienable dowry" of all human beings that can never be lost under any circumstances. Instead, human dignity should be interpreted as a fragile potential for "embodied self-respect" – a potential that has to be fulfilled and self-actualized by the persons in question *themselves* under occasionally precarious life conditions (Pollmann 2005). Or to put it differently: Human dignity is misunderstood when it is presupposed to be an already "inborn" and, therefore, indefeasible value. In contrast, it must be taken as a highly vulnerable and, therefore, threatened capability to lead a life worth living

[2]"The dignity of the human being is untouchable. To respect and protect it is the compulsory task of all state power," Article 1 (1) *Basic Law* for the Federal Republic of Germany (*Grundgesetz*) from 1949 [*my translation, A.P.*].

in self-respect. And from this position it follows that *violations* of human dignity – such as humiliation (Chapters 3 and 4), instrumentalization (Chapter 5), degradation (Chapter 6), debasement (Chapter 7), torture (Chapter 8), rape (Chapter 9), slavery (Chapter 14) or poverty (Chapters 11 and Chapter 12) – should be reinterpreted as attacks on the person's abilities and options to gain and express self-respect in social life.

I will proceed in five steps, and the first step will be an historical review: Although the triumphal procession of human dignity, especially in international human rights law, can only be traced back to the second half of the twentieth century, the very *notion* of dignity is obviously much older (17.2). The most remarkable philosophical puzzle today is that there are at least four competing, but seldom differentiated, conceptions of this one main concept of dignity, and, as I will show, only one of these four conceptions will make sense of universal "human rights" to have one's dignity protected (17.3). In order to prove this, different interpretations of the "grounding" relationship between human dignity, on the one hand, and human rights, on the other, can be given. And, here again, only one of four interpretations seems to be the correct one, although it is the most unpopular (17.4). I will then propose my own view of the substantive *content* of human dignity, which will be an explanation of the idea of embodied self-respect (17.5). These considerations will lead us to a crucial but persistently ignored philosophical insight: One must differentiate between "possessing" and "protecting" human dignity. Not all human beings already possess the *same* dignity, I will argue, but that is why they all have exactly the same *rights* to its protection (17.6).

17.2 Four Historical Episodes

If we take a closer look at the use of the term human dignity in philosophical and legal debates, we become aware of a striking contradiction: On the one hand, most interpreters assume that dignity is something "inherent", something that cannot be lost, for it is a kind of "natural", "inborn" and, therefore, "inalienable" worth or value simply given by being human. And, as a result, human beings simply *have* dignity, just because they belong to the human species. But on the other hand, it cannot be denied that there are, in fact, fundamental and violent attacks on human beings causing damage to, or even loss of, dignity. People who are humiliated, debased, exploited, discriminated, tortured or raped do not seem to be mistaken to describe these vicious experiences as "violations" of their dignity. The philosophical question then is: How is it possible to deprive someone of something that is inborn or inalienable in principle? Or when it comes to the legal question of basic constitutional rights: Why should something that we cannot lose anyway be protected by the state and its authorities? If all human beings already *have* human dignity in an inalienable way, why should state institutions have the compulsory task of protecting it?

As it will be shown later, this puzzle rests on confusion between the ideas of "possessing" and "protecting" human dignity. But in order to clarify this puzzle we have to start with the historical *roots* of this confusion. As a brief philosophical history of the term “human dignity” reveals (Menke and Pollmann 2007: ch. 5 and 6, Bayertz 1996, Wetz 2005), this history must be reconstructed in at least four major steps – resulting in very different conceptions of human dignity.

(a) *Roman Antiquity*: In Roman antiquity the Latin term “*dignitas*” was reserved for high-ranking persons in public life bearing special responsibilities, gaining special benefits or extraordinary accomplishments. Persons in exalted social positions with very important functions or duties – like statesmen, politicians or generals – were awarded a high reputation explaining not only their fame but also their dignity. One will find this use of the term, for instance, in the writings of Cicero. Although Cicero is also said to be the first author who talked of a very *special* kind of dignity that all human beings seem to have in common (Cancik 2002), by far the most *popular* use of the term at that time singled out specific “dignitaries” from amongst the masses.

(b) *Christianity*: It was Christian theology of the middle ages that explicitly gave the term a universalistic shift. The ancient idea of a special dignity that only privileged persons would have was *generalized* by transferring this idea to the exalted role *the* human being was said to play in the realm of nature as the “pride of god’s creation”. From now on, every human being just by being human – that means despite all individual differences – was supposed to simply have a dignity on divine, natural and metaphysical grounds, a dignity that other creatures in this world would not have for only human beings were created in “god’s image” (Soulen and Woodhead 2006).

(c) *Early Modernity*: In Italian Renaissance, especially with Pico della Mirandola, and later with the Enlightenment movement, above all with Immanuel Kant, this already universalized notion of dignity was more and more *secularized* by “freeing” it from theological implications. Not that Pico or Kant were not Christian in their religious beliefs, but their philosophy made an important distinction: They were both convinced that as human beings we do not owe our dignity to the fact that we reflect a divine splendor but because we *ourselves* are capable of something great: of “reason” and “moral autonomy”. And therefore we are *god-like* and worthy of exaltation (for Pico: Trinkaus 1995: ch. 10, for Kant: Hill 1992).

(d) *After 1945*: Things changed profoundly after 1945 – at least from a human rights perspective. The hubris, or self-idolatry, of the renaissance and enlightenment notion of humanistic dignity as quasi-godly autonomy was turned almost into its opposite by the monstrous experiences of fascist barbarism and Stalinist terror. Something must have been wrong with moral autonomy for something like this to become possible. It was only then, after the Second World War, that what can be called the human rights notion of dignity appeared: From now on, all human beings were said to have special rights to the protection of their dignity, since totalitarian inhumanity had proven the extreme violability of these rights and also the fundamental fragility of human dignity – to the point of its total extermination. It is primarily this notion of human dignity that we can find in the human rights declarations and treaties adopted by the United Nations (UN) after 1945 (Menke and Pollmann 2007: part III, Dicke 2002).

To say that it is "primarily" this notion of human dignity that was implemented in the UN human rights treaties is to concede that the three former interpretations of dignity are also still in use today. As we will see in the following part of this paper, some interpreters still stick to the ancient particularistic notion of dignity, while others are convinced that only theological groundings of dignity will work, whereas a third group still relies on humanist or Kantian accounts (see, e.g., the discussions in Bayertz 1996, Malpas and Lickiss 2007). Nevertheless, from a human rights perspective, a deep and fundamental break has to be bookmarked within the history of dignity. European totalitarianism brought about a fundamental, decisive turn within modern human rights thinking – a turn towards dignity. It was not until 1945 that, what we can call, the political presence of human rights *in the light* of human dignity began. It goes without saying that there had been philosophical reflections on both human rights and human dignity before, but to state that they are *intertwined* is a rather new idea (Menke 2007). For more than 200 years the human rights discourse got along without the founding idea of dignity, whereas for more than 2000 years the talk of dignity did not imply that the idea of equal rights could be derived from it. It is the experience of a human catastrophe so monstrous that shocked the history of both human rights and human dignity to its very foundations, and against which the Universal Declaration of Human Rights from 1948 is targeted (see Morsink 1999). In its preamble we are reminded of the "barbarous acts which have outraged the conscience of mankind". Therefore the global commitment to human dignity, as well as the new international human rights regime, was grounded on some kind of worldwide promise that things like this would never happen again (Johnson and Simonides 1998).

17.3 Four Different Conceptions of Dignity

Following a discussion of a famous methodological essay by Walter Bryce Gallie (1956), we have to differentiate between philosophical "concepts" and "conceptions": Central terms like "truth", "art", "freedom" or "justice" stand for basic philosophical notions (concepts) that are "essentially contested", as Gallie says – since we will always find many different and even disparate substantial interpretations (conceptions) of these main philosophical ideas that the discussion will not agree on. "Dignity" also seems to be such an essentially contested concept, and, in direct accordance to the four stages of its history that we have just reconstructed, there are at least four different conceptions of its substantial *meaning*. In other words: There might already be an almost global consensus on the worth of the "dignity" concept as such, but by far no common *use* of the term. This can be demonstrated by referring to recent debates in bioethics on the dignity of the human embryo (Beyleveld and Brownsword 2001, Stoecker 2003, Damschen and Schönecker 2003, President's Council on Bioethics 2008). These discussions have been centered on two main sets of problems (Pollmann 2005): Firstly, who does in fact count as a member of that group of beings who are supposed to already *have* dignity as well as corresponding basic rights? Does *every* human being participate in that group and from the very beginning? Or should we interpret dignity as some sort of a salient feature that has to be accomplished and can only be ascribed to special human beings that we call "persons"? Secondly, is it true that the term "dignity" stands for an inalienable and "absolute" worth that cannot or must not be graded, a worth that everyone has in exactly the same and equal way? That means, should we really say that a 14-day old embryo has exactly the same human dignity as a grown-up adult? Or can, or even must, we distinguish – legally and morally – between different "degrees" of having dignity?

In the first set of questions we are confronted with the problem of distinguishing between human beings in the "full" sense (persons) and "other" human forms of life, where only the first may then have dignity. In the second set of questions, we have to face the fact that the dignity of two different human beings could be accomplished or realized only to a different degree or extent, even *if* every human being already – without exception – would participate in human dignity from the very beginning. A combination of these two sets of problems leads us to four different conceptions of dignity. And somehow surprisingly,[3] these four conceptions correspond directly to the four main historical interpretations given above.

[3]The explanation for this is quite simple: The three older conceptions have "survived" and are still in common use today.

(a) *Achievement*: The first group of interpreters, often following a path-breaking legal study on the sociological function of constitutional rights by Niklas Luhmann (1965), seems to simply adopt the ancient use of the term by assuming that a person can only be awarded dignity when she lives a public life worthy of social respect. She has to play social "roles" and, therefore, gain the status of dignity as a kind of earned merit. So dignity must be understood as deriving from social "achievements" that have to be made in social life, retained by certain social efforts and defended against interpersonal offenses as well as self-inflicted forfeits (Brennan and Lo 2007). From there it follows, firstly, that not all human beings can have dignity, but only "persons" who can achieve this special status. So the human embryo obviously does not belong to the group of those who possess dignity. And it follows, secondly, that all persons do not have dignity in exactly the same way, but only "more or less" depending on the degree of factual achievement.

(b) *Dowry*: The opposite group of interpreters, which is indeed the biggest one, is convinced that dignity is given from the very beginning of every human life and in each case in exactly the same non-graded way. This assumption is grounded on a premise, which was, and still is, characteristic of theological or metaphysical conceptions of dignity: Grading different forms of life or periods of human development must be forbidden since it would miss the divine, natural or metaphysical worth of the human life form as such. Therefore, dignity has to be understood as some kind of a gift or "dowry" by human nature – a natural gift that even the human embryo can count on. Whether in a given case a theological, metaphysical, anthropological, or even biological argument is presented, they all agree on the premise that every human being has dignity from the very beginning and in exactly the same way – just by being human (Lee and George 2008).

(c) *Capacity*: The third group of interpreters is influenced by, and committed to, the Enlightenment notion of dignity. Not all human beings, but only persons with a special property or "capacity" can have dignity. This position wants to draw a morally significant line between certain "pre-forms" of human life, on the one hand, and those stages of human development, on the other, in which typical characteristics of human persons come into existence. In the Kantian tradition, for instance, one might think of the capacity for moral rationality and autonomy (Shell 2008). For other thinkers, less demanding properties are relevant: such as a "capacity to suffer pain" or a "conscious interest in living" that a 12-week embryo might not yet have (e.g. Hoerster 2002). This view explicitly denies that every human being already has dignity "from the start", but, nevertheless, when a human being becomes a person, she also gets her full, non-graded dignity.

(d) *Potential*: The fourth group does agree with the second by assuming that, indeed, every human being already participates in human dignity. But at the same time it is conceded that we can differentiate between different degrees of its realization. The central argument here is that although every human being – as a member of humankind – has an individual "potential" to live a life in human dignity, the question whether we really are able to fully unfold this potential or capability is dependent upon the concrete circumstances of our life. In other words: How far a human being will be able to actually realize his capability of dignity is always dependent upon decent or humane life conditions (Pollmann 2005, Nussbaum 2008). Therefore, human beings live in dignity sometimes "more" and sometimes "less", and that is why human dignity should not be seen as a natural gift that every one simply has and cannot lose anyway but rather as a fragile possibility, a possibility of human flourishing (Kass 2008).

Dignity	Accomplished	Given
Graded	Achievement (Roman antiquity)	Potential (after 1945)
Non-graded	Capacity (early modernity)	Dowry (Christianity)

17.4 Four Relations Between Dignity and Rights

All four epochal uses of the term "dignity" are in philosophical, but also common use today. And depending on whether we interpret dignity as an achievement, a dowry, a capacity or a potential, we seem to be led to different decisions: what members of humankind will belong to the "inner circle" already possessing dignity and also corresponding human rights? All human beings? Only persons? Not all persons? What makes this decision even more complicated is the fact that the conceptual relation between possessing human dignity, on the one hand, and claiming corresponding human rights, on the other, is quiet unclear. The central question here is: What particular philosophical role does human dignity play within the realm of human rights? And the other way around: What exactly is the conceptual function of human rights for preserving human dignity? Constitutional and international lawyers debating this question (Meyer and Parent 1992, Kretzmer and Klein 2002) have shown that – again – four different alternatives must be distinguished when it comes to explaining and interpreting this interrelation.

(a) *The Ground of Human Rights*: The first interpretation rests on the assumption that the idea of dignity is the normative basis from which human rights can be derived. Following this interpretation, dignity is not itself a human right but the justificatory "ground" from which to deduce and proclaim concrete human rights. It is *because* human beings have dignity or equal worth that they *also* have special human rights (Gewirth 1982). So dignity must be understood as a presupposition for having human rights – as their necessary, but also sufficient condition. And human rights are indispensable imperatives deriving from human dignity. For that reason, human dignity and human rights must be seen as two sides of the same coin: A person has either both of them or she has none. Yet still dignity and rights are not the *same* since the role of dignity for having concrete rights is about the same as that of the foundations of a house on which its walls rest and rely upon (see Dicke 2002).

(b) *A Special Human Right*: Following a second interpretation, human dignity should not be taken as primordially grounding the idea of human rights but rather as a right in itself – even though a very special one – for this right tells the legal system what the most important human good is that needs protection in constitutional and international law (see Benda 2000). This can be seen as a historical insight due to the barbarism of the twentieth century: However important all the other rights may seem – like rights to liberty and security, to freedom of speech and religion, or even to life – they are all of *less importance* compared to the top-priority right to the protection of dignity. Therefore, dignity should not be seen as the "first" reference point to human rights but rather as their "last": Whatever state authority might do to its citizens, whatever reasons there might be to restrict or even suspend one or the other basic legal claim, there is at least one human right that simply must not be violated in any way – and that is the right to have one's own human dignity protected (Klein 2002).

(c) *Dignity as the Sum of Human Rights*: The third interpretation takes the notion of dignity as the aggregate or "sum" of human rights. For the latter are taken as simply spelling out in detail what it would mean to live a life in dignity. In consequence, the Universal Declaration is to be interpreted as a "list" of necessary aspects of human dignity. Or to put it differently: If you had an idea of the realization of human rights, you would at the same time have a detailed picture of a life in dignity. Both would not just be two sides of the same coin, but strictly the same: Dignity *is* the sum of human rights. This interpretation goes along with a provocative reading of the relation between dignity and rights. However rich in tradition and well-established the term "dignity" might be, as a legal reference point it is dispensable or even superfluous for it does not add anything to the idea of human rights (Macklin 2003). There is nothing *more* to the idea of human dignity than human rights – and the other way around – and that is why the older human rights declarations of the eighteenth century were able to get along without dignity (Maritain 1943).

(d) *Dignity as the Purpose of Human Rights*: The fourth interpretation starts by sharing important intuitions of the three others. Similar to the first one, it states that dignity is the decisive normative reference point in relation to human rights, but like the second interpretation, it also claims that the protection of dignity is a right in itself that claims something special. In addition, it indeed follows the third interpretation by conceding that human rights could get along without the notion of dignity; it *could*, but then, it is said, we would no longer stick to the specific and contemporary interpretation of human rights after 1945 – as a constitutional, but also international law shield against arbitrary rule and totalitarianism (Menke 2007). As a result, the historical commitment to human dignity that we can find in the relevant legal documents should be seen as some sort of a "second preamble" or as the explicit *reason*, why we proclaim all other human rights today: as necessary legal conditions for living a life in dignity.[4] In consequence, human dignity is the goal or "purpose" of human rights. And in accordance with the fourth conception of

---

[4]This should not be confused with the central, but somehow opposite, premise of the first interpretation, that human dignity is the necessary condition for human rights.

dignity mentioned above, the realization of human rights would help the realization of a human potential to dignity (Pollmann 2005, Nussbaum 2008, Kass 2008).

17.5 Embodied Self-Respect

In each part of this chapter, four different alternatives have been presented concerning the historical roots (17.2) substantive meaning (17.3) and legal function (17.4) of human dignity. In each case I will follow the fourth interpretation:[5] First, I adopt the historical postwar view that the common use of the dignity notion profoundly and decisively changed with the year 1945. I then assume that human dignity should be seen as a potential that needs to be carried out and realized. And for that reason, human rights shall be seen as implemented with the purpose of legally protecting this fragile potential for human flourishing. But even if the reader were to unresistingly follow me in that, a question remains: Do we already have an answer to the central philosophical question of what the special *content* of human dignity is? Or to put it differently: What exactly is shown or portrayed in the photographs by Pfannmüller and Klein (2008) reproduced here?

Let us consider more precisely the argument that I have just sketched: That human rights are meant to guarantee the legal preconditions of human dignity obviously means more than just the protection of "mere" living. As cynical as it may sound, arbitrary imprisonment (Chapter 10), bonded labor (Chapter 14), extreme forms of humiliation (Chapters 3 and 4), rape (Chapter 9) and even torture (Chapter 8) *can* be in accordance with bare survival or viability. Human rights call for life of a "higher" quality. And it is exactly this higher form of life that is suggested by the idea of a human life "in dignity". Still, what is the concrete substance of that idea? The postwar notion of human dignity sketched above rests on the universalistic assumption that simply every human being, from whatever country or culture she may come or whichever language she speaks, is a highly vulnerable being that is dependent on the legal and social protection of her dignity. And as long as we – from whatever country or culture *we* might come or whichever language we speak – all use the term "human"[6] for identifying certain rights and a certain dignity as universal, we presuppose common human characteristics, claims and also interests in moral respect and legal protection that help us justify corresponding rights (Höffe 2007: part 3). For that reason, we should now focus on the question of what *kind* of common characteristics, claims and interests we can universally presuppose. For there must be certain or typical human traits and interests that give us reason to speak of a dignity of the "human" being. But what particular features might these be? A number of potential characteristics, claims, and interests are listed below. The ascending order of these potential candidates reflects the extent to which they are contested in contemporary debates on dignity. The notion of dignity as "embodied self-respect" that I will propose should bring all those characteristics, claims, and interests together. Although I cannot go into detail here, I believe that all of these are important common features when it comes to a substantial picture of human dignity.

[5]What I cannot demonstrate here is that every other combination seems possible but less plausible.

[6]Although, of course, in different languages.

(a) *Basic Characteristic*: When we first ask for the primordial or basic characteristic that makes us all count as actual, or at least as potential, holders of human dignity, one response is simply the fact of being human as such. The almost trivial premise is therefore: Our mere belonging to the human species[7] is, by definition, already sufficient to qualify us, at least *potentially*, as the owners of human dignity and, therefore, as addressees of human rights protection. In other words: Being human "by nature" is enough to be a possible candidate for human dignity (Lee and George 2008).

(b) *Equality*: It is not just the simple fact of being human that makes us count as candidates for dignity but the normative claim that we all should count as human beings in the same way. Critics of that claim could indeed be convinced that, although we are all human beings, some of us might still be of different moral worth: e.g. if men were of higher value than women; if believers would count more than atheists; if adults were of more worth than embryos, etc. But the notion of human dignity seems to imply the opposite as it is closely connected to the idea of "equality" (Menke and Pollmann 2007: ch. 6) – either in the sense of an

[7]Some animals might also have dignity, but, by definition, no *human* dignity.

equal *possession* of human dignity or at least in the sense of an equal *right* to its protection.[8]

(c) *Respect*: The distinctive form of social recognition that we claim to be entitled to when we mutually adjudge moral or legal equality to other persons, we call "respect" (see the discussion in: Dillon 1995). From this it follows that social respect is *egalitarian* from the beginning and should be terminologically distinguished from "esteem" due to individual and special efforts or personal achievements (Honneth 1995: part II). When a person sees herself respected as an "equal beneath equals" she is treated decently or in a humane way; that means treated as a being of equal worth and from human "flesh and blood" – and not as a mere thing, machine or animal (Margalit 1996: part II).

(d) *Self-Respect*: From the experience of mutual respect may result a very special form of personal self-relation that is of vital importance for the idea of dignity. This kind of self-relation *reflects* equal social recognition into the "inner world". And we usually call this particular form of incorporated social appreciation "self-respect". Persons gain self-respect in social relations if they feel convinced that they are really equal beneath equals; that they are – as human beings – exactly of the same worth as every other human being (Margalit 1996, Statman 2000).

(e) *Expression of Self-Respect:* Whereas self-respect is first and foremost an inner self-relation, people want to authentically express or "embody" self-respect in social life. What counts here as a representative expression of self-respect is mainly the outward appearance of a person or how she acts and behaves in public; a behaviour that can obviously be sometimes more and sometimes less in accordance with her inner conviction of equal worth (see Spaemann 1987). What other people do ascribe to this person, if they ascribe incorporated self-respect, is "dignified demeanor", "spine" or an "upright posture". And it is in this respect that people sometimes complain that a particular person has lost or "forfeited" her own dignity by acts of self-degradation (Kass 2008).

(f) *Vulnerability:* It is this very important fact that people want to express and embody self-respect in public life that makes them assailable and vulnerable. People need decent life conditions to live a life in dignity (Margalit 1996, Nussbaum 2008). So if people "vegetate" in deep inhuman or derogatory circumstances, such as involuntary pain, poverty, slavery or tyranny, how can they maintain their self-respect? How should a person even gain – far less express – her self-respect in social life if her existence is devastating or if other people "kick" her although she is already down? Typical forms of such disrespect are called "discrimination", "instrumentalization", "debasement", and above all "humiliation" (Statman 2000).[9]

If we sum up these six important characteristics, we see quite a disturbing picture: Although the protection of human dignity can be seen as a universal good that is in all human being's interest, just because we are human (a) and, furthermore, equally human (b), this human interest in protection of dignity can only be satisfied if other

---

[8] I will come back to this crucial difference in the last part of this paper.

[9] See also the contributions to Part I of this volume.

people do respect our equal worth as human beings (c). Moreover, this interest will only be fully satisfied if the person in question is guided by a strong feeling of self-respect (d) and when she is capable of expressing and embodying self-respect in public life (e). That again presupposes that she must have adequate and decent life conditions so that a life in dignity – one in "embodied self-respect" – becomes available (f). This quite complex conception of dignity might seem disturbing, since it appears to imply the assumption that human dignity might be some kind of an "attitude" based on self-respect. Accomplishing and keeping dignity would *also* be an undertaking *of one's own responsibility*. But that is in fact the way human dignity should be seen: A concrete loss of dignity *can* be the result of social disrespect or humiliation, but *finally*, as I will show in the next two steps, it has to be interpreted as a lack or absence of self-respect.

(g) *Personal Responsibility*: Although other people as well as state authorities are obliged to respect our dignity, it is obvious that they often do not do so, and then it comes to minor or major attacks on our self-respect. Being confronted with devastating life conditions, it might sometimes be hard to uphold our dignity, but however vigorous or serious these attacks might be, it is almost never strictly *impossible* to resist them (Margalit 1996). Even under tyranny, torture or in the Nazi concentration camps, some people have been able to withstand humiliation and to keep their embodied self-respect and, therefore, their dignity.[10] From this it follows: Whether we keep or lose our dignity is – at least *also* – due to our ability and power to preserve it (Pollmann 2005, Spaemann 1987).

[10]In a TV interview, a holocaust survivor once answered the question of how she managed to survive the concentration camp as follows: "Because I never lost my dignity."

(h) *Lacking Causality*: Therefore, we have to concede that there are no simple causal or "automatic" relations between interpersonal attacks on human dignity and its factual loss. People might often be victims of massive assaults and rights violations, and there is always a high risk of losing dignity due to a withholding of recognition. Human rights violations *are* human rights violations because they attack our self-respect.[11] Nevertheless, no other person will be able to completely deprive us of our dignity as long as we do not give up our self-respect. Here we find the truth of the stipulation in Article 1 of the German *Basic Law*: "The dignity of the human being is untouchable". Embodied self-respect cannot be lost if we refuse to give it up. In the end, we all have to keep our *own* dignity, and however cruel it may sound, our dignity cannot be stolen without some kind of forced "cooperation", since, for the humiliation to be effective, people somehow have to "agree" that they themselves are not of equal worth (Margalit 1996: ch. 7). To put it briefly: There is no loss of dignity without a loss of embodied self-respect (Pollmann 2005).

At this point we have to avoid a misunderstanding that seems likely: The argument just sketched does *not* imply that the victims themselves are in part – let alone completely – to blame for their loss of dignity. Although they have to contribute to its preservation, it is not their "fault" if they lose their self-respect due to aggressive assaults by others. For psychological, social, or physical reasons, some persons might simply have more strength or mental power than others to preserve their self-respect (see Honneth 1995). This, of course, does not mean that these persons themselves are fully "in charge" of safeguarding their own dignity. It is true that a person will only be able to live a life in dignity if aggressive others do not affect the quality of her life so seriously that a loss of self-respect becomes inevitable. Acts of disrespect, discrimination, or humiliation are still vicious threats to personal dignity since they constrain the social leeway of a life in embodied self-respect (Spaemann 1987).

17.6 Possessing and Protecting Dignity

Every human being can be regarded as *equal* insofar as we can presuppose that they all have the same fundamental human interest to live a life in dignity. But at the same time, people are *different* in the extent to which they are able to factually realize their potential for embodied self-respect. Therefore, we must concede that not all human beings – and not even all persons – will have *full* dignity, but, as equal human beings, all *participate* in human dignity and will have corresponding interests in legal protection. At this point, a decisive but often ignored difference has to be marked: We have to distinguish between the problem of whether people actually possess dignity and to what extent from the related, but divergent, question

[11] Although most of the contributions to this volume will not really share this double assumption of "personal responsibility" and "lacking causality", most of the violations that are discussed here can still be reconstructed as attacks on self-respect.

of whether we all have exactly the same rights to its protection. In the end, such dignity rights only become reasonable and meaningful as *human rights* if we strictly distinguish between these two aspects. But why is that?

From reasons I have sketched in the third part of this chapter, human rights should be seen as legal guarantees or shields for human dignity, for the latter is not the primordial "ground" for human rights but their aspired "purpose". Human rights, it was said, shall allow us space to live an upright life in embodied self-respect – without discrimination, degradation, humiliation, etc. All human beings already participate in that potential for embodied self-respect, but not all human beings are allowed to fully realize it. That is why *all* need human rights. In other words: Since human dignity is a fragile good, it is dependent on legal protection, and claiming universal human rights simply means that everybody should have the opportunity to live in embodied self-respect – at least *as best as possible*.[12] We can presume, by proxy, that all human beings, even if they are not seen to count as "persons", do have a vital interest in humane and decent social treatment, and that is why we can also presume a common or universal interest in the legal conditions for realizing dignity – as long as the latter is taken as a capability for embodied self-respect that all human beings want to make the most of.

This human rights conception of dignity as a human potential combines plausible intuitions of the three other conceptions – achievement, dowry, personal capacity – by avoiding their particular disadvantages; what is in fact convincing about the achievement-conception is the premise that human dignity has to be accomplished and realized in real life. But it would be wrong to assume that people themselves are *fully* responsible for the respect or merits they obtain in public life. In contrast, most violations of dignity are the result of vicious treatment by *others*, which the achievement-conception misses. The correct intuition of the dowry-conception is the claim that all human beings have an equal worth just by being human – an equal worth that we cannot deprive them of by any plausible or compelling reasons. But this claim to equality is not *itself* what we call the dignity of the human being, for the latter would mean a life in which equal respect could be individually expressed and literally embodied in social life. Finally, a reasonable observation of the capacity-conception is the fact that, predominantly, those who are persons will have the best chance of realizing their potential to embodied self-respect. However, the conclusion that, therefore, only persons could reclaim corresponding *rights* would be misguided and wrong. For people who already live a life in full dignity might need those rights least of all.

---

[12] Although I cannot go into detail here, this means something different for grown-up adults, embryos, the mentally-ill, disabled, comatose or even dead people. That is why the popular, but wrong claim that all these human beings are "born" with the same dignity should be reinterpreted as a normative claim about the opportunities all human beings *should* have, not as a description of what capacities they *actually* have (Brennan and Lo 2007).

This important point helps us to avoid a second major misunderstanding that can be called the "ought-implies-can-fallacy". That would be the mistaken view that a person can only *have* certain rights to the protection of her dignity, if, and only if, she can effectively *use* these rights. From this false perspective it would then follow that, for instance, embryos, the mentally-ill, comatose, or dying people would not posses rights, e.g. to freedom of expression, movement, peaceful assembly or political participation. But why should that be the necessary consequence? Let us consider a concrete counter-example and think of a healthy adult who is kept imprisoned in her own house by a tyrannical spouse. She will not have the chance to give her vote on Sunday's federal election, that is true, but would one say that she therefore does not *have* a human right to vote? Of course not. She does have this right. Its possession is completely independent from her actual capability to use it. And so it is in general: All human beings simply have these rights just by being human – and this goes *in particular* for those who are "not yet" (like embryos), "not at the moment" (like comatose or imprisoned), not "fully" (like the mentally-ill), or "not anymore" (like the dying) able to live a life in dignity and fully use corresponding rights.

This leads us to a solution to the terminological contradiction I started with: Why should the legal system declare the protection of something that human beings cannot lose anyway? One should not make the mistake of extrapolating from universal and categorical human rights – which indeed all human beings have just by being human – to a likewise universal and categorical possession of dignity. Instead, every human being has human rights because we are all deeply vulnerable and able to realize and embody our dignity only to different extents. We can even lose our self-respect and dignity, so legal protection is needed *particularly* where the dignity of a human being is in acute or severe danger. Once again: Not all human beings, and not even all persons, have full dignity, but due to the moral and also political claim[13] that they should all count as legally equal, they all have the same universal rights, which have to be respected, protected and fulfilled. To state it briefly: *Because* human beings do not already have equal human dignity, they all have equal human rights.

References

Bayertz, Kurt. 1996. Human dignity: Philosophical origin and scientific erosion of an idea. In *Sanctity of life and human dignity,* ed. Kurt Bayertz, 73–90. Boston, MA: Kluwer Academic Publishers.

Benda, Ernst. 2000. The protection of human dignity: Article 1 of the Basic Law. *SMU Law Review* 53: 443–453.

Beyleveld, Deryck, and Roger Brownsword. 2001. *Human dignity in bioethics and biolaw.* New York, NY: Oxford University Press.

Brennan, Andrew, and Yeuk-Sze Lo. 2007. Two concepts of dignity: Honour and self-determination. In *Perspectives on human dignity: A conversation*, eds. Jeff Malpas and Norelle Lickiss, 43–58. Dordrecht: Springer.

Cancik, Hubert. 2002. 'Dignity of Man' and 'Persona' in stoic anthropology: Some remarks on cicero, De Officiis 1 105–7. In *The concept of human dignity in human rights discourse*, eds. David Kretzmer and Eckart Klein, 19–39. New York, NY: Kluwer Academic Publishers.

Damschen, Gregor and Dieter Schönecker, eds. 2003. *Der moralische Status menschlicher Embryonen: Pro und contra Spezies-, Kontinuums-, Identitäts- und Potentialitätsargument.* New York, NY: de Gruyter.

Dicke, Klaus. 2002. The founding function of human dignity in the universal declaration of human rights. In *The concept of human dignity in human rights discourse*, eds. David Kretzmer and Eckart Klein, 111–112. New York, NY: Kluwer Academic Publishers.

Dillon, Robin S., ed. 1995. *Dignity, character, and self-respect.* New York, NY: Routledge.

Gallie, Walter Bryce. 1956. Essentially contested concepts. *Proceedings of the Aristotelian Society* 56: 167–198.

Gewirth, Alan. 1982. *Human rights: Essays on justification and applications.* Chicago, IL: University of Chicago Press.

Hill, Thomas E. 1992. *Dignity and practical reason in Kant's moral theory.* Ithaca, NY: Cornell University Press.

Höffe, Otfried. 2007. *Democracy in an age of globalisation.* Dordrecht: Springer.

Hoerster, Norbert. 2002. *Ethik des Embryonenschutzes: Ein rechtsphilosophischer Essay.* Stuttgart: Reclam.

Honneth, Axel. 1995. *The struggle for recognition: The moral grammar of social conflicts.* Cambridge, MA: Polity.

Johnson, M. Glen, and Simonides, Janusz. 1998. *The universal declaration of human rights: A history of its creation and implementation 1948–1998.* Paris: UNESCO.

Klein, Eckart. 2002. Human dignity in German law. In *The concept of human dignity in human rights discourse*, eds. David Kretzmer and Eckart Klein, 145–160. New York, NY: Kluwer Academic Publishers.

Kretzmer, David and Eckart Klein, eds. 2002. *The concept of human dignity in human rights discourse.* New York, NY: Kluwer Academic Publishers.

[13]For a discussion of the central philosophical problems of further justifying this fundamental human rights claim see Menke and Pollmann (2007: ch. 2).

Lee, Patrick, and Robert P. George. 2008. The nature and basis of human dignity. In *Human dignity and bioethics*, ed. President's Council on Bioethics, 409–433. http://www.bioethics.gov/reports/human_dignity/human_dignity_and_bioethics.pdf. Accessed 13 Jun 2009.

Leon R. Kass. 2008. Defending human dignity. *Human dignity and bioethics*, ed. President's Council on Bioethics, 333–349. http://www.bioethics.gov/reports/human_dignity/human_dignity_and_bioethics.pdf. Accessed 13 Jun 2009.

Luhmann, Niklas. 1965. *Grundrechte als Institution: Ein Beitrag zur politischen Soziologie*. Berlin: Duncker & Humblot.

Macklin, Ruth. 2003. Dignity is a useless concept. *British Medical Journal* 327: 1419–1420.

Margalit, Avishai. 1996. *The decent society*. Cambridge, MA: Harvard University Press.

Maritain, Jacques. 1943. *The rights of man and natural law*. New York, NY: Charles Scribner's Sons.

Menke, Christoph. 2007. From the dignity of man to human dignity: The subject of rights. In *Values and norms in the age of globalization*, ed. Ewa Czerwinska-Schupps, 83–94. Franfurt, Main: Lang.

Menke, Christoph, and Arnd Pollmannn. 2007. *Philosophie der Menschenrechte. Zur Einführung*, Hamburg: Junius.

Meyer, Michael J. and William A. Parent, eds. 1992. *The constitution of rights: Human dignity and American values*. Ithaca, NY: Cornell University Press.

Morsink, Johannes. 1999. *The universal declaration of human rights: Origins, drafting, and intent*. Philadelphia, PA: University of Pennsylvania Press.

Nussbaum, Martha. 2008. Human dignity and political entitlements. In *Human dignity and bioethics*, ed. President's Council on Bioethics. http://www.bioethics.gov/reports/human_dignity/human_dignity_and_bioethics.pdf. Accessed 13 Jun 2009.

Pfannmüller, Günter, and Wilhelm Klein. 2008. *Unantastbar. Von der Würde des Menschen*. Frankfurt, Main: Zweitausendeins.

Pollmann, Arnd. 2005. Menschenwürde nach Maß. *Deutsche Zeitschrift für Philosophie* 53: 611–619.

Shell, Susan M. 2008. Kant's concept of human dignity as a resource for bioethics. *Human dignity and bioethics*, ed. President's Council on Bioethics, 333–349. http://www.bioethics.gov/reports/human_dignity/human_dignity_and_bioethics.pdf. Accessed 13 Jun 2009.

Soulen, R. Kendall and Linda Woodhead, eds. 2006. *God and human dignity*. Grand Rapids, MI: Eerdmans.

Spaemann, Robert. 1987. Über den Begriff der Menschenwürde. In *Das Natürliche und das Vernünftige*, 77–106. München: Piper.

Statman, Daniel. 2000. Humiliation, dignity and self-respect. *Philosophical Psychology* 13, 523–540.

Stoecker, Ralf, ed. 2003. *Menschenwürde: Annäherung an einen Begriff*. Wien: Öbv & Hpt.

Tiedemann, Paul. 2007. *Menschenwürde als Rechtsbegriff. Eine philosophische Klärung*. Berlin: BWV.

Trinkaus, Charles Edward. 1995. *'In our image and likeness': Humanity and divinity in Italian humanist thought*. Notre Dame: University of Notre Dame Press.

Wetz, Franz Josef. 2005. *Illusion Menschenwürde: Aufstieg und Fall eines Grundwerts*. Stuttgart: Klett-Cotta.

Index

P. Kaufmann et al. (eds.), *Humiliation, Degradation, Dehumanization,*
Library of Ethics and Applied Philosophy 24, DOI 10.1007/978-90-481-9661-6,